AMERICAN
DYNASTY

AMERICAN DYNASTY

Aristocracy, Fortune, and the Politics of Deceit in the House of Bush

KEVIN PHILLIPS

VIKING

VIKING

Published by the Penguin Group
Penguin Group (USA) Inc., 375 Hudson Street,
New York, New York 10014, U.S.A.
Penguin Books Ltd, 80 Strand, London WC2R 0RL, England
Penguin Books Australia Ltd, 250 Camberwell Road, Camberwell, Victoria 3124, Australia
Penguin Books Canada Ltd, 10 Alcorn Avenue, Toronto, Ontario, Canada M4V 3B2
Penguin Books India (P) Ltd, 11 Community Centre, Panchsheel Park,
New Delhi–110 017, India
Penguin Books (N.Z.) Ltd, Cnr Rosedale and Airborne Roads,
Albany, Auckland, New Zealand
Penguin Books (South Africa) (Pty) Ltd, 24 Sturdee Avenue,
Rosebank, Johannesburg 2196, South Africa

Penguin Books Ltd, Registered Offices: 80 Strand, London WC2R 0RL, England

First published in 2004 by Viking Penguin, a member of Penguin Group (USA) Inc.

7   9   10   8

Copyright © Kevin Phillips, 2004
All rights reserved

LIBRARY OF CONGRESS CATALOGING-IN-PUBLICATION DATA
Phillips, Kevin P.
American dynasty : aristocracy, fortune, and the politics of deceit
in the house of Bush / Kevin Phillips.
p.   cm.
Includes index.
ISBN 0-670-03264-6
1. Bush, George, 1924–   2. Bush, George W. (George Walker), 1946–   3. Bush family.
4. United States—Politics and government—1945–1989.   5. United States—Politics and government—
1989–   6. Presidents—United States—Biography.   7. Politicians—United States—Biography.
8. Aristocracy (Political science)—United States—History—20th century.   9. Wealth—
Political aspects—United States—History—20th century.   10. Political corruption—
United States—History—20th century.   I. Title.
E882.P48 2004
973.928'092—dc22
[B]   2003061299

This book is printed on acid-free paper. ∞
Printed in the United States of America
Set in Minion
Designed by Francesca Belanger

To the memory of President Dwight D. Eisenhower, whose words in his 1961 farewell address once again demand attention and respect:

This conjunction of an immense Military Establishment and a large arms industry is new in the American experience. The total influence—economic, political, even spiritual—is felt in every city, every state-house, every office of the Federal Government. We recognize the imperative need for this development. Yet we must not fail to comprehend its grave implications. . . .

In the councils of government we must guard against the acquisition of unwarranted influence, whether sought or unsought, by the military-industrial complex. The potential for the disastrous rise of misplaced power exists and will persist.

We must never let the weight of this combination endanger our liberties or democratic processes. We should take nothing for granted. Only an alert and knowledgeable citizenry can compel the proper meshing of the huge industrial and military machinery of defense with our peaceful methods and goals so that security and liberty may prosper together.

January 17, 1961

PREFACE

This book has changed a lot—in length, indignation, and its hitherto unpublished information—since I began writing it in December 2002. My original ambition was to identify and explain the Bush-related transformation of the U.S. presidency into an increasingly dynastic office, a change with profound consequences for the American Republic, given the factors of family bias, domestic special interests, and foreign grudges that the Bushes, father and son, brought into the White House.

Unfortunately, in examining two Bush presidencies and the family's four-generation pursuit of national prominence and power—and in doing so through a lens that highlighted elite associations, dynastic ambitions, and recurring financial and business practices—I found a greater basis for dismay and disillusionment than I had imagined. The result is an unusual and unflattering portrait of a great family (great in power, not morality) that has built a base over the course of the twentieth century in the back corridors of the new military-industrial complex and in close association with the growing intelligence and national security establishments. In doing so, the Bushes have threaded their way through damning political, banking, and armanents scandals and, since the 1980s, controversies like the October Surprise, Iran-Contra, and Iraqgate imbroglios, which in another climate or a different time might have led to impeachment.

I am not talking about ordinary lack of business ethics or financial corruption. During the late twentieth century, several other presidents and their families displayed these shortcomings, and the public has become understandably blasé. Four generations of building toward dynasty, however, have infused the Bush family's hunger for power and practices of crony capitalism with a moral arrogance and backstage disregard of the democratic and republican traditions of the U.S. government. As we will see, four generations of involvement with clandestine arms deals and European and Middle Eastern rogue banks will do that.

American Dynasty is on the one hand a book about economics, history, and politics in the era that covers the two Bush presidencies. But it is also a portrait of four Bush (and Walker) generations—their ambitions, financial practices, scandals, and wars. It brings into focus many circumstances and relationships that have not previously been examined together and seriously discussed, for reasons that are both unusual and unfortunate. During the late 1970s and 1980s, the Bush clan in a sense flew under the radar of critical biography and investigation. The first two published biographies of George H. W. Bush—*George Bush: A Biography* (1980) by Nicholas King, a former Bush press secretary, and *George Bush: An Intimate Portrait* (1989) by Fitzhugh Green, a CIA-connected Bush social chum—were friendly treatments that had no room for warts. Neither did the 1991 *Flight of the Avenger* sequence of books lionizing his record in World War II. Unfortunately, this puffery managed to preempt more serious book-length exploration.

The first major objective study, *Marching in Place* (1992), by *Time* reporters Dan Goodgame and Michael Duffy, dwelt critically on his 1989–92 presidential record but came out too late to affect the political climate that defeated Bush in 1992, and it got little attention. *George Bush: The Unauthorized Biography,* published in 1992 by allies of Bush-hating Lyndon LaRouche, tended to submerge its massive, and often revelatory, research in snowdrifts of paranoia, and no serious readers or reviewers gave it much credence.

By 2000, naturally, biographies of the younger Bush, even critical ones, devoted little attention to anything other than his own career. Thus the first three generations of the family escaped multidimensional and skeptical scrutiny, save for a professional, but essentially friendly, biography by historian Herbert Parmet entitled *George Bush: The Life of a Lone Star Yankee* (1997). Now that the Bushes have become a presidential dynasty, for however long, they will command more probing attention, but the national interest would have been better served had that occurred in the 1970s.

Few have looked at the facts of the family's rise, but just as important, commentators have neglected the *thread*—not the mere occasion—of special interests, biases, scandals (especially those related to arms dealing), and blatant business cronyism. The evidence that accrues over four generations is extraordinarily damning. This is especially true of the Bushes' ties to the Wall Street financial world and the military-industrial complex.

But considering an additional relationship may explain even more. After four generations of connection to foreign intrigue and the intelligence community, plus three generations of immersion in the culture of secrecy (dating back to the Yale years of several men in the family), deceit and disinformation have become Bush political hallmarks. The Middle Eastern financial ties of both Bush presidents exemplify this lack of candor, as do the origins and machinations of both Bush wars with Iraq. Appendix B in this volume reviews the family's penchant for secrecy and for cleaning and locking up government records.

It doesn't help that the major media have tended to use kid gloves with the family. In 1999, longtime reporter Robert Sherrill, writing in the *Texas Observer,* contrasted this treatment of the Bushes with how "when Richard Nixon's brother Donald—my poor, damn dumb brother, Nixon called him—used his name to pry a loan of $205,000 from billionaire Howard Hughes, the mainstream press raised a stink that lasted years." The Bushes have also benefited from the Democrats' apparent reluctance to investigate the connections, misdeeds, and malfeasances of a popular president such as George W. Bush. Others have made the point that if a Clinton-era special counsel was necessary for Whitewater, why not a Bush-era special counsel for Enron?

As a former longtime Republican who came of political age during the Nixon years, I take the point about double standards. My own distaste since the 1960s for what George H. W. Bush seemed to represent—a career built on support from a vague "elite" rather than merit or democratic selection—had a Republican genesis. It drew on views prominently, although not decisively, voiced within the GOP. Dwight D. Eisenhower had warned—in words quoted in this volume's opening pages—about the future threat that might come from the military-industrial complex. Richard Nixon's dislike of Bush's elitist economics leaped out in an endorsement Nixon made of my 1990 book, *The Politics of Rich and Poor.* Ronald Reagan had personal qualms about his running mate that some say he never lost. Fellow Texans John Connally and H. Ross Perot were both disdainful of Bush. John McCain kept this tradition alive in his 2000 view of the younger Bush.

Few prominent Republicans voiced similar qualms as the campaign for the election of 2004 began. Moreover, inasmuch as the elder Bush turned me into a political independent, I have to admit that I can no longer attribute my own unhappiness with the dynastic, economic, religious, and war politics of George W. Bush to my earlier Republican molding alone.

I must also acknowledge that the party of my youth and middle age has changed enormously. For fifteen years after I published *The Emerging Republican Majority* in 1969, I supported the GOP campaign argument that public policy had gone too far in trying to squeeze religion out of American life. Now the voter backlash against that early squeeze has so reversed the national discussion that the *opposite* threat is crystallizing: there is a Republican Party dangerously dominated by southern fundamentalist and evangelical constituencies, willing to blend biblical theology into U.S. Middle Eastern policy and attach faith healers to the advisory structure of the U.S. Food and Drug Administration. The research I did on politics and religion in writing chapter 7 was a revelation to me, as I hope it will be to readers.

That the Bushes have many qualities to commend them as a private family—community involvement, generosity to those who work for them—is not really the point. They are not a private family. They are a public family, and one that is writing a new definition of the presidency. They are bending public policy toward family grudges and interests. What matters is their policy and conduct in that emerging role. The further evidence, since 9/11, of the United States' becoming an embattled imperium, even showing faint specklings of garrison state thinking, only doubles the stakes.

True, the dynastic trend in the United States goes deeper than the Bushes. If Hillary Clinton runs for president in 2008, the failings and lingering grudges of her family's own would-be dynasty will be fair game. And thus we may learn—for better or worse—more about the transformation and perils of American politics. This book, however, is about the dynasty we already have and what it stands for. This is the direction in which national politics and national discussion must turn first.

CONTENTS

Contents

AMERICAN DYNASTY

The Bush-Walker Family Tree

(Not all family members are represented.)

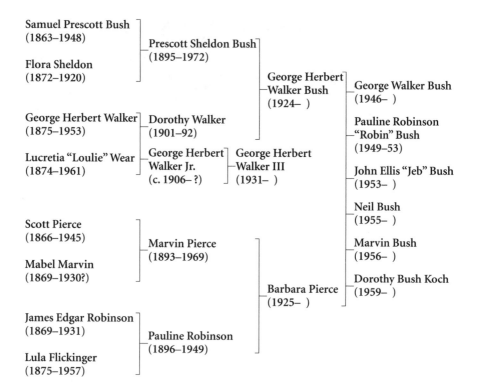

Samuel Prescott Bush
(1863–1948)

Flora Sheldon
(1872–1920)

Prescott Sheldon Bush
(1895–1972)

George Herbert
Walker Bush
(1924–)

George Walker Bush
(1946–)

George Herbert Walker
(1875–1953)

Dorothy Walker
(1901–92)

Pauline Robinson
"Robin" Bush
(1949–53)

Lucretia "Loulie" Wear
(1874–1961)

George Herbert
Walker Jr.
(c. 1906– ?)

George Herbert
Walker III
(1931–)

John Ellis "Jeb" Bush
(1953–)

Neil Bush
(1955–)

Scott Pierce
(1866–1945)

Marvin Pierce
(1893–1969)

Marvin Bush
(1956–)

Mabel Marvin
(1869–1930?)

Barbara Pierce
(1925–)

Dorothy Bush Koch
(1959–)

James Edgar Robinson
(1869–1931)

Pauline Robinson
(1896–1949)

Lula Flickinger
(1875–1957)

Introduction

Concern about a U.S. dynastic presidency first emerged in 2000, prompted by skeptics of the Bush succession, as well as by amateur historians unnerved by analogies to the seventeenth-century English Stuart and nineteenth-century French Bourbon restorations. The topic gained force and more widespread credibility when the 2002 elections confirmed George W. Bush's popularity and when the war of early spring 2003 displayed his personal commitment to resuming his father's unfinished combat with Iraq's Saddam Hussein. Controversial wars and geopolitical ambitions, after all, have frequently originated as dynastic ambitions.

Other institutional aspects of a family-based presidency warrant national attention. Dynasties tend to show continuities of policy and interest-group bias—in the case of the Bushes, favoritism toward the energy sector, defense industries, the Pentagon, and the CIA, as well as insistence on tax breaks for the investor class and upper-income groups. By inauguration day of 2001, Houston-based Enron had a relationship with the Bush clan going back a decade and a half. Families restored to power also have a history of seeking revenge against old foes as well as recalling longtime loyalists and retainers. George W. Bush's record has included retiring such taunters of his father as Texas governor Ann Richards (in 1994) and House Speaker Newt Gingrich (Bush helped to force him out after the 1998 elections) and appointing former officials dating back not just to his father's term but to the Ford administration of 1974–76, a virtual incubator of the Republican Party's Bush faction.

This dynasticism was hardly a phenomenon unique to the United States. In the first few years of the twenty-first century, the restoration of old European royal houses was discussed in Serbia, Bulgaria, Romania, and Italy. As in the United States, the principals were political conservatives.

Another questionable aspect of dynastic control is the effect of biological inheritance. History is all too familiar with hereditary traits like the Hapsburg chin and the Tudor temper. Some pundits have queried whether heredity might likewise explain certain behaviors shared by the two Bush presidents—frenetic activity, scrambled speech, the hint of dyslexic arrangements of thought.[1] Although the press has been reticent to pursue such matters, they do have a genuine relevance. Three, perhaps four, generations of Bushes have displayed great capacities for remembering names, faces, and statistics. *Dallas News* reporter Bill Minutaglio, a biographer of the younger Bush, discovered that George H. W. Bush "went so far as to tell his spokesman Marlin Fitzwater to gather together the photographs of the Washington press corps so he could memorize all their names; the Bush men were always startlingly better than anyone else at memorizing names." At the same time, both father and son have shown little talent for conceptualization or abstraction. Is it a coincidence? Dynasty, with its subordination of individual achievement to gene pools and bloodlines, always involves a gamble on the nuances of heredity.

In the United States, as we will see, the twentieth-century rise of the Bush family was built on the five pillars of American global sway: the international reach of U.S. investment banking, the emerging giantism of the military-industrial complex, the ballooning of the CIA and kindred intelligence operations, the drive for U.S. control of global oil supplies, and a close alliance with Britain and the English-speaking community. This century of upward momentum brought a sequence of controversies, albeit ones that never gained critical mass—such as the exposure in 1942 of Prescott Bush's corporate directorship links to wartime Germany, which harked back to overambitious 1920s investment banking; the Bush family's longtime involvement with global armaments and the military-industrial complex; and a web of close connections to the CIA, which began decades before George Bush's brief CIA directorship in 1976. Threads like these may not weigh heavily on individual presidencies; they are many times more troubling when they run through several generations of a dynasty.

We must be cautious here not to transmute commercial relationships into a latter-day conspiracy theory, a transformation that epitomizes what historian Richard Hofstadter years ago called the "paranoid streak" in American politics. (Try a Google Internet search for "George Bush and Hitler," for example.) On the other hand, worries about conspiracy thinking should not inhibit inquiries in a way that blocks sober examination, which often more properly identifies some kind of elite behavior familiar to sociologists and political scientists alike.

The particular evolution of elites within nations that became leading world economic powers over the last four centuries is a subject I have discussed in several previous books, especially *Wealth and Democracy* (2002). The rise of a nation's "establishment" to its zenith is invariably an accretive process, not a successfully executed sequence of plots. Still, "old-boy" networks or their equivalents usually play a significant role in maintaining a group in power.

Treating the Bush presidencies as growing out of a four-generation interaction with the so-called U.S. establishment is, in a word, essential. Likewise, dealing separately with the administrations of George H. W. and George W.—or worse, ignoring commonalities of behavior in office—is like considering individual planets while ignoring their place within the solar system.

Four examples are illustrative. One is the repeated use of family influence in arranging or smoothing over difficulties in the military service of three generations of Bushes: Prescott, George H. W., and George W. Similarly, the involvement of four Walker and Bush generations with finance—in several cases, the investment side of the petroleum business—helps to explain their recurrent preoccupation with investments, capital gains, and tax shelters. George W. Bush's 2003 commitment to ending taxation of dividends was simply an extension of his father's frequent calls for reducing capital gains tax rates as the solution to any weakness in the national economy. Third, the family's ties to oil date back to Ohio steelmaker Samuel Bush's relationship to Standard Oil a century ago, while its ultimately dynastic connection to Enron spanned the first national Bush administration, the six years of George W. Bush's governorship of Texas, and the first year of his Washington incumbency. No other presidential family has made such prolonged efforts on behalf of a single corporation. Finally, there is no previous parallel to the relationships between the Bushes and the CIA and its predecessor organizations, which began in the invisible-ink and *Ashenden, Secret Agent* days of George Herbert Walker and Prescott Bush. Quite simply, analyzing separately the two Bush presidencies risks losing sight of such essential and revealing leitmotifs.

Arguably, a clan *lacking* such continuity of interests and relationships probably could not have succeeded in establishing a dynastic presidency. It would not have developed the requisite links to the establishment. It should be noted that the term "dynastic" is used here to describe a *fact*, not a theory: namely, the succession of 2000, in which the eldest son of a defeated president was eight years later chosen by his father's party and inaugurated as the next president. Such inheritance has no American precedent; it trespasses, at least spiritually, on the governance framed by Washington, Franklin, Jefferson, and Madison. Hereditary rulers were to be feared, the founders knew, even when, like the fifteenth-century Medicis of Florence, they initially chose to keep the framework of the Republic in place.

While the election of 2000 became an obvious pivot by marking a full-fledged family restoration, the election of 1994 must be considered a secondary milestone, for it served to anoint formally eldest son George W. Bush, already the most logical choice to follow in his father's footsteps. Winning the Texas governorship that year established him as the family political heir over his younger brother, who lost a statehouse bid in Florida. Sharing his father's name, looking eerily like him, and having a similar electoral base in Texas, George W. was able to embody a much more resonant promise of "restoration" among voters than could have been managed by his younger brother Jeb. Also to the point, the 1994 elections suggested the motivational potential for a restoration: namely, the moral anger of a large portion of the American electorate—pollster Gallup came to call them "the repulsed"—with the new president, Bill Clinton. Not a few voters felt apologetic, survey takers found, for having turned the elder Bush out of office in 1992.

Were history to posit a "Bush era," lasting from George H. W. Bush's triumph in 1988 through 2008, the two family presidencies might well define the entire two decades, turning the Clinton years into the political equivalent of sandwich filler. On the other hand, were Senator Hillary Clinton to achieve in 2008 a second restoration, this one Clintonian, public perception might well lurch toward some American equivalent of the fifteenth-century Wars of the Roses, during which the English Crown was contested by the houses of York and Lancaster.

National politics, in short, has begun to take on the aura of a great family arena. Of the four wives of the major-party presidential nominees in 1996 and 2000, two quickly gained U.S. Senate seats: Hillary Clinton in 2000 and Elizabeth Dole in 2002. A third, Tipper Gore, decided not to make a Senate bid in Tennessee. Other seats in the U.S. Senate, in the meantime, began to pass more like membership in Britain's House of Lords.

Regionally, the prime example of family continuity in national government has been New England. In Rhode Island, Republican Lincoln Chafee took the Senate seat of his father, John Chafee, when the latter died in 1999. Next door, Edward Kennedy occupies the Massachusetts Senate seat vacated by his brother when he became president, and just to the west in Connecticut, Senator Christopher Dodd sits where his father sat from 1958 to 1970. Parenthetically, both senators from New Hampshire are the sons of former governors. One of those from Maine is the wife of a former governor.

Dynasticism, then, is clearly not just a peculiarity of the Bush presidency. Yet there was a vital catalyst in the 1996–98 jelling among Republicans of a commitment, backstopped by favorable national polls, to running the Bush family's eldest heir for the presidency. It helped to legitimize a larger trend, broadening its momentum.

In this context, religion furnished another critical engine for a Bush triumph. To many Republicans and independents, the Bush family appeal was renewed in 1993–94 by ongoing revelations of Clinton's moral turpitude and his eventual impeachment. Perhaps because of how this tide of moral outrage had come to arouse southern fundamentalist constituencies, George W. Bush began to emphasize and display unusual personal religiosity. He cast himself as the prodigal son, brought back to God after waywardness and crisis. From 1994 to 2000, he repeatedly used such biblically inflected language about good and evil that one could almost hear the words of Daniel and Jeremiah. So close did he draw to evangelical and fundamentalist Protestant leaders that in 2001, the *Washington Post* suggested that the new president had virtually replaced evangelist Pat Robertson as the leader of the U.S. Religious Right. To have suggested any similar role being assumed by his father would have been laughable.

In contrast to the sophisticated 1990s dialogue saluting globalization, Internet democracy, and the supposed end of history, much of the world's population, especially its poor and dispossessed, was participating in a quite dissimilar expression—a swell of fundamentalist and evangelical religion, often with a strong admixture of nationalism. While a few nations were actively seeking restorations and the resumption of power by kings, this larger trend, affecting Protestants, Catholics, Eastern Orthodox Christians, Jews, Muslims, Hindus, and Buddhists alike, dwelled instead on prophets and pharaohs, awaited or feared ones (red calves, Mahdis, and Antichrists), holy cities, and desecrating unbelievers, along with more ominous events like jihads, end times, raptures, and ultimate Armageddon.

Well might embattled Americans, weary of warfare in the Holy Land, yearn for the simple "family" issues propounded in the cultural politics of the 1980s and 1990s—most of which were used in a calculated courtship directed at low- and middle-income voters stressed by two-earner households, lengthened work hours, and day-care and tax pressures. Unfortunately, by the time these day-to-day issues were overshadowed by stock market crashes, terrorism, and war in the early 2000s, little net economic progress had been made. If anything, the stress on ordinary families was now even greater.

Thus the irony: The dominant "family-related" trend taking the United States into the twenty-first century turned out to be a form of classic *reaction*. In economics, it favored aristocracies of both capital and skills, from Wall Street to major-league baseball. Family values were brandished to save multimillionaires from the federal inheritance tax. In politics, "family" bred dynasties and elite entrenchment. Even more broadly, amid the fear of additional barbarian attacks in the 9/11 vein, Americans slid toward another historical reversal: allowing the eighteenth-century republic to be reconceptualized as an embattled twenty-first-century imperium, threatened by dangers and strains not unlike those that plagued third- and fourth-century Rome.

The central purpose of this book is to interweave several strands of analysis and thought that need to be considered together if we're truly to understand the perilous state of the American political system. One is the political and religious fundamentalism that has gained strength as the new century has unfolded. A second is the ever-changing importance within the United States of different economic sectors and elites—from investment banking and oil to the military-industrial complex. The third is the twentieth- and early-twenty-first-century emergence of the Bush family, which this volume seeks to track along a trajectory of American wealth and power through the heydays of Wall Street investment banking, Ivy League clubdom, and Texas petropolitics and into the post–World War II emergence of the CIA and rise of the national security state.

Until now, our political history has embodied a different, midcentury-flavored saga centered on careers of men like Dean Acheson, Robert A. Lovett, and W. Averell Harriman, who played their starring national roles from the late 1940s to the early 1960s. Now a new dynasty warrants a different national story. The Bushes and their initially more influential Walker family in-laws were also "present at the creation," to use Acheson's term, but in secondary capacities. The family stepped into public visibility only in 1952, when Prescott Bush, managing partner at Brown Brothers Harriman, for many years the nation's biggest private investment bank, won election to the U.S. Senate from Connecticut. He also became a favorite golf partner of President Eisenhower, also impressing the then vice president, Richard Nixon.

When Nixon, in turn, won the presidency in 1968, he would treat George H. W. Bush, a first-term congressman, as befit the son of Prescott Bush. The younger Bush had also been commended to Nixon by former Republican presidential nominee Thomas E. Dewey, probably the one man most responsible for convincing Dwight Eisenhower to take Nixon as his running mate back in 1952. Thus did the Nixon administration become the all-important career elevator for the little-known U.S. representative from Houston.

Eastern patricians, even the oil-stained variety, were rare in the Nixon entourage—and for that matter, rare in national Republican elective politics. Nixon wore them as badges of social acceptance; he had taken one, former U.S. senator Henry Cabot Lodge of Massachusetts, as his vice presidential running mate in 1960. Eight years later, he let the name of George H. W. Bush make the vice presidential rumor mills, less because of any possible appeal Bush might have in Texas than for the socioeconomic reassurance he would offer to New York and Connecticut Republican donors and Ivy League clubland.

Appointments to the United Nations (1970) and the Republican National Committee (1973) brought Bush cabinet and Nixon-inner-circle status, maintaining the Washington visibility critical to his future. Nixon valued Bush's family connections, gung ho spirit, personal likability, and social outreach. Similar considerations helped to guide President Ford's 1975 selection of him to head the CIA, a famous repository of Yale alumni. Bush wanted to be—and perhaps was—taken as qualified for the cabinet in the unelected, bred-to-it manner of a Curzon, Cecil, or Lansdowne in Edwardian England.

This, to be sure, is getting ahead of our story. What made it possible to consider Bush for vice president in 1968, almost out of the blue, was that some fifty years earlier, his two grandfathers—George Herbert Walker, a well-connected St. Louis financier, and Samuel Prescott Bush, a wealthy Ohio railroad equipment manufacturer—had managed to implant themselves and their descendants in the eastern establishment. This helped Prescott Bush get ahead, much as later connections helped George H. W. and George W.

To tell their tale, *American Dynasty* unfolds like this: Chapter 1 introduces the Bushes as our "not-quite-royal family." I'm not being facetious here. The Bush royal connections documented in *Burke's Peerage* and elsewhere have nourished the self-image of both chief executives. However, the real founding father of the Bush clan was not a Bush, but a Walker— George H. Walker, for whom both the forty-first and forty-third presidents are named.

If Samuel P. Bush made money and connections in World War I, which he did, Walker made more of each. Afterward, he was wooed in 1919 by Averell Harriman to run an ambitious set of investments about to be cobbled together in the postwar political maelstrom of 1920s Germany and Russia. Over two decades, father-in-law Walker helped steer Prescott Bush to the top of what became the Brown Brothers Harriman of midcentury— rich, full of Yale Skull and Bonesmen, London-linked, politically influential, and intimately wired through several of its top partners to the postwar birthing of the CIA. During the first half of the twentieth century, the United States had evolved its own version of "permanent government" akin to the British model. Although this establishment peaked from the 1920s through the 1950s, its influence lingered, to George H. W. Bush's critical advantage.

Chapter 1 concludes the family portrait with the two-decade-long ideological and religious transformation that proved so important to the presidential restoration in 2000. Consummated by George W. Bush, this change from Connecticut pinstripes and Episcopal church pews to Texas cowboy boots and fundamentalist religious alliances conveniently mirrored the late-twentieth-century migration of the U.S. population and of political power. It must be counted as one of the most successful makeovers in modern history.

Chapter 2 examines the underlying cultural and economic forces that helped to make dynastization of wealth and politics a turn-of-the-twenty-first-century reality. Pseudoaristocratic taste caught hold in the United States of the 1980s through the ersatz British clothing and furnishings of Ralph Lauren and the success of magazines like *Architectural Digest* and *Yachting,* as well as the chic of the Bloomingdale's–Metropolitan Museum– Diana Vreeland Chinese and French fashion party circuit patronized and promoted by President and Mrs. Reagan. Celebrity culture sought out stardom in everything from baseball and rock music to the corporate executive suite, while in economics, a kindred winner-take-all ethos widened the chasm between top and middle earners. The bull market in stocks between 1982 and 1999, in which the Dow Jones Industrial Average pole-vaulted by some 1,300 percent, gilded the fortunes of the top 1 percent of American families by tying the escalation of wealth to stock ownership. This convergence of economic and cultural favoritism furthered the rise of great-family politics in the United States.

Chapter 3 considers the Bush restoration in the election of 2000 from two separate perspectives: its genesis in U.S. domestic politics and its European historical analogies. The similarities between the United States at the end of the Clinton years and the England of 1660–61 and the France of 1814–15 suggest the parallel forces at work. The English in the 1640s and the French in the 1790s had executed their kings and expelled their ruling houses. Within two decades or so, the regicides in each nation had worn out their moral and political welcome, creating support for bringing back the old royal houses.

The American electorate's overthrow of George Bush in 1992 brought in Bill Clinton. However, Clinton's 1993–94 moral disrepute, peaking with his 1998–99 impeachment, enabled a Republican restorationist campaign, strongest in the evangelical and fundamentalist South, that rallied just enough voters to inaugurate the born-again George W. Bush. Economic conservatives, meanwhile, supported a Bush reinstatement for oil, defense, and Wall Street–based reasons. When Bush took office in 2001, a parallel to Stuart and Bourbon arrogance quickly emerged in the new regime's insistence on ideological conservatism despite the lack of any such national mandate. Restoration drinks from its own special psychological well.

The first three chapters lay out part 1's framework of family, dynasty, and restoration. Part 2 turns to the origins, nature, and bias of Bush economic policies and relationships to governments. Chapter 4 begins with a portrait of Texanomics—its cultural harshness and fiscal regressivity. It also plumbs the irony of how the state has managed to reconcile the free-market mythology with world-famous crony capitalism and preeminence in pressing for federal bailouts in the 1980s and 1990s.

The four-generation Bush and Walker involvement in the investment business antedates the family's arrival in Texas, but since George H. W. Bush and his family moved to oil country, their business behavior has become increasingly aligned with the state's stereotype, thriving on family connections, cronyism, paper entrepreneurialism, tax shelters, and government influence. On a national basis, however, the harsh reputation of Lone Star State economics—confirmed by official data on environmental quality, education, and income distribution—has obliged the family's presidential office seekers to wear "kinder and gentler" policies and "compassionate conservatism" as velvet cloaking.

Chapter 5 moves from the duality of harshness-cum-compassion to the 2001–4 mind-set of a regime headed by two former Texas-based energy company chief executives, captaining the most energy-dominated national administration in U.S. history. A survey of the mutual assistance of the Bush family and Enron since 1985 is followed by a look at the crony capitalism unfurled during Cheney's stewardship of the Halliburton Corporation. As we will see, Enron and Halliburton shared many interests and biases.

Chapter 6, the final economic profile in part 2, returns to the interrelationship of the Bush dynasty and the rising military–national security–industrial complex—from World War I through the tumult of the twentieth century to the complex's early-twenty-first-century metamorphosis in the upthrust of terrorism and homeland-security issues. This is a chapter in which many forces come together. One subsection focuses on World War II and the enlargement and mutation of the early military-industrial complex, including the absorption of Germany-savvy U.S. business, financial, and legal elites into the OSS, the CIA, and kindred agencies in the 1940s. George H. Walker, Prescott Bush, Brown Brothers Harriman, and their Yale and Wall Street colleagues were all important actors in this drama.

Another section of chapter 6 looks at the first three generations of the Bush dynasty—from Samuel Bush, George Walker, and Prescott Bush through George H. W. Bush—and their involvements with the national security establishment. Too little attention has been paid to the strong connections developed between the Bush family and the CIA many years before George H. W. Bush ran it. Under George W. Bush, the CIA has flexed more muscle than ever.

Part 3 turns to another theme: the politics, geopolitics, and wars that have arisen, at least in part, out of the restoration psychology and fundamentalist theology of George W. Bush. The implications here are still taking shape.

Part of what restored the Bushes to the White House in 2000 through a southern-dominated electoral coalition was the emergence of George W. Bush during the 1990s as a born-again favorite of conservative Christian evangelical and fundamentalist voters. His 2001–4 policies and rhetoric confirmed that bond. The idea that the de facto head of the Religious Right and the president of the United States can be the same person is a precedent-shattering circumstance that has barely crept into national political discussion. Chapter 7 looks at the thirty-year rise of the Religious Right in U.S. politics and how the Bush family has adjusted its religious intensity and shifted denominational identifications to ride that trend.

Recall, however, that the United States has by no means been alone in undergoing a recent surge in religious fundamentalism and nationalism. Chapter 7 documents related trends in many other nations and cultures: Islam from North Africa through the Middle East to Indonesia and the Philippines, nationalistic Buddhism in Japan, right-wing Hinduism in India, militant Judaism in Israel, and the icons-and-incense Orthodox Christianity of Eastern Europe and Russia. The apparent intensity of religious fundamentalism in the United States—polls reported that almost half of U.S. Christians believe in Armageddon, and the states of Arizona, New Mexico, and Colorado succeeded in getting Washington to renumber U.S. Highway 666 because fundamentalist Christians worried about its satanic symbolism—demonstrates that not all of the world's religious radicalism has loci in the Middle East and Central Asia.

Chapter 8, in turn, takes some of the religious and political links profiled in chapter 7 and examines their role, along with oil, armaments, and domestic political considerations, in the emergence of a new U.S. foreign policy, one that blends biblical bluntness about an "Axis of Evil" with skepticism, if not hostility, to the United Nations and an embrace of preemptive warfare. The fact is that any emergence of a U.S. "crusader state" stands to profit important economic interests even as it pleases religious fundamentalists.

Chapter 9, "The Wars of the Texas Succession," examines the first and second wars with Iraq from a Bush dynastic standpoint. Texas presidents have now launched the last three U.S. wars: Vietnam, the Gulf War of 1991, and the 2003 war to overthrow Saddam Hussein. The latter two reflect a unique set of circumstances. They were the first pair of U.S. wars to be fought by father-and-son presidents, and were caused in part by a misconceived U.S. arms buildup in Iraq undertaken by Bush as Reagan's vice president and then as president himself. They also reflected a two-generation

Texan preoccupation with U.S. Middle Eastern and Caspian oil interests. "The War of the Texas Succession" thus has a geopolitical as well as a family-based foundation.

Finally, the afterword offers a short conclusion, which recalls the ways in which the founding fathers thought the American Republic might go astray. That the object of their labors might follow the pathway of the Florentine, Dutch, and other republics toward great-family and dynastic leadership was a real concern to them.

Just how dynastic the U.S. future will be, and with what consequences, remains to be seen. The tendencies may be nipped in the bud; the first decade of the twenty-first century may turn out to be an anomaly. What can be said today is that the circumstances of the United States in these tumultuous years have taken a turn that would have surprised and presumably appalled the nation's founding fathers. As was the development of the so-called imperial presidency in the 1960s, the emergence of a dynastic presidency is contrary to the American political tradition, and the shorter its duration the better.

PART I

Family, Dynasty, and Restoration

CHAPTER 1

The Not-Quite-Royal Family

It is hardly too early to examine the nature of the Bush dynasty, and why—at the moment at least—it has largely escaped the antagonism that led the founders to fear any hereditary titles. Such sentiment prompted political foes to compare the Adamses to the Stuart kings of Britain and the Kennedys' adversaries to warn that eight years of Jack, eight years of Bobby and eight years of Ted would, after all, conclude in the Orwellian 1984.

New York Times, 2002

Most dynasties are defined and circumscribed by region. The Roosevelts rode as high and far as the national fortunes of New York State. . . . The Kennedys acquire an outlier state or three, but Massachusetts remains their feudal domain. Not the Bushes. Their success is found in an essential rootlessness.

Washington Post, 2001

The power of the American presidency—and, for that matter, its awesome centrality in the world—burgeoned in the first years of the twenty-first century, especially after the terrorist attacks of September 11, 2001. An earlier muscle flexing during the peak years of the cold war with the Soviet Union had led to the imperial presidency of the 1960s. That culminated in Watergate, and the stature of the president understandably weakened after the scandal.

The unnerving crisis of a terrorist attack within its borders led the United States to a new sense of empire and disdain for international restraints. Sweeping doctrine was involved, going far beyond the ad hoc White House grasping of the sixties. Another distinctive feature of the turn-of-the-century mood was its sudden turn to esteeming family and inheritance—the election of a man with the same looks, name, manner, and party as his ex-presidential father, chosen through a process that wound up traducing the democratic will of the American electorate. In 2000, George W. Bush became the first president since 1888 who had not won at least a plurality of the popular votes. After losing by more than five hundred thousand ballots, he was chosen by a four-vote margin in the electoral college, courtesy of a 5–4 decision by the U.S. Supreme Court.

Most twentieth-century presidents put in office by tight margins sought to be conciliatory to make up for want of a popular mandate. Not the Bush administration. Eschewing any inhibition based on lack of national consent or legitimacy, it governed from the start with an ideological edge. Family credentials and a powerful financial donor network had been the basis of the new president's nomination, and family connections quickly became a fount of federal appointments, including two for children of the five pro-Bush Supreme Court justices: Janet Rehnquist, daughter of the chief justice, became inspector general of the Department of Health and Human Services, while Eugene Scalia, son of Justice Antonin Scalia, became solicitor of the Department of Labor.[1]

Other important party families likewise enjoyed favor. The Bush White House helped to anoint Elizabeth Dole, wife of the GOP's 1996 presidential nominee, for nomination and election as U.S. senator from North Carolina. Colin Powell, who might have contended for the 2000 nomination himself, became secretary of state and saw his son named chairman of the Federal Communications Commission. The twenty-eight-year-old son of Senator Strom Thurmond of South Carolina was nominated for U.S. attorney in that state, despite being just three years out of law school.

Old Bush loyalists returned to Washington like exiled Stuarts flocking back to the London of Charles II in 1660. Richard Cheney, defense secretary in the previous Bush regime, was now vice president. Donald Rumsfeld and Cheney had, respectively, been chief of staff and deputy chief of staff in the Ford White House of 1975. Rumsfeld, who had also been secretary of defense in 1976, came back to the Pentagon a quarter century later. Andrew Card, whose relations with the senior George Bush dated to the Republican National Committee of 1972, was appointed White House chief of staff. Karl Rove, a political aide to the Bushes over the same period, took up the post of chief White House political adviser.

The imperial presidency of the 1960s had also bred dynastic loyalty. John F. Kennedy was scarcely in office before he named his brother Robert as U.S. attorney general and managed to pass his Massachusetts Senate seat to his youngest brother, Edward, who only just met the age requirement. But neither of the brothers succeeded in his own later presidential bid— Robert Kennedy fell to an assassin's bullet in 1968, while Edward Kennedy was defeated by incumbent Jimmy Carter in the 1980 Democratic presidential primaries. Lyndon Johnson and Richard Nixon, the other two incumbents sharing the imperial zenith, might have been tempted to follow suit, save that their brothers were ne'er-do-wells and their only children were daughters.

The result was to leave the dynastic presidency to make its appearance almost without warning, to a nation preoccupied with the millennium and a bursting stock market bubble.

A Confusion of Dynasties

George W. Bush doubtless found renewed discussion of the dynasty issue an acceptable price tag of his political victory in the 2002 elections. But a probing spotlight had been turned on. The *New York Times,* above the fold on the front of its November 10, 2002, "Week in Review" section, blazoned a half-page color picture of Air Force One with the simple, stark legend: "Defying Expectations, a Bush Dynasty Begins to Look Real."

Not so, replied Republican pollsters: Rather than perceiving the continuity of a dynasty, the public viewed presidents number forty-one and number forty-three as separate entities. More candor had come from the Bushes themselves, both *père et fils,* almost two years earlier. On inauguration day, George H. W. Bush had jokingly referred to his son as "Quincy," reminding everyone that he was not the first president's son to succeed to the republican purple. The former president later furnished a laudatory quote for a book conveniently entitled *America's First Dynasty: The Adamses, 1735–1918.*[2]

The Adamses, however, do not furnish a meaningful analogy. A quarter of a century separated the two presidents, and Quincy (as he is familiarly known) was put in office by a different political party from his father's. Nothing about his controversial election (by the House of Representatives) fortified his office, which he lost after one term. Still, the Adams example was welcomed in Bush-era Washington: See, father-and-son presidencies are as American as apple pie! A Kennedy analogy was also at hand. Early in 2001, George W. Bush invited the Kennedy family to a preview of *Thirteen Days,* a movie about the 1961 Cuban missile crisis. In November, he dedicated the new U.S. Justice Department building named for former attorney general Robert Kennedy; Senator Edward Kennedy, in attendance, expressed his pleasure. The message was unsubtle: Democrats, too, have dynasties.

Thomas Jefferson and James Madison would not have rested that easy in 1789 or in 1800, when memory was fresh of overthrowing a king in the American Revolution. The hint of a hereditary chief executive would have been inflammatory. But by 2001, ten generations had passed since the debates of the early Republic.

By the late twentieth century, thinkers had begun to posit that American voters, in ceremoniously choosing and inducting a president, were actually in psychological hot pursuit of a king. Public attitudes had been further conditioned by the familiarity of media-bestowed titles of democratic "royalty"—dukes of the baseball diamond and queens of country music. The loss of John F. Kennedy Jr. in a 1999 airplane crash was treated as the death of a royal prince. The peril that this popular-culture royalism might carry over into the selection of leaders was ignored beyond political science seminars.

The 2000 election gave new impetus to dynasticism. Besides the Supreme Court's role and the implications of the second Bush's being chosen just eight years after his father and by the same party establishment, genealogy had become a national hobby. Americans looking for great-great-grandparents were thronging records offices from Donegal and East Anglia to Palermo. The Bushes themselves proudly drew attention to their English royal blood, a lineage upheld by the arbiters in London. John Adams, a signer of the Declaration of Independence, would have choked; John F. Kennedy, grandson of a Boston saloonkeeper, would have heard Irish ghosts laughing uproariously.

The two Georges, however, cherished their Plantagenet and Tudor forebears. Early biographies of George H. W. Bush stressed the seventeenth-century New England roots on both the Bush and Walker sides of the family, alleging that Senator Prescott Bush and his family descended from English king Henry III. Then, after George H. W. had won the 1988 presidential election, London-based *Burke's Peerage,* the world's authority on royal lineage, all but bowed.

Harold Brooks-Baker, publishing director of *Burke's,* allowed that some other U.S. presidents had royal connections, "but none as royal as George Bush." Rather than to Henry III, he traced Bush's family history to Mary, the sister of King Henry VIII, who became part of the Bush family tree by wedding the duke of Suffolk.[3] Queen Elizabeth, Brooks-Baker pronounced, was thus the president's distant cousin.

In 2002, an American company, MyFamily.com, also traced George W. Bush and Winston Churchill to a common ancestor, fifteenth-century Northamptonshire squire Henry Spencer.[4] This pleased the second President Bush, who had placed a bust of Churchill on his desk in 2001.

To call the Bushes a "not-quite-royal family" captures the between-ness of their position. While no American presidential family can actually be royal—the Constitution, to begin with, specifies that "No title of nobility shall be granted by the United States"—the Bushes' triple predilection for royal genealogy, restoration, and an unacknowledged dynasty is an extraordinary coincidence. Biographers have also been reminded that Barbara (Pierce) Bush is descended from the fourteenth president, Franklin Pierce, which gives her son presidential genes on both sides of his family. Barbara Bush said of her eldest son in 2000 that "he should be president," at least implying his descent as a credential.

The chairman of the 2000 Republican presidential campaign, Donald Evans, went so far as to call the Bushes "America's Family." Certainly they have appeared to presume entitlement. Before Prescott Bush was elected to the U.S. Senate from Connecticut in 1952, he had decided that a mere seat in the House of Representatives was not worth giving up his managing partnership at Brown Brothers Harriman for. Five or so years after Prescott Bush went to the Senate, George H. W. Bush's nascent ambitions seem to have locked in on that same upper house, hoping for a family continuity.

Stephen Hess, who in 1966 published the book *America's Political Dynasties,* thirty-six years later agreed that the Bushes should be considered a dynasty, but an "accidental" one. True enough, in the sense that the accident of Bill Clinton's moral shortcomings and impeachment may have been a precondition for Bush's accession in 2000. Even so, the speed and seriousness of the family's efforts to make George W. Bush governor of Texas in 1994 and to do likewise for his brother in Florida more than hinted at its higher goals. Goaded by their father's defeat, the next generation of Bushes laid plans to come back.

The Founding Father: George Herbert Walker

There is more of George Herbert Walker than of anyone else in the names of both George Herbert Walker Bush, his grandson, and George Walker

Bush, his great-grandson. We may say the same of his role in the Bush family's midcentury success. In 2003, George H. W. Bush provided material for a laudatory book about his father, Prescott Bush, identifying him as the first U.S. senator to be both father and grandfather of a president. In this case, "legacy" was the term he preferred to "dynasty." Financially, however, George H. Walker, a generation older, was the clan's founding father, much as Joseph P. Kennedy was the economic enabler of his political brood. Some in the Walker family implied the same, emphasizing how much attention and career assistance George Herbert Walker and George Herbert Walker II gave to two generations of Bushes.

Both the Walkers and the Bushes were old and prosperous families even in the mid–nineteenth century. The first Bush to attend Yale was the forty-third president's great-great-grandfather, James Smith Bush, in the 1850s. He went on to become an Episcopalian minister in Staten Island, New York, and his son, Samuel Prescott Bush, learned engineering at nearby Stevens Institute of Technology in New Jersey. The Walkers were wealthier, though. Great-great-grandfather David Walker had built the largest dry goods import firm west of the Mississippi. Much of his business was with Britain, where he also sent his son, George Herbert Walker, to school during the 1880s.

For political reasons, office seekers in the Bush family have frequently misrepresented their social and economic status. Senator Prescott Bush pretended that modest income kept his father from sending him to law school after he graduated from Yale in 1913. George H. W. Bush purported to have "interviewed" for his first job. George W. Bush chose to portray himself as a young man molded and Texified by San Jacinto Junior High School. The historian Herbert Parmet, in his biography *George Bush: The Life of a Lone Star Yankee,* described the tactical genesis of this class denial:

> Prescott's recorded reminiscences, given in 1966, present, somewhat disingenuously, a hint of genteel poverty, undoubtedly a habit cultivated by one who had spent the bulk of his previous two decades canvassing for votes among ordinary people. To deny the realities of his background, the stature of his father as a leading industrialist of the day, was consistent with perpetuating the myth of the self-made man. Prescott had been a U.S. Senator from Connecticut at the time he gave the interview and was practiced at minimizing his pedigree. He claimed that his father did not have enough money to put him through law school, a notion of financial limitations not

only at variance with his career and lifestyle but also one strongly rejected by those who knew anything about him.[5]

In fact, Samuel Bush had become wealthy as the president of Buckeye Steel Castings, a railroad-equipment-manufacturing firm, which he headed from 1908 until his retirement in 1927. It was a fair-sized steel plant, sprawling across many acres and specializing in railroad couplings and other steel castings needed by the large Morgan-, Harriman-, and Rockefeller-controlled rail systems. Frank Rockefeller, the brother of John D. and William, who went into Great Lakes iron ore and steel, preceded Samuel Bush as Buckeye's president from 1906 to 1908.[6] Through Buckeye, Bush had ties to the Rockefeller family, with its Standard Oil and National City Bank holdings.

Prominent in Ohio railroading as well as steel, Bush became a director of the Pennsylvania Railroad's Ohio subsidiaries, of the Hocking Valley Railway and the Norfolk and Western Railway, and of the Huntington National Bank. From 1917 to 1918 he served on the War Industries Board, where he was in charge of the forgings, guns, small arms, and ammunition section and later the facilities division. Besides founding the Ohio Tax League, Bush became the first president of the National Association of Manufacturers and a director of the Federal Reserve Bank of Cleveland. He built an imposing house with lavish gardens in the Columbus suburb of Bexley and sent his children east to boarding school—the girls to Connecticut's Westover, the boys (including Prescott) to Episcopalian St. George's in Newport, Rhode Island. The family spent summers in fashionable seaside Watch Hill, Rhode Island.[7]

Several hundred miles away in St. Louis, George H. Walker was becoming richer. By 1914, his investment firm, G. H. Walker and Company, founded in 1900, had become one of the more important in the Mississippi Valley. The principal history of U.S. investment banking has described the forces involved: "During the first decade or so of the 20th century the supply of domestic capital seeking investment also grew rapidly. Between 1900 and 1910, banking assets more than doubled, increasing from $10.7 billion to $22.4 billion, and many country banks in the Middle and Far West, which previously had invested almost exclusively in farm mortgages, started buying railroad, industrial and utility bonds. . . . The increase in funds for investment led to a growing interest in securities throughout the country."[8]

Walker got off to a quick start by buying and reselling companies like

Laclede Gas and the New Orleans, Texas and Mexico Railroad.[9] Success with various railroads in and around Texas—also including the St. Louis, Brownsville and Mexican, as well as several local lines absorbed into the Burlington and Santa Fe systems—brought Walker to the notice of E. H. Harriman, owner of the vast Union Pacific system; his son Averell; and Texas judge Robert S. Lovett, who took charge of the UP after E. H. Harriman's death in 1909. Walker's English schooling and relationships also piqued the interest of J. P. Morgan and Company, which took some of his underwritings and used his firm in securities syndicates. St. Louis, at that time, was the major financial center in the south-central United States and the nation's fifth-ranked city in investment banking.

The Republican Party preference Walker would display during the 1920s was hidden in his earlier St. Louis career. He was involved in both business deals, including the 1904 St. Louis World's Fair, and Democratic mayoral politics alongside two other well-known figures—ex–Missouri governor David Francis, later (1893–96) secretary of the interior, and millionaire St. Louis businessman Robert Brookings, who would go on to found Washington's Brookings Institution. When war broke out in Europe, Walker's connection to the House of Morgan became profitable; when the United States entered World War I in 1917, his connections to Francis, Brookings, Harriman, and Lovett became invaluable.

Steadfastly isolationist, parts of Missouri remained opposed to entering the conflict even after Washington declared war. Dozens of townships were still German-speaking. Not a few banks refused to participate in marketing British bonds. Such views were not shared by Walker and his pro-British friends. J. P. Morgan and Company, chosen in 1914 by Britain and France as their commercial agent for purchasing war supplies in the United States, carried out this function by establishing within the firm its famous Export Department under Morgan partner Edward Stettinius Sr. George H. Walker, with his knowledge of midwestern industrial production and railroad transportation, took on a minor but lucrative regional advisory role. Allied wartime purchases through Morgan ultimately came to $3.2 billion, a staggering sum more than four times the entire U.S. federal budget in 1914.[10]

When the United States finally entered the war, British purchases no longer went through Morgan but were handled by the Allied Purchasing Commission affiliated with the War Industries Board. Walker's luck was such that Robert Brookings went to Washington to become chairman of that board's Price-Fixing Committee. Judge Lovett, in turn, took over as the board's priorities commissioner. In addition, Brookings and Lovett also served as two of the three board members of the Allied Purchasing Commission. Chairman Bernard Baruch was the third.[11]

David Francis, appointed in 1916 as Woodrow Wilson's ambassador to Russia, occupied another privileged position in the web of wartime information and munitions contracts. The title of a recent biography of Francis, *Standing on a Volcano,* referred to his task of hammering out a commercial treaty with Russia, as well as advising on U.S. bank loans to the Russian government. In 1917, on his advice, the United States gave the Russian revolutionary government under Aleksandr Kerensky a $325 million credit, to be spent on war matériel from the United States.[12] George Walker kept in touch with Brookings, Lovett, and Francis, exchanging information, influencing war contracts, and placing friends and acquaintances in jobs from Washington to St. Petersburg. Future partner Averell Harriman, for his part, put aside railroading to build ships for the war effort, setting up near Philadelphia with a contract to construct forty freighters for the federal Emergency Shipping Corporation.[13] Not surprisingly, he remained in contact with his fellow wheeler-dealer.

In 1919, convinced to direct his postwar ambitions toward Germany and Russia, Harriman persuaded the ubiquitous "Bert" Walker to become president of a new Wall Street investment banking firm, W. A. Harriman and Company, being organized by the Harriman family with the collaboration of the Rockefeller-headed National City Bank and the Morgan-connected Guaranty Trust. Besides helping to guide the Harriman railroad interests, Walker would backstop Averell Harriman's own grand plans, which ranged from a participation in Germany's once-proud Hamburg-Amerika steamship line to oil and manganese interests in the Russian Caucasus. Walker moved to New York, and for more than a decade not only helped to run W. A. Harriman and Company but helped to direct separate Harriman personal and family investment vehicles like the Harriman Fifteen Corporation, the Silesian-American Corporation, and Harriman International. These, it would turn out, would be the more controversial enterprises. St. Louis newspapers described Walker in awed terms as the man responsible for assembling Harriman's overseas empire.[14]

In 1904, Walker and his father had built a summerhouse on what became Walker's Point in Kennebunkport, Maine, where they had begun vacationing in the 1890s. George Walker's eldest and favorite child, Dorothy, was born there in 1901. By the end of the 1920s—at his peak he was a director of seventeen corporations—he also had a home in Santa Barbara, California; an opulent residence at 1 Sutton Place in Manhattan; a country mansion on Long Island; and "Duncannon," a ten-thousand-acre South Carolina lodge and preserve where the younger Bushes would hunt doves and quail and shoot skeet.[15] Some winters saw him take a house in Aiken, South Carolina, just a few miles from the polo field where Averell Harriman—a dedicated, eight-goal player—ran his string of ponies. (For a short time, Walker and Harriman had a stable together on Long Island, racing horses under their own colors.)

Like Harriman, Walker sometimes took his extended family south in a private railroad car. One Bush granddaughter described the happy times at Duncannon, remembering "the wonderful food and the care taken over the slightest things, like the trimmed edges of the grapefruit. We were waited on by the most wonderful black servants who would come into the bedrooms early in the morning and light those crackling pine-wood fires."[16]

Walker was flinty—an amateur heavyweight boxing champion in his youth—and something of a pirate in business. He was a lover of golf and Scotch whisky, a notable ladies' man—he courted and married Lucretia Wear, a famous beauty of the 1890s who had already attracted the St. Louis–bred fashion writer Condé Nast—and a bear to members of his own family. Years later, granddaughter Elsie Walker called him "a tough father, a tough old bastard. . . . There really wasn't a lot of love on the part of the boys [her father and uncles] for their father."[17]

When his daughter Dorothy—like her father a hard-charging athlete—met Prescott Bush in St. Louis in 1919, Walker quickly warmed to him as a fellow golfer and sportsman who was also handsome, smooth, and polished in an Ivy League way, something Walker was not. Dorothy and Prescott married in 1921, and after Prescott Bush had several years' experience elsewhere, he came to work for his father-in-law at W. A. Harriman and Company as a vice president in 1926. With the added assistance of his own Yale and Harriman connections, he became Walker's heir apparent, emerging as one of the managing partners in the merged firm of Brown Brothers Harriman by the mid-thirties.

If George H. Walker was something of a second father to Prescott Bush, the same and perhaps more can be said of the relationship of his son

George Herbert ("Uncle Herbie") Walker Jr. to Prescott's son George H. W. Bush. While the successful public careers came on the Bush side of the family, the financial assistance and business mentoring was dispropor- tionately on the Walker side. Many years later, when his uncle was dy- ing, George H. W. sent an emotional letter telling him how much he had needed him "as my father, my brother and my best friend."[18]

Having to acknowledge and accept the influence and money of two Walker generations cannot always have been easy for Samuel Bush and then for Prescott Bush. In Greenwich, even after Prescott and Dorothy Bush had been married for almost two decades, the title to the big house on Grove Lane was in the name of Dorothy Walker Bush. Only in 1981, when George H. W. Bush became vice president, did the Walkers, prompted by the security-minded invasiveness of the Secret Service, suggest that he pur- chase and move into the big family house on Walker's Point in Kenne- bunkport. One can easily imagine this longtime economic subordination spurring a compensating Bush drive for office and political power.

At the same time, however, the Bushes rode steadily higher as the main historical currents of 1917–60 created a new U.S. global hegemony and a domestic military–national security complex. These developments meshed with the almost simultaneous maturation of an American establishment drawn in part from the management of two world wars but also reflecting the interwar golden era of the preparatory school, Harvard-Yale-Princeton, investment banking, diplomatic service, and Wall Street legal axis that columnist Joseph Alsop rightly called the "WASP Ascendancy."[19]

The Twentieth-Century Heyday of the Old-Boy Network

Whether such claims for the rise of an American aristocracy are exagger- ated or not, the early and mid–twentieth century did see a partial Amer- ican equivalent—in some ways, a transatlantic imitation—of the prior British Ascendancy, rooted in Eton and Harrow, Oxford and Cambridge, the Guards, the Foreign Office, and the like. Over the years, dozens of its participants have nostalgically described everything from the cutlery at Harvard's Porcellian Club to the portions of the Connecticut Gold Coast deemed most acceptable in polite society. During the fifties and sixties, the name Bush did not show up in these various memoirs, recollections, and chronicles of white-shoe America. Only in the seventies did it begin to creep into sentences and footnotes, but by the eighties it commanded paragraphs and pages, and now the white-shoe racks in the Bush closet have become a literary staple.

George H. W. Bush's first biographer, Nicholas King, a Harvard man who worked for Charles Bohlen at the U.S. embassy in France and then for Bush himself at the United Nations, may have reflected the family's own 1980 perceptions of their network's heyday when he started: "At the close of the 1930s and on the eve of the Second World War, these [prep] schools were at their apogee. They set the academic standards and their graduates dominated the major Eastern colleges, especially the Ivy League. They also brought the famous 'old boy networks' to the peak of their power. To be a graduate of Andover is no doubt still of some importance to the world, but then it had special significance."[20]

Within the upper tier of prep schools and colleges, clubs and secret societies were considered the innermost sanctum. Andover's AUV (Auctoritas, Unitas, Veritas—Authority, Unity, Truth), to which George H. W. Bush belonged, was the acme at that school until the secret societies were abolished after World War II. Its code of secrecy was a teenager's preparation for what might follow in college. At Harvard, so important was Porcellian that rejection by it provided Franklin D. Roosevelt's unhappiest recollection. Theodore Roosevelt was so proud of being in the "Porc" that he boasted of it to Germany's Kaiser Wilhelm. In this same decade, Grotonian Averell Harriman helped lead a move to Yale as a protest against Groton-Porcellian clique-ism at Harvard. At Yale, "the most legendary of all college clubs was Skull and Bones. To be tapped by Bones in that era was akin to canonization. . . . The clocks [at Bones] were set five minutes fast to symbolize that Bonesmen started life a leg up."[21]

Columnist Joseph Alsop, himself a Porcellian man, still upheld the ascendancy of that era's WASP schools in a late-1980s retrospect: "I don't know quite how to define it without sounding a fool except to say that it really was an ascendancy—in fact, an inner group that was recognizable as a group."[22] John McCloy, chairman of the Chase Bank and prominent enough in the 1950s to be thought of as the establishment's unofficial chairman, protested that he really wasn't, because of his middle-class origins. "Yes, of course," he acknowledged, there was an establishment. "They were Skull and Bones, Groton, that sort of thing. That was the elite. . . . I always had it in mind, even to this day, that I was not really a part of that."[23]

That three generations of Bushes *have* been "part of that" is central to the family's ascent.

Friend and foe alike have tied success at the network's schools to three essential underpinnings: good family, good attitude (loyalty to the school and to one's peers), and good skill at sports. Rough edges made for a poor fit. Prescott Bush (St. George's 1913, Yale 1917, Skull and Bones) and George H. W. Bush (Andover 1942, Yale 1948, Skull and Bones) fit well, thereby unfolding a kind of red carpet on which they could later walk comfortably through the upper echelons of American life.

Prescott Bush's skill in athletics—he excelled in tennis, was captain of the baseball team, and played a championship-level golf game—made him stand out in his class, impressed his future father-in-law, and aided his subsequent career. Imposing at six feet four inches, polished and courtly, he was a man who conveyed integrity and did well with clients and customers— more a meeter-and-greeter than the clever sort who pioneered innovative transactions or stratagems. "Movie-star handsome, tall and athletic," in the words of his biographer, "he was a rain-maker, earning his money primarily by charming and snaring potential clients."[24] As managing partner of Brown Brothers Harriman, he sat on an impressive array of corporate boards—Prudential Insurance, Pan American Airlines, CBS, the Simmons Company, Dresser Industries, Pennsylvania Water and Power, and the Vanadium Corporation of America—where his business, social, and government connections were valued.[25]

Besides golf, though, what Prescott Bush seemed to like most of all was singing. Alsop recalled many hours of choruses and bothy ballads at Harvard's Porcellian, but it was at Yale that song was particularly emphasized as a facet of male bonding—witness the prominence of the Whiffenpoofs and a host of lesser imitators with names like the Grill Room Grizzlies. Throughout Bush's busy investment career, he sang in different clubs and quartets, often traveling to do so. According to one former Yale Glee Club president, "It was his ear, his enthusiasm and his concept of a second bass part in a quartet which revolutionized barbershop singing."[26] Besides singing with the Whiffenpoofs, he brought them along on the Senate campaign trail. Even for many Connecticut voters it was a bit too much Old Blue.

Fitzhugh Green, another George Bush biographer, characterized the elder Bush as a man who "believed in principles, but left no substantive footprints. He offered no particular vision, except that of a life of rectitude and of music—always music, shared with the young."[27] As a senator, Bush enjoyed his ten years on the Hill but made little legislative mark, a charge akin to the one later directed at his son. Still, fellow legislators respected the influence he had both in Wall Street circles and as one of President Eisenhower's favorite golfing partners. It also helped, as one colleague observed, that he looked like "a Roman senator."

The career benefits of Groton, AUV at Andover, and Skull and Bones were enormous, as the Bushes would discover in everything from bull and bear to cloak-and-dagger. Yet in some ways, the products of such schools were unsuited for the battlefields of elective politics. Cyril Connolly, an English Old Etonian, observed that these institutions tended to instill a state of permanent adolescence in their alumni, arresting aspects of personal development and extending a taste for wine, song, pranks, initiations, oaths of secrecy, inner sanctums, and other rites of loyalty far into middle age.[28]

As a twenty-three-year-old new army captain in 1918, Prescott Bush foolishly sent a joke letter to his hometown newspaper, the *Columbus State-Journal,* announcing that he had been awarded the Distinguished Service Cross, the Victoria Cross, and the Legion of Honor on World War I's western front for saving the lives of Generals Pershing, Foch, and Haig by bringing down an almost fatal artillery shell with his bolo knife.[29] His parents had a little explaining to do. Earlier that year, together with four other officers-cum-Bonesmen, he was said to have plundered Geronimo's grave near Fort Sill, Oklahoma, to take the Apache chief's skull back to the Skull and Bones Vault at Yale. Even at age fifty-seven in 1952, introducing presidential candidate Dwight Eisenhower at Yale, he wore a collegian's raccoon coat, acting like a cheerleader until students started calling "Down, Bush."[30]

George H. W. Bush had his own distinctive preppy streak. In addition to his famous narration while playing horseshoes—a triumphant "Mr. Smooth does it again" with each ringer—his recurrent bursts of enthusiastic schoolboy phraseology even as president were sometimes described as "Bush-speak." His enthusiasm extended to schoolboy games. The U.S. ambassador to Kenya, Robinson McIlvaine, after a 1971 visit by the Bushes to Nairobi, recalled how Bush would sit down with McIlvaine's niece and her youthful friends to play "thumper," a game like slapjack in which players had to bang on the carpet when a particular card turned up. The slow thumper lost the hand. Bush, captivated, would ask in subsequent Christmas cards who had been the best thumper recently. One year, said McIlvaine, he enclosed a picture of Nikita Khrushchev banging his shoe on the Soviet desk in the UN General Assembly with a note: "You see, we play Thumper at the United Nations, too."[31]

A study of the first Bush administration by two *Time* reporters revealed further evidence of that adolescent streak. "He cued up exploding golf balls made of chalk for unsuspecting visitors at Kennebunkport. On Halloween 1988 he donned a rubber George Bush mask and walked through his campaign plane exhorting passengers to 'Read my lips! Read my lips!'" He was also a man who "howled with laughter when he played the twenty-dollar-bill-on-the-end-of-a-string trick on unsuspecting waiters at the Chinese embassy; who would greet visitors to the Oval Office by placing a wind-up mechanical bumblebee on the floor and letting it buzz around; who walked around the White House with a voice-activated stuffed monkey that socked itself on the head whenever the commander in chief began to talk."[32]

George W. Bush, in turn, is sometimes portrayed as having developed such tendencies in a fraternity-boy vacuum, without noting this larger family heritage—for example, his penchant during the 2000 campaign for doing imitations of Dr. Evil, the campy villain in the movie *Austin Powers: The Spy Who Shagged Me.* Journalist Frank Bruni, in his 2000 campaign book *Ambling into History,* referred to him as "part scamp and part bumbler, a timeless fraternity boy and heedless cutup," and recalled one campaign episode in which Bush "took his [airplane hot towel], cleaned his hands with it, and then did something less expected: draped it over his entire face and then turned abruptly toward me. He was, at this point, the presumptive Republican presidential nominee . . . and he was playing a toddler's game of peek-a-boo."[33] By then such antics were third-generation stuff.

None of this clowning seems to have compromised family ambition. Prescott Bush's political career was both gentlemanly and, in its way, successful. His wife later said he had wanted to be president, believing that if he had started in politics at an earlier age, he might have been.[34] More likely, such an effort would have failed because of his Wall Street background and certain World War II controversies, to which we will return. Perhaps his son knew, understood, and internalized what his father had privately desired.

Certainly George H. W. Bush's political career and style resembled his father's. It is not clear that he cared much about politics before his father went to the Senate in 1952. But as Prescott Bush's second term passed the halfway mark in 1959–60, his son was beginning to prepare for a political career in Texas. He held off running for office until he had accumulated enough money to be independent and could bear the expense of public service while maintaining personal comfort. Like his father, he made his first political bid for a U.S. Senate seat, starting close to the top. This is the period that may have inculcated dynastic hopes.

Like his father, Bush had been a notable athlete, both at Andover and at Yale. He captained baseball teams in both places and, in his own words, later half considered being "a tennis bum."[35] He became a big man on campus at Andover—one might think of the two columns of club memberships and extracurricular activities listed under his picture in the 1942 Phillips Andover yearbook as his first résumé—by epitomizing popularity, good attitude, and school spirit. He would do so again at Yale, albeit attending after World War II as a married man, which made him less of a joiner.

Confronting burning issues or making ideological commitments was not part of his early political makeup. Bush's 1964 and 1966 election campaigns employed heavy advertising to downplay issues and elevate the candidate's personal appeal, casting him as a young family man on the go, hard at work in shirtsleeves and tie with a suit jacket carelessly thrown over his shoulder, Kennedy-style. Ironically, such image making provided a fair clue to what Bush would be in office: lithe, athletic, handsome, personable, and ambitious—always seeking friends and striding purposefully toward the approval of authority figures able to bestow his next nomination or appointive office.*

In the more cynical seventies and eighties, assessments of the legislative and policy achievements in George H. W. Bush's résumé generally concluded that it came up short. His preppy watchband would provide an opportunity for caricature assassination. His reputation for glad-handing and promoting, the political equivalent of school spirit, became a tired stereotype. Surveying Bush's 1971–72 service as U.S. ambassador to the

---

* Cousin Ray Walker, a psychiatrist, described George H. W. Bush this way: "He always placated his father. Then, later on, he placated his bosses. That is how he relates—by never defining himself against authority."[36]

United Nations, even sympathetic biographer Green described him as "so enthusiastic and thorough in his official entertaining that the mission protocol officer called him 'the Perle Mesta of the U.N.' He didn't stop with the big ceremonial parties. He took a dozen or so members of the U.S. Economic and Social Council with him one night to sit in his Uncle Herbert Walker's box at Shea Stadium to watch the Mets play baseball. He took others for Sunday meals at his parents' house in Greenwich, Connecticut."[37] Wordy speeches in the UN General Assembly often found the U.S. ambassador at work penning his trademark short thank-you notes to fellow delegates and others.

When he was chairman of the Republican National Committee in 1973–74, his behavior was much the same, as he covered the country "like a Republican brush salesman for a total of 124,000 miles, giving 118 speeches and 84 press conferences. Wherever he went he passionately insisted that no White House hand had been in the Watergate jam pot."[38] Like his father, he was more charmer than thinker.

By now his image had begun to suffer. In 1972, *New York* magazine included Bush in its list of "The Most Over-Rated Men in New York." In 1974, Bryce Harlow, an old Washington hand who was helping Gerald Ford to pick a vice president, felt obliged to point out George Bush's essential duality. On the one hand, the popular Bush had garnered the most support in an informal survey of Republicans in Congress, the GOP National Committee, the cabinet, and the White House staff. On the other hand, said Harlow, many of the nation's top leaders "regarded him as intellectually 'light.'"[39]

It was no longer enough, apparently, to be Poppy Bush, "the greatest kid in school," navy combat pilot at twenty, son of a U.S. senator who had headed a major Wall Street investment bank. Vietnam and Watergate had changed the nation's political and cultural yardsticks. The up elevator of the old establishment—of the World War II "Wise Men" and the newer "Best and Brightest" of the Kennedy era—had lost much of its power.

Perhaps surprisingly, however, the change turned out not to matter. Bush served two additional short stints in high offices—as chief of the U.S. mission to the Chinese government in Beijing (1974–75) and then as director of the Central Intelligence Agency (1976). There, he helped to convince his old associates in Congress to stop investigating the CIA. Just as important, his appointment reassured senior CIA officialdom: No Bonesman from Yale, whose father had been an intimate associate of both Allen

Dulles and Robert A. Lovett, would let them down. Yale history professor Gaddis Smith has observed that "Yale has influenced the CIA more than any other university, giving the CIA the atmosphere of a class reunion."[40] Bush kept the faith, although some faulted him for picking agreeable rather than talented top aides.[41]

By 1978, he had decided to run for president. Biographers have acknowledged how some individuals and audiences he told of his plans in 1977–78 were taken aback: President of what? they asked. What corporation? No, the reply came: president of the United States. Bush clearly lacked the usual election victories and obvious geographic bases. His own base was more diffuse and establishmentarian: old friends and old fortunes. One of those friends admitted, "We had a terrible time keeping the UN ambassadors from forming a club for George Bush, or keeping the CIA from organizing support for him. That would not have been very helpful."[42] What he also had, besides his résumé and social cachet, was the support of much of Gerald Ford's 1976 organization, including campaign manager James A. Baker III, Bush's old Houston chum. So, despite the skepticism at bourbon-and-sirloin venues like the Republican Men's Club of Texas, his candidacy was far from being merely fanciful.

True, Ronald Reagan drubbed George H. W. Bush in the 1980 nomination race. The former California governor also developed enough distaste for his challenger to refuse at first to consider him for vice president. Yet Bush, who had won a pivotal early caucus in Iowa, also won Connecticut and Massachusetts in midseason. Thereafter, he managed to triumph in two later primaries in Pennsylvania and Michigan with the help of Ford-connected state party organizations. Reagan, after spending heavily in the early contests to overwhelm his multiple foes—Bush, John Connally, John Anderson, Howard Baker, Bob Dole, and Philip Crane—was drained of cash by late April. A relative handful of primary and caucus victories and several hundred delegates were enough to make Bush the runner-up. Thereafter, the need to mend a breach with the GOP's old eastern establishment wing obliged a reluctant Reagan to turn to him as a running mate.

For Bush the real prize, of course, lay in staking his claim to the political and governmental succession. Eisenhower's vice president, Richard Nixon, had gone on to be the next Republican chief executive. Nixon, in turn, was succeeded by *his* last vice president, Gerald Ford. Never elected to any office higher than two terms in the House of Representatives from the

Seventh District of Texas, George H. W. Bush was now in place to achieve the same ultimate promotion. If the old establishment of midcentury was fading, its credentials had lasted just long enough to bring one of its own to the brink of power.

The American Politico-Economic Establishment and the Two World Wars

The power structure that emerged in World War I and reached the height of prestige during the Second World War and the two following decades was obviously far more than just a social phenomenon. Groups like Skull and Bones were a clubby symptom but hardly a driving force. Part of the new establishment came from the organization and hierarchies of national mobilization that had been established during the two wartimes—years that, quite simply, had realigned the world.

These were the broad tracks along which the Walker and Bush families climbed, financially and politically. Over the years they led the family to an involvement with the mainstays of the twentieth-century American national security state: finance, oil and energy, the federal government, the so-called military-industrial complex, and the CIA, the National Security Agency, and the rest of the intelligence community. From just 5 to 10 percent of U.S. gross domestic product in 1914, these sectors' share in 1950 may have reached as high as 30 percent, bringing a parallel transformation of America's interest-group and power structures.

Some scholars of the U.S. military-industrial complex date its origins back to the construction of a large steel-clad navy in the 1880s and 1890s, which made serious demands on government spending, heavy industry, and metallurgy. Most agree that the future complex took definable shape during the First World War, even though the disarmament treaties of the 1920s and neutrality sentiments of the 1930s kept military outlays too low to sustain preparedness until rearmament began in 1939–40.[43] After Pearl Harbor was attacked in 1941, many who had cut their teeth during the 1917–18 mobilization were given much larger war-related responsibilities, cementing earlier elite credentials.

Franklin D. Roosevelt's own role in 1917–18 as assistant secretary of the navy had included a lot of hard bargaining over war contracts. FDR had been caught up in, if not always impressed by, that mobilization. As president, if he didn't know those involved in the current effort from his years at Groton and Harvard, many were familiar from Woodrow Wilson's wartime Washington. Both wartime mobilizations created lasting networks.

Bernard Baruch, who had run the War Industries Board (WIB) in which Samuel Bush, Judge Robert S. Lovett, Clarence Dillon, and Robert Brookings had all worked, renewed his engagement in the early 1930s, helping to brainstorm the National Recovery Administration and drawing up FDR's Interwar Industrial Mobilization plan. He came out of retirement on a limited basis in 1943 to become chief policy consultant to the federal Office of War Management (OWM), and FDR at one point flirted with reinstalling him in the top job.

Averell Harriman, finished with shipbuilding, kept his financial stakes in Brown Brothers Harriman and his other investments but jumped into the New Deal by working with two former WIB officials, Hugh Johnson and Herbert Bayard Swope, in the National Recovery Administration in New York and then Washington. He went on to become FDR's emissary to Churchill and Lend-Lease administrator, then ambassador to Russia, ambassador to Britain, and, after World War II, secretary of commerce and mutual security administrator.

When World War II came, well-connected investment firms virtually doubled as Washington placement bureaus. Judge Lovett's son Robert A. Lovett, one of Prescott Bush's partners at Brown Brothers Harriman, became assistant secretary of war for air under Secretary Henry Stimson. Another Brown Brothers Harriman alumnus, Artemus Gates, took over as assistant secretary of the navy for air. From Dillon Read, the Wall Street firm that Clarence Dillon had turned into a powerhouse after his War Industries Board service, James Forrestal became undersecretary of the navy in charge of its economic activities and procurement. Others at Dillon Read who joined the mobilization included Paul Nitze (later national security adviser), William Draper (later chief of the economic section for the postwar U.S. military government of Germany), Ferdinand Eberstadt (later vice chairman of the War Production Board and a founding father of the CIA), and C. Douglas Dillon (Clarence's son).

Harriman was not the only high climber. Forrestal became secretary of the navy in 1944 and secretary of defense in 1947. Edward Stettinius Jr., whose father had been the Morgan partner in charge of the 1914–17 purchase of U.S. arms and munitions for the French and British, had a series of key jobs: head of the War Resources Board in 1939, director of the Priorities Division of the Office of Production Management in 1941, under-secretary of state in 1943, and finally secretary of state in 1944. Lovett was named undersecretary of state, then undersecretary of defense, and finally became secretary of defense in 1951. So strongly had he come to epitomize establishment thinking that in 1961 John F. Kennedy, seeking exactly that gravitas after his hairbreadth victory, offered Lovett his *choice* of cabinet positions—State, Defense, or Treasury. When Lovett declined for health reasons, Kennedy took as treasury secretary C. Douglas Dillon.[44]

Some chroniclers have profiled the 1917–60 emergence of "the Wise Men" and others in terms of links forged at universities and clubs, not least the Skull and Bones hegemony at Brown Brothers Harriman (Averell Harriman, E. Roland Harriman, Robert A. Lovett, Artemus Gates, Prescott Bush, and several others). However, the argument for an elite at least partly shaped by war priorities and mobilization service seems almost as compelling. In later years, Lovett reminisced about his father's "Manhattan and Locust Valley dinner parties attended by old friends from the War Industries Board, where he heard discussions about industrial mobilization and offered his own ideas on the importance of airplanes to the nation's transportation and defense."[45] Professor Robert Sobel, in *The Life and Times of Dillon Read,* noted that for Clarence Dillon, "the WIB experience was a watershed event . . . creating a community of interests and shared experiences second in Dillon's case only to that of Harvard."[46] Grosvenor Clarkson, secretary of the Council of National Defense, an early forerunner of the WIB, later recalled, with only some exaggeration, that "the War Industries Board of the United States had in the end a system of concentration of commerce, industry, and all the powers of government that was without compare among all the other nations, friend or enemy, involved in the World War."[47]

In any event, the opportunities offered by Wall Street in the post–World War I era were little short of mind-boggling. Britain's *Manchester Guardian* had seen the change coming as early as 1917: "The war has radically transformed the relations between the United States and Europe. . . . The United States by the end of this war will have wiped out most of its debt to foreign investors. It will have a currency of unimpeachable magnitude. The American bankers will have acquired the experience they have hitherto lacked in the international money market. . . . It can hardly be doubted that under these circumstances, New York will enter the lists for the financial leadership of the world."[48] By 1919, the transfer of financial power was speeding up. Sterling's postwar weakness had obliged the British Treasury to impose an informal embargo on British merchant banks' making foreign loans, which in effect moved a great deal of international business to New York. The world was about to become America's financial oyster.

As U.S. bankers and businessmen cast their eyes overseas, shrewd law firms took on attorneys with war-era experience. Dean Acheson, who would climb the ladder from assistant secretary of state for European affairs in 1941 to secretary of state in 1949, wrote his own first book about the legal concepts developed by the War Labor Board.[49] The name partners of the new Washington law firm he joined in 1922, Covington, Burling and Rublee, were respectively a well-connected Maryland congressman, the general counsel of the wartime Shipping Board, and an attorney who had worked with the Council of National Defense and with the French on the Allied Maritime Transport Council.

On Wall Street, three of the law firms interacting with the future military-industrial and national security complexes were Cravath, Henderson and de Gersdorff; Sullivan and Cromwell; and Donovan, Leisure. Heading the latter was "Wild Bill" Donovan, the World War I Congressional Medal of Honor winner who would go on to organize the World War II Office of Strategic Services (OSS), which served as the embryo of the CIA. The Cravath firm, meanwhile, drew its momentum from Paul Cravath's 1914–17 prominent drumbeating alongside the Morgan interests on behalf of the Allies, followed by his visibility in bankrolling the new Council on Foreign Relations in 1919.

At Sullivan and Cromwell, the moving force was John Foster Dulles, soon to be joined by his younger brother Allen. Both were grandsons of Secretary of State John Foster and nephews of Woodrow Wilson's wartime secretary of state, Robert Lansing. John Foster Dulles worked for the War Trade Board, thereafter attending the Versailles peace negotiations of 1919 as counsel to the U.S. Reparations Committee. A little later, Bernard Baruch, with whom Dulles had served on the Reparations Committee, arranged for the young lawyer to ghostwrite a book on the Versailles treaty. Brother Allen also went to Versailles, as a State Department representative assigned to the redrawing of central European boundaries.[50] After the Republicans took the White House back in 1952, John Foster Dulles would become secretary of state, and Allen Dulles director of the CIA.

During this period some of the most ambitious men on Wall Street spent months or years in Europe, drumming up bond issues (to sell in the cash-flush United States) and potential industrial participation or acquisitions for American companies. Walter Isaacson and Evan Thomas described this up-Rhine and down-Danube commercial treasure hunt in *The Wise Men,* their study of Harriman, Lovett, Acheson, McCloy, et al.: "While the rest of the country slept in deep isolation, a close-knit clique of Wall Street bankers and lawyers, most of whom had traveled through Europe as children, met in the clubs of London and Paris and Berlin as friendly competitors putting together suitable investments for their firms. In a private and profit-seeking capacity, they were rebuilding a war-ravaged Europe in a manner as grandiose as many of these men would employ a world war later with the Marshall Plan."[51] The House of Morgan had a strong residual advantage in Britain and a lesser one in France but indulged a wartime legacy of distaste for Germany. Thus it was to Germany, the postwar republic, that an important group of Wall Streeters turned their particular attentions.

The most prominent were Averell Harriman, George H. Walker, Clarence Dillon, and the Dulles brothers. They often worked together in the 1920s, when ambitions were most grandiose, and in the 1930s, when embarrassing German relationships had to be sorted out, restructured, and even hidden. Many men with these particular involvements, or their family members, went on to become pillars of the U.S. national security and intelligence establishments during and after World War II.

Almost from the start, American investments of the 1920s in both Germany and Russia were controversial. Harriman, Walker, Dillon, and the Dulleses were variously criticized for customer chasing, reckless lending (many of the German redevelopment bonds underwritten went bad in 1929–32), and even aiding previous or potential enemies. The investments were also on a large scale. Through one or another financial vehicle, the Harriman firms arranged a major shareholding in the Hamburg-Amerika line, set up a U.S. bank to serve the German Thyssen steel interests, bought a one-third interest in the principal German-owned coal and zinc mines in Poland (through a holding company called the Silesian-American Corporation), and took a position in Germany's transatlantic cable company.

In 1925, their friendly rival, Dillon Read, helped to refinance the Thyssen steel interests with a $15 million bond issue and then followed in 1926–27 with $70 million in bond issues for the Vereinigte Stahlwerke (United Steelworks), a massive cartel of German coke, coal, iron, and steel producers.[52] During World War II, it would produce some 40 percent of Germany's steel plate, sheeting, pipes, and tubes. James Forrestal, who became Dillon Read's president in 1938, was for several years an officer of General Aniline, the cloaked U.S. subsidiary of I. G. Farben, the German chemical giant.[53] Partner William Draper, who handled some of the German business, was also codirector of a Dillon subsidiary, the German Credit and Investor Corporation of New Jersey, which specialized in U.S. investments in Germany.[54]

By the late 1930s, Brown Brothers Harriman—the former W. A. Harriman and Company—and Dillon Read were two notable active investors in a Germany rapidly rearming under Adolf Hitler. It is an irony, but not a coincidence, that by 1943, many of their best-known partners and executives—from Averell Harriman and James Forrestal to Robert Lovett, Douglas Dillon, William Draper, and David K. E. Bruce—were major figures in the Washington war effort or the Office of Strategic Services, as were the two Wall Street lawyers with the largest German practices—the two Dulleses. John Foster Dulles, as a board member of International Nickel, actually had helped work out that firm's prewar cartel agreement with I. G. Farben to provide Germany with a steady supply of nickel for armor plating. When Wall Street firms and major multinational corporations like General Motors, ITT, and Ford needed to rearrange German holdings, it was to these two that they turned. Prescott Bush, who handled much of the German work at Brown Brothers Harriman, used their services. In Allen Dulles's office notes of January 1937, the clients requiring cloaking of assets were short-handed as "Brown Brothers Harriman–Schroeder– Rock."[55]

The U.S. Justice Department had begun probing German-connected companies and investors in 1941, but Pearl Harbor and the U.S. declaration of war against both Germany and Japan put government investigations into overdrive. In early March 1942, a special Senate committee began public hearings on cartel agreements between U.S. and German firms. Before long William S. Farish, the chairman of Standard Oil of New Jersey, had pleaded no contest to charges of criminal conspiracy between his company and I. G. Farben. In keeping with cartel agreements, Standard had withheld from U.S. authorities information on the production of artificial rubber.

Secretary of War Stimson, a man with strong establishment ties—Andover, Yale, Skull and Bones, and service in both Republican and Democratic cabinets—asked President Roosevelt in March 1942 to stop the investigations because they would interfere with companies engaged in the war effort. However, that didn't stop the inquiries being made by the alien property custodian under the Trading with the Enemy Act of December 1941.

None of this would have been happy news for Prescott Bush at 59 Wall Street. In 1938, the firm had been collaterally involved in a German transaction—shipping tetraethyl lead needed by the Luftwaffe—by the Ethyl Corporation, of which Farish was a director and which was half owned by Standard Oil of New Jersey.[56] In 1941, the *New York Herald Tribune* had featured a front-page story headlined "Hitler's Angel Has $3 Million in U.S. Bank," reporting that steel baron Fritz Thyssen had channeled the money into the Union Banking Corporation, possibly to be held for "Nazi bigwigs."[57] UBC was the bank, nominally owned by a Dutch intermediary, that Brown Brothers Harriman ran for the German Thyssen steel family. Prescott Bush was a director.

In August 1942, the property of the Hamburg-Amerika line, for many years partly owned by the Harriman and Walker–controlled American Ship and Commerce Corporation, was seized under the Trading with the Enemy Act. On October 20, the alien property custodian seized the assets of the Union Banking Corporation. Eight days later, with UBC's books in hand, the government acted against two affiliates, the Holland-American Trading Corporation and the Seamless Steel Equipment Corporation. In November, the government seized the assets of the last major entity connected to Harriman, Walker, and Bush—the Silesian-American Corporation.

Politically, the significance of these dealings—the great surprise—is that none of it seemed to matter much over the next decade or so. A few questions would be raised, but Democrat Averell Harriman would not be stopped from becoming federal mutual security administrator in 1951 or winning election as governor of New York in 1954. No innuendo would keep John Foster Dulles from being appointed to a U.S. Senate seat in 1949 or becoming U.S. secretary of state in 1953. Nor would Republican Prescott Bush and his presidential descendants be hurt in any of their future elections.

It is almost as if these various German embroilments, despite their potential for scandal, were regarded as unfortunate but in essence business as usual. Or more plausibly, that at a high governmental level, such roles were unofficially reclassified as an intelligence function—a "tell us what you know about Germany" obligation. Those in the American legal and financial community who had decades of experience with Germany and well-placed connections there doubtless were considered to be important wartime national security assets, however questionable some of their overseas dealings. In any event, a surprising number of the descendants of men who had dealt with Germany—William S. Farish III, William Draper III, and Joseph Verner Reed Jr. (grandson of Remington Arms chairman Samuel Pryor, earlier a director of both UBC and American Ship and Commerce)— turned up as close personal advisers or high-level appointees in the George H. W. Bush administration.

Chapter 6 will look at these connections in more detail. For now, suffice it to say that besides its dynastic roots in the early years of the military-industrial complex, the Bush family and circle were quietly important in the midcentury emergence of the U.S. intelligence community. These connections go back more than three decades before George H. W. Bush's thirteen brief months as director of the Central Intelligence Agency from December 1975 to January 1977. National security as well as political connections would be vital to the family's success and standing over the quarter century following the end of World War II.

Paternal Footsteps Followed and Rejected: The Four-Generation Making of the Bush Dynasty

Dynastic persistence usually depends more on heredity than on bonds of affection. Among England's eighteenth-century Hanoverian kings, for example, eldest sons generally disliked their fathers. George II and George IV set up rival courts as Prince of Wales or prince regent before their fathers died. Three centuries earlier, English and French kings and Turkish sultans executed siblings, nephews, and cousins with hardly a thought.

By contrast, the dynastic houses of the United States, particularly the Kennedys and Bushes, have presented themselves with thoroughly warm, benign imagery: handsome and large extended families interrupting happy barbecues and brisk touch-football games to campaign for one another, burbling with a civic enthusiasm that might have been scripted by the Hollywood of the 1950s or drawn by Norman Rockwell as a *Saturday Evening Post* cover. Little press attention, however, is ever paid to the families' dark sides: the hereditary dysfunctions, crowds of old retainers, allied families and networks, supplicants for a second or third generation of favors, and the kind of persisting domestic or international vendettas that color the histories of the royal houses of Europe.

Any serious look at the Bush succession must be through these lenses. After four generations of wealth, the family has lost whatever nodding acquaintance its ancestors born in the 1860s might have had with Horatio Alger. By the mid-twentieth century, connections and crony capitalism had become the family economic staple, with emphasis on the rewards of finance, and instinctive policymaking fealty to the investment business. The Bushes have produced no college presidents or stonemasons, no scientists or plumbing contractors—generally speaking, their progeny have become almost exclusively financial entrepreneurs.

These recurrent economic biases are part of the subject matter of chapter 4. This chapter's focus, keyed to dynastic success itself, is on how four generations have sought to elevate the family, and the degree to which the heir in each generation—Prescott Bush Sr., George H. W. Bush, and George W. Bush—has imitated (or not imitated) the career path of his father. The putative answers begin to fill in some interpretive gaps. Fathers and sons have not always been as supportive as appearances suggested.

George Herbert Walker and Samuel Bush made their successes by leaving their fathers' vocations—respectively, dry goods and the Episcopal ministry—and striking out on their own. Neither was a particular role model for his own sons; both provoked some degree of filial resentment or distance. Prescott Bush talked about his father not having money for him, and did not go back to Columbus, Ohio, to work (save for a brief period after his mother died in an auto accident). He may have found more of an economic, political, and athletic authority figure in father-in-law George Herbert Walker. On the other hand, Prescott Bush may well have resented, by 1942, the nest of cobra eggs that his father-in-law had left under the names Union Banking Corporation, American Ship and Commerce, Silesian-American, and the rest. Former Justice Department official John Loftus suggests such disillusionment in his book *The Secret War Against the Jews.* Other chroniclers have avoided the subject.

What George H. W. Bush, in turn, was trying to do when he went from Andover into naval aviation training rather than Yale—and then when he went with Dresser Industries, an oil services company, rather than staying in New York with Brown Brothers Harriman—is also grist for interpretation. Was he rejecting that world or just trying to get out of his father's long eastern and Ivy League shadow?

Loftus, citing unnamed sources in the intelligence community, contends that the eighteen-year-old George H. W. Bush, in becoming a naval aviator, was trying to redeem the family honor from the German taint.[58] The greater weight of evidence, judged by the views of biographers, is that he had a great respect for his father, proudly following his path through Yale and Skull and Bones. Besides, at age eighteen, just out of Andover and with no college under his belt, he depended on his father's help to arrange an underage and unqualified entrance to the naval air program. While in theory this entrance would have appeared impossible, it might have been quite manageable with a telephone call from Prescott Bush to one of three fellow Yale and Skull and Bones men (the secretary of war, the assistant secretary of war for air, or the assistant secretary of the navy for air).

Indeed, when the new Yale graduate went to Dresser in 1948 instead of into investment banking, supposedly wanting no part of "getting a job with Dad's help and through Dad's friends," being hired was once again a mere paternal word away—a conversation between Prescott Bush, then a Dresser board member for eighteen years, and Dresser chairman Neil Mallon, yet another Bones comrade, whose own posting had originated two decades earlier on the whim of the management group at W. A. Harriman and Company. The managers had just bought and refinanced Dresser, and were looking for someone to run it. In neither case was the Bush apple falling too far from the tree.

The official history of Dresser Industries (1979) does not in fact sustain the legend that Bush struck out boldly for the wilds of Texas: "[Prescott] Bush's own regard for Dresser had been passed to his son, George, who, following World War II, had worked for [company treasurer Rudolph] Reimer in the Cleveland headquarters, then for Pacific Pumps and Ideco [two subsidiaries] before becoming an independent oil producer in Texas."[59] The upscale side of Midland, where Bush wound up living, quickly became a kind of Cambridge or New Haven South. Half of his friends in the oil business were transplanted Ivy Leaguers. The town's newly paved streets were named after Ivy League colleges: Millionaires lived along Princeton and Harvard Streets (as George W. later would). Small Midland, by itself, supported Harvard, Yale, and Princeton Clubs.

Interestingly, although Bush's independent oil ventures in Texas were family funded, only a relatively small stake ($50,000) came from his father.

The larger flow, another $350,000 in 1950 and $500,000 in 1953, came from the friends and clients of George Herbert Walker Jr.—Uncle Herbie— whose own children resented how much attention he (like his own father) seemed to concentrate on the Bushes. Where George H. W. Bush indisputably took after his own father, not after his Walker relations, was in preferring public office and in heading off toward politics once he had enough money to be independent. He also continued his father's national security interests in taking up the CIA directorship in 1975, as well as by (usually) being a New England–type Republican fiscal conservative and social moderate disinclined to wear ideological cowboy boots. His initial presidential nomination bid in 1980, instead of counting on the oil states or the South, looked hopefully toward early-voting Iowa and beyond to northeastern states.

Despite a much-advertised taste for pork rinds and country music, George H. W. Bush wound up even more of a Yale caricature than his father had been in 1952, in his raccoon coat cheerleading for Eisenhower. In 1988, after George H. W. lost the Republican caucuses in Iowa, he made the extraordinary excuse that his supporters were busy on the golf course or at air shows or debutante parties. That same year, Washington's Gridiron Club spoofed him with not inappropriate lyrics: "If your daughter's in cotillion and your son's enrolled at Choate and your wife is worth a million, I'm sure to get your vote."[60]

Son George W. Bush, despite making the Connecticut-to-Texas transformation with sagebrush panache, took his father as a role model. In 2000, Elizabeth Mitchell, executive editor at *George,* the magazine begun by John F. Kennedy Jr., published a book called *W: Revenge of the Bush Dynasty.* Her principal thread was a pursuit not only of how much he resembled his father but of how he had consciously sought to imitate him and follow in his career footsteps: "Some of the twinning of mannerisms could be downright spooky to friends. Of course, they shared the same first and last names. Always people would be doing somersaults to distinguish between them. George and Georgie. George Senior and Junior. Big George and Little George. George and George W."[61]

Besides their physical resemblance, George W. shared his father's tendency to play golf for speed and to mix up his sentences with something resembling verbal dyslexia. Actual dyslexia ran in their family; in 2000, writer Gail Sheehy marshaled a case that George W., like his brother Neil, had it.[62] However, the Sheehy hypothesis was never really pursued. Father and son also had a striking ability to remember people's names and faces and to memorize things, especially baseball batting orders, starting lineups, and fraternity members. For both—and apparently for Prescott Bush and Great-grandfather Bush, too—unusual memory was a great asset, both in retail politicking and in retaining data and information.

Like his father, George W. Bush went to Andover, and like his father and grandfather, he attended Yale. Like his grandfather, who played first base, and his father, who did likewise, George W. also made Yale's varsity baseball team, albeit only as a third-string pitcher. Also like his father, he became president of Yale's Delta Kappa Epsilon fraternity. Chronicler Mitchell noted that his engagement to a Houston girl named Cathy Wolfman "so echoed George W.'s parents' history that even some of his friends noticed. Cathy had been a Smith girl, as Barbara was, although she transferred to Rice University for her last years. George W. was 20 years old, the same age his father had been when he married. . . . They made the decision over Christmas vacation, the same holiday season when his parents wed. They planned to spend senior year in New Haven together just like his parents had."[63] However, the engagement was later ended.

At Yale, both his grandfather and father were tapped by Skull and Bones, and so was George W. After graduating, he became a military pilot like his father, with some similar help from family influence. In early 1968, before his graduation, a friend of his father's spoke to Texas lieutenant governor Ben Barnes. The lieutenant governor, in turn, contacted the commander of the Texas Air National Guard, Brigadier General James M. Rose, with the result that George W. jumped the several waiting lists involved. After taking five weeks of basic training, he was discharged as an enlisted man, recommended for a second lieutenancy the next day, and given pre-training permission to spend September to November working in the campaign of successful GOP Florida Senate candidate Edward J. Gurney.

It had been against navy regulations in 1942 to place eighteen-year-old George Bush in flight training, and the Los Angeles Times found a similar bending of the rules twenty-six years later. George W. did not qualify for either a direct commission or flight training.[64] Tom Hail, the historian of the Texas National Guard, explained that direct commissions were "for doctors only, mostly because we needed extra flight surgeons."[65] The air force flight-instruction program was also a favor, because such expensive training would not normally be given to a green candidate who had shown no professional commitment. The Texas Air National Guard arranged for George W. to train on F-102 fighters, dated aircraft being phased out of frontline service. He knew that he would not go to Vietnam; indeed, his own unit in Texas was being shut down even as he finished flight training.

George W. thereupon went to work in his father's unsuccessful 1970 Senate campaign, after which he found a job traveling for Stratford of Texas, an agribusiness firm run by fellow Yale Skull and Bonesman Richard Gow, who had been with his father at Zapata Petroleum. In 1972, he attached himself to another family friend, former Republican deputy national chairman James Allison Jr., in another losing effort—the Alabama U.S. Senate campaign of former postmaster general Winton M. Blount. Twenty-six years old in mid-1972, George W. was stumbling, falling far behind in his effort to walk in his father's footsteps.

At some point late in 1972, his father got him a different kind of job, working with minority children in the Professionals United for Leadership League (PULL), an organization that the elder Bush chaired. George W. seems to have stayed in this job through the summer of 1973 until he went off to Harvard Business School. Few explanations have been offered for this unusual employment, but J. H. Hatfield, in a hostile 2000 biography entitled *Fortunate Son,* made a charge never substantiated (or, for that matter, comprehensively refuted): that after a 1972 arrest in Texas for possession of cocaine, George W. worked at PULL for some months as part of a deal by which his record was later expunged by the court.[66]

A degree from Harvard Business School put Bush back on a meaningful career trajectory, and shortly after graduating in 1975, he got back on his father's old track by deciding to seek his fortune in familiar Midland. A few years later, the 1980 census would peg Midland as the richest town in America, with the highest per capita income and the highest level of Rolls-Royce sales.[67] Like his father teaming with John Overbey in 1950, George W. decided to begin on his own by being a landman—the person who prowls the maps and records at the county courthouse for potentially oil-productive land rights and then locates the owner to strike a deal.

In 1977, he named his mini-enterprise Arbusto—Spanish for Bush—but he got married that year and wound up doing no drilling until 1979. Once again, he was thrown off his father's vocational timing in 1978 by a local opening for the U.S. House of Representatives. Instead of waiting to make enough money to become financially independent before going into politics, he launched a campaign for the West Texas seat being vacated by longtime conservative Democrat George Mahon.

He won the nomination, defeating a Reagan supporter, Odessa mayor Jim Reese, who then declined to back him in the general election. Bush lost in November to conservative Democrat Kent Hance but took a respectable 47 percent to Hance's 53 percent. Battle lines for the 1980 Republican presidential race were already being drawn, and some pro-Reagan Republicans tried to tie George W. to his father's internationalist and eastern establishment connections. Like his father in the Senate races of 1964 and to a lesser extent 1970, George W. was dismissed as too preppy, too Yalie, to be truly Texan.

In 1979, his uncle Jonathan, who headed a small New York investment firm named J. Bush and Company, put together a drilling fund for his nephew at the same time as he was raising money for the accelerating presidential bid of George W.'s father. Arbusto, now headquartered in the same Midland Petroleum Building where George H. W. Bush had started Zapata a generation earlier, got a pot of $565,000 from Uncle Jonathan's investors. However, the wildcatting didn't go well, and oil prices, after peaking in 1980, dropped in 1981 and 1982. As his father's prominence had increased, George W. renamed the company Bush Exploration. He went back to family friends for more money—oil investments, even ones with empty holes, were useful as tax shelters—and came up with $4.7 million, including $1 million from Philip Uzielli, an investor with several Bush connections, and $172,550 from William H. Draper III, a fellow Bonesman.

Arbusto, the joke went, had turned into Ar-Bust-o. Its investors took big nominal losses (in the $3 million range) even while Bush got a salary and office operations money. In 1984, a Cincinnati-based group, including a Yale classmate, decided to buy out Arbusto and hire George W. to run the group's oil interests in Midland. The vice president's son—his father was now laboring in Washington for energy deregulation—became chairman and third-largest owner of the company, Spectrum 7 Energy Corporation, with 16 percent of the stock.[68]

By 1986, oil prices had plummeted; the oil business was a disaster, and so were the finances of Spectrum 7. A major outlay for stripper wells had failed, and Bush started looking for another financial angel. As the *Observer* of London would later note, "Whenever he's struck a dry well, someone has always been willing to fill it with money for him."[69] This time it was Harken Energy, a small Texas firm with high-powered connections that was then gobbling up other small oil companies on the verge of bankruptcy. Harken offered a swap: one of its shares for every five of Spectrum 7. None of the Cincinnati investors seemed to mind, so the deal closed on September 30, 1986. George W. got stock worth about $530,000, a Harken directorship, and a two-year consulting arrangement at $80,000 per year, which later rose to $120,000 a year. Bush senior now being within hailing distance of the White House, the would-be influence buyers grew more substantial: Over the next few years, Harken would turn out to have links to Saudi money, CIA-connected Filipinos, the Harvard Endowment, the emir of Bahrain, and the shadowy Bank of Credit and Commerce International.

The Harken deal also gave George W. something else: freedom to do what he wanted beyond attending the occasional Harken board meeting. His choice was to help in the campaign his father, about to finish a second term as Reagan's vice president, was beginning for the 1988 Republican presidential nomination. By this point, George W. Bush had spent almost two decades as an adult trying to follow in his father's footsteps and generally lacking the necessary luck or skills to do so. But between 1986, when his father began running for the presidency, and 1992, when he was driven from it, the political dynamic changed. So did George W. Bush.

The connection to the old establishment, whose red carpet his father had walked so successfully through potentially hostile Nixon and Reagan administrations, had by now become a liability. The mocking Gridiron stanzas would be paralleled in newsmagazine covers about the "wimp factor," and in scathing 1991 public resentment of George H. W. Bush's inability to relate to grocery prices or scanners. Such themes would recur during the 1992 New Hampshire GOP presidential primary in taunts hurled by challenger Patrick Buchanan at "King George" and the "Walker's Point" elites. The vote share that Bush received that November was the worst for a sitting president in eight decades.

But only a little more than a year after the dust of 1992 had settled, George W. Bush was running for governor of Texas in the 1994 election. Moreover, he was now displaying a cultural and political persona quite unlike his father's, one that promised a real chance to restore both his family and the Republican Party to power in 2000.

Bush still relied on the four mainstays of his father's establishment: finance, oil and energy, the military-industrial complex, and the national security–intelligence community. These power bases were quite compatible with the increasingly southern base and the conservative ideological evolution of the Republican Party. What was different was Bush's nonelite demeanor: the cow country accent, the rumpled clothing, the chewing tobacco, the style of religiosity, the moral fundamentalism, the outsider language, the disdain for the Harvards and Yales, the six-gun geopolitics, and not least the garb of a sinner rescued from drink and brought to God by none other than evangelist Billy Graham.

To understand this transformation, consider the tale of George W. Bush *not* following in his father's footsteps. From a fairly early age, he was more of a rascal and less of an Ivy League gentleman in training, a Texas cutup with a Texas drawl. At Andover, he could manage to become a Big Man on Campus type only by rowdy wit—his nickname was "the Lip"—and by postures like making himself "Stickball Commissioner." One of the few unassigned books he read was Barry Goldwater's *Conscience of a Conservative*. As president of the DKE house at Yale, he got in trouble for lifting a Christmas wreath from a store and for branding pledges as an initiation.

In contrast to his father's fond Ivy memories, he came away from Yale with a grudge against its fashionable campus liberalism. At Harvard Business School, one girlfriend recalled, he didn't fit the Charles River MBA norm: "While they were drinking Chivas Regal, he was drinking Wild Turkey. They were smoking Benson and Hedges, and he's dipping Copenhagen, and while they were going to the opera, he would listen to Johnny Rodriguez over and over and over and over."[70]

Friends recalled several years of bombast and wastrelism after he returned to Texas in 1975. Before he got married in 1977, a worst-dressed award was named after him at the local country club. He had been an Episcopalian as a youth, but he joined Midland's First Methodist Church after being wed there. The worse things got in the oil business and with his bourbon habit, the more attention he paid to Bible study classes. "I believe my spiritual awakening started well before the price of oil went below $9 [per barrel]," he told one interviewer, but 1986 was "a year of change when I look back at it."[71] That was when he found God and, right after his fortieth birthday, put away the Wild Turkey bottle.

An ivied Episcopal faith had not helped George H. W. Bush get along with the Southern Baptist rural Democrats of Texas any more than it had endeared him to the fundamentalists, evangelicals, Pentecostals, and premillennialists who filled the battalions of the Religious Right critical to the Reagan-era national GOP. By contrast, a decade after being saved by Billy

Graham, an evangelized and fundamentalist-leaning George W. would reply "Jesus Christ" when asked what philosopher had most influenced him. Bible Belt televangelists, some of them his father's persecutors, became his proud hosts from Longview to Lubbock. In New Hampshire and other Yankee states in 1988, the younger Bush frequently made a bad impression with his Texas twang, cowboy boots, and wad of chewing tobacco dribbling a small brown stream out of the side of his mouth.

He was, in short, almost a caricature overcorrection of several of his father's greatest political weaknesses. However, party power brokers assumed the roughness could be polished. By 1997, a considerable number of the big donors, business and financial magnates, powerful lobbyists, and Republican hierarchs who had supported his father were concluding that with a George W. Bush matured by six years as governor of Texas, they could preempt the Republican nomination in 2000. Then, by tapping the public's moral hunger and Clinton fatigue, they could win the presidential election and govern the United States further to the right than George H. W. Bush would have imagined. Finance, oil, the military-industrial complex, and the national security–intelligence community would return to the nation's highest councils.

Fulfillment of this strategy would mark one of the most extraordinary role changes by a major American political family in the country's history. George H. W. Bush had lost the presidency in 1992 partly because he struck voters as an upper-class man with little sense of the rest of the country, never a winning position in U.S. politics. Voters have generally responded best to more interesting or complicated politicians—witness the dualities posited by mid-twentieth-century historian Richard Hofstadter in many of the most influential: Thomas Jefferson ("the aristocrat as a democrat"), William Jennings Bryan ("the democrat as a revivalist"), Theodore Roosevelt ("the conservative as a progressive"), and Franklin D. Roosevelt ("the patrician as an opportunist").[72]

It's not hard to define a similar duality for George W. Bush. Because of his family, his initial characterization must be conservative, aristocrat or patrician, although his demeanor from boyhood revealed practically nothing of the patrician. Let me propose three possible posttransformation nouns to accompany the first term: revivalist, evangelist, or fundamentalist. Taken together, his self-certainty, religious conviction touched with messianic hints, and a tendency to both doctrinal extremes and black-versus-white simplicities suggest a striking new pairing on the Hofstadter chart: *the aristocrat as a fundamentalist.*

But we are getting ahead of our story. It is the presidential election year of 2000, and the modern United States is on the brink of an entirely unprecedented prospect: American political and economic dynastization.

CHAPTER 2

The Dynastization
of America

If you want a short conversation with George the First, mention the Bush dynasty. "We don't think that way," he says repeatedly.

Duty, Honor, Country, 2003

Even more than money, political inheritance mocks our pretenses to equal opportunity.

Michael Kinsley, "Dad, Can I Borrow the Scepter?" 2002

Only a few years into the twenty-first century, the "end of history," a concept that had been popular with many in the 1990s, had all but vanished from political dialogue. Religion, family, war, and greed, arguably the four horsemen of human nature, had resumed their place in history's cavalcade.

Yesterday seemed to return at a full gallop. The collapse of the Internet bubble deflated the promise of a cyber-democracy, once supposedly at hand. The twin towers of finance and technology, in the form of Manhattan's World Trade Center, were felled on September 11, 2001, by the crashes of two hijacked jetliners orchestrated by suicidal members of a little-known Islamic terrorist group based in far-off, primitive Afghanistan.

As Americans lost faith in technology after 9/11 and the NASDAQ crash, they were cast by some in the popular press as turning for comfort to *Lord of the Rings* fantasy and medievalism. Across the Middle East and the Indo-Pakistani subcontinent, religious factions—from Israel's National Religious Party to Turkey's Justice and Development Party to India's Bharatiya Janata Party—won control of national or state governments or assumed a pivotal role in ruling coalitions. In Europe, a political union of church and state was resurrecting disestablished monarchies from Italy to the Balkans.

The business cycle, left for dead by neophiliacs in the late nineties, struck back only months after the millennium. Consumer confidence withered as stocks began their greatest market swoon since the Great Depression. Corporate chief executive officers went from cult to culprit status, following Wall Street into the docks of both public opinion and federal and state law enforcement. For many months, the largest market gains accrued not to growth stocks but to the glittering fetish of Assyrian kings and medieval alchemists: gold.

While this turn-of-the-century cultural and political climate was more favorable for dynasties and other old ways of thinking, it did not simply bespeak a return to authority and traditionalism. The psychologies involved were more complicated, though some did hark back a generation to more basic conservative trends.

That previous powerful rightward shift had represented the 1970s and 1980s backlash against the excesses of midcentury U.S. (and Western) economics and culture. The progressive and socialist provocations were multiple. Secular-minded elites had insisted on divorcing government from religion and moral standards. A Center-Left cultural and political correctness, in turn, had sought to resolve discrimination and inequalities by social prescription—quotas, subsidies, guidelines, semantic reclassification (welfare recipients as "clients," criminals as "victims," the poor as "economically deprived"), and sociologically based judicial rulings.

In the economic sphere, leftist thinking was resented for intruding on marketplace functions and pushing taxes to levels that sapped incentive. Overall, argued the Right, an ideology of too much government had become an embedded force and had subsequently stagnated. After decades of rule making, the Center-Left had developed a 1970s and 1980s sclerosis, much as the conservative and laissez-faire economic elites of 1914 or 1929 had before they were shouldered aside.

As this antiliberal countertide swelled, it introduced its own neoaristocratic and market philosophies, which came to dominate North America and Western Europe under Ronald Reagan and Margaret Thatcher. By the millennium, these forces, in turn, had gone from an initially sober, if sometimes narrow, insistence on a greater role for religion, personal responsibility, markets, and wealth to a turn-of-the-century ideology indulging its own excesses.

One excess was the emergence during the 1980s of a cultural "luxury fever" nourished by the rising stock market and soaring circulation of publications like *Architectural Digest,* which promoted a conscious imitation of aristocracy. In tandem came an expanding national preoccupation with celebrity and an acceptance of a winner-take-all ethos for society, with its top-heavy allocation of America's vocational rewards.

By the 1990s, critics began to deplore the lopsided control of politics by an elite of large political contributors. The Right was also mobilizing religious conservatives to bolster a corporate and financial agenda. Some observers hypothesized a new U.S. global military and de facto imperial role—visible first in the gunboat-and-missile diplomacy of the eighties—captivating a republic hitherto ill at ease with concepts of empire. After the stock market crash, popular economic utopianism tailed off. Following September 11, public opinion became conspicuously more accepting of the crisis side of imperialism: stronger government in Washington, U.S. global hegemony, Pax Americana, and even a doctrine of preemptive military strikes. But we are concerned here with the cultural corollaries.

Aristophilia and the Rise of American Gentrification

A stickler, to be sure, could trace the trappings of empire and dynasty back to the 1960s—to Kennedy's misty Camelot, Johnson's proclamation of a Great Society from Mississippi to the Mekong, and Nixon's *Prisoner of Zenda* uniforms for his White House guard. Still, the more defining watershed followed the inauguration of Ronald Reagan in 1981. Democratic president Jimmy Carter, cultivating smallness and rejecting the imperial presidency of the sixties, had reduced highway speed limits, hinted at a national malaise, and worn a sweater in a national television speech urging energy conservation. President and Mrs. Reagan, in complete contrast, wanted to rebuild U.S. might, restore the economic incentives of the Roaring Twenties, and bring back fashion, high society (California-style), and conspicuous consumption.

Their arrival in Washington began with inauguration festivities costing a record $16 million, an outlay that critics found redolent of both Edwardian England (it featured the dated formality of a morning "stroller suit") and Versailles (the lavish thoughtlessness of the affair). Following the inaugural hubbub, Ronald and Nancy Reagan became patrons of what one cultural historian described as an "aristocratic movement" spanning the worlds of White House, communications media, fashion, department store, and museum.[1] The Reagans and their California friends embraced a series of exhibitions and dinners organized under the aegis of *Vogue* and *Harper's Bazaar,* the Metropolitan Museum of Art, Bloomingdale's, and Neiman Marcus and in honor of designers like Yves Saint Laurent, Pierre Cardin, Oscar de la Renta, and Ralph Lauren. Pretentious in a manner that would have been rejected by the first-family Eisenhowers, Kennedys, and Nixons (albeit for different reasons), these affairs glorified the gowns of the Chinese Ching dynasty, the eighteenth-century ancien régime, the 1890s French Belle Epoque with its own eighteenth-century revival, and the equestrian costumes of the eighteenth- and nineteenth-century English gentry.

In late 1984, when the Costume Institute of the Metropolitan opened a "Man and the Horse" exhibit, its sponsorship by Polo/Ralph Lauren filled the Met's galleries and museum stores with posters, photos, riding gear, and pseudo–English country house furnishings bearing the Polo logo. This attention, amplified by a national advertising campaign, gave a princely boost to what might be called the Imitation Buckinghamshire wing of the American aristocratic revival. Even two decades later, the style propagated by Lauren in the 1980s was still appealing enough to spawn new imitations, such as the "British Gentry" line put out by North Carolina–based Thomasville Furniture.

Despite the prevalence of these accoutrements of instant gentrification, we can hardly posit an aristocratic revival based solely on Polo, *Harper's Bazaar,* and Nancy Reagan's alleged yearnings for Marie Antoinette. A greater sense of the popular mood can be gleaned from the ties between the Reagans, the Republican Party, and the most-watched television series in the United States (and for a while, the world): *Dynasty.* Consider the case made in the mid-1980s by California cultural historian Debora Silverman:

> There is a mutually reinforcing connection between popular opulent fashion and the dual roles of White House Nancy Reagan on one hand and the television fantasy of "Dynasty's" Krystle Carrington on the other. In the weekly evening show, Krystle is the devoted wife of a rich and loving "entrepreneur" and her sartorial splendor, like Mrs. Reagan's, is presumed to be the natural physical expression of her husband's competitive success in the marketplace. "Dynasty" began programming during the week of the first Reagan

inaugural in 1981, and exploited the confusion between fantasy and reality by occasionally featuring recognizable political figures, such as Henry Kissinger and Gerald Ford, as guests at some of the extraordinarily lavish parties attended by the Carrington clan. "Dynasty" has been complemented by a new popular show, "Lifestyles of the Rich and Famous," which purports to tell true stories of the rich. "Dynasty" fashions, along with perfume, jewels, accessories, and lingerie, are now marketed as department store signature items and advertised to consumers as a way to "share the luxury," "share the treasures," and "share the magic" of the Carrington characters' staggering riches by buying their imprint.[2]

Thinly disguised soap opera was, of course, for the masses. But many well-off Americans who would have scoffed at *Dynasty* accessories happily gentrified their lifestyles by striding, sailing, eating, or drinking through the lavish worlds offered by upscale magazines like *Architectural Digest, Yachting, Gourmet,* and *Wine Spectator.* By 2001, the four had a combined circulation of some 2.2 million, up 500 percent since conspicuous consumption had regained élan in the early 1980s. While the million or two richest American families might not have hereditary titles in the British or European manner, they could nonetheless try to live like lords. In earlier eras, when the leading world economic powers were Holland and Britain, such consumption traits, especially attention to French furniture, fashions, wine, and cuisine, had also accompanied heydays of aristocracy and class polarization.

More revealing still, the hunger of Americans for lineage, titles, and royal genealogy was open enough to need little confirmation from the proliferation of highly rated French restaurants or 120-foot yachts. The Republic of Franklin and Jefferson has seen its share of architectural and cultural revivals associated with "aristocratic" taste—Philadelphia's late-eighteenth-century Palladian villas, the Federalist style of early-1800s New England, which was followed by the Colonial Revival of the late nineteenth century, with its new membership societies emphasizing British aristocratic or colonial antecedents. The last two decades of the twentieth century began another such broad-based revival.

Once again, Americans pursued a mounting fascination with ancestry and genealogy—this time, through Web sites, search engines, and endless family histories, as well as proliferating research libraries at church, historical, and genealogical societies. The preservation of historic properties ballooned, as did public fascination with history itself—the huge audiences commanded by television documentaries, and the comparable sale of books about kings, presidents, explorers, battles, and wars, most involving dead white men of dubious political correctness.

A further symptom may surprise even the genealogically engaged: America's swelling national interest in hereditary entitlements. *The Hereditary Society Blue Book,* a listing that dates back to seventeenth- and eighteenth-century groups like the Ancient and Honorable Artillery Company of Massachusetts and the Welsh Society of Philadelphia, reveals two principal chronological groupings.[3] The first, of some sixty-five organizations formed during the Colonial Revival from the 1880s down through 1914, includes the Colonial Dames of America, the Holland Society of New York, and the General Society of Mayflower Descendants. The second set, representing some fifty societies founded since 1980, features groups like the Descendants of Founders of New Jersey, the Society of Kentucky Pioneers, and the Society of Descendants of the Alamo. Other directories list the dozens of Scottish clan societies, as well as extended family groups like the Poindexter Descendants Association and the Society of Descendants of Robert Livingston.

What was new in the twentieth century was organizations requiring that members have demonstrable ties to gentry, nobility, or royalty. The first, founded in 1902, was the Plantagenet Society (open to descendants of all Plantagenet kings), followed in 1903 by the Order of the Americans of Armorial Ancestry. In 1911 came the Order of Colonial Lords of Manors in America; in 1931, the Society of Descendants of Knights of the Garter; and in 1938, the National Society of the Lords of Maryland Manors. A group collected around an unusual bond, the Descendants of the Illegitimate Sons and Daughters of the Kings of Britain, joined them in 1950. Since 1980, hereditary organizations have been introduced such as the Descendants of Knights of the Bath, the Society of American Royalty (largely preoccupied with the descendants of Hawaiian kings and queens), and in 1995, rather prophetically, the Presidential Families of America.[4]

Just as revealing, especially over the last two decades, has been the ever more brisk trade in titles of nobility (loosely speaking). Most of the obtainable cachets—Lord of the Manor of Twistle or some such—represented a profitable coming together of mail-order and Internet entrepreneurialism, research into the titular nooks and crannies of British law, and the status hunger of (mostly, but not entirely) American purchasers. More or less si-

multaneously, demand also grew for directories of foreign royalty and nobility. The publishers of *Burke's Peerage* came to do a surprising portion of
their business in the United States, documenting noble and royal ancestries
for the Smiths and Joneses as well as the Bushes. The *Almanach de Gotha,* a
German registry that had stopped publication in 1944, started up again in
London in 1998. Cockayne's *Complete Peerage,* long out of print, was reis-
sued in 2000, partially to meet U.S. demand.

Coats-of-arms research and reproductions also flourished. Gift shops
in British castles sold as many heraldic decals and refrigerator magnets to
Americans as to Britons, if not more. But other circumstances spotlighted
the U.S. nuances. The cities of Lancaster and York, Pennsylvania, despite
the largely German ancestry of their populations, took as civic badges the
red rose of Lancaster and the white rose of York, symbols of the two royal
houses that fought England's fifteenth-century Wars of the Roses. Charlotte, North Carolina, a rebel and Presbyterian hotbed during the American Revolution, turned Tory by adopting a crown as its symbol, styling
itself the Queen City after the monarch for whom it was originally
named—Charlotte of Mecklenburg, the wife of George III. Other towns
and counties in North Carolina followed suit: Craven County displayed the
arms of the earl of Craven, one of the original Carolina proprietors; the
chic coastal town of Beaufort took on the heraldry of that English ducal
family.

The increasing American acceptance of hierarchy could also be seen in
other areas. In 1995, two professors, Robert Frank and Philip Cook, published a revelatory book entitled *The Winner-Take-All Society.* In it, they
documented a group of "markets in which small differences in performance often give rise to enormous differences in economic reward. Long
familiar in entertainment, sports and the arts, these markets have increasingly permeated accounting, law, journalism, consulting, medicine, investment banking, corporate management, publishing, design, fashion and a
host of other professions."[5]

As the two scholars explained, advances in technology and communications had combined with freer movement of populations and commerce
between states and nations to make it possible for the stars in a given profession or vocation to achieve almost instantaneous national or global
stature (as opposed to being restricted by yesteryear's more confining geography). As a result, the gap in repute and reward between the top and
even the high middle, only a hairbreadth of luck or talent down, became

much greater than before. Here was yet another trend supporting the emergence of an economic aristocracy.

Even the day-to-day peerage of commercial parlance—a lexicon comprising expressions like "Texas tort kings," "queens of country music," "movie moguls," "imperial corporate CEOs," and "Wall Street Masters of the Universe"—made peerage and monarchy user-friendly, muting any national echo of the founding fathers' worries about aristocracies and hereditary rulers. Dynasties, the ultimate aristocratic expression, have been at least as visible in Hollywood and the performing arts as in Washington. In 2001, writer Daniel Gross noted the parallel:

> When the Academy Award nominations were announced last Monday, the list included two second-generation representatives of Hollywood royal families: Jeff Bridges, son of actor Lloyd and brother of Beau, was nominated for Best Supporting Actor; and Kate Hudson, daughter of Goldie Hawn, is a contender for Best Supporting Actress. Hudson and Bridges are but two of many stars who are sons, daughters, and grandchildren of respected pros.[6]

The advent of celebrity was also integral to the "aristophilia" apparent by the century's end. The inauguration of a movie actor as president was quickly followed by articles like "The Meaning of Celebrity" (1983) and by Richard Schickel's 1985 book *Intimate Strangers: The Culture of Celebrity*. Ronald Reagan's unusual background helped to rearrange the relationships of politics and imagery.[7] He was not just the first actor to become president; he was also the first proponent of restoring traditional morality to have been married to two different Hollywood actresses. In an age of celebrity, image was more than a match for fact.

The mock aristocracy of celebrity had a revolving door. Some of the early celebrities of the eighties had actually exited by the new century, especially the business entrepreneurs ennobled by new 1980s magazines like *Entrepreneur* and *Inc.* Wall Street investment bankers, the erstwhile Masters of the Universe, saw their prestige shrink with their 2002 or 2003 bonuses. The *New York Times* noted that corporate CEOs, once heroic figures, had lost their appeal as subjects for the book-buying public. But stars in many other galaxies, including politics, continued to glow.

For U.S. presidents, celebrity status is in fact a well-established phenomenon. In *The American Presidency* (1956), Clinton Rossiter suggested that of the nation's dozen principal folk heroes since the Revolution, half had been presidents.[8] In 1898, historian Henry Jones Ford observed that "American democracy has revived the oldest political institution of the race, the elective kingship. It is all there: the prerecognition of the notables and the tumultuous choice of the freemen."[9] Abraham Lincoln's secretary of state, William H. Seward, expressed much the same idea to a British journalist in 1868: "We elect a king for four years and give him absolute power within certain limits, which after all he can interpret for himself."[10]

Theologian Michael Novak, in his 1974 study *Choosing Our King,* observed of the U.S. chief executive that "we may wish it otherwise, but he is king—king in the sense of decisive, symbolic focal point of our power and destiny."[11] In 1993, Lewis Lapham, the editor of *Harper's,* added more recent factors to the analysis: "The wish for kings is an old and familiar wish, as well known in medieval Europe and in ancient Mesopotamia, but its recent and cringing appearance in late twentieth-century America, in a country presumably dedicated to the opposite premise, coincided with the alarms and excursions of the Cold War, with the presidency of John F. Kennedy, and with the emergence of the theatre of celebrity."[12] Recent presidential families have come to breed multiple, even dynastic celebrityhood.

Perhaps the ultimate insinuation of U.S. aristophilia and de facto monarchism came from the London publishers of *Burke's Peerage.* On the day before the 2000 presidential election, they predicted that George W. Bush would win because he had more royal blood than his opponent—and because the candidate with the most royal blood always won U.S. presidential contests. George W. Bush was even more "royal" in ancestry than his father because his mother's royal connections included French Bourbon and several Scandinavian monarchs, as well as members of the Russian, Spanish, and German monarchies.[13] American comments on this alleged electoral dynamic were apparently not sought.

Since the election, of course, the events of 9/11 and their ramifications have focused more attention on global terror and the imperialization of U.S. international behavior. Theses that in the Reagan era depended on vague aristocratic revivals and the supposed resemblance between the choice of a king and a U.S. president were developed with a much grander sweep. All too soon, Washington found itself in a wide-ranging conversation about Roman-style empire, preemptive war, and the transformation of American politics into an arena of great families and rival dynasties.

Religion, Imperialism, and Reaction

Historically, these three concepts have proven to be interdependent—kings have been succored by the type of religion that required bishops, imperialism has thrived under the power of the scepter, and dynastic restorations have ushered in reactionary politics. Thus, even a partial transformation of American political culture in any one of these spheres stood to have momentous consequences. The twentieth-century United States, by and large, functioned in keeping with its definition as a republic led by a popularly elected chief executive. Now, in a twenty-first-century political framework, readjusting to new threats, it showed glimmerings of an empire determined to strike back, even though the latter-day legions wore Kevlar instead of Roman breastplates.

At first blush, the sort of religion that has successfully gained popularity over other denominations in the United States since the 1970s—Pentecostal, evangelical, fundamentalist, and even charismatic—would not seem to be the sort connected with monarchy, at least in the old European style of the High Church Anglicanism of imperial Britain or the ancien régime Catholicism of the Bourbons. However, the transforming forces working on the body politic over the last few decades have begun to create a new king-and-bishops equation. To begin with, the putative imperium of the early twenty-first century bears more relation to Professor Walter McDougall's American "Crusader State," with its proselytizing ideology and its biblical analogies, than to any European pomp-and-liturgy type of empire.[14]

In McDougall's formulation, U.S. crusadership has had two phases: the Old Testament America (defensive and eye-for-an-eye), which lasted from 1783 to 1898, and the New Testament America (ameliorative and proselytizing), which began with William McKinley, Theodore Roosevelt, and Woodrow Wilson. Writing in 1995, McDougall could not have anticipated the Protestant denominational mainstays of the Bush Crusader State, with its seething desire to take preemptive action against the portion of the Axis of Evil represented by Iraq, but we can identify them easily enough.

The pillars of the Republican Moral Restoration of 2000 and the ensuing Crusader State had very much the same especially supportive core: evangelical and fundamentalist Protestants, a group that included roughly a quarter of all Americans. For them, the inaugural slogans of restoring trust and helping wounded travelers on the road to Jericho segued all too easily into the 2002 and 2003 rhetoric of launching preemptive strikes to smite the evil tyrants of the Middle East before they could smite first. It was, after all, a matter of Scripture. The prelates of this biblical Crusader State—figurative prelates, of course—were of a very different cloth from the old establishment ministers of metropolitan U.S. churches with well-rooted ivy, weathered brick, and 1790 cornerstones. They were, rather, the Billy Grahams, Pat Robertsons, Jerry Falwells, and Bob Joneses, with their flocks of many millions singing "Onward, Christian Soldiers."

Americans' growing perception of their country as an empire beset by barbarians, far from being irrelevant to domestic politics, not only reflected new national circumstances but helped to mold a new mood. While part of this imperial reinterpretation reflected the reality of mobilizing against terrorism as early as the 1990s, well before 9/11, scholars of history and international affairs had begun to examine how the post–cold war United States, no longer countered by the Soviet Union, was assuming the role of global hegemon that its leaders and people had always denied was its ultimate goal. Even a lengthy treatise would be insufficient for a full examination of this theme, but as a foundation for discussing a dynasticizing presidency, several developments require brief note.

Professor Charles Maier, emeritus director of Harvard's Minda de Gunzburg Center for European Studies, sketched the core of the evolution of imperial attitudes in a 2002 article, "An American Empire?" A decade ago, he argued, the very concept of empire had aroused "righteous indignation" because the United States was "an empire that dared not speak its name":

> But these days, on the part of friends and critics alike, the bashfulness has ended. "The Roman and British empires have had their day. Why should we begrudge the new American Empire the right to protect its citizens from a jealous and hostile world," writes a former British European Union official to the *Financial Times*. The historian Paul Kennedy cites the overwhelming preponderance of military power the United States possesses. In full agreement, the Bush administration has vowed to preserve that decisive margin against any rivals.

By 2003, it was a truism that whereas multilateral U.S. policies had suited the multipolar world that was the context for the cold war, the Pax Americana that would be needed to meet the challenge of terrorism might have to be as arrogantly unilateral as the long-ago Pax Romana. Professor Maier found another U.S.-Roman parallel in how "from the Colosseum to the Super Bowl, in the West at least, empires particularly rely on the sports of the amphitheater that reward star players with fame and fortune"—and employ them, along with the glory of empire, to divert popular attention from rising inequality within the realm.[15] Empire and aristocracy, in other words, are mutually supportive institutions.

Conversely, the summer disarray, guerrilla warfare, and continuing U.S. casualties in Iraq that followed George W. Bush's May proclamation that the military battle was over somewhat cooled public enthusiasm and the manner in which "empire" was discussed. So did the international polls that showed diminished respect for the United States. Indeed, some experts began likening the Bush-era United States not to Rome or Britain but to short-lived right-wing nationalist imperial ventures like the pre–World War I Germany of Kaiser Wilhelm and the imperial Japan of Emperor Hirohito two decades later.[16] These were cautions, although not serious parallels.

Chroniclers of pop culture drew on more exotic wellsprings to chart the drift toward imperium. As J. R. R. Tolkien's *Lord of the Rings: The Two Towers* dominated U.S. movie box offices in January 2003, the editors of *Time* argued in a cover story that as technology had lost its promise of utopia in the NASDAQ crash, Americans had slipped into a blacker, more pessimistic attitude—a return to the moral clarity of good and evil as represented in fantasy and medievalism.[17] Some twenty-five thousand Americans, *Time* noted, already belonged to the Society for Creative Anachronism, a California-based organization given to styling its leaders as knights and baronesses and dedicated to re-creating the lifestyle of sword- and ax-bearing premodern Europe.

Whether merely a manifestation of pop culture or a reflection of deeper currents within the American psyche, this mood swing did have a logic, some of it perverse. Three and four decades earlier, many sociologists, anxious to define racial and social injustice in terms of victimization and deprivation, had authored naive government interventions that had helped lose a generation of American voters to liberal politics. By the late nineties, however, a new breed of sociologists, historians, and cultural anthropologists had turned their research in the opposite direction, studying evidence for such illiberal behavior as a historical revival of paganism in the United States and Europe, a reemerging politics of racial and ethnic differences, even the persistence of occultism. Lurking in all of these cultural phenomena, scholars found, was the surprising twenty-first-century revitalization of concepts—race, the notion of an exotic and impenetrably foreign Orient, and cultural and religious nationalism—reckoned by earlier twentieth-century modernists to be ebbing in the age of the airplane and the telephone.[18]

While no one seriously contemplated a second coming of Attila the Hun or a displacement of Christianity by Wotanism, this kind of serious sociological attention to the unpleasant underpinnings of history, one might argue, was putting the relevance and realpolitik back into a discipline partially discredited in the seventies and eighties by a reemerging worldwide emphasis on markets. Renewed attention to the darker aspects of life helped to prepare sociology for a rematch with a familiar foe: conservative exaltation of markets and economic man, now increasingly unrealistic. Market theology can be almost childlike in its ignorance of subjects like the Koran, suicide bombers, and Carpathian ethnography.

The limited discussion in the United States of the global reignition of religion and nationalism was paralleled by inattention to one of its effects in Europe: the rise of movements, mostly on the political Right, to restore kings, pretenders, and royal houses exiled for over fifty years to the disestablished thrones of Italy, Serbia, Bulgaria, and Romania. The restoration of George W. Bush in the United States had company. In Bulgaria, Simeon II, deposed as a boy in 1946, returned in 2001 as prime minister, not as king. Elsewhere, reestablishment of the monarchy was at issue. By 2002, the Italian parliament had allowed the exiled royal claimant of the House of Savoy to begin visiting Italy again. In Serbia, the deceased father of Crown Prince Alexander had lost his throne in 1945 after the proclamation of the People's Republic of Yugoslavia. In 2001, Alexander got his palace back, if not his crown. King Michael, the Romanian claimant, allowed to return to a local château, had actually ruled Romania as a boy before being expelled by the Russians in 1947.

It is more than eerie. A disturbing sidebar to the political culture of these restorations was how many of the would-be monarchs, royal houses, and supporting factions had been on the fascist side in World War II. Italy's House of Savoy was banished in part for backing Mussolini and supporting his 1938 race laws targeting Jews. In Bulgaria, Simeon's House of Saxe-Coburg-Gotha fought through much of the war as an ally of Nazi Germany. The Serbian factions backing the potential Alexander II evoked memories of World War II massacres and ethnic battles still commemorated after six hundred years. The Romanian House of Hohenzollern-Sigmaringen, supported by the Iron Guard movement that blended rural Eastern Orthodox religion with folkish nationalism, fought most of World War II on Hitler's side.[19]

Unfair as it may be to lump together the Houses of Karadjordjević, Saxe-Coburg-Gotha, Savoy, and Hohenzollern-Sigmaringen, they suggest the dark side of the global political force that has buoyed dynasty and restoration. The analogy to the English-speaking nations is obviously limited, but the caveats cannot be entirely ignored. And now, we must turn to the different encouragement given to aristophilia during the 1980s and 1990s by *economic* forces.

The Economic Dynastization of America

Part of the unwelcome message of economic and political dynastization lies in its very success: its two-decade flight under the radar of those who grew up believing that the democratic values of World War II and Franklin D. Roosevelt had become an inextricable part of the national social fabric. Instead, the upheavals of the 1980s and 1990s consigned many of these midcentury values to an ideological limbo, and many older Americans found the changing *über*-philosophy difficult to grasp.

Much the same thing had happened after the Civil War, when aging Jeffersonians and Jacksonians steadfastly believed that the egalitarian values of the early nineteenth century persisted despite the rise of corporations. They had been captivated by the post-1783 elimination of the old British legal structure of entail and primogeniture, which kept estates intact under one heir at death. In the 1820s, even the Federalist Noah Webster paid tribute to the revolutionary principles: "An equality of property, with a necessity of alienation, constantly operating to destroy combinations of powerful families, is the very soul of a republic."[20] Not until the 1880s did it become clear that the new power of corporations, with their prolonged legal existences and constitutional rights equivalent to those of individuals, had simply mooted the old rules and provided the framework for the rise of a new aristocracy. The reforms and shibboleths of a hundred years earlier had become irrelevant.

To be sure, the four decades between the rise of Theodore Roosevelt and the death of Franklin D. Roosevelt had proved that the Americans of that era could wield the progressive income tax and the estate and gift tax to achieve much of what the Jeffersonians had accomplished by ending the system of entail and primogeniture. Yet any assurance that these egalitarian principles were enduring was short-lived. No president of the 1970s or 1980s ever reiterated FDR's blunt 1935 proclamation that "the transmission from generation to generation of vast fortunes by will, inheritance, or gift is not consistent with the ideals and sentiments of the American people." By the Reagan era, just as during the late-nineteenth-century Gilded Age, new and different currents had begun to erode prior democratic institutions.

In assessing such transformations, the cultural politics are not easy to separate from the economics. However, if the early pages of this chapter concerned the cultural forces buoying aristocratic and hierarchical leanings, those that follow examine the economic dynastization of America. Since the 1980s, the two have gained in force together.

During this period, the role of the stock market and the corporation in the creation of American wealth exceeded their importance in any previous boom. Although large blocks of wealth were still concentrated in corporations that were privately held rather than publicly traded, the great asset growth of the eighties and nineties rode to glory along the extraordinary trajectory of the Standard and Poor's, Dow Jones, and NASDAQ indexes.

That stock market basis of wealth had been less true a century earlier, when more of it was held in land, urban real estate, partnerships, and unincorporated businesses. Even so, as the great trusts were organized during the 1890s and the first decade of the twentieth century, often dozens if not scores of unincorporated businesses would be gathered in, paid for with stock in the new megafirm. This new entity, in turn, was often valued at several times the sum of its parts, especially if the resulting combination approached monopoly potential. When J. P. Morgan organized U.S. Steel in 1902 with an unprecedented $1.2 billion capitalization, he made dozens of new millionaires from among the major entrepreneurs of greater Pittsburgh alone, with the results visible in everything from garish mansions to ostentatious luxury purchases.

In the mid–twentieth century, some revisionist historians looked back at those decades and attributed the emergence of progressivism, including widespread support for graduated taxes and antitrust regulation, at least in part to the disgust of the older Boston, New York, and Philadelphia gentry with the easily made millions and vulgar opulence of the Gilded Age nouveaux riches. To a considerable extent, wealth divided politically. The Adamses, Lodges, Roosevelts, Van Cortlandts, Shippens, and Whartons, with their individual $600,000 and $1.3 million fortunes tied to law, real estate, or inheritance from a merchant prince grandfather, could not begin to compete with the new riches being spun off by railroads and the oil, steel, sugar, and beef trusts, with a commercial swagger they came to deplore. Consider, for example, the old-family annoyance in Theodore Roosevelt's 1898 remark that "with [Brooks] Adams' contempt for the deification of the stock market . . . all generous souls must agree."[21]

No full parallel can be drawn with the 1980s and 1990s. In the United States, old money rode that stock market escalator almost as successfully as the emerging Internet, telecom, and software magnates. Over the long term, the old-money hold on financial dominance was better, given the transience of the lead enjoyed by the new money at the peak of the technology bubble. Between mid-1982 and 1999, for example, the Dow Jones Industrial Average rocketed some 1,200 percent, and the increase in the size of the thirty largest family and individual U.S. fortunes measured by *Forbes* was approximately similar. Stock ownership, as much as or more than actual entrepreneurialism, was thus an essential component of wealth.

Stock ownership's benefits, however, were massively concentrated at the apex of the American economic pyramid. Despite the claims for a "Republic of Shareholders" that crowded the editorial page of the *Wall Street Journal,* the paper's news columns told the true story: "For all the talk of mutual funds and 401(k)s for the masses, the stock market has remained the privilege of a relatively elite group. Nearly 90% of all shares were held by the wealthiest 10% of households. The bottom line: that top 10% held 73.2% of the country's net worth in 1997, up from 68.2% in 1983. Stock options pushed the ratio of executive pay to factory worker pay to 419:1 in 1998, from 42:1 in 1980."[22]

Succinctly put, the two-decade stock market boom, together with the tax advantages that accrued to investment income over earned income, became the motive force of a new national economy. It enabled the top 1 percent of Americans, who held some 40 percent of the nation's individually owned stock, to pull up and away from the rest of the citizenry. Their share of U.S. household income, including capital gains, doubled, from 10 percent in 1980 to 20 percent in 1999. More than a million households inhabited this golden circle. By comparison, the average household income in the middle quintile of the population stagnated, and many at the bottom lost ground. (Fuller details on these trends and changes can be found in my 2002 book, *Wealth and Democracy: A Political History of the American Rich.*)

The aristocratizing factor of this trend is hard to escape. Moreover, because the sheer disproportion of share ownership and wealth rose steadily as one approached the top of the top 1 percent, the income and wealth gains near its apex—roughly one hundred thousand households, the highest one-tenth of the top 1 percent—were likewise disproportionate. The annual incomes of these households began at well over $1 million. Entry-level net worth was pegged in the $12 million to $14 million range.

Still more extraordinary gains were racked up by the highest one-hundredth of the top 1 percent. Two economists, Thomas Pinketty and Emmanuel Saez, calculated that this group of roughly thirteen thousand tax-paying households had a minimum income of $3.6 million and an average income of $17 million. Their share of total U.S. household income increased almost fivefold between 1970 and 1998, jumping from 0.7 percent to over 3 percent, a stunning ratio.[23]

A wealth pyramid, albeit less precise than a block of data, is in order here. The divisions within the top 1 percent of American incomes can be likened to the hierarchy of nobility and gentry of yore. At the apex, the princes of the *Forbes* list increased their money tenfold during the eighties and nineties, while below them the approximately thirteen thousand peers of the economic realm registered something like a fivefold increase. A notch down, the broader top one-tenth of 1 percent—one hundred thousand or so knightly households—enjoyed probably a tripling. In the bottom half of the top 1 percent came the $300,000–$500,000 households—the minor gentry, esquires, and counselors—who averaged perhaps a doubling. Most of the serious economic dynastization of the United States has involved the top one-tenth of the 1 percent—the thirteen thousand. Moderately rich extended families, where $30 million to $50 million is spread over four to eight households, would be in the next tier down.

Even among clans where many relatives were barely on speaking terms, a certain unity of purpose developed in sharing financial services. Between 1937 and 1999, four of America's richest families—the Rockefellers, Mellons, du Ponts, and Phippses—increased their combined net worths from between $2 billion and $4 billion to roughly $38 billion without enjoying ownership of any new, cutting-edge industry. What they took advantage of was the financialization of America and the entrenching tools that burgeoning investment firms offered to U.S. wealth holders. Elaborate trust arrangements, sophisticated family offices, lucrative private placements, exotic hedge funds equipped to bet as easily on bear claws as on bull stampedes, and other varieties of hereditary portfolio armor emerged as the latter-day equivalent of the entail and primogeniture that Jefferson, Madison, and their allies had extinguished in the new nation two centuries earlier.

Forbes magazine was a particularly proud chronicler of these developments. For example, 120 years after the death of Commodore Cornelius Vanderbilt, the forty-three descendants of one of his great-great-grandsons, William A. M. Burden, were reported to enjoy a comforting half billion dollars thanks to their family office and its management of their pooled funds. Other families like the Bells of General Mills, the grain-trading Cargills, the Ziff publishing dynasty, and the Pratt clan of Standard Oil set up versions of the private (family) trust companies permitted under the laws of states like Delaware, Wyoming, and South Dakota. And this account leaves out the well-known large repositories: U.S. Trust, Bessemer Trust, Northern Trust, the Trust Company of the West, and so on.[24]

In 1937, a muckraking journalist named Ferdinand Lundberg contended that sixty families, bolstered by ninety of lesser rank, controlled much of the top echelon of U.S. business. As of 1999, there was a much richer, much larger group of households that fell into that category while remaining just as distant from the economic problems and pressures of the ordinary American family. Since the 1980s, the United States has replaced France as the major nation with the largest gap between the rich and the poor. Wealth and income stratification—the hardening of the economy's arteries—was world-class and worsening.

The Princeton economist Alan Krueger wrote in 2002 that "if the United States stands out in comparison with other countries, it is in having a more static distribution of income across the generations with fewer opportunities for advancement."[25] Indeed, a sequence of economic studies found a rapid rise in how much of a father's earnings advantage passed to his sons. In the 1980s, it had been 40 percent; by the late 1990s, it was 65 percent. Of the major Western nations, only Britain had as little intergenerational mobility.

Several decades of tax policies favorable to the upper brackets and their investments had already aided stratification. However, legislation enacted in 2001 to phase out the estate tax by 2010 heralded further concentration. Lisa Keister, author of *Wealth in America,* cited estimates that without the progressive rates in the estate tax of the nineties, the share of U.S. wealth owned by the top 1 percent in 1998 would have been 43 percent instead of 38 percent.[26] Working from population and actuarial tables, forecasters expected record dollar levels of estates to pass to heirs between 2001 and 2020, a prospect that spurred upper-bracket pressure for tax "relief." Given that fully half of the federal estate tax was paid in 1999 by the 6.6 percent of estates over $5 million and a quarter by the 467 estates worth more than $20 million, its full elimination promised to be the ultimate enabler of wealth dynastization.[27]

According to the Center on Budget and Policy Priorities, the disappearance of the estate tax threatened a mammoth ten-year $740 billion revenue loss during the post-repeal decade after 2012. Looking ahead seventy-five years, the center guessed that the revenues sacrificed by estate tax repeal would equal nearly 40 percent of the entire projected shortfall of the Social Security Trust Fund. Even some of the nation's richest men found these priorities appalling. Billionaire investor Warren Buffett worried that "without the estate tax, you will in effect have an aristocracy of wealth, which means you pass down the ability to command the resources of the nation based on heredity rather than merit."[28]

A Politics of Great Families in the United States?

The mutation of the erstwhile "family" issue in U.S. politics did not go unnoticed. Economics columnist Paul Krugman concluded one wry examination of the new regime by noting that "for years, opinion leaders have told us that it's all about family values. And it is—but it will take a while before most people realize that they meant the value of coming from the right family."[29]

Not surprisingly, the growing concentration of wealth also gave rise to a parallel concentration of political power, to the benefit of corporations and other large donors. This had also occurred in other U.S. boom periods—the post–Civil War Gilded Age and the Roaring Twenties—because businessmen and financiers invariably want to buy access, favoritism, or permissive regulation while the economic partying is at its merriest. Between 1980 and 2000, the dollars pouring into the presidential-year arena of federal elections roughly trebled; the cost of running for open House and Senate seats jumped by 500 percent. Over 40 percent of the individual contributions over $200 came from donors with incomes in the top 1 percent.

Ballooning election costs generally increased the dependency of office seekers on rich donors. However, there were exceptions, and three of the most important neatly echoed the themes of the era: celebrities; men and women rich enough to fund their own campaigns; and the brothers, sisters, sons, daughters, and spouses of well-known politicians able to bank on their name recognition and access to money. By 2002, the evidence was clear.

The most impressive example had come in the spring and summer of 1999, when national fund-raisers and major donors tied to former president Bush—not a few had connections going back three decades—joined with the Texas contributor base of Governor George W. Bush and the smaller Florida contingent of Governor Jeb Bush for a blitzkrieg that, according to the description of one disheartened foe, "sucked the oxygen right out of the atmosphere." As chapter 3 will explain, it was the opening salvo of the Bush restoration.

The other two major dynasties were also well funded. With the help of her husband's donors, Hillary Clinton raised $40 million and won a solid victory in New York's gold-plated 2000 U.S. Senate race. In Rhode Island that year, the fund-raising prowess that allowed Congressman Patrick J. Kennedy to flood the state with money—$2.7 million for the two Democratic House winners of 2000 versus under $300,000 for the Republican losers—so impressed other House Democrats that they made him chairman of the Democratic Congressional Campaign Committee.[30]

Cash, however, is not the sole currency of dynasties. "The only thing better than money for a political campaign is free media," one pundit opined, "and aristocratic politicians simply make better copy."[31] Commentator Michael Kinsley observed that "a political name is inherited wealth of the most plutocratic sort. A childhood or marriage steeped in politics is good training and brings useful connections. But mainly, an established name is the political equivalent of a commercial brand. 'Brand extension,' as it is called, means using the reputation of an established product to help peddle a new one. There is a certain logic to the notion that if Kleeneze is a good laundry detergent, then a dishwater detergent named Kleeneze will be good too. But the power of brand extension operates more on a sub-rational level of sheer name recognition." He went on to conclude, "The notion that Jones Jr. will make a good senator because Jones Sr. did is less a rational assumption than a primitive instinct."[32]

Unfortunately, primitive instinct seems to have intensified, given the electorate's increasingly frequent support of family dynasts. After Republican Lincoln Chafee was named to his father's Rhode Island Senate seat, Democratic congressman Patrick Kennedy made this joke at a local roast: "Now when I hear someone talk about a Rhode Island politician whose father was a senator and got to Washington on his family name, used cocaine and wasn't very smart, I know there is only a 50-50 chance it's me."[33]

Once again, numbers will reveal how the politics of family has been spreading. Some 77 of the 535 members of the 107th Congress elected in 2000 were relatives of senators, representatives, governors, judges, state legislators, or local officials. Moreover, blacks, Hispanics, and environmentalists were playing the family game as well as the millionaire clans. Mario Diaz-Balart joined his older brother Lincoln in the U.S. House, both being Cuban American Republicans from Florida. In California, Mexican American Democrat Linda Sanchez won her first term in Congress as a Democrat with some help from the repute and connections of her four-term sister, Loretta.

In the West, where the Udall name has favorable associations with environmental fidelity, Mark Udall, son of longtime Arizona congressman Morris Udall, won a House seat in nearby Colorado. His cousin Tom, son of former secretary of the interior Stewart Udall, got elected from New Mexico. Presumably local voters inferred at least some philosophic resemblance.

Nevertheless, one family had come to overshadow all the others. Along with ten to twenty minor "dynasties," and a senior duo in the second tier— the Kennedys and Clintons, the two other families that had elected a president—one alone held first-tier status: the Bushes. In addition to their principal credential of having elected two presidents in close succession, they had also gained control of two of the four biggest states and developed their extended family into an entourage akin to the lesser royals who deputized for Britain's House of Windsor.

Biographer Bill Minutaglio, a Texas newspaperman, has researched this topic most fully. During the first eighteen months of the George H. W. Bush administration, he reports,

> Bushes and Walkers helped lead fifteen of the forty-one presidential delegations that flew, usually on official Air Force jets, to special international ceremonies. Nancy Bush Ellis would lead the U.S. delegation to Athens in honor of 2,500 years of democracy in Greece, and she represented her

brother on a visit to the leaders of Western Samoa; Jonathan Bush represented his brother and the United States in the Ukraine during a ceremony
marking attacks against Soviet Jews and he also attended the 1989 presidential inauguration in Argentina; William Bucky Bush represented the United
States during Malta's independence celebrations, and then traveled to Turkey
to honor the patriarch of the Eastern Orthodox church.

Other siblings, sons, and daughters went to Benin, Bolivia, Paraguay, Gam-
bia, and Morocco; presidential nephews and cousins attended ceremonies
in Guatemala and Poland.[34]

In addition, seventy-one members of the extended Bush-Walker family
came to Houston for the 1992 Republican National Convention; dozens
served as delegates or surrogates at functions spread throughout the city.
Twenty-five were brought onto the Astrodome stage for "Family Values
Night."[35] The Kennedys would undoubtedly have marshaled similar ranks
if they had won the presidency again in the eighties or the nineties, a feat
they were unable to accomplish. It was the Bushes who managed the first
American restoration—and they did so in the context of circumstances
that marked a major upheaval in the nation's political culture.

CHAPTER 3

The First American Restoration

If this is a dynasty, why did the voters take away his [George H. W. Bush's] job and give it to Bill Clinton in 1992? . . . The question continues to be an open wound.

Bush biographer Mickey Herskowitz, 2003

This is not a family that would be taking over the world if they were not in politics. But they're good at becoming president. It's a curious niche.

Longtime Bush aide, quoted anonymously in the Washington Post, 2001

Like his father's, W.'s basic message is: Trust me, I've been bred for this job.

Maureen Dowd, New York Times, 2000

Perhaps because the Bushes, in contrast to the insouciant Kennedys, were loath to be identified as a dynasty, neither father nor son ever offered any perspective on the 1992–2000 roller-coaster behavior of Americans in throwing out one Bush president, embracing an antagonistic insurgent, and then restoring the eldest Bush son and heir to the White House—or at least creating a stalemate in which the U.S. Supreme Court would do so. The family's own explanation for the scarring defeat in 1992 blamed "vendettas"—one by the Republican primary challenger, Patrick Buchanan; the second by computer billionaire Ross Perot, who decided to run in the general election as an independent.

Neither Perot nor Buchanan was a fan of George H. W. Bush's "country club," CIA, and old-boy-network brand of Republican politics. Perot privately called Bush a "wimp" and a "rabbit." Grudges did exist. Yet their campaigns can no more be dismissed as simple vendettas than could

Theodore Roosevelt's third-party Bull Moose belligerency in 1912. That year, Roosevelt split away most of the Republican Party's progressive wing, especially in the West, with his attacks on the institutional and economic conservatism of the GOP establishment and President William Howard Taft. The two progressive candidates, TR and Woodrow Wilson, together got 69 percent of the total ballots cast nationally, with Socialist Eugene Debs pulling another 6 percent. Taft took just 23 percent, the worst showing for a Republican presidential nominee since the party's formation in 1854.

George H. W. Bush's defeat in 1992, while less severe, bore some relation. It must be understood in order to fathom how remarkable it was for a restoration to occur eight years later. Democratic nominee Clinton and Reform Party contender Perot together drew 62 percent, shrinking Bush's portion of the total vote to slightly over 37 percent, the worst reelection showing for a president since Taft. (Even the hapless Herbert Hoover had drawn 40 percent in 1932.) As chapter 4 will suggest, Bush's greatest weakness was economic. Republican primary opponent Buchanan drew first blood in the New Hampshire primary, denouncing the president as an elitist ("King George") unconcerned with ordinary people's jobs and urging state voters to "dump his tea in the harbor." Even the *Washington Post* and *New York Times* noted the effectiveness of Buchanan's "little guy" economics.

Perot, in turn, savaged the administration's high budget deficits and blamed free-trade policies for exporting jobs. The employment data were indeed grim. Although the 1990–91 recession had officially ended in March 1991, white-collar joblessness, in particular, kept rising through the end of 1992, touching levels not seen since the late 1930s. Climbing stock indexes may have earned kudos on Wall Street, but Main Street remained unimpressed. In the longer term, Perot's criticism of Bush's deficits helped to shape the fiscal policies of the Clinton administration, just as TR's demands in 1912 had whetted Woodrow Wilson's subsequent progressivism.

What portion of this the Bushes understood is unclear. They did, however, comprehend that the 1988–92 drop in George H. W.'s share of the total presidential vote—a slump of 16 percentage points, from 53.4 percent to 37.4 percent—represented a severe earthquake on the political equivalent of the Richter scale. Since the first Republican-Democratic presidential contests in the 1850s, declines of 15 points or more had occurred just four times—undercutting the Democrats between 1856 and 1860, the Republicans between 1908 and 1912, the Republicans again between 1928 and 1932, and the Democrats between 1964 and 1968. Indeed, the convulsions of 1856–60, 1928–32, and 1964–68 figured among the major political realignment sequences of U.S. history; the spasm of 1908–12 was the Theodore Roosevelt exception.

Judged by these precedents, the electorate's dismissal of George H. W. Bush was either a party realignment opportunity waiting for fulfillment— one that Bill Clinton wasted over two terms—or the rare sort of nonre- aligning convulsion in the TR manner. To dismiss the event as merely the result of vendettas is simply inadequate. The precipitous fall in George H. W. Bush's job approval rating from a crest of 89 percent in March 1991, fol- lowing the apparent triumph over Iraq's Saddam Hussein, to just 40 to 45 percent in the primary season a year later (and 35 to 37 percent by mid- summer) was revealing in itself. No other American president had ever lost so much public confidence so quickly.

University of Texas professor Walter Dean Burnham, a distinguished scholar of U.S. political realignment, observed that "whatever else 1992 was, at its center was the landslide rejection of an incumbent president. . . . George Bush belongs to a specific, if select group of presidents who, ini- tially elected with high hopes and considerable popular support, achieved spectacular failure on the job. Including Bush, there have thus far been six such cases across the history of the American presidency."[1]

The significant question, then, is not how George H. W. Bush got trounced in 1992, but why his public esteem recovered steadily thereafter, enabling within only eight years the first restoration of a ruling family to the U.S. presidency. The two relevant precedents—furnishing partial, al- beit imperfect, parallels—come from modern European history. However, before turning to these, it is useful to examine two other essential factors: the unappreciated depths of Bush family ambition and self-importance dating back a half century, and the emergence of Bill Clinton in the 1990s as an object of loathing among many Republican and conservative inde- pendent voters.

Pride, Ambition, and Pretentiousness

Whatever the nature of destiny, biography is its explanation. In 2003, a book about Senator Prescott Bush, prepared with the cooperation of his family, was published under the title *Duty, Honor, Country*. Its author, Mickey Herskowitz, a Houston sportswriter long known to the Bushes, had originally been approached in March 1999 "to put together a quickie campaign biography that would appear to be in [George W.] Bush's own words."[2] The thesis that emerged in 2003, captured in the title, was that Prescott Bush's code of honor, integrity, and duty lived on as a family legacy, inspiring its multigenerational commitment to public service. No message could be clearer: "legacy" is the family's preference over "dynasty" as a description of its hold over American politics.

Indeed, the book spotlights an even earlier progenitor of faith and probity: Prescott Bush's grandfather James Smith Bush, the Episcopal minister who in the 1850s became the first of the clan to graduate from Yale. Because he so compellingly embodied these qualities, James Bush was "clearly the founding father."[3] Surprisingly, George Herbert Walker, whose dollars underwrote the efforts of several generations of Bushes, is shouldered aside with a few paragraphs. Accounts of his taste for luxury are interlaced with descriptions of his "raw drive," toughness, and penchant for drinking and gambling. He was "a man considered by some to be coarse," and he "intimidated his family as well as his business rivals."[4]

This portrait has a whiff of revisionism to round out its ingratitude. The single photograph of him included in the book shows a tough-looking young man holding a rifle and is captioned "George H. Walker serving in a posse June 1900."[5] Perhaps readers are expected to think that the vile and coarse Walkers are alien to the Bush legacy.

Duty and public service do make cameo appearances in the Bush saga, fulfilling the stern instructions on those New England school walls. However, so do vanity, ambition, and pretentiousness. Among the pictures from the family scrapbook that appear in *Duty, Honor, Country* is one showing the George H. W. Bushes entertaining Queen Elizabeth and Prince Philip; the caption helpfully explains that "the Bushes are descended from British royalty."[6] A half century of such preening must be taken seriously as an index of a family's image of itself.

As early as the late 1940s Barbara Bush talked to friends about becoming first lady.[7] As we have seen, Prescott Bush's wife, Dorothy, said that her husband, during his decade in the Senate, had wanted to be president, an ambition he probably developed years before he retired in 1962. His sense of office was such that his grandchildren were instructed to call him "Senator," not "Grampa." Precisely when George H. W. Bush caught the itch is not known, though by 1963, son George W., at Andover, had begun to speak of his father's goal to be president.[8] In the mid-1960s, according to an associate, George H. W. Bush neglected long-range business planning at

Zapata Offshore because of his preoccupation with becoming a senator like his father.[9] The Bushes' commitment seems no less persistent than the Kennedy drive; the difference is that while the Kennedys joked about their ambitions, the Bushes have dissembled.

Those in proximity, however, sensed the quiet compulsion. Concern over George W.'s modeling himself on George senior helped motivate his fiancée, Cathy Wolfman, to break off the engagement in 1969—or so friends said.[10] Dynastic ambition popped up elsewhere in the family in 1981 when insurance executive Prescott Bush Jr. announced a primary challenge to the incumbent Republican U.S. senator from Connecticut, liberal Lowell Weicker. The two families, both hailing from Greenwich, had had something resembling a Corsican feud, aggravated in 1980 by Weicker's refusal to endorse George H. W. Bush for vice president. Prescott Bush Jr. raised almost a million dollars, some from the family. But he withdrew from the race after several months, as his essentially issueless candidacy became bogged down in perceptions of another Bush seeking office as destiny fulfillment.

Despite his minimal governmental experience, George H. W. Bush's presidential hunger was common knowledge by 1968, when Richard Nixon helped by letting him be mentioned as a possible vice presidential choice. In 1970, Bush—then a candidate for the U.S. Senate—was cited by Washington columnist David Broder as a possible replacement for Vice President Spiro Agnew as Nixon's running mate. In 1974, Bush campaigned to be picked as the new vice president when Gerald Ford ascended to the Oval Office after Nixon's resignation, but Nelson Rockefeller took the prize. In 1975, after Rockefeller announced he would retire the following year, Bush's renewed hopes were scotched. To get him confirmed in 1975 as CIA director, Ford had to exclude him from the 1976 vice presidential selection. After leaving the CIA in early 1977, Bush began laying the groundwork for a 1980 presidential race.

Such consistent ambition, rarely ameliorated by a particular cause or issues agenda, is hard to reconcile with the New England school mottoes of duty, public service, and noblesse oblige. While some biographers have argued that the Bushes displayed no dynastic intention until the late 1990s, the larger pattern seems reasonably clear. One of his own cousins interpreted George H. W. Bush's compulsion for office as an extension of his chronic popularity seeking and habitual thank-you notes. Ray Walker, a psychoanalyst, told the Los Angeles Times in 1987 that "he needs to be president, that's for sure. There's no choice for him, really. For him, it's the absolute confirmation."[11]

George W.'s second-generation attempt to follow in parental footsteps is revealing, both for the parallels already detailed and in light of some obvious pitfalls he faced. During the 1980s, when cousin John Ellis saw Bush seeming to hurry, he would sometimes call out to him, "Primogenitor, baby."[12] His father's surprise choice of Dan Quayle as his 1988 vice presidential running mate, therefore, must have come as something of a shock. One biographer noted that by election day, "for months George W. had endured inquiries into the fact that he and Dan Quayle had both been members of the same national fraternity and had both gained admission to the national guard. Campaign observers also began hearing relentless, creeping suggestions that aside from being about the same age, the pair were remarkably similar in their upbringing and personalities: handsome descendants of old-money captains of industry, less-than-stellar university students, deemed extraordinarily charismatic and charming by their old time college mates, big-time golfers."[13] Some older Republicans had a different but related take: Quayle, they said, actually reminded Bush senior of *himself,* right down to the occasional lime green pants and madras jackets. To George H. W., journalists who mocked Quayle's dubious intelligence were merely spiteful; for a while, at least, he believed Quayle was being unfairly dismissed.

As for the succession, the post–World War II practice in the Republican Party had been to promote sitting vice presidents for open presidential nominations, which could have made Quayle the favorite for 1996. An eldest son struggling with press comparisons with his father's choice might have felt displacement pangs (perhaps not surprisingly, a number of mid-1992 reports would place George W. in that year's brief dump-Quayle movement). However, in late 1988, with Quayle ascending to the vice presidency, George W., then serving as his father's liaison to the Religious Right, must have felt that he needed a strategic advisory. He requested a report, eventually forty-four pages long and nicknamed "All the President's Children," examining how the offspring of past presidents had been perceived by voters and the media. The record wasn't reassuring, especially when it cited such precedents as Franklin D. Roosevelt Jr.'s failure in his run for governor of New York.[14]

George W. was in fact already considering a statehouse bid in Texas, but his own soundings came back negative. He lacked credentials of his own, and as a further disincentive, his mother advised him not to run for governor in 1990; doing so while his father was president would cause political problems. While he heeded her warning, his father's reelection defeat two years later, both liberated him to run in 1994 and energized him for the larger challenge ahead.

During their father's term, both of the president's eldest sons had pondered statehouse races—George W. again in Texas and Jeb in Florida. Early in 1993, each supposedly telephoned a different parent—George W., his mother; Jeb, his father—to discuss his plans for 1994. But whereas Jeb announced in June 1993, the firstborn was more cautious. Now managing partner of the Texas Rangers baseball team, a career credential well chosen for both business and Texas leadership imagery, George W. waited for November's off-year elections in New York City, New Jersey, and Virginia. This barometer was made favorable by a GOP sweep. On November 8, he announced his candidacy for governor.

Besides freeing the two brothers' ambitions, their father's reelection defeat also cried out for revenge—especially in Texas. Dynasty now had a second spur. The incumbent Democratic governor, Ann Richards, a friend of the Clintons, had created an uproar at the 1988 Democratic National Convention with her mocking speech about George H. W. Bush being "born with a silver foot in his mouth." Victoria Clarke, the president's 1992 campaign press secretary, said that getting even for his father's defeat became a particular motivation for George W. The Bushes "will probably get very mad if they ever read this, but I think what [George W.] is doing and how effectively he is doing it has a lot to do with how much he cares about his father."[15] Jeb, she said, had always been politically committed, even before his father was "wronged."

Uncertainty about the family political succession—would the nod go to the firstborn prince, who inherited sarcasm from his mother ("I have my daddy's eyes and my mother's mouth"), or to the younger one, who had a legacy of seriousness from his father?—ended in November 1994, when George W. won in Texas and Jeb lost in Florida. Although the Sunshine State was manifestly more liberal—Clinton would carry Florida in 1996 while losing Texas decisively—that was beside the point. Jeb Bush had been widely regarded as the better politician, yet George W. Bush was the one to grab a major governorship.

As a result, he made himself the heir apparent, although his brother's family had some difficulty accepting that. Amid the inauguration festivities of January 2001, George P. Bush, Jeb's eldest son, told a reporter, "No one would have picked my uncle. If you came up to any close member of my family six years ago and said my uncle wanted to be president, they'd probably laugh in your face. We were really surprised."[16]

In 1995, however, the timing of George W.'s decisive step remained uncertain. Nineteen ninety-four had delivered a massive midterm repudiation to Bill Clinton, as well as to the sort of glitzy, celebrity-type liberal politics represented by Ann Richards. The giddy Republicans taking over Congress in 1995 felt sure they would defeat Clinton in 1996, and the new president's reelection bid in 2000 would postpone a Bush opportunity. This scenario became less likely, however, as the field of presidential hopefuls took flesh—Senate majority leader Bob Dole, Texas senator Phil Gramm, magazine publisher Steve Forbes, commentator Patrick Buchanan, and Tennessee governor Lamar Alexander. The convenient candidacy of fellow Texan Gramm, who had wide energy-industry support, provided a temporary hitching post for a governor unable to run in 1996 after only two years in office. Dole captured the nomination but lost in November after a less than impressive campaign. In the skies over the Texas state capital, however, the political stars once again came into alignment.

At this point, it becomes necessary to return to the key point raised earlier in this chapter: What had strained the sourness from the public's memory of the Bushes and of the economic circumstances under which George H. W. Bush had left office?

Bill Clinton: Bubba as Ogre?

Much of the rehabilitation of the Bush image between 1992 and 1996 came as a reaction to the moral tarnish that had already begun to accumulate on Bill Clinton, the "bozo" who had defeated him. Clinton had managed to keep innuendo at bay during the 1992 campaign, partly because of the Perot diversion, partly because of the electorate's economic preoccupation, and partly through his own repeated insistence that nothing in his background was amiss. Had what later became common knowledge been revealed during the campaign, Clinton might well have been too crippled to win. This realization fueled Bush family bitterness.

Almost immediately upon his arrival in the Oval Office, the public faced a media barrage of Clinton controversies and scandals, from the new president's decision to admit gays into the military to allegations of financial and sexual misbehavior. George H. W. Bush might not know much about milk or bread prices or hard times in Peoria, but few doubted his gentlemanly demeanor. As Clinton's administration battled an apparently endless string of accusations, polls showed public estimates of his predecessor rising again. If the Bushes had begun to think of Clinton as a liar and usurper, so had many other Americans.

From 35 to 37 percent in mid-1992, the former president's approval climbed to 45–55 percent at the time of Clinton's inauguration in January 1993, and 55–60 percent when the midterm elections came in November 1994.[17] In addition to the White House scandals, Bush also benefited as blame for the still-weak economy shifted to Clinton and the Democrats, and unpopular Republican economic policies were no longer front and center.

More encouragement came when voters turned back to the Republicans in the 1994 elections, capped by the Texas gubernatorial victory of the ex-president's eldest son. However, the deeper explanation for the 1994 congressional election results lay in a powerful voter angst. While most Republicans preferred a self-congratulatory interpretation that reaffirmed their own ideology and programs and the 1988–92 Bush legacy, historically turnovers of that magnitude had predominantly reflected the negative feelings of voters. Before the Democrats' painful loss of 8 Senate and 52 House seats in 1994, the party in the White House had taken four comparable post–World War II drubbings: In 1946, Democrats lost 11 seats in the Senate, 54 in the House. In 1958, Republicans gave up 13 in the Senate, 47 in the House. In 1966, Democrats lost 7 in the Senate, 48 in the House. In the Watergate year of 1974, the Republican body count was 3 in the Senate and 43 in the House. Three times out of four, an important part of the impetus was disapproval of a president—Harry Truman in 1946, Lyndon Johnson in 1966, and Richard Nixon in 1974.

That was also the motive force in 1994, and the worst Democratic defeats and anti-Clinton vituperation came in Dixie. The GOP's previous big congressional advances below the Mason-Dixon line had likewise come when home folks soured on Democratic presidents of southern origin, usually over their racial and cultural liberalism, embarrassing behavior, or manifest weakness in foreign policy. The biggest of those Republican inroads came under Johnson (in the 1964–68 elections) and Carter (in the 1978–80 elections). Nineteen ninety-four's negative landslide against Clinton was the culmination of three decades of regional transformation. The

Bubba-as-ogre phenomenon was already building, voiced especially in the views expressed in fundamentalist pulpits and at annual meetings of the Southern Baptist Convention.

Cultural politics had in effect laid a trap for the Democrats. In the 1960s and thereafter, as conservative Republicanism flexed its muscles, the only way that the Democrats could win the White House was to follow what could be called the good-ole-boy script. Liberal presidential candidates from the North invariably lost, from Hubert Humphrey and George McGovern to Walter Mondale and Michael Dukakis. Democratic success came only for those who could counter GOP appeal below the Mason-Dixon line by taking the role of a more populist or progressive, but still Bubba-talking, brand of southerner, as in the cases of Johnson, Carter, and Clinton himself.

If Clinton represented the Bubba of Bubbas, the zenith of the Dogpatch White House, part of the caricature had taken form in the presidency of Lyndon Johnson. Besides uncouth demeanor, he had a black-sheep brother, Sam Houston. Good-ole-boy brothers would turn out to be reliable hallmarks of late-twentieth-century Democratic White Houses: Sam Houston Johnson; Billy Carter, who took money from Libya and had a beer—Billy beer—named after him; and finally Roger Clinton, an attention-seeking rock musician who had done time on a drug charge.

More tellingly, between 1994 and 1998, Clinton himself became a loathed figure for roughly two-fifths of the U.S. population, much as Johnson had been because of the war in Vietnam. Gallup would later term these critics "the repulsed."[18] Clinton had grown up in a broken home in an Arkansas gambling town—Hot Springs—that had a national reputation for loose law enforcement, loose cash, and loose women, and Republicans insisted he had absorbed predilections for all three. As the criticism became relentless, the eighteen months leading up to the 1994 elections began to resemble a moral merry-go-round.

The White House travel office scandal was the first round of the attack, followed by the suicide of White House counsel Vincent Foster, then the appointment first of Robert Fiske and after him Kenneth Starr as special prosecutor to investigate the involvement of Bill and Hillary Clinton in Arkansas's failed Whitewater real estate development. Next came the accusation by ex–Arkansas state employee Paula Jones of sexual harassment by Clinton while he was governor of Arkansas, followed by his own response claiming presidential immunity against her lawsuit. Republicans overdid their traditional-values indignation, but southerners were particularly mortified by a misbehaving president who spoke with their own accent.

In 1994, when southern voters handed the Republicans solid majorities of the region's seats in Congress, they gave the GOP control of both the House and Senate for the first time since 1953–54. The party's changing geographic base, in turn, worked to deepen and Dixiefy its conservatism. The Republicans controlling Congress in 1953–54 had been overwhelmingly northern. Four decades later, the largest party bloc in the Congress was southern, and so was the GOP congressional leadership. The president pro tem of the Senate was Strom Thurmond of South Carolina, the majority leader, Trent Lott of Mississippi; in the House, the Speaker was Newt Gingrich of Georgia, and the majority leader and majority whip were both Texans, Dick Armey and Tom DeLay. All but Armey were Southern Baptists.

Indeed, part of the new militance was church-driven. Instead of Episcopalians, Methodists, and Presbyterians, the congressional Republican Party was now dominated by the fast-growing Southern Baptists, many of whom belonged to that denomination's newly ascendant conservative faction, the Southern Baptist Convention (SBC). Over the next four years, the congressional GOP would absorb from the SBC a doctrinal fervor that went well beyond mainstream white southern views, on issues that included the Bible as the literal word of God (65 percent of Southern Baptists agreed), the basic wrongness of premarital sex (63 percent), and the invariable wrongness of homosexuality (90 percent).[19]

To this new GOP constituency, Clinton was anathema, and state and national Southern Baptist Conventions were soon humming with denunciatory resolutions. Because some 80 percent of southern white evangelical Christians voted Republican for Congress in 1994, few party strategists underestimated this bloc's importance. Among the fourteen states in the greater South—the former Confederacy plus Kentucky, Missouri, and Oklahoma—the SBC share of the population was 30 percent or more in six (Mississippi, South Carolina, Alabama, Georgia, Tennessee, and Oklahoma) and 25 percent or more in three others (North Carolina, Arkansas, and Kentucky).[20] In these fourteen states, white evangelical, fundamentalist, and charismatic Protestants probably totaled 35 percent of the electorate; in the nation as a whole, the figure was closer to 25 percent.

In Texas, with a 20 percent SBC population share, George W. Bush and his political adviser, Karl Rove, had discerned a similar drift in the state's

1988–94 voting returns. In 1994, the Anglo counties where Bush made sizable local gains over his father's 1988 Texas presidential victory were small-town and rural areas dominated by Southern Baptists and other unfashionable denominations. Such locales had furnished President Eisenhower's ten weakest non-Hispanic counties in 1956, when he carried Texas easily because of heavy urban and suburban support. Nixon and Reagan improved GOP strength, but the final switch awaited the nineties. In 1994's gubernatorial race, six of these counties backed George W. Bush, whereas his father had carried only one in 1988. That same year, the Religious Right also took over the Texas Republican Party, as prayer breakfasts drew bigger crowds than hospitality suites, and the convention opened with a "Grand Old Prayer Session."[21]

Bush also targeted Bill Clinton in his 1994 gubernatorial campaign, well aware that only 35 to 40 percent of Texans approved of the president. In the days leading up to his critical television debate with Ann Richards, he reminded voters at every campaign stop how she had headed the Democratic National Convention that nominated Clinton in 1992.

Come 1996, Republican leaders griped at losing a second presidential election to Clinton, yet they took heart from his inability to capture 50 percent of the three-way vote (the results: Clinton, 49 percent; Dole, 41 percent; Perot, 8 percent). That outcome suggested Clinton might well hurt the Democratic nominee four years hence. At the time, survey takers also reported that former president George H. W. Bush had climbed to some 60 percent approval in national polls. In trial heats looking ahead to 2000, his near namesake, the governor of Texas, led Vice President Albert Gore, the presumed Democratic choice, by roughly 10 points. Not a few of those backers thought they were voting for Bush's father.

In retrospect, strategist Rove acknowledged having first contemplated a George W. Bush presidential race in 1994 and having planned for it in 1996.[22] Certainly the arrangements were taking shape by 1997, and then Clinton's impeachment and Bush's strong reelection in 1998 generally buoyed party calculations. By that point, most voters had forgotten or set aside their 1992 dissatisfaction with Bush economics. And with the boom and bull market in stocks predicted to continue through 2000, GOP strategists doubted that any old economic resentments would resurface. The converse—that a strong economy would boost the Democrats—pointed the GOP toward its obvious major countertheme: the nation's need for moral renewal after disillusionment with Clinton.

Texas might even serve as the model of how to fashion a victory. With luck, the successful Bush-orchestrated alliance between the Corporate Right and the Religious Right in the second-biggest state could be repeated nationally. Given the inevitability of morality as a 2000 issue, there was no plausible GOP strategy that did not include the Religious Right. The drawback was the flip side of the coin: the potential for a backlash in the Northeast, Great Lakes, and Pacific. Were Bush to be seen as the creature of the Religious Right, he would lose.

After two decades of Bush candidacies and incumbencies, the national GOP political and financial leadership of the late 1990s was closely intertwined with the family and its chief fund-raisers and advisers. Conservative editor William Kristol assessed the situation more bluntly: "The Bush network is the only genuine network in the Republican Party. It *is* the establishment."[23] Because of George W.'s dynastic credentials, Republican corporate, financial, and party leaders knew they could safely ignore his cowboy boots, mangled sentences, global inexperience, and reputation as a prodigal son—a curriculum vitae and image that would have doomed a similar officeholder named Smith or Jones. The candidate himself, however, as one Texas journalist reported, had a nagging private worry . . . *Won't the nation be resistant to the notion of a Bush dynasty?*[24]

But throughout 1999, his consistent 10- or 12-point lead in the polls hinted at the possible Republican equivalent of a coronation. The moneymen would write their checks; a steady flow of congressmen and governors would come by in small delegations to express their support. Foreign dignitaries from his father's orbit—former Canadian prime minister Brian Mulroney, Qatar's foreign minister Sheikh Hamad bin Jassim bin Jabr al-Thani, and such like—would visit the governor's mansion in Austin, staging a tableau vivant of presumed foreign policy dialogue. Momentum would build.

Strategists could also count on the Republican Party's innate respect for hierarchy. Of the other nomination possibilities or contenders, half had been part of the 1988–92 Bush administration: Vice President Dan Quayle, National Security Adviser Colin Powell, Education Secretary Lamar Alexander, Labor Secretary Elizabeth Dole, Housing and Urban Development Secretary Jack Kemp. Most, probably, would have to step aside as the ranks of congressmen and senators endorsing the heir apparent grew to 100 and then 125.

Money itself likewise commanded deep bows in the Republican Party.

As the early contributions raised by the Bush campaign soared above $25 million in June 1999, and surpassed $50 million by Labor Day, rivals fell by the wayside, complaining that Bush fund-raisers had taken the distributor caps from their financial engines. (Even John McCain, after a ringing February primary victory in New Hampshire, would not have enough in the bank to survive through the March primaries.) Only a Bush, riding his family name and machine to a solid national poll lead, could have preempted donations and party support to this degree.

These assets are almost impossible to overstate. In 1978, when George W. ran for Congress, he had raised a disproportionate amount of his money from his father's allies and his mother's famous Christmas card list. He did so again in 1999, sending out one of his first presidential-race mailings over Barbara Bush's signature and also tapping into his father's network. "That has been very important," chief fund-raiser Don Evans admitted. His contacts "enabled us to get into cities in the spring and get people energized. That played an important part in laying the foundation."[25] Contributor lists obtained by the *Dallas Morning News* showed the names of many with longtime ties to the Bush family.[26] In addition, George W. raised huge sums from companies doing business in Texas, and tapped his brother's donors in Florida, making it his number three state in early dollars raised.

As for the actual mobilization of the electorate behind the promise of a restoration of national morality, that would be pursued through both hard and soft themes—using quiet harps as well as brash trumpets. The clarion calls were left to the Republicans in Congress, especially in the House of Representatives, where stalwarts had exulted over Special Prosecutor Kenneth Starr's findings. In 1998, they turned Starr's case against Clinton into articles of impeachment, which passed the House in December but failed to achieve a conviction in the Senate in February. The failure of this strategy, which was confirmed by GOP 1998 midterm election losses, lay in shrill, clumsy management and rampant hypocrisy. Republican House leaders, led by Speaker Newt Gingrich, were inept in developing a legal case against Clinton, and recklessly sought *expulsion* of the president, rather than mere censure, on essentially moral grounds, at a time when Gingrich and his supposed replacement, Speaker-designate Robert Livingston, were themselves soon to leave office amid charges of adultery. One fundamentally weak element in the impeachment drive was that so many Americans simultaneously wanted to reject the impeachers.

Wisely, George W. Bush kept his distance from that issue, and spoke instead about bringing integrity and honesty back to the Oval Office. It was enough for him to look stern and then say, to huge applause, "When you elect me I will swear to uphold the dignity and honor of the office to which I was elected." He also ran a television commercial called "Pictures." In it, parents would come up, hold out photographs of their children, and tell him how they wanted their children to be able to respect the White House again.[27]

Other background themes effectively contrasted the moral standards and reputation of the Bushes with those of Clinton. Before the election of 1988, George H. W. Bush had visited that year's Christian Booksellers' Association convention in Dallas to talk about *George Bush: Man of Integrity,* a book that discussed the family's close relationship with evangelists Billy Graham and Jerry Falwell. In 1995, at George W.'s gubernatorial inauguration, Billy Graham had referred to "the moral and spiritual example his mother and father set for us all."[28] George W. had discussed his own religious awakening in his 2000 election tract, *A Charge to Keep.* Over the years, Barbara Bush, with her books about her family and dogs, had established herself as something of a national grandmother. As we have seen, George W.'s campaign chairman called the Bushes "America's Family."

Back in 1981, the symbolism of a television show like *Dynasty* might have been acceptable to the Reagans, but two decades later, Republican officials had a warmer kind of screen image in mind for the Bushes. "When you're talking about Clinton fatigue, part of it is that we loved Ozzie and Harriet," explained Ron Kaufman, George H. W. Bush's former political director. "We really did. People want *Little House on the Prairie* to be real, and the Bushes represent that."[29]

By 2000, scarcely a leaf on the tree of Bush family moral rectitude had been left unexamined. George W. Bush proudly recalled how, in the early 1960s, his grandfather, in a commencement address at Rosemary Hall, the Connecticut girls school, had criticized Nelson Rockefeller for the shamelessness of the man's then-controversial divorce: "Have we come to the point in our life as a nation where the governor of a great state—one who perhaps aspires to the nomination for president of the United States—can desert a good wife, mother of his grown children, divorce her, then persuade a mother of four youngsters to abandon her husband and their four children and marry the governor?" Prescott Bush asked. "Have we come to the point where one of the two great political parties will confer on such a one its highest honor and greatest responsibility?"[30] Four decades later, George W. claimed almost from the first days of his exploratory committee that he, in contrast to Clinton, had been faithful to his wife.

An old friend allowed to reporters that Billy Graham was among those who had urged George W. to run: "Reverend Graham has told [George W.] that he has to do it. Because of where America is today."[31] To much of the Christian Right, such sentiments hardly seemed presumptuous, and George W. himself was certainly primed to express the requisite personal religiosity. On December 13, 1999, at a debate leading up to Iowa's Republican presidential caucuses, the moderator asked the assembled GOP hopefuls "what political philosopher or thinker" they most identified with. The Texas governor alone—and not the two evangelicals, Alan Keyes and Gary Bauer—hastened to interpret this question in a religious vein, replying, "Christ, because he changed my heart."[32]

The biblical role into which he so easily and comfortably fell was that of the prodigal son (Luke 15:11–24)—a wayward sinner, in this instance reclaimed from near-alcoholism or worse and brought to God and salvation with the help of preacher Graham in 1985, just a year or so before his fortieth birthday. This vision of a preacher-assisted conquering of a man's demons was surely more appealing to believers than the metamorphosis of an Ivy League oilman who, some suspected, had turned to religion when the bottom fell out of the oil market. Besides, it kept the publicly renounced demons from rearing up again, midcampaign, with political pitchforks.

The possible exception, referred to earlier, lay in the unsubstantiated rumor that in late 1972 at age twenty-six, George W. had been arrested in Houston for possession of cocaine. At his father's request, a judge supposedly agreed to expunge the court record, provided young Bush did voluntary community service at a local youth project. The job, in fact, did happen; he worked at a community center for a number of months. For a few days in mid-1999, after the rumor was reported on Salon.com, the Internet was abuzz. However, the writer who published the allegations in a book, J. H. Hatfield, had a criminal record, which discredited both him and his story.[33]

Whether a quarter-century-old cocaine arrest would have destroyed George W.'s political career is conjectural. The devil-may-care precedents of Shakespeare's Prince Hal and other roistering heirs suggest that it might not have. And many, if not most, fathers would have tried to help a son who found himself in a similar situation. Still, further investigations raised a number of legal queries. First, there was the issuance in March 1995, entirely out of sequence of renewal date, of a new Texas driver's license to George W. Bush. Cynics suggested that in Texas, a peculiar motivation might have applied here: namely, to eliminate some of the record of past infractions collected under state law as an informational attachment to driver's licenses. The new one was issued, deleting portions of the record, two months after Bush had become governor and had named an old friend to head the license-issuing agency, the Texas Department of Public Safety.

The second intriguing discovery, brought to light in 2000, was that George W. had interrupted the fulfillment of his Air National Guard obligations for almost a year, beginning in May 1972. One reason, journalists suggested, might have been to avoid taking a required air force physical examination that was subject to random drug testing. Senior officers seem to have covered for him; he was not discharged or drafted, as he might have been. Questions have been raised about Bush aides allegedly tampering with the air force files.[34] The substance of these events is not in doubt.

Neither episode proved there had been any cocaine-related arrest, and the exculpatory explanation accepted by the press for George W.'s volunteer service at PULL, the Houston inner-city group, was that George H. W. Bush himself had arranged it after his eldest son had turned up one night after driving while intoxicated. Further pursuit of this issue by the major media in the United States was negligible, although pointed coverage did run in the *Sunday Times* of London. Among U.S. newspapers, the closest attention came in the *Boston Globe* of May 23, 2000:

> Still, the puzzling gap in Bush's military service is likely to heighten speculation about the conspicuous underachievement that marked the period between his 1968 graduation from Yale University and his 1973 entry into Harvard Business School. It is speculation that Bush has helped to fuel: For example, he refused for months last year to say whether he had ever used illegal drugs. Subsequently, however, Bush amended his stance, saying he had not done so since 1974.[35]

From a broader evidentiary standpoint, cocaine usage was no longer the issue. Had a cover-up been proved—a disposal of or tampering with records akin to the cover-ups for which Richard Nixon and Bill Clinton were pursued—it might have scuttled any plausibility of a Bush-led moral restoration. Clinton and Bush would have become fellow scamps, not dragon and putative Saint George. The extended adolescence of a dauphin or Prince of Wales is benignly tolerated; the politics of moral supremacy requires a stricter standard.

In the end, the family claim to probity generally succeeded, giving George W. Bush a wide lead over Democrat Gore as the candidate better equipped to restore morality to the nation. Between mid-1999 and election day 2000, the favorability ratings of former president Bush remained between 50 and 65 percent. Clinton's ratings as a moral man and moral leader fell into the 20 to 25 percent range.

It is easy to argue that as president, William Jefferson Clinton—in Arkansas, his nom de pool hall had been plain Bill—did indeed achieve the depths of ignominy needed to bring on a traditionalist vengeance. Beyond congressional Republicans, only a few critics, from writer Jude Wanniski on the Right to commentator Christopher Hitchens on the Left, ever used extreme terms like "monster" to describe Clinton. However, this phraseological escalation had a late genesis: the February 1999 television interview run by NBC News (after the Senate impeachment trial was over) in which Arkansas housewife Juanita Broaddrick accused Clinton of forcibly raping and biting her two decades earlier. Polls taken after Broaddrick's interview showed roughly six out of ten who had watched believed her.[36]

To judge how public doubts about Bill Clinton affected a 2000 Bush restoration, one must examine the opinion data for 1999 and 2000, not the numbers during the heat of the autumn 1998 impeachment process. The Broaddrick accusation was only one factor. In 1998, Clinton had profited from the public's judging him not alone but against the unpopular, pro-impeachment House GOP leaders, from Gingrich down. By 1999 and 2000, both Gingrich and the threat of immediate presidential removal had fallen off the table. Nor was there any question, as in 1998, about Bill Clinton, with his 80 percent national approval for managing the economy, being forced from office while the stock market teetered during its high-wire walk. As these potentially disruptive ramifications of impeachment faded, the public's moral distaste for Clinton—79 percent thought him guilty of perjury, 53 percent of obstruction of justice—came more to the forefront.[37]

In May 1999, months after the Broaddrick television interview, a Fox News–Opinion Dynamics poll found George W. Bush crushing Clinton himself, not just Gore, by 56 percent to 34 percent in a theoretical matchup. In December 1999, polling by the Gallup Organization found 50 percent of the public supporting the House decision to impeach Clinton, up 15 points from the original postimpeachment sampling in December 1998. In July 2000, ABC News found 45 percent now favoring the impeachment, up 10 points from what that network had measured in December 1998. Similarly, in July 2000, a nationwide poll for the Associated Press found 40 percent of U.S. voters picking honesty and truthfulness as the most important quality in a president, up 10–15 points from previous elections.[38]

If 38 percent of Americans were what Gallup called "repulsed" by Clinton in 1998, by the end of 1999 and into 2000, this number must have been between 40 and 45 percent—a brutal backdrop for the presidential candidacy of Clinton's personally selected vice president. We also know that the distaste of swing voters for Clinton in summer pre–Democratic convention polls helped convince Gore to pick moralizing Connecticut senator Joseph Lieberman, who had briefly considered endorsing impeachment, as his running mate.

As chapter 7 details, Republican gains and support levels in the 2000 presidential election were greatest among those who attended religious services at least once a week. Voters who never attended services, by comparison, were lopsidedly Democratic. Some experts tied anti-Clinton (and thus anti-Gore) attitudes to religiosity. Georgetown University scholar James Reichley, author of *Religion in American Public Life,* told a Texas forum that "the rejection of Gore was based on the belief of many voters that the White House had violated ethical and moral norms that had been based on Judeo-Christian moral tradition. That was by far the most important religious factor in the 2000 elections."[39]

Even out of office, Clinton continued to be a Beelzebubba figure for the American Right. Washington's annual Conservative Political Action Conference sold every kind of anti-Clinton bumper sticker and enmity paraphernalia short of voodoo dolls. Setting aside Broaddrick's allegations, there is no doubt that Clinton was the first president to use the Oval Office as a venue for being fellated by a White House intern, the first to have his DNA tested for an (unrelated) paternity suit, and the first to have his foreign policy motivations both previewed and satirized by a Hollywood comedy (*Wag the Dog*). To many Republicans and conservative independents, men and women who despised the forty-second president, George W. Bush had become a rare rallying point for notions of restoration, legitimacy, and personal responsibility. Thus did the stakes of the 2000 contest transcend those of ordinary presidential elections.

Royal Martyrs and Revolutionary Monsters: The Restoration Parallels

Back in 1960 or 1980, Americans could fairly have observed that *republics* don't restore ruling dynasties; only kingdoms and empires do. However, amid the turn-of-the-century speculation about the United States' becoming more imperial in its culture and attitudes, it is appropriate to consider two especially useful European analogies to the events and psychologies of U.S. politics between 1992 and 2000. The overthrow of George H. W. Bush in 1992, the moral dissatisfaction with his insurgent successor, and the rising drumbeat among conservatives to replace the usurper with the blood heir of the older ruler are about as close as the American Republic is likely to come to a transatlantic version of the English Stuart (1640–60) and French Bourbon (1789–1815) revolutionary dethronements and subsequent restorations.

The following is a very simplified portrait of the basic parallels. Amid widespread political and economic resentment that turned to revolution, King Charles I of England and King Louis XVI of France were eventually executed, in 1649 and 1793, respectively, and were soon replaced by revolutionary strongmen, Oliver Cromwell and Napoleon Bonaparte. Although both were able leaders, Cromwell and Bonaparte became devil figures to out-of-power royalists, and the frequency of war and crisis under their rule wore on increasingly tired nations. Eventually, after Cromwell's death and Napoleon's 1812–15 military defeats, restoration triumphed. The Stuart heir, son Charles II, was brought back to the throne in England, and the Bourbon heir, brother Louis XVIII, in France.

Needless to say, the motivations and convulsions of a twentieth-century republic cannot precisely, or even very closely, match those of kingdoms in earlier centuries. U.S. presidential elections are not guillotines, however sharp the edge of lopsided defeat might feel to a William Howard Taft, Herbert Hoover, or George H. W. Bush. But as we have seen, Bill Clinton became something of a moral devil figure to some 40 percent of Americans, especially churchgoing Christian conservatives. They responded to the stratagems of the Bush faction of the Republican Party to organize a moral and political restoration around the former president's eldest son. Revealingly, the Bush restoration mirrored some behaviors and mind-sets visible earlier in the Stuart and Bourbon reenthronements.

Restoration, of course, has one central impulse: to recover the past.

Each time, that has involved a return of the courtiers, cronies, and preju-
dices of the expelled dynasty, often the very figures that had helped to incite
the earlier expulsion. Because chapters 4–6 will assess the recurrent financial and economic sectoral biases of the Bush family, the following pages
will simply address the restorationist aspect of Bush cabinets, cronies, and
federal appointments. Loyalty has counted more than talent—admittedly
an abstraction, where politics is concerned—in filling most cabinet and
upper subcabinet jobs.

Richard Cheney's selection as vice president—recommended by
George H. W. Bush in a summer 2000 conversation with his about-to-be-
nominated son—is a case in point. As the Texas-based chief executive of a
major oil services corporation, Cheney duplicated rather than complemented George W. in state of residence, intraparty faction, and industrial-
sector bias. He brought no constituency outreach. The outweighing
dynastic consideration was the historical need to surround a restored
monarch with some of his father's skilled counselors. Cheney, who had
been White House chief of staff under Gerald Ford (1976) and defense secretary under the elder Bush, headed this list. His role would be to do for
George W. Bush what the earl of Clarendon, a principal adviser of Charles I,
did for the early reign of Charles II.

To manage twenty-first-century military preparedness and geopolitics,
the Bush administration reached back to the final years of the Vietnam
War. Donald Rumsfeld and Richard Cheney, as chief of staff and deputy
chief of staff, respectively, had presided over the machinery of the Ford
White House in the spring of 1975. This was the bitter April when Saigon
finally fell to the North Vietnamese, followed several weeks later by the
mishandling of the rescue of the SS *Mayaguez,* an American merchant ship
seized by Cambodia. If this defining Vietnam background is extended to
include Cheney's prominent involvement in the 1991 Gulf War, it becomes
clear that few regimes have chosen top defense strategy teams whose thinking has been so shaped by the experience of old wars and by an anxiousness
to wipe away their lingering embarrassments.

Indeed, so many senior appointees in the second Bush administration
had done service under Gerald Ford that David Hume Kennerly, the official White House photographer during that administration, told the *New
York Times* in 2002, "I feel like Rip Van Winkle. It's like I woke up twenty-
five years later, and not only are my friends still in power, they're more
powerful than ever."[40]

Still another set of old faces—from Elliott Abrams, in the mid-1980s an assistant secretary of state, to Cheney himself, back then a helpful member of a congressional investigating panel—reflected the family's loyalty to the *alte Kameraden* of the mid-1980s Iran-Contra scandal. George H. W. Bush had pardoned Abrams and several other participants as one of his last acts as president. Several others may have earned their recommissioning under the second Bush by earlier service in having kept the Iran-Contra stain from seeping under his father's vice presidential door in 1988. Calvin Trillin, writing in *The Nation*, captured the liberal critique in verse:

> So Elliott Abrams (the felon) is back,
> And Poindexter's now a big cheese
> High level appointments now favor the guys
> With rap sheets instead of CVs.[41]

In addition to rewarding old loyalists, dynasties are known—the Stuarts and their retainers somewhat, the Bourbons and their retainers more stereotypically—for forgetting no slight and savoring revenge. One sidebar to the rise of George W. Bush has been the steady elimination of old political foes—Jim Hightower and Ann Richards in Texas; Texas Republican state chairman Tom Pauken; House Speaker Newt Gingrich (George W. Bush helped to force him out in 1998, in part as payment for Gingrich's 1990 embarrassment of Bush senior over taxes); Albert Gore, one of the two 1992 regicides; and Senate Republican leader Trent Lott, a Reagan rather than Bush factionalist. Lott's throat was quickly cut in 2002 when his foolish remark about Strom Thurmond and segregation handed the White House a sharp knife.

Indeed, the Machiavellian Bush role in the eliminations of Speaker Gingrich and Senate leader Lott—both replaced with easygoing, collaborative successors—underscored yet another frequent restoration policy: to rebuild executive (royal) prerogative and influence at the expense of the legislative branch. Well indexed in both Stuart and Bourbon histories, prerogative expresses itself less as a definable program than as a presumption of entitlement, a hallmark of successful reassertion. New assumptions of authority in war making and secrecy and a bent for unilateralism have been to the George W. Bush dynastic presidency what executive privilege and impoundment were to the imperial presidency portrayed by Arthur Schlesinger in 1974.

"Secrecy," argued *Newsweek*, "is another old family trait (both [Bush presidents] were Skull and Bones at Yale) in vogue again in Washington. Recall Cheney's secret energy task force, the secret detentions of suspected terrorists and a decision by Bush—terribly harmful to professional historians—to keep the documents of his father and other presidents secret."[42]

As they have moved toward success, restorations have also usually drawn their forces from particular geographic areas, regions where conservatism and traditional religion were most intense. In the British Isles, the dethroned Stuarts found their strongest support in Ireland, Scotland, parts of Wales, and the north and west of England, where rural populations overlapped with High Church Anglicans and Catholics. In France, staunch backing for the Bourbons could be found in the poor and rural arch-Catholic west of France—Vendée, Poitou, Anjou, Maine, and Brittany. For George W. Bush, the analogous locus of his restoration was the South, the part of the United States most given to tradition, family, military service, religion (especially fundamentalist or evangelical Protestantism), a rural gentry, and a lingering regional taste for social events featuring kings, queens, and courts.

The southern colonies of the mid-seventeenth century, appropriately, took the royalist side in the English civil war and cheered the Stuart Restoration in 1660. When another attempt at a Stuart restoration failed in the Britain of 1745, thousands of defeated Scottish Highlanders set sail for the American South, settling in the Cape Fear Valley of North Carolina. In 1861, Confederate secretary of state Judah P. Benjamin, himself British-born, had to deny a report that he had approached British authorities about the South returning to the old flag and monarch. It would have been inappropriate, really, had the first American restoration been centered anywhere else.

Restoration and Presidential Legitimacy

In any theory of democratic belief, "restoration" and "presidential legitimacy" are not terms that go well together. If anything, restoration, with its dependence on family and inheritance, necessarily promotes attitudes that, in a political system like that of the United States, undercut popular sovereignty. Democratic legitimacy is necessarily drawn into question when succession via dynasty is accepted. So it was in 2000—and the convoluted legal and judicial processes by which George W. Bush satisfied the electoral mandates of the U.S. Constitution in 2000 added to the strain. It took the events of September 11 to mute what could have been a drawn-out legitimacy debate.

If elements of "de-democratization" were inherent in plans to put a former president's eldest son in the same White House chair just eight years after the father's departure, a further blow to popular governance came through what pundits wound up calling 1999's "money primary." This was the unprecedented attempt, especially on the Republican side, to bank a decisive disproportion of available party contribution dollars on behalf of an anointed nomination favorite. Other contenders, it was assumed, would either withdraw or wind up lacking sufficient funds to last through more than a few primaries. Even for the GOP, the substitution of checkbook balloting by party contributors for a decisive primary-day pulling of vote levers by rank-and-file party registrants represented a major break with tradition.

Prior practice, quite simply, had been to accept the vox populi. In the nine open GOP presidential nomination races between 1936 and 1996—"open" in the sense that no Republican sat in the White House to run again, or to try to select the nominee (Reagan did not try)—big donors had never managed that kind of overwhelming financial control. Some degree of competition always extended through the spring of the election year, giving party rank-and-filers a prolonged opportunity to stir excitement through the primary season. Of the four out of nine such Republican nominees who went on to win in November, all of them—Eisenhower in 1952, Nixon in 1968, Reagan in 1980, and Bush in 1988—had won the first-in-the-nation Republican primary in New Hampshire, the state whose town meetings, church halls, and cracker barrels made participatory democracy into a Norman Rockwell *Saturday Evening Post* cover.[43]

That pattern was broken by George W. Bush in February 2000. On primary day, he was crushed in New Hampshire by John McCain, whose thin bankroll required him to visit every mountain hamlet and weekly newspaper, speaking of the peril in American politics' putting out a For Sale sign. But powerful message notwithstanding, the Arizona senator's prospects subsequently withered, for he had too little money to meet too many organizational and advertising demands as the hurtling campaign calendar brought four primaries and caucuses in the week beginning on February 28, twenty-five in the week beginning on March 6, and six in the week beginning on March 13. The overthrow of the New Hampshire barometer—that no New Hampshire GOP primary loser could go on to win both the nomination and then the presidency—powerfully expressed the shifting balance between grassroots democracy and the combined forces of dynasty and money.

One key moment in the race had been Bush's decision to reject federal matching funds for his qualifying private campaign contributions. This decision put him outside the federal legal constraints on campaign spending up through the summer nominating conventions, allowing him to overwhelm the Democrats in organization building and image making from January to August. True, cascading dollars could not preempt a serious general election in the same way. Even so, the prospective omnipotence of the money factor in politics, innately favorable to the Republicans, further encouraged Bush-era Republicans to try to turn the dance of the dollars into a constitutionally protected exercise. Giving money to office seekers and even spending it on elections, they contended, was a form of political speech protected by the First Amendment. Opponents replied that the exaltation of donors would undercut the role of voters.

The dilution of participatory democracy arising out of the 2000 election would worsen as the Florida recount unfolded, and the result fed the ideological cocksureness that would become so visible in the early months of the Bush administration. If the lack of a popular mandate from the election seemed unimportant to the Bush team, that view may have been encouraged by the most surprising language in the Supreme Court's 5–4 decision upholding Bush's election, indicating that, in the American democracy, the public had no constitutional right to participate in electing a president.

Florida: A Failure of Democracy?

Let us stipulate: Rarely have the forces of restoration been overly preoccupied with voter participation or other such democratic niceties. In the United States of 2000, the dynastic element of this distemper affected both parties. Gore's own rise to the Democratic presidential nomination was much like Bush's: a career owed to parentage, as well as to the support of major institutionalized fund-raising capacities (his own and Clinton's). If Gore's periodic populist rhetoric during the campaign had a staged, opportunistic quality, so did his response to the Florida electoral developments. Trite recitations of civic concern found more voice than democratic outrage.

If support for a dynastic restoration requires an element of fervor, so does upholding the thwarted will of the people. Anger is a prerequisite, as Andrew Jackson, the first Tennesseean to run for president, demonstrated when he took up the political equivalent of his dueling pistols after the election of 1824. His fury came from having been counted out of the presidency, despite a large edge in the popular vote, when a hung electoral college forwarded the final decision to an anti-Jackson U.S. House of Representatives. Gore, the first Tennessee presidential candidate ever to have been a member of the Harvard Board of Overseers, declined to fight in the Jackson tradition.

The irony was that by November 9, just two days after the 2000 balloting, multiple circumstances had demanded a call for boldness. First, the election arena had narrowed to Florida alone, a state governed by a second Bush dynast, the nominee's younger brother, whose allies and appointees administered the state election laws and certified election outcomes. Second, Florida also happened to be one of three states that the Republicans had arguably stolen in the recount of 1876, the last previous instance of a hung presidential election. Democrats could reasonably have used that precedent to talk about Florida's Jeb Bush administration and its return to a Grand Old Electoral Crime Scene. Third, Republican nominee Bush had fallen several hundred thousand votes behind in the national popular vote. Were he to be chosen president, he would be the first chief executive not to have won a mandate through the popular vote since Benjamin Harrison in 1888. Each was an argument with which Democrats could have challenged Bush's democratic illegitimacy.

One contextual argument never raised during the Florida recount—a further symptom of national inattention to the dynastic backdrop—was the so-called October Surprise of 1980. This was the episode leading to accusations in 1991–92 that vice presidential nominee George H. W. Bush, twelve years earlier, had participated in the Reagan-Bush campaign's arrangements to have anti-American Iran hold its U.S. hostages, seized in 1979, until January 1981, instead of releasing them by November 1980 in a deal that could have reelected Democrat Jimmy Carter. The elder Bush and the 1980 campaign manager, Bill Casey, were alleged to have worked with an anti-Carter faction of present and former CIA operatives, some of whom had broad international experience in election tampering. The considerable evidence for these charges is weighed in chapter 9, but they are also relevant in this discussion of the Bush family's commitment to the democratic election process.

From an immediate legal and procedural standpoint, however, the 2000 recount confronted Democratic strategists with a can of worms. A Gore victory in Florida, where Bush's statewide lead appeared to be between 600 and 1,800 votes, was not to be expected from any routine recount of machine-accepted ballots. Localized potential for tipping the scale was thought to exist in four counties (Miami-Dade, Palm Beach, Broward, and Volusia) where apparent inaccuracies or mishandled ballots justified a hand count. Cautious advisers favored the limited, four-county remedy expected to involve only a short delay. A few bolder souls—at a November 11 meeting, for a fleeting historical moment, Gore himself was one—briefly favored demanding a full statewide recount but then backed away. This would have included a hand count and individual review of the 175,000 ballots not accepted or tabulated by the machines.

Such was the scope of serious battle. Of these rejected presidential ballots, most fell into two categories: *undervotes* (some 60,500, where the choice for president was left blank or marked inconclusively) and *overvotes* (roughly 105,000, with more than one choice for president written or punched). Both offered opportunities to qualify ballots because both kinds of spoilage were capable of being exaggerated or misread by computers. A mere undervote, dismissed by pin-striped consiglieri, might not be deficient after all, but could be a legitimate, red-blooded American ballot marking, countable and entitled to full constitutional protection. So might a humble overvote. Two or three thousand of these worthies, resurrected from the wastebasket, might change the name and party of the president-elect.

Achieving this magnitude of recount required a Jacksonian level of indignation. The Republicans, too, were racing to court, and the uncertain public was still open to suasion. The critical rejections by voting machines were centered in counties and precincts sharing at least one of three characteristics: a ballot design that misled (especially Palm Beach County's so-called butterfly ballot), the use of outdated punch-card voting systems, or a high ratio of befuddled voters (largely minority groups and the elderly) who were unable to understand the ballot. Some of these voters had also been unable to get explanatory assistance or make officials comprehend that they had spoiled or double-punched a ballot and needed the substitute allowed in most jurisdictions.

Such precincts tended to be heavily Democratic. As early as 1988, the National Bureau of Standards had recommended that punch-card ballots be done away with because of "inaccuracy or fraud in computerized vote-tallying."[44] Their particular effects on minority voters might even amount to a violation of constitutional rights. In any event, where they remained in use, hand counting was sometimes necessary.

Texas, in a 1997 election law reform Governor George Bush himself had signed, stipulated not only that hand counting was in order when questions arose but that it should be carried out generously. That required accepting various degrees of punching or indentation that "show a clearly ascertainable intent of the voter to vote."[45]

A week after the election, the Florida Supreme Court, which claimed the ultimate jurisdiction over interpreting the state's own election laws, could plausibly have been asked by the Democrats to consolidate the several cases brought. For example, it could have then ordered (1) a limited four-county hand recount of the undervotes alone; (2) a full statewide hand recount of all 175,000 machine discards; (3) a hand recount of all machine rejects confined to the twenty-five counties using punch-card voting rather than more sophisticated systems; or (4) a recount in all counties where at least 3 percent of the ballots were machine rejected (the state average was 2.85 percent, with the highest percentage, 12.3 percent, occurring in black-majority Gadsden County). Practically speaking, the full statewide recount, not much more trouble to local election boards than any other alternative, was by far the most plausible and least discriminatory remedy.

In retrospect, in a full statewide recount some 20,000–30,000 of the machine-rejected overvotes and undervotes might well have qualified under the Texas-type criteria. If so, judging from newspaper samplings made then and later, Gore should have won about two-thirds, enough for a statewide victory by somewhere between 5,000 and 8,000 votes. There were good reasons for the GOP's Florida recount team, led by ex–secretary of state James A. Baker III, to fight hand recounts tooth and nail, which is exactly what they did.

Let me step back a moment. The question of voter intention, while a chimera, also merits some consideration. Of the 175,000 supposedly spoiled ballots, 6,000 were cast by (mostly elderly Jewish) voters in Palm Beach County who, confused by the local butterfly ballot, overvoted by punching slots for both Gore and third-party nominee Patrick Buchanan; another 3,000 were cast by Palm Beach County residents who overvoted for both Gore and Socialist David McReynolds. Obviously, they were almost all Gore voters, but such ballots were decisively spoiled. In Miami-Dade, some 1,700 ballots were punched out of kilter and not counted, but a study months later identified a 316-vote edge for Gore.[46]

Then there were the substantially mistaken "scrub lists" put out by a GOP company hired by the Florida Elections Board to purge voter rolls of deceased persons, ex-felons, and the like, which wound up costing thousands of qualified voters, mostly blacks, their registration and their chance to cast a ballot. This was most evident in black sections of Duval County (Jacksonville). By comparison with the number of possibly thwarted Bush backers, tens of thousands more citizens trying to vote for Gore seem to have been confused, turned away from the polls, or told that they had been delisted. If eligible Florida voters trying to vote for Albert Gore rather than George W. Bush had constituted a definable and legally recognizable yardstick, the vice president would have won.

Legally, however, there is no such yardstick. Frustrated Democratic dalliance with civil rights lawsuits and demands for a partial revote in Palm Beach County were unrealistic. All of these proposals won substantial television attention and had an element of moral triumph. But in terms of overturning Bush's hairbreadth victory, preoccupation with chimeras and piecemeal remedies in South Florida was fatal.

At this point, given the large stakes of the 2000 election, a harsh retrospect is in order: How much did the leading Democrats not know or not understand (and for how long) about a group of factors critical in Florida? Were they familiar with the Bush-signed Texas hand recount law, the pivotal nature of the 175,000 undervote and overvote universe, and the plausibly disqualifying connections between the 2000 Florida state elections board and the Bush campaign? It is hard to avoid concluding that top Democrats were outsmarted by the much larger, better financed, and shrewder Bush Florida recount team.

To head his Florida effort, Gore picked former secretary of state Warren Christopher, a pin-striped international lawyer from San Francisco, along with the national Gore campaign chairman, former secretary of commerce Bill Daley, son of Chicago mayor Richard Daley, famously said to have stolen enough votes in 1960 to keep Richard Nixon from carrying Illinois. Fairly or not, Daley's Chicago connection made him a historical punching bag for Republican recount spinners. Perhaps worse, neither Christopher nor Daley knew Opa-locka from Okeechobee. The cracker courthouse cliques and Everglades swamp foxes lined up with the Republicans most assuredly did.

During the initial week of postelection jockeying, the Republicans shrewdly worked to imprint their own Florida edge on the public's mind, insisting, in essence, "We have already won both the election and the recount." The Democrats, timid about seeming obstructionist and barred by Gore's own antecedents from sassing dynastic entitlement, paid little attention to the GOP's double-barreled Florida vulnerability. This encompassed the Republican voting rights abridgements and, most of all, the banana republic ethics of letting the presidential vote totals be pawed, sorted, and manipulated by election officials reporting to (a) the cochair of the state Bush campaign (Secretary of State Katherine Harris) and (b) the Republican presidential nominee's younger brother (Florida governor Jeb Bush).

The collusion of Harris, Jeb Bush, and the Bush presidential campaign has since been loosely documented by computer evidence of e-mails and the existence of a war room staffed by GOP operatives within the Florida secretary of state's office. Trials and investigations later established Harris's complicity in a systemic purge of voter rolls tantamount to civil rights violations.[47] But Gore's Florida recount team seems not to have understood the imperative of quickly establishing the election-tampering culpability of state officials.

Last but not least, the Gore forces became trapped in legal sideshows (Palm Beach butterfly discussions) and niggling tactics. On November 17, the Florida Supreme Court staged a brief rescue by rejecting Republican attempts to stop the embattled ballot reviews in Broward, Miami-Dade, Palm Beach, and Volusia Counties and enjoining Katherine Harris from certifying her unofficial Bush margin. On November 21, the court's fuller decision lengthened the recount deadline to November 26 and encouraged county officials to take a broad-minded view of qualifying ballots. It was a fleeting victory, though, because no statewide recount was ordered (Gore had not asked), undervotes alone were mentioned (not overvotes), and no clear standard for recounting was stipulated. The petard of their own making on which the Democrats would shortly be hoist was already in place.

The Gore camp's neglect of the overvotes was particularly blameworthy, for they were almost certainly the ball game. In Volusia and Gadsden Counties, recounts found major gains for Gore in the supposed overvotes.

In Jackson County, on the Georgia line, it turned out that election authorities had fixed 300 overvotes, most for Bush, by affixing blank labels to cover the extra markings.[48] A survey by the *Orlando Star-Sentinel* found that in Lake County, another Republican stronghold, the machine-rejected overvotes yielded a pickup of 131 net countable votes for Gore.[49] A *Washington Post* survey found that in Florida's eight largest counties, Gore "was by far most likely to be selected on invalid overvoted ballots, with his name punched as one of the choices on 46,000 of them. Bush, by comparison, was punched on 17,000."[50] The ballots rejected by the machine but easily ascertainable by visual examination would have given Gore the election.

Wily Republicans, for their part, had filed suit in federal district court on November 11, with an eye toward getting the controversy up to the U.S. Supreme Court. This partly repeated what the GOP had done in 1876 to resolve the tight Hayes-Tilden presidential race. Florida, South Carolina, and Louisiana, the last three states still occupied by federal troops following the Civil War, each certified rival Democratic and Republican slates of electors. The meeting of the U.S. Senate to count electoral votes, scheduled for December, was postponed to await resolution by a special fifteen-member electoral commission in early February 1877.

The commission had seven Democrats and seven Republicans from Congress, with a somewhat independent Republican Supreme Court justice, Joseph P. Bradley, as the fifteenth and swing member. When voting time came, he sided with the GOP, giving Republican Hayes a razor-thin 185–184 margin in the electoral college.[51]

Something similar would happen again in 2000, when the Republican U.S. Supreme Court, by a vote of 5–4, awarded Florida to Bush, giving him a 271–267 margin in the electoral college. A single Republican Supreme Court justice provided the one-vote margin upholding the actions of the Republican state authorities in Florida. The Florida Supreme Court, their federal superiors ruled, had gone too far in making its own law. On top of which, it had accepted recount procedures that violated the equal protection clause of the Fourteenth Amendment to the U.S. Constitution, and it had failed to provide a workable standard.

The U.S. Supreme Court, alas, is a political body insistent on pretending otherwise. As one chronicler noted, "Speculation about political biases fills the air. Does it matter that Scalia's son works for [Bush counsel] Olson's law firm? Or that Thomas's wife is collecting resumes for the new

Bush administration? Or that Thomas himself owes his job to Bush's pop? Or that O'Connor and Rehnquist clearly want to retire, and clearly want to do so when a Republican is in the White House?"[52]

Gore's lawyers seethed because they had been paying little attention to the Fourteenth Amendment, believing—as some dissenting Supreme Court justices would themselves soon argue—that the possible federal equal protection issue was too ephemeral to justify overturning a state supreme court's interpretation of its own state laws. It was too much of a reach. One dissenter, Justice Ruth Bader Ginsburg, protested that the high court had overturned such interpretations only three times before—in 1813, 1958, and 1964. Moreover, she added, the majority's embrace of a supposed December 12 deadline for finalizing the recounts was also gratuitous. Congress could wait until December 27, when it was to request certified returns from states where there still weren't any electors, or January 6, when it was scheduled to confirm the validity of the electoral vote.[53] In 1877, as we have seen, Congress waited until February.

Even Republican-appointed justices David Souter and John Paul Stevens came down against the position taken by the Bush recount team, rejecting the equal protection basis for federal jurisdiction as "not substantial." Stevens delivered his much quoted, stinging indictment: "Although we may never know with complete certainty the identity of the winner of this year's presidential elections, the identity of the loser is perfectly clear. It is the Nation's confidence in the judge as an impartial guardian of the rule of law."[54]

The crazy quilt of local recounts pursued and limited remedies sought in Florida ultimately gave the Court's pro-Bush majority a plausible, if wobbly, peg on which to hang a ruling it was probably determined to reach. The irony, as Republican lawyers privately admitted, was that the equal protection argument would not have worked against a full statewide recount, the demand Gore briefly considered on November 11 partly because of its bold clarity.

Enough of technicalities; they have been necessary to tell a story that also matters on a much larger political and philosophical scale. American electoral crises of this magnitude, invariably high-powered moments in history, tend to define their major participants. Jackson made his mark in 1824, staked out his claim, and swept into the White House in 1828. The 1876 election left Republican winner Rutherford Hayes mocked as Old Eight to Seven and His Fraudulency. Samuel Tilden, the Democrat counted out, was no duelist like Jackson, but Democrats made so strong a case for Republican misbehavior that people assumed that the wronged Tilden would run again in 1880 and win. He didn't run, but largely because of age.

The 2000 outcome, by contrast, made the Republicans look strong and decisive while putting Gore and the Democrats in a negative spotlight. By temporizing and dragging things out, yet never sounding any persuasive clarion, they lost public opinion. Jake Tapper of Salon.com, who wrote an exhaustive five-hundred-page book, *Down and Dirty,* about those five crucial weeks, began his preface with a harsh assessment all too well supported by the unfolding events: "Democrats were capricious, whiny, wimpy, and astoundingly incompetent. Republicans were cruel, presumptuous, indifferent and disingenuous."[55] The Bush lawyers knew they had to win, and their ability to do so must have produced considerable hubris.

The Bush high command certainly had a better sense from the start of the Florida recount's importance and the need to pour in huge resources and work in tandem with state officials. When recount expense papers were finally filed in 2002, just days before fines could have been levied, it turned out that the GOP had spent $13.8 million on lawyers, salaries, travel, and hotels, compared with $3.2 million spent by the Gore organization.[56] Roughly one hundred lawyers were sent to Florida and Texas, and frequent use was made (with recompense) of Enron and Halliburton corporate aircraft.

By the summer of 2001, it was clear that, on top of their recount skills, the Republicans had indulged in some vote tampering. The *New York Times* reported in July that just after the November election, as Florida teetered in the balance, GOP operatives worked to get a large number of overseas absentee ballots, many of them military, some apparently procured after election day, accepted by collaborative local election boards in Republican counties despite failure to comply with local election laws, in many cases because of late postmarking. Of 2,490 overseas ballots, the *Times* found 680 not in compliance, 80 percent of them in counties Bush carried. Yet all were counted in reaching Bush's final margin of 537 votes.[57]

The effort to purge the voter rolls, in turn, involved a program authorized by state authorities up to and including Secretary of State Katherine Harris. Over the years, some 17 percent of Florida's voting-age black males have been disenfranchised as ex-felons—Florida and Texas are the two harshest states in this respect—but many of the names provided in the 2000 purge were inaccurate, so many delistings made were improper. After

U.S. Civil Rights Commission hearings, ChoicePoint, the company providing the faulty lists, agreed to give the NAACP $75,000 for "past and future efforts to further the electoral opportunity of Florida's minority voters."[58] The NAACP, in turn, noting that eighteen of the nineteen precincts in the state with the highest rates of rejected ballots in 2000 were black-majority precincts using punch-card systems, sued the state of Florida to end their use.

Enlarging the probability that George W. Bush really didn't carry the Florida popular vote was the expanding margin by which he had fallen short nationally. By New Year's, the deficit had risen to 530,000 votes, up from 200,000 on the morning after election day. Here, too, the Democrats let a major talking point slip away. Eventually, after September 11, the national news media consortium handling the unofficial reexamination of undervotes and overvotes abandoned any further efforts to detail what had really happened in the Sunshine State. Bush's ratings soared in the public mood of rally-round, and the major legitimacy debate that had begun during the winter of 2000–2001 was suspended.

The consortium's autumn actions came in for much more cynical scrutiny overseas than at home. Leading U.S. newspapers generally commented that (1) the public had lost interest in the Florida recount even before 9/11, and (2) more yardsticks of consortium vote counting put Bush ahead than put Gore ahead; but in any event, the tabulation of overvotes was being suspended. Outside the United States, reports generally expressed the view that the overvote count showed a large Gore lead, but that to publish this and destroy the legitimacy of Bush's presidency was impossible after 9/11. The staunchly conservative *Daily Telegraph* of London noted that although the tabulation was ready in late August, it "appears to have been sacrificed on the altar of patriotism and a perception that America needs to be led into war by a strong president. . . . French and Canadian newspapers suggest that the black-out can only raise suspicions, and the issue is being increasingly aired on the Internet."[59] The correctness of this surmise was apparent by mid-2003, as war-related doubts about George W. Bush grew. Some 38 percent of nationwide respondents in a *New York Times/ CBS News* poll said that he was not "a legitimately elected president."[60]

While proper in that strained postattack period, or at least inevitable, the suspension of the consortium's examination also squelched press discussion of the administration's legitimacy. Nor did commentators dwell on the extent to which the glaring weakness of the Democrats during the five-week political and constitutional crisis must have encouraged an already cocky incoming Bush administration. What could have been a debacle of Bush legitimacy turned out to be a celebration of ideological and tactical triumph. Many of the GOP lawyers and spokespersons involved were rewarded when high administration posts were handed out, as well they should have been. In addition to securing the presidency, they kept any debate from focusing on issues of restoration, legitimacy, and a thwarted popular plurality in a context tailor-made for raising such themes.

Such success could only have encouraged a Bush administration already half convinced of an entitlement dating back to the maelstrom of the nineties—a legitimacy interrupted by Clinton's 1992 false pretenses and usurpation, and requiring no validation by the electorate or by any election-day popular-vote margin. Obviously, this was not a view that could be voiced, but Antonin Scalia, the ultraconservative justice whom George W. Bush especially admired, had hinted at related beliefs during two separate stages of the U.S. Supreme Court's December deliberations. On December 8, in language better suited to a seventeenth-century royal prerogative court, he wrote the opinion granting a stay of the Florida recount because counting votes "of questionable legality does in my view threaten irreparable harm to petitioner [Bush], and to the country, by casting a cloud upon what he claims to be the legitimacy of his election."[61]

Then on December 11, the five-justice majority holding for Bush declared that "the individual citizen has no federal constitutional right to vote for electors for President of the United States unless and until the state legislature chooses a statewide election as the means to implement its power to appoint members of the Electoral College."[62] The Court then added that even after giving the choice of electors to the public, a state legislature could take the selection into its own hands. Harvard historian Alexander Keyssar, author of *The Right to Vote: The Contested History of Democracy in the United States,* called this "one of the stranger developments of the post-election conflict: the blunt expression of a legal argument denying that Americans actually possess a right to vote in presidential elections."[63]

Part of Scalia's objection to democracy, amplified a year later, was that it got in the way of a return to an eighteenth-century interpretation of the U.S. Constitution. Speaking at the January 2002 Pew Forum on Religion and Public Life, he opined that as written in 1787 the Constitution reflected natural or divinely inspired law that the state was an instrument of

God. "That consensus has been upset," he said, "by the emergence of democracy." He added that "the reactions of people of faith to this tendency of democracy to obscure the divine authority behind government should not be resignation to it but resolution to combat it as effectively as possible."[64] Stuart and Bourbon ultraists pronouncedd kindred thoughts after those restorations.

The reluctance of American politicians to put a historical framework around the events described in this chapter is understandable enough. Restorations have been volatile periods, and as we will see, the dynasties returned to power have carried too much baggage from the past—political, economic, and diplomatic—to survive for very long.

PART II

Crony Capitalism, Covert Operations, and Compassionate Conservatism

CHAPTER 4

Texanomics and Compassionate Conservatism

Between 1964 and 2000, the state of Texas was home to three elected presidents (Lyndon Johnson, George H. W. Bush and George W. Bush), two vice presidential candidates (George H. W. Bush and Lloyd Bentsen), and one independent presidential candidate (H. Ross Perot), who in 1992 received 19 percent of the vote—more than any third-party candidate since Theodore Roosevelt in 1912. The Lone Star State, having long been known for its exports of cotton, oil and cattle, was now exporting presidents and would-be presidents.

Michael Lind, *Made in Texas,* 2003

The Bushes are political migrants. . . . They maintained their political hegemony by moving west. The Rockefellers did the same thing, but they picked the wrong states.

New York University professor Mitchell Moss, 2001

L ittle about Texas has recommended it as a state from which to recruit the nation's cultural, economic, or governmental leadership. Stalled for a generation by the legacy of the Civil War, Texas began the twentieth century as a relative backwater, counting a population of 3 million and a combined agricultural, mineral, and industrial output roughly on a par with that of Indiana. But after four generations of rapid, helter-skelter growth, it entered the twenty-first century as the second-most-populous state in the Union, home to 21 million people. Epicenter of the nation's oil and energy industries, Texas is also the Southern Baptist buckle on the U.S. Bible Belt. Arguably most significant of all, the onetime nineteenth-century republic of Stephen Austin, William Travis, and Sam Houston seems to have become the emerging incubator of American presidents.

With only half as many residents per square mile as California, the Lone Star State is still filling in its sprawling landmass, equal to the combined size of New England, New York, New Jersey, Pennsylvania, Ohio, and Illinois. The watershed of the state's rivers is even bigger, an outreach of siphons. The Rio Grande, constituting Texas's southwestern border, gathers in the Rocky Mountains of Colorado. The Red River, rising near the New Mexico–Texas border, crosses the Panhandle plains, spends five hundred miles as Texas's northern border with Oklahoma, and thereafter flows through Louisiana into the Mississippi River. The state has an ego to match its acreage. Having wrested its freedom from Mexico at gunpoint in 1836, Texas is also unique in having been a separate country before settling for statehood in 1845, which may help to account for part of its overscale self-esteem.

By the early 2000s, the state's distinctiveness—which was less the mystique of cattle, land, and oil described by Edna Ferber in *Giant* than a pervasive "don't-fence-me-in" culture and economics—had begun to exert a national influence that Americans, whether in New Jersey, Minnesota, or Oregon, could no longer dismiss. When the term "Sun Belt" crept into national parlance in the late 1960s to describe the new conservative power axis stretching from Florida through Texas to California, it was the Pacific colossus that first took front rank. Between 1952 and 1988, whenever the Republicans occupied the White House, either the vice president (Nixon from 1952 to 1960) or the president (Nixon, 1968–74; Reagan, 1980–88) was a Californian, except during the short Ford interregnum after Watergate. Since 1988, though, the GOP has not nominated a Californian for either office. Texans have taken the party and national helm.

The transfer involved much more than a mere migration of power within Sun Belt conservatism. The dynastization of Republican politics under the Bushes has, rather, truncated the latter-day Sun Belt, creating a more chicken-fried and fundamentalist-flavored axis extending from Texas to Florida and dominated by those two states, which have risen to number two and number four in the nation's population. Both California and the Arizona of Bush's archrival, John McCain, have edged away from the Austin-Tallahassee mind-set, as befits states with more northern cultures and less influential fundamentalist or evangelical populations.

New preoccupations have accompanied the redrawn geography. Race, while remaining a powerful underlying factor in voting divisiveness, is no longer a determining issue. Those battles have already been fought and have redrawn southern loyalties over some three decades. Beyond a few flare-ups over keeping the old Confederate Stars and Bars in several southern state flags, the old debate has slackened.

To cite the themes that have particularly roiled Congress under Clinton and Bush—taxes, the federal budget, the environment, gun control, campaign finance, government support of religion, military readiness and preemptive attacks, homeland security, and unilateralist foreign policy—is to illustrate that extreme thinking was no longer routinely the province of the old Dixiecrat states from South Carolina to Louisiana. On two-thirds of these subjects, the "ultra" views now came from Texas think tanks, congressional delegations, and political rhetoric, including that of the Bush White House. The Texas origins of America's first serious presidential dynasty only underscored the salience of three of its distinguishing mindsets: Texanomics, crony capitalism, and the need of both Bush presidents to dress their Texas-rooted agendas in "kinder, gentler" imagery and supposed "compassionate conservatism."

Texanomics: Economics, Culture, and Morality

According to turn-of-the-century data, metropolitan New York City, greater Los Angeles, and the San Francisco Bay area were more economically stratified than Texas, because of the extremes of wealth and income that were a product of their finance, communications, and high-technology industries. But on a statewide basis, most years saw Texas join Louisiana and New York as the three states with the greatest polarization—the widest gaps between the average family incomes of the top fifth and bottom fifth of the population. Between the late 1970s and the late 1990s, inequality increased in the Lone Star State, as in most sections of the country, because incomes at the top soared while those in the middle and at the bottom stagnated or slid.

However, stratification in Texas had some distinctive nuances. According to the Washington-based Urban Institute, Texas ranked worst among the fifty states in inequality among children.[1] Some 3.1 million Texans—a high 15 percent of the state's population—were officially classified by the federal government as poor because they earned less than $15,260 a year for a family of three.[2]

In part, this pervasive poverty was a result of Texan unwillingness to spend money to ameliorate the state's rich-poor gap. Data for 2000 compiled by the U.S. Census Bureau ranked Texas forty-ninth in state taxes and fiftieth, dead last, in per capita state spending. Yet as the economy weakened in 2001 and 2002, choruses of state officials called for even further budget cuts and reductions in state services. Richard Vedder, an economist at the business-financed Texas Public Policy Foundation, told a conference of state legislators that "Texas should be proud of being last in government spending per capita. It means you're delivering state services most efficiently."[3]

In contrast to Californians or New Yorkers, upper-bracket Texans, especially oilmen and latter-day *hacendados* in land or cattle, have worried less about these socioeconomic divisions and been less embarrassed by them. Texan civic culture, more akin to that of Mexico, Venezuela, or Brazil, has accepted wealth and its benefits with minimal distraction by either guilt or noblesse oblige.

Here it is important to note that George W. Bush is the first president to clearly represent this kind of low-tax, low-service, high-economic-stratification brand of southern economic conservatism since the little-remembered Zachary Taylor of Louisiana won the election of 1848. Part of George H. W. Bush's politics was still influenced by northeastern Ivy League conservatism, and the other three southerners elected to the White House since Taylor—Lyndon Johnson, Jimmy Carter, and Bill Clinton— were moderate Democrats with partial populist streaks that put them at odds with George W. Bush's Texas elite conservatism. But in 2000, this revolution was not as obvious as it should have been.

During the boom years of the 1990s, as many Americans participated in a nationwide worship of market forces and embraced theologies of social Darwinism, traditional Texas practices and viewpoints began to be viewed as more mainstream. Gone was the 1980s image of the state shaped by the two most visited tourist attractions in East Texas: the Kennedy assassination site and the robber-baron lair at Southfork, where the hit television drama *Dallas* had been filmed. By 2000, opinions popular in Waco, Lubbock, or McAllen had become less likely to arouse suburban New Jersey, less likely to appall Cupertino, California. White House aspirants from Texas profited from a reduced risk of having home-state attitudes, remarks, or old speeches thrown in their faces.

By broad criteria of taxation, social welfare, and spending, though, Texas had become the national capital of a politics that edged toward survival of the fittest. The evolution of "Texanomics," a useful shorthand term for the state's fiscal practices, has drawn as much on culture as on economics. The two—and "culture" in this context encompasses conservative religion—interacted to help define what Texas's political and economic power structure wanted government to do or, more typically, wanted it not to bother with. During the 1990s, George W. Bush, as governor, struck a resonant chord by calling for "personal responsibility" to replace the guilt and government programs left over from the sixties, thereby reducing welfare to a level where charities and religious groups could take over. Save for the new phraseology, this was bringing philosophic coals to Newcastle.

Texas, as the twenty-first century opened, probably left more issues and circumstances unregulated—uncorrected, unameliorated, unassuaged—than any other state. One might figuratively blame something in the water; water itself, vital to parched areas like West Texas, symbolized the mindset. Texas is one of the few states that continue to acknowledge the right of capture; even groundwater is a private property right.

Or consider the state's biggest city, steeped in decade after decade of hostility to zoning. As summed up by Bush biographer Herbert Parmet, "The Houston of George Bush's political baptism was one of free-flowing, everything-goes, unrestricted pell-mell growth. Limits were practically 'subversive.' The city that had kept sprawling after the war could not be restrained or even rationalized by urban planning. Efforts at public modification opened its authors to charges of 'socialism' or even 'communism.' Money was king in the most uninhibited sense, and the accumulators [were] the new emperors in a modern frontier anarchy."[4]

Hand in glove with opposition to zoning has been a downplaying of environmental concerns. The eastern side of Harris County, which includes Houston, is home to nearly half the petrochemical capacity in the United States. In 2000, New York Times reporter Jim Yardley began a story this way: "Houston, Tex.—For decades, the stench of the nearby refineries never seemed to concern city leaders here. The hot summer breezes often carried a brown haze over the downtown skyline, and with it, an odor that the business elite regarded as the sweet smell of money. 'Smell that,' went a popular refrain during the 1960s. 'That's prosperity.'"[5] Change has been slow.

Money in politics, meanwhile, has been controlled about as well as guns, which is to say hardly at all. Texas has been the Wild West of campaign finance, a 268,581-square-mile Dodge City, wide open to donors giving any amount of money to any nonfederal candidate, so long as it was declared. The Texas legislature meets for only 140 days every two years, initiating a soapbox derby in which some fifteen hundred registered lobbyists

spend about $250 million—at least, $250 million was the sum reported—
to convince 181 legislators which bills should be sped to the finish line.[6]

The state's elected judiciary is scarcely less available to those whose
pockets jingle. According to poll takers, some 79 percent of Texas attorneys
said campaign contributions influenced judicial decisions, either fairly or
very significantly. Between 1994 and 1998, the ten state supreme court
judges facing election raised 52 percent of their campaign kitties from
lawyers, law firms, and litigants filing appeals with the high court during
that period.[7]

If conservatives in the Texas congressional delegation have tried to
bring the Texas attitude toward guns and political contributions to Washington, equal attention has been devoted to recasting the federal tax system
in the (regressive) Texas style. The latter has famously kept the income tax
wolf from the hacienda door by stinting government and raising revenues
through regressive options like the sales tax. Local progressives blame these
strictures for everything from the state's weak education system to unre-
lieved child poverty, although the message of minimal government also
pours out of other state institutions.

Through the 1980s and 1990s, powerful Texans in Washington openly
promoted a flat-rate income tax or some version of a national sales tax as a
federal-level substitute for taxing income. Their ranks included Senator
Phil Gramm, House Ways and Means Committee chairman Bill Archer,
House majority leader Dick Armey, and Deputy Treasury Secretary Charls
Walker. Governor George W. Bush, who backed Gramm's 1996 presidential
ambitions, had expressed his own vague interest in such tax schemes. By
the early 2000s, speculation was shifting toward a so-called federal consumed income levy. Taxing only outlays for consumption, while excusing
money saved or invested, would further grease the wheels of wealth accu-
mulation.

Over the years Texas multimillionaires and billionaires have become
notorious for making extreme proposals that sounded good over drinks at
the Petroleum Club but somehow miscarried in the popular press. In the
1950s, for example, oilman H. L. Hunt advocated that citizens' voting
power be proportionate to the taxes they paid. In recent years, some Texans
in Congress have not been far behind in their views. Armey, in his 1995
book *The Freedom Revolution,* compared Franklin D. Roosevelt to Stalin
and Mao.[8] In the early 2000s, the wide-open Houston suburbs sent to Con-

gress an extraordinary pair of representatives. One was Ron Paul, an ex–Libertarian presidential candidate who became known in the House as Dr. No. He described the United States as "a police state that is totally out of control." The second was Tom DeLay, who became House majority leader when Armey retired in 2002. Formerly the operator of a pest control company, DeLay called the federal Environmental Protection Agency a "Gestapo" and urged its abolition.

As the nation's leading energy producer, Texas has been responsible for some of the nation's worst environmental problems, notably air pollution— Houston overtook Los Angeles as the smoggiest U.S. city in 1999—and hazardous wastes in the chemical districts alongside the Houston Ship Channel. Dozens of books, reports, and special studies weighed the impact of George W. Bush's environmental policies as governor, but after forty or sixty pages, even the East Texas volume of spillage, emissions, particulates, and toxics lost its force through sheer banality. In any case, there was disagreement over whether Bush had bettered things (one ranking showed Texas's worst-in-the-nation toxic release rating for 1994–97 improving to fifth place in 1999) or simply perpetuated the odorous status quo. (The new ranking added more industries, whereas under the old calculus Texas would have remained number one.) *Time* magazine in 2000 caught the Texanomic essence: "Bush let industry write an anti-pollution measure, and believes voluntary plans, not regulation, can clean up air and water. No wonder Texas has a world-class pollution problem."[9]

The problem existed before Bush, to be sure, but his view of privatization as panacea was hard to overstate, as it was carried over into other areas of his government. One initial target was the giant, incurably liberal University of Texas in Austin; a second was the state's multibillion-dollar system of administering health care, housing, and other assistance to the poor and elderly. Ultimately the university was not seriously challenged, and the contracting out of social welfare administration was thwarted by the Clinton administration.[10] Managing to hand over state environmental regulation to the polluting industries was less of a milestone, but success in Texas did help shape a similar Bush commitment in Washington.

By the late twentieth century, Texas cultural and economic biases, advanced by presidents and members of Congress, had also impressed themselves on two other national policies: immigration control and trade law. Over the years, Texas business has always wanted low-cost labor—workers for the state's warehouses, sweatshops, crop fields, domestic service, and sales counters. Local industries, some of them refugees from northern taxes, regulation, and unions, thrived on both low wages and taxes kept down by minimal public services. In addition to laws inimical to unions, the proven solution for keeping costs down has been Mexican laborers—either illegal immigrants or temporary guest workers brought in under the pre-1964 bracero program. Their presence in the Texas labor market also applied downward pressure on other wages.

Many employers preferred the illegals, who were compliant as well as cheap. As governor, George W. Bush opposed efforts to deny undocumented aliens public education and health care, but compassion was hardly a paramount motive: Low-wage labor was simply too important to discourage. Arguably, taxpayer-provided services were a subsidy of sorts to the labor attitudes of the farmers, ranchers, and business owners who employed the illegals. It was no coincidence that within weeks of his 2001 inauguration, Bush as president endorsed a harsh labor agenda—less regulation of workplace safety, relaxation of rules against the federal government doing business with companies that violate labor laws, and permission for states to opt out of minimum-wage increases. The AFL-CIO's national political director was moved to quip that "George Bush makes Ronald Reagan look like Mother Jones."[11]

Late-twentieth-century Texans also revived the old southern preference for a U.S. free-trade regime beneficial to the region's commodity exports. However, the North American Free Trade Agreement of the 1990s had some important variations, preeminently access by U.S. corporations to low-cost labor *within* Mexico. That idea had nineteenth-century roots. In the fifteen years before the American Civil War, most Texans, who had become U.S. citizens after 1845, had joined with other southerners in favoring the annexation and U.S. statehood of nearby tropical lands—northern Mexican states like Sonora, Chihuahua, Coahuila, Tamaulipas, and even Yucatán, together with Cuba and possibly Nicaragua.

The goal was both political and economic. Once incorporated into the United States, these lands would become slave-owning societies—only Spanish Cuba still allowed slavery in 1860—managed by southerners. Besides the sugar, rice, tobacco, fruits, and coffee that could be grown there, southern investors also coveted the region's railroad routes and mines. Even more important, four to six new states would have sent enough new U.S. senators and congressmen to Washington to prevent the growing northern strength in Congress from crippling slavery and shifting national control to Yankee industry.

Even though they came to naught, these earlier efforts established a state agenda: Texas, from the first, has been impelled by economic geography to pursue some control over Mexico's resources and workforce. With George H. W. Bush as president, Texas and the South resumed this ambition through the North American Free Trade Agreement. Much as northern and labor critics predicted, the first decade of NAFTA produced a major realignment of U.S-Mexican industrial and trade relationships.

The old trade surplus in favor of the United States, based on American firms selling manufactured goods below the Rio Grande, vanished as U.S. companies set up low-cost subsidiaries in the northern Mexico *maquiladora* districts. Automobiles, machinery, electronics, apparel, and furniture, previously manufactured in the United States but now made in Mexico by U.S. companies employing $1.50-an-hour labor, began flowing back to U.S. consumers. From a trade deficit of $1.7 billion in 1993, Mexico rocketed to a trade surplus of $23 billion with the United States in 2001 and $31 billion in 2002. Save for the packaging materials sold to the Mexican plants to facilitate the return of finished goods, the only net U.S. export gains came in agribusiness and bulk commodities like cereals and organic chemicals.[12]

The job losses for U.S. industry centered in high-wage sectors, mostly in the North. The Texas economic elites, by contrast, collected pesos and dollars in two pockets: first, through the state's huge agricultural and chemical sectors, and second, through the further enrichment of Texas banks, law firms, accountants, transportation companies, investment bankers, and upper-bracket investors in Mexico and the U.S. *maquiladora* enterprises. Sam Houston, who had advocated a protectorate over Mexico on the floor of the U.S. Senate in 1858, never lived so see that, but NAFTA fulfilled some of the same Tejano ambitions.

Texas, in short, is an unusual American state, and many of its economic and cultural preferences are not those of the nation as a whole.

The Bush Family, the Finance Sector, and Low-Growth Economics

Both Bush chief executives, number forty-one and number forty-three, have been powerfully influenced and biased by their Texas milieu, especially in economic matters. One of George W.'s old friends told a Texas biographer that "Midland is probably where he first got the mistaken idea that doing well in business is the solution to America's problems, that is, what's good for business is good for America. 'Opportunity and business fortune for all' isn't really true for everyone. But it was for them [the Bushes]."[13]

Yet their family ideology and economic orientation have a much deeper taproot—the Bush-Walker bent for finance, specifically the securities business and its locus on Wall Street, in the Northeast, and in the traditions and sensibilities of old school and college classmates. If Oxford and Cambridge, Eton and Harrow typically sent their sons to Parliament, the Foreign Office, MI6, or the Indian civil service, the American institutions mentioned in chapter 1 sent theirs to J. P. Morgan, Brown Brothers Harriman, Kidder Peabody, the State Department, the Chase Bank, and Guaranty Trust. In the late 1940s, several platoons also diverted—one should not think they deserted—to Midland, the Ivy League beachhead in a boom-flushed state where the larger oil and oil service firms still had major ownership ties to Wall Street and the East.

Which brings us to the myth of George H. W. Bush forsaking the family's Wall Street roots for the tumbleweed and dust devils of the Permian Basin. The Texas relocation is fact; the forsaking of Wall Street connections is illusion. As noted earlier, *Initiative in Energy: The Story of Dresser Industries,* a semiofficial corporate history published in 1979, described George H. W. Bush as beginning his industry career in 1948 with Dresser Industries in Cleveland, Ohio, where it was then based.[14] He had previously gotten nowhere in interviews with Procter and Gamble in Cincinnati. Rudolph Reimer, for whom he first worked, was the Ohio-based company controller and fiscal strategist.[15] Prescott Bush's firm, when it was still W. A. Harriman and Company, had financed Dresser, and the senior Bush had been the firm's man on the Dresser board since 1930. How many weeks or months into his employment Bush relocated to Texas—there and in California, he put in over two years learning the company ropes—is not entirely clear.

In late 1950, when George H. W. wanted to leave Dresser to set up in the oil business on his own, his father's close associates there gave their blessing and provided ongoing career assistance. The family was a magic carpet. Uncle Herbie at G. H. Walker and Company rounded up the investors for the partnership his nephew had arranged with John Overbey, a small-time lease and royalty operator in Midland, the West Texas oil capital. Virtually every biographer of both Bushes has dwelt on the Midland phenomenon— the post-1945 influx of Ivy Leaguers who hailed from the upper-class East and had access to family capital. The college types in Midland, Overbey noticed, had "all had a chance to be stockbrokers and investment bankers. And they had all wanted to learn the oil business instead."[16]

In fact, the oil fields of the Permian Basin represented one of the century's great American wealth opportunities, which nobody knew better than the New York capitalists.* John Younger, another Midlander, pointed out that "one of the Getty boys was here. One of the members of the Mellon family. People whose parents were running brokerage houses."[17] Overbey himself was overwhelmed by what he recalled as "the dizzying whirl of a money-raising trip to the East with George and Uncle Herbie: lunch at New York's 21 Club, weekend at Kennebunkport where a bracing Sunday dip in the Atlantic off Walker's Point ended with a servant wrapping you in a large terry towel and handing you a martini."[18]

Perceptive observers discerned a kinship of sorts between the securities business and the landmen, like George H. W. Bush, who worked the arbitrage between their payments for oil leases and the expected royalty income. Skill was important, but so was luck. "Of all the professionals to compare him to," one chronicler reported, "the oil man is most like a stockbroker in cowboy boots."[19]

Moreover, like much of the investment sector, the oil business of that boom era derived its capital through a cosseting cornucopia of federal tax shelters. Whereas ordinary dividends and interest were taxed at a top rate of 80 to 90 percent, investments in oil enjoyed preference piled on preference. First, income from a strike would be partly tax-free because of the 27.5 percent oil depletion allowance. On top of that, as much as 70 percent of the cost of bringing in a well could be deducted as an intangible drilling expense against taxable income in the same year. Hugh Liedtke, George H. W.'s principal partner from 1953 to 1959, besides being the Amherst- and Harvard-educated son of Gulf Oil's chief counsel, was also a tax shelter whiz who "began trading oil-producing properties in a way that permitted the eventual owner to defer his tax liabilities until the field was depleted,

---

*Indeed, by the millennium, only one state, Alaska, had produced more oil and gas than the Permian Basin of West Texas.

much like taxes in IRA accounts are deferred until someone's retirement. These deals proved particularly popular with Liedtke's stable of well-heeled investors back in Tulsa."[20]

Revealingly, another close friend of Prescott Bush's, who had agreed to hire George H. W. before the new Yale graduate opted for Dresser instead, was Ray Kravis, a rich Tulsa oil and gas developer.[21] Although his son Henry became famous in the 1980s for the leveraged buyouts run through his firm, Kohlberg Kravis Roberts and Company, the father, too, had been a legend on Wall Street. Back in the late 1920s, Kravis had pioneered a special tax-shelter arrangement through which oil properties could be "packaged" and sold in a manner that reduced the tax on the profits to 15 percent from the normal 81 percent rate applied to oil properties.[22]

Firms like Brown Brothers Harriman, Goldman Sachs, and Bear Stearns relied on Kravis's ability to assess oil properties with a combined geological, accounting, and tax expertise. Alan Greenberg, later the chairman of Bear Stearns, recalled that in the 1950s and 1960s, "no one investing in oil in those days made a move without consulting Ray Kravis."[23] Clearly, Prescott Bush was well placed to put his son into the brainbox of the oil industry, not its toolshed, and that financial foundation always remained important during George H. W. Bush's stint as a Connecticut Yankee in King Petroleum's Court.

During the 1950s, working at Zapata Petroleum, the company he and his uncle's investors owned with the Liedtke brothers, George H. W. was again principally occupied on the money side. Instead of finding oil or drilling, as he recounted to the *Texas Monthly,* he was "stretching paper"— turning over debt and making new terms with the creditors.[24]

When he decided to split away from Zapata Petroleum in 1959, Bush bought the firm's Zapata Offshore subsidiary to run largely on his own, albeit with the help of a further $800,000 raised by his uncle. In the early 1960s, federal tax strategy, ever central, had taken on some new twists. Zapata Offshore was in the business of providing offshore drilling platforms and rigs, mostly under contract to Gulf, Standard of California, and Royal Dutch Shell. These operations were based in the eastern Caribbean and the coastal waters off Mexico and Kuwait, as well as off the U.S. coast. Company operations lost money in the early years but bounced back in the early and mid-1960s. After-tax profits, however, involved not just successful operations but shrewd utilization of offshore subsidiaries—in Bush's case, a half dozen with names like Zapata de Mexico, Zapata International, Seacat Zapata, and Zapata Overseas.[25]

By 1964, as noted, George H. W. Bush was spending less and less time on the business, as politics, not moneymaking, moved to the top of his agenda. While his investors made profits in the late 1960s, Bush, after selling his interest to new management, never cleared any great sum, despite some heady days. In the mid-1950s, Zapata Petroleum had hit oil with well after well in the West Jameson Field near Midland, and the stock had quadrupled to $23, making him a paper millionaire for a while. But after he was elected to Congress in 1966, his filings put his net worth at roughly $1 million. While good, it was hardly a spectacular showing for a man who had come to boom-poised Texas with such powerful connections and so much access to capital.[26]

When Bush left the government in 1977, after a decade of holding federal office and the Republican national chairmanship, he did not go back to Midland and the oil fields. Instead, he accepted corporate directorships at Eli Lilly, the drug firm; Purolator, a company controlled by his close friend Nicholas Brady; Texas Gulf Sulphur; and Dallas-based First International Bancshares, the biggest Texas bank holding company, and its British affiliate, First International Bancshares of London. Besides making him chairman of the executive committee, First International offered European connections and paid well; so did the tax-sheltered oil and real estate partnerships well-heeled friends put him into. Thirty years after leaving for Texas, he was back in more or less the same business his father and so many of his schoolmates had pursued.

The commercial saga of George H. W. Bush's siblings and sons, especially the forty-third president, will be told shortly in conjunction with the family's involvement with crony capitalism, government connections, and bailouts (ostensibly overseas phenomena, but in truth as prevalent in the United States as in Rome or Bangkok). This involvement also became a part of Bush economic culture. To resume our immediate topic, though, the point is that over four generations, the vocation of the Bushes has been essentially financial, sometimes with a flow of petroleum or a whiff of natural gas. This background, transcending their Texas experience alone, explained much of their economic worldview: what they perceived to be a good economy, the yardsticks they used to measure it, and what policies they pursued in the White House to promote the necessary outcomes.

The beginning of the Bushes' financial background had come with George H. Walker, for over forty years president or chairman of two major investment firms, W. A. Harriman and Company and G. H. Walker and Company. Prescott Bush, in turn, started at W. A. Harriman and Company in 1926 and later became the managing partner of Brown Brothers Harriman. George H. W. Bush mostly did the financial side of oil until he wound up with First International Bancshares. Of his three brothers, Prescott junior headed Prescott Bush and Company and was also closely associated with Asset Management International Financing and Settlement Limited. Jonathan likewise had his own investment firm, J. Bush and Company, and later became president of RIMCO (Riggs Investment Management Company). Brother William (Bucky) was president of Boatmen's Bank in St. Louis and then a principal of Bush and O'Donnell Investments. Brother-in-law Scott Pierce was president of the brokerage firm E. F. Hutton until he had to resign when the company was charged with mail fraud.

Of George H. W.'s four sons, Marvin worked for Mosley, Hallgarten in Boston, then at Shearson Lehman, and finally wound up running the hedge fund section at Virginia-based Winston Partners. Neil, sullied by his tenure as a director of Colorado's looted Silverado Savings and Loan, went on to do investment deals through his Interlink Management Corporation. Jeb, who began his career at Texas Commerce Bank, went to Miami and got into investments (IntrAmerican Investments) and the real estate business, participating in controversial financing of office buildings through savings and loan institutions that later became insolvent, all prior to becoming governor of Florida.

George W.'s business career, as we have seen, was spent primarily in obtaining new financing or lining up rescuers for his unsuccessful oil and gas ventures. This was not difficult, for whenever he drilled a dry hole, as one wit observed, someone always filled it up with money for him. At Yale, what he had really wanted to be was a stockbroker—and not just any old stockbroker, but one who struck paper gold. "He wanted to be rich," remembered Houston friend Doug Hannah. "He wanted to possibly be a stockbroker because his great-uncle and uncle were stockbrokers. . . . George and I would sit around in the summertime, in the evening, and dream about opening our own stock brokerage firm. We all wanted to be partners."[27] Following in his father's footsteps meant Texas and oil, but even at his first exploration firm, Arbusto, his secretary told a biographer, his interest was less in oil than in pitching to investors: "My suspicion was that he enjoyed raising money more."[28]

No previous presidential family has been so wholeheartedly involved with a single economic sector over multiple generations, yet with so little scrutiny of the resulting narrowness of its public policy views. If representing Texas for ten or twenty years stamped a senator's or congressman's view of the national agenda, what would have been imprinted on a presidential family by a century of working to increase the wealth of a small slice of Upper America?

In terms of the U.S. economy, the implicit model followed during both Bush presidencies can be summed up in one phrase: *investment-driven*. Investment drove the economy, and what fueled investment was tax advantage. Reduction of the capital gains tax rate became a recurrent Bush drumbeat. Low interest rates were good because they reliquefied investors and financial institutions. Federal budget deficits, although troubling, were acceptable as an alternative to raising taxes or to squelching investment-friendly tax cuts. High debt levels and current account deficits, while less than desirable, were not a threat if accompanied by substantial investment in the United States. If one accepted the arguments of White House economists, high current account deficits, especially the record levels of the second Bush administration, were principally a reflection of how much foreigners wanted to invest in the United States.

The usual perception of Bush policy has been that it is primarily the product of upper-class bias rather than the expression of a coherent ideology. Conservative writer Fred Barnes was unusual in crediting George H. W. Bush with strong views, calling him "a supply-sider of a sort—a corporate supply-sider." Bush had less interest in the abstract effect of marginal rates, but "providing tax incentives for business is something else again. He loves them."[29] *Time* correspondents Michael Duffy and Dan Goodgame distilled a similar Palm Beach and Park Avenue essence:

> Bush believes that in economic policy what is good for wealthy investors and business executives is good for America. He believes that taxes must be kept low on capital gains and on top marginal incomes, so that members of the educated and monied elite—which he sees as the creative force in the economy—will have an incentive to risk their capital. . . . He believes, implicitly, that taxes need not be low on the wages or savings accounts of ordi-

nary Americans, who are not a creative force in the economy and who anyway have no choice but to work and scrimp.[30]

Politically, this blend of supply-side theory and investment-sector
fealty has not resonated with the public, which senses its favoritism to the
Forbes 400 or the S&P 500 over the workforce of 135 million. Like the liquidity pumped out at intervals by Chairman Alan Greenspan and the Federal Reserve, tax cuts aimed at stimulating upper-bracket investment have
a record of bypassing declining industrial centers and urban slums, and
even middle-class neighborhoods full of two-earner households mired in
credit card and mortgage debt.

The first Bush administration was a textbook example of these biases.
Consumer confidence and employment data showed householder income
expectations plummeting and white-collar jobs contracting from 1990
right through the autumn of George H. W. Bush's 1992 reelection defeat.
This happened despite rising stock market indexes, aided by Federal Reserve policy, and despite government data that showed the overall economy growing. Median-income householders were simply not the growth
beneficiaries.

Their low priority was confirmed elsewhere on the tax front, as when
both Reagan and Bush had accepted a rapid upward ratcheting of the FICA
(Social Security and Medicare) tax burden on middle-income families, especially two-earner ones. After big rises under Reagan, under Bush the
level of individual income up to which the tax was applied climbed from
$48,000 in 1989 to $55,500 in 1992, while the rate imposed escalated from
7.51 percent to 7.65 percent. The self-employed fared even worse. Investors
were the class for whom the president kept seeking relief through a reduction in the tax rate on capital gains. In 1990, when a growing budget deficit
forced a small tax increase, the president took personal pains to see that the
top rate on the highest earners did not go above 31 percent. Instead, he insisted that the highest marginal rates be placed on upper-middle-income
taxpayers, those whose adjusted gross incomes fell into the $120,000–
$300,000 "bubble" range, in which itemized deductions and exemptions
were phased out.

Another hallmark of the senior Bush's four years was a continuation of
the Reagan administration's support for "investment" that most non-supply-
side economists believed favored luxury consumption, excessive real estate
construction, and pursuit of profit in mergers and leveraged buyouts. Far

from being distant, faceless manipulators, some of the best-known practitioners of the eighties takeover and leveraged buyout game included old Oil Patch *compañeros* quite well known to George H. W. Bush. One was Hugh Liedtke, whose Pennzoil Corporation (built around what began as Zapata Petroleum) tried to take over Getty Oil and wound up collecting several billion dollars from Texaco. A second was raider T. Boone Pickens, whose principal pirate vessel, Mesa Petroleum, had evolved from the Hugoton Production Company. Hugoton had been acquired by Pickens after a connection set up by Hugh Liedtke and Zapata Petroleum. Bigger still was Henry Kravis, freewheeling son of the Ray Kravis who had been enlisted to introduce the George H. W. Bush just out of Yale to the many-splendored structure of oil and gas deals. Bush, in the White House, was a friend and ally.[31]

Equally symbolic of the new mind-set pervading Washington was the emergence of Team 100—the president's 249-member inner circle of $100,000-or-over donors—as an open parade of influence seekers. Johnson and Nixon had had similarly wealthy donors, but Bush formalized the group, prompting the magazine of Common Cause to run a special April-May 1992 issue on "George Bush's Ruling Class."[32] The favors and special rulings described on behalf of Team 100 members ranged from federal grants and emergency federal water allocations to sweetheart arrangements for buying up the assets of failed savings and loan associations seized by the government.

If anything, the second Bush administration, emboldened by its Florida recount victory, leaned even further in the direction of investment-focused economics. Although official gross domestic product data indicated a recovery in 2002 and 2003, employment continued to slump, and consumer confidence kept reaching new lows until it spiked in April during the Iraq war. Skeptical economists like Stephen Roach of Morgan Stanley suggested that George W. Bush was repeating his father's economic recovery without job creation.

There was no mistaking the bias: The son's antilabor proposals were even stronger; FICA taxes were allowed to bite ever harder on the middle class; and the federal pension legislation enacted in 2002 left the time bomb of massive underfunding still ticking within corporate America's shaky retirement systems. Bush's tax reduction proposals, far bolder and bigger than his father's, reflected unprecedentedly open favoritism to the rich. While the blueprint to end double taxation of dividends was technically complex, because the top 1 percent of the population collected 40 percent of the dividends, they stood to receive roughly that proportion of the benefits. The legislation that was ultimately passed simply slashed the tax on dividends, avoiding any exotic mechanics.

As chapter 2 has discussed, only large estates (over $1 million) still paid inheritance taxes in 2001, so the full estate tax repeal quickly orchestrated by the White House and GOP Congress was stark class legislation. As for the tax bracket reductions voted in 2001, they gave 36 percent of their full-term benefit to the top 1 percent. The abandonment of these revenues sent the federal budget deficit soaring, adding to the fiscal policy resemblance between the first and second Bush regimes.

If this portrait of the George W. Bush administration seems to leave out Enron, Halliburton, and the other errant companies to which the White House had ties, the omission is only temporary. They are the subject matter of chapter 5.

However, the economic weaknesses of 1989–92 and 2001–3 went beyond the Bush family's biases and their investment-model perception of the U.S. economy. Hauteur and lack of interest in the commonweal also exuded from another modus operandi, associated with Texas and the Sun Belt by public perception but actually much broader in its origins. This is the practice of crony capitalism: government favors for the well connected, and publicly financed rescues for private financial interests. During both Bush administrations, such practices flourished to a degree that mocked their ostensible commitment to free markets.

Crony Capitalism: Government Connections, Private Deals, and Public Bailouts

Samuel P. Bush, a relative progressive in his younger days, has been cited in economic studies by business historian Mansel G. Blackford for the interest the engineering-trained Ohioan showed in scientific management, labor policy, and the welfare of his employees as president of Buckeye Steel Castings during the decade before World War I.[33] Most of the subsequent Bushes, by comparison, have shown much more inclination to be dealmakers, rainmakers, or, in the most recent generations, influence brokers.

Prescott Bush was a bit of each. While he owed most of the positions he achieved in the 1920s and 1930s to relatives and old-boy networks, he was not fundamentally a trader or speculator, but an investment banker who developed long-term relationships, particularly on the boards of companies like Pan American Airlines, CBS Broadcasting, and Dresser Industries. His taste for politics may have developed because many companies on whose boards he sat were in regulated industries (Pan Am and CBS) or dealt with government through highly classified activities. Dresser and the Vanadium Corporation of America, for example, were both involved in the World War II atomic bomb project. Like Brown Brothers Harriman in the 1940s and 1950s, Prescott Bush himself seems to have been close to the defense establishment. He certainly had influence in those quarters.

Both George H. Walker and Prescott Bush grew up when the line between business activity and political office holding was only loosely drawn. Walker's old friend, U.S. ambassador to Russia David Francis, mixed public and private business both in handling the St. Louis World's Fair of 1904 and later in a 1916 private U.S. bank loan to Russia, parts of which were handled through Francis Brothers and Company in St. Louis.[34] As late as World War II, Averell Harriman kept his Brown Brothers Harriman partnership and Russian stock and bond portfolio while serving in Moscow as U.S. ambassador.[35]

As for Prescott Bush, aside from the German-linked companies set up by George H. Walker, little about his business career was controversial. So, too, for George H. W. Bush in his early years. His father and uncle arranged his jobs or took care of the financing he needed. However, there was no apparent influence peddling of the sort so visible among his children and at least one sibling once his own election as vice president and then president brought the family ship into Opportunity Cove.

Between the 1960s and the 1980s, crony capitalism sometimes took the form of dollars from the CIA or from other government agencies and federal programs enlisted by the CIA. Zapata Offshore, the international drilling subsidiary that passed under Bush's principal control when he left the larger Zapata framework in 1959, operated within surveillance distance of Castro's Cuba and was said by some to be CIA supported. Other CIA-favored entrepreneurs seem to have gotten access to Export-Import Bank loans, savings and loan associations, and government housing and Medicare programs.

George H. W. Bush's 1979–80 campaign for the presidency and election to the vice presidency also opened dual spigots. Jonathan Bush, a Wall Street investment consultant, raised money for his brother's presidential campaign during the same conversations in which he raised money for his nephew George W.'s ill-fated Arbusto oil venture.[36] Any devil would necessarily be in the details.

The 1983–85 period saw the vice president's three oldest sons, George W., Jeb, and Neil, all play the influence game. After the implosion of George W.'s original oil and gas business, largely funded in the late 1970s by what one participant called the "A-Team" of Connecticut and New York Bush supporters, he arranged the 1984 merger noted earlier with Spectrum 7 Energy Corporation, headed by a Yale classmate, William DeWitt Jr. When his stewardship didn't help Spectrum 7, which lost substantial amounts of money, George W. negotiated a second acquisition of his enterprise in 1986, this time by a larger concern, Harken Energy.

Harken was described in the *Texas Observer* as having "direct links to institutions involved in drug-smuggling, foreign currency manipulation and the CIA's well-documented role in the destabilization of the Australian government."[37] Bush received over $500,000 in stock for the deal, annual consulting fees, and, presumably, the unmistakable message that his financing rested on his name and connections.

Jeb and Neil were also busy making money the old-fashioned way: by trading on an influential father. Arriving in Miami in 1980, Jeb was soon involved in Florida GOP politics (as Dade County chairman), the affairs of the Cuban émigré community, and the real estate business, all of which overlapped. His principal business contacts were well-heeled Nicaraguan contras or CIA-connected Cubans. With one, Armando Codina, he bought an office building in 1985 with financing by a local savings and loan, Broward Federal. A few years later, Broward's failure put in the hands of the federal Resolution Trust Corporation the loan (by then in default) secured by the Bush-Codina office building. Conveniently, the two investors worked out a deal with federal regulators that avoided foreclosure for a payment of $500,000, leaving the remaining cost of their unpaid loan ($4.1 million) to be picked up by taxpayers.[38]

A second deal saw Jeb contract in 1985 with a subsequently convicted wheeler-dealer, Camilo Padreda, to find tenants for the latter's empty office building. That same year, receiving a $75,000 fee as a real estate consultant, he helped Miguel Recarey, the head of International Medical Centers (IMC), by lobbying the federal Department of Health and Human Services to exempt IMC from restrictions that would have limited its flow of Medicare patients.[39]

Neil, the third son, found a way to conjoin the opportunities of JNB Exploration, the "oil company" he set up in 1983, and Silverado Savings and Loan, the large Denver-based S&L whose board he joined in 1985. During his board tenure, Silverado made over $200 million in loans, later largely defaulted, to Neil's two partners in JNB Exploration, a pair of high-rolling GOP and George H. W. Bush contributors named Ken Good and Bill Walters. Neil, who did not tell Silverado about his close business connections to Good and Walters, had received a $100,000 loan from Good with no obligation to pay it back. Cherry Creek National Bank in Denver, owned by Walters, gave JNB Exploration a $1.5 million line of credit, from which JNB paid the then vice president's son $550,000 between 1983 and 1988.[40]

By 1988, all three Bush sons were grazing in lush pastures. George W., as a director of Harken, met with Arkansas banker Jackson Stephens, a major Reagan-Bush contributor, to raise $25 million for Harken by bringing in Saudi real estate tycoon Sheikh Abdullah Bakhsh as a board member and major investor. Supposedly, bankers close to Stephens, Inc., also helped recommend Harken to the government of Bahrain (as well as to the new Bush-appointed U.S. ambassador to Bahrain) for a Persian Gulf gas and oil exploration contract. This came through in 1989.

In 1988, George W. also began angling for a prominent role in the acquisition of the Texas Rangers baseball team, which was being sold by oilman Eddie Chiles, an old friend of his father's. The deal did not go through easily, despite Bush's love of the sport, but it was finally concluded in 1989 on three pivots of cronyism. The first was the help in arranging meetings and financing given to Bush by baseball commissioner Peter Ueberroth, a family friend mentioned during 1988 as everything from a potential Bush cabinet member to a long-shot vice presidential choice. Number two was the investment participation of Texas billionaire moneyman Richard Rainwater, a major Reagan-Bush contributor, who was pitched on the basis of respect for the new president.[41]

Last, but certainly not least, was the arrangement by which the city of Arlington, Texas, agreed to finance a new $191 million stadium for the Rangers with a bond issue paid for by a small sales tax increase. The stadium was to be deeded over to the baseball consortium in twelve years, after the Rangers group had paid $60 million, in annual payments of $5 million. Critics argued that the weakness of the deal negotiated for Arlington by then mayor Richard Greene reflected his vulnerability as a defendant in two federal lawsuits filed by federal regulators regarding his role as an executive in two failed savings and loan institutions.[42]

What sold investors was the highly rewarding stadium deal, which depended on the city of Arlington's pushing the sales tax increase through in a special election and then stretching its power of eminent domain to seize the necessary land for what was mostly a private purpose. Bush became the managing partner, benefiting from the project's helpful Texas political symbolism and exposure. Ueberroth shot down the notion that the president's son had been the deal's architect: "George W. Bush deserves great credit for the development of the franchise," Ueberroth said. "However, the bringing together of the buying group was a result of Richard Rainwater, Rusty Rose, Dr. Bobby Brown and the commissioner."[43]

While raising the connections ante, the election of George H. W. Bush as president in 1988 also turned up the spotlight on his sons' and brothers' business dealings. George W.'s relationship with Harken Energy and the reasons for Harken's Persian Gulf contract became a favorite news discussion topic. Neil's machinations with Silverado were the stuff of headlines, as were the reports of how the Reagan-Bush administration had squelched action by federal regulators in 1988 to keep the scandal from becoming an issue in that year's election.[44]

Jeb's first big gambit with his father in the White House became a topic pursued by journalists in both Florida and Texas. In 1988, he set up a company with David Eller, a Broward County GOP fund-raiser, for the overseas marketing of flood control pumps made by Eller's MWI Corporation. Then in 1989, he and his wife, Columba, went on a marketing trip to Nigeria, where they were received in style by Nigerian president Ibrahim Babangida. According to Nigerian press reports, Jeb pledged that his father would increase aid to developing countries.[45] Deals were struck, and by 1992, the Florida pump company had secured $74 million in U.S. Export-Import Bank financing—a large amount for a country Ex-Im loan officers considered a bad risk. "I didn't get paid for the Nigeria business," Bush told the *Palm Beach Post* in 1994. "I have not made a dime on business with Nigeria." But by checking tax records, the *Post* found that the "Bush-El" partnership paid Jeb at least $300,000 for his participation in a second pump-marketing venture.[46]

By 2002, the Bush-Eller relationship was looking even more dubious. Prosecutors charged that MWI used more than one-third ($28 million) of the Export-Import Bank loan to pay bribes to Nigerian officials and grease the palms of MWI insiders. Although Bush claimed he had nothing to do with the Nigerian deals, he had visited Nigeria twice and MWI marketing videos obtained by the *St. Petersburg Times* emphasized the company's Bush connections.[47]

Neil, too, took quick advantage of his father's position, and the *St. Petersburg Times* described his spirited return to self-aggrandizement. After he shed JNB Exploration, "his next company, Apex Energy, was formed with a personal investment of $3,000, plus a $2.3 million loan from the federal government's SBA [Small Business Administration] program. Like JNB, Apex went belly-up with few assets to repay the SBA. Afterward, Bill Daniels, a Colorado cable-TV magnate and prominent contributor to President Bush, offered Neil a job."[48]

By this point, one of the president's brothers was also crowding onto the stage. Prescott junior, who had tried to run for the U.S. Senate from Connecticut in 1982, abandoned these efforts and instead pursued business and investment opportunities in Asia and elsewhere. In February 1989, just weeks after his brother's inauguration, he arrived in Tokyo to court clients, thereafter flying to China, where he had a 30 percent interest in a Japanese proposal to build an $18 million resort and golf course near Shanghai. His family contacts cemented the arrangement.

That same year, following Beijing's brutal crackdown on demonstrators in Tiananmen Square, Asset Management, a U.S. company, paid the president's brother $250,000 to consult on the firm's arrangement to provide $300 million worth of Hughes Aircraft satellites to China for use in setting up its internal communications network. In November, Congress passed sanctions specifically barring the export of U.S. satellites to China unless the president found the sale "in the national interest." But in December, George H. W. Bush did indeed lift the sanction on the $300 million deal, citing "the national interest" as a justification. Prescott's third Asian project that year was to arrange a buyout of Asset Management by West Tsusho, a Japanese investment firm promising a $250,000 finder's fee when the deal closed.[49] Newspapers reported that Japanese police were investigating West Tsusho's ties to organized crime.

Another of George W. Bush's uncles, his mother's brother Scott Pierce, had to resign in 1985 as president of E. F. Hutton after the brokerage firm was charged with multiple counts of mail fraud. In 1991, Uncle Jonathan's investment firm, J. Bush and Company, was fined $4,000 for doing business in Connecticut without proper registration.[50] Authorities in next-door Massachusetts fined the company $30,000 for failing to register as a broker-dealer and barred it from trading with the public for one year.[51]

During the 2001 ruckus over Enron, the Center for Public Integrity turned up an internal Securities and Exchange Commission document prepared in 1991 suggesting that George W. Bush himself had violated federal securities law at least four times in the late 1980s and early 1990s in selling Harken Energy Company stock while serving as a director of that company.[52] The case for considering his large $848,000 sale of Harken stock in mid-1990 as an insider-trading violation was later strengthened when the *Boston Globe* reported that a week before his sale, Harken lawyers had advised him of the insider-trading risk.[53]

As for Jeb Bush, the limitations of his ethical framework became clear in the late 1980s when two of his principal Miami business associates were indicted. Camilo Padreda pleaded guilty to defrauding the Department of Housing and Urban Development of millions of dollars during the 1980s. When agents of the Department of Health and Human Services determined that Miguel Recarey had been defrauding Medicare through overcharging, false invoicing, and embezzlement, the onetime head of International Medical Centers fled to Venezuela.[54]

Even before the Bushes inaugurated their second president in 2001, they had become the first presidential family to stake out what can best be described as overseas commercial spheres of influence. The Persian Gulf was clearly preeminent among them, thanks to the wars and armaments deals of the 1980s and 1990s, as well as ex-president George H. W. Bush's close relations with the Saudi and Kuwaiti royal families. Sons Marvin and Neil had also made commercial visits.

China was also significant, a relationship begun during Bush's 1970s tenure as chief of the U.S. mission. With George H. W. Bush in the White House, brother Prescott junior was the principal visitor, but Chinese president Jiang Zemin entertained even Neil Bush at dinner when he visited in late 2001 to promote his newest company.

Within the Western Hemisphere, Mexico had been important to George H. W. Bush during his Texas oil days, but by the late 1990s, he was paying more attention to Argentina because of a close relationship with Carlos Menem, the former president turned wealthy businessman and arms dealer. Sons Neil and George W. Bush also had Argentine dealings.

All in all, if presidential family connections were theme parks, Bush World would be a sight to behold. Mideast banks tied to the CIA would crowd alongside Florida S&Ls that once laundered money for the Nicaraguan contras. Dozens of oil wells would run eternally without finding oil, thanks to periodic cash deposits by old men wearing Reagan-Bush buttons and smoking twenty-dollar cigars. Visitors to "Prescott Bush's Tokyo" could try to make an investment deal without falling into the clutches of the *yakuza,* or Japanese mob.

But obviously, the situation is nothing to joke about. During the Asian currency crises of the late 1990s, the crony capitalism of countries like Korea became cartoon fodder in the U.S. business press. Although the problem is less prevalent in the United States, its pervasiveness in the political and commercial annals of the Bush family may help to explain the lack of civic commitment in the economic policies of two Bush presidencies.

Compassionate Conservatism: The Three Bush Generations

If hypocrisy is the tribute vice pays to virtue, compassionate conservatism is the policy hypocrisy uses to disguise economic vice. While it has been three generations in the making, its rhetorical embrace by the Bushes has come to display less and less genteel upper-class pretense—the need to relate to meat-loaf incomes and middle-class medical costs—and instead to manifest a higher and higher ratio of outright deception: saying one thing and meaning another.

Over the decades in which the Bushes have held senatorial, cabinet, vice presidential, and presidential office, they have periodically sought to underplay their wealth and connections. Since 1988, two much-repeated phrases—George H. W. Bush's "kinder and gentler nation" and George W. Bush's "compassionate conservatism"—have emerged as supposed touchstones of worthy intentions and commitment to those less fortunate. From time to time, the same phraseology has been employed as a segue from harsh campaign tactics to the warmer, fuzzier imagery used to reposition a Bush who has just won an election. What seems to have changed, slowly but significantly, is the motivation behind the veneer.

Merely ducking the aura of wealth, of course, was hardly more than politics as usual. We have already seen how Prescott Bush spoke of a father who didn't have the money to send him to law school and how George H. W. employed empathy-seeking references like "high school" and "job interview." Preferring to discuss "legacy" rather than "dynasty" is just as logical a tactic. The recurring thread of true deception in both Bush administrations has come with the cotton candy webs of questionable compassion and negligible noblesse oblige spun around an essential preoccupation with business and financial economics. At other times, this hollow compassion has been brought into play as a gauzy distraction—for example, after George H. W.'s outspoken opposition to civil rights legislation in his 1964 Texas Senate race, or after his 1988 use of the controversial Willie Horton advertisements, and later by George W. following his 2000 visit to Bob Jones University in South Carolina.

The original, mild version of the family's public ethos began with Prescott Bush, whose representation of midcentury Connecticut required much less artifice than did catering to the family's later southern electoral base. His principal handicap in Connecticut politics was high cultural—being a Wall Street investment banker, an Episcopalian of the Social Register variety, and a resident of Greenwich, the upper-income suburb home to so many lions, leopards, and jackals of Manhattan's business and financial districts. Although candidates of this stripe rarely sought statewide office, when they did they almost inevitably lacked popular appeal in the ethnic, largely Catholic industrial towns clustered along the riverbanks, where the old mills and factories had made brass, machine tools, clocks, and firearms during the nineteenth century.

Narrowly defeated in his first Senate race in 1950, Prescott Bush had been hurt among the Catholic two-fifths of the Connecticut electorate by last-minute charges linking him to family planning and birth control. Squeaking through on a second try in 1952, with critical assistance from Dwight Eisenhower's presidential coattails, he had tried to minimize the connotations of his rich-family, Wall Street résumé by seeming less stuffy and emphasizing his involvement in charitable, educational, and civil rights causes.

This was a plausible enough stratagem. Besides being a Yale trustee, Prescott Bush had for years been state chairman of the United Negro College Fund, a cause heavily backed by the Chase Bank and other pillars of the New York financial community. His commitment to the internationalist wing of the Eisenhower-era GOP was clear, not least because Brown Brothers Harriman had boasted of investments in some forty countries. Together with his Yale and Skull and Bones disdain for the establishment-baiting Senator Joseph McCarthy, these positions won the Connecticut senator the label of Republican moderate.

That description may, however, be misleading. *Congressional Quarterly,* in its two-decade history, *Congress and the Nation 1945–1964,* cited only four of Prescott Bush's legislative maneuvers—one to protect northeastern industry (1956), a second to restrict Kennedy trade legislation (1962), a third to restrict public housing (1956), and a fourth to cut funds for the National Institutes of Health (1961). All except the first reflected the dominant conservative position among Senate Republicans.[55] His conservatism was also evident in matters of business, finance, labor, and national security, his opposition to "socialized medicine," and a moral probity that verged on the puritan.

Before his 1962 attacks on Nelson Rockefeller for his divorce, Prescott Bush had stopped speaking to his own brother for having left his wife and children to take up with a Philadelphia society woman.[56] By 1964, three generations of Bushes—Prescott, George H. W., and George W.—were all reading *Conscience of a Conservative* and supporting Arizona senator Barry Goldwater for that year's Republican presidential nomination.[57] Nelson Rockefeller, Prescott clearly believed, was a cad.

For George H. W. Bush, resettled a thousand miles away, there were pluses and minuses in pursuing the same gentlemanly, albeit slightly camouflaged, politics. On the one hand, Texas had more opportunity because there were fewer rivals for Republican nominations. But the need for cultural pretense was a drawback. In 1989, even son George W. would begin mentioning a vital difference between him and his father: the elder Bush had been acculturated by Greenwich Country Day School, whereas he had learned to speak and think Texan at San Jacinto Junior High School.

George H. W. Bush's own transition to Lone Stardom had definite rough patches. Biographers have recounted episodes such as how he was laughed at for wearing Bermuda shorts in Baptist West Texas and the advertising in one early campaign that featured him walking with a poodle straining at the leash. Incumbent Democratic senator Ralph Yarborough, who easily beat back Bush's challenge in 1964, did so partly by mocking him as a Connecticut carpetbagger. The single Texas office he was able to win—two terms as U.S. representative from Houston's silk-stocking district—involved a constituency rich with oil millionaires, private planes, and a high ratio of college graduates. River Oaks was a place where prep schools, foreign cars, and modified northern accents were acceptable.

But Texas was more than River Oaks and comparably rich Midland. Against the statewide backdrop, George H. W. Bush's cultural schizophrenia continued to be a political Achilles' heel, an unstable mix of genteel northeastern moderate conservatism and the two-gunned Texas brand, with its radio preachers, chemical smog, and Goldwater buttons. In 1980, Bush had remained eastern enough—memberships in organizations like the Trilateral Commission and the Council on Foreign Relations were threaded through his résumé—to aim his presidential campaign at early northern primaries and caucuses. Between 1985 and 1988, however, he signed up Lee Atwater, a good-ole-boy political adviser from South Carolina; reassured televangelists Jim and Tammy Faye Bakker that he occasionally watched their *P.T.L.* (Praise the Lord) *Club;* and published *Man of Integrity,* a tome testifying to his born-again status and close relationships with southern preachers. Primaries in the Old Confederate South were to be his March 1988 political firewall should things go poorly in the early Iowa and New Hampshire contests.

In 1984 and thereafter, however, the perception of him by Republican and journalistic elites had become less favorable. The business, financial, and free-market core of his beliefs, if kept generalized, was acceptable in almost any plausible Republican administration, while cultural and moral issues were accepted as the window dressing he switched as needed. His shifting positions in these areas, in fact, dated back two decades. After flirting with the John Birch Society, condemning civil rights legislation, and embracing Goldwater during the 1964 campaign—he later told his Episcopal minister that he regretted taking "some of the far right positions to get elected"[58]—Bush thereupon changed in 1965 to endorse Lyndon Johnson's Great Society.[59] Then, between 1968 and 1973, he curled up to Richard Nixon to secure two cabinet-level appointments: the United Nations post and the Republican national chairmanship.

When the press perceived him as pandering in the mid-1980s for Ronald Reagan's endorsement in 1988, however, their view of his fundamental character weakness was ignited. Columnist George Will concluded in 1986 that "the unpleasant sound Bush is emitting as he traipses from one conservative gathering to another is a thin, tinny 'arf'—the sound of a lapdog. He is panting along Mondale's path to the presidency."[60] Of the many names Texas politicians have been called, "lapdog" is rare—and the image stuck fast, capped in 1987 by *Newsweek*'s devastating cover story "Fighting the Wimp Factor."

By the spring and summer of 1988, the disaffection of swing voters had put Democratic nominee Michael Dukakis well ahead in the national polls. However, Bush struck a reasonably successful middle-of-the-road note in his acceptance speech to the August GOP convention and again in the weeks that followed. While making new environmental and educational commitments, he also promised not to raise taxes. Government was too big, he argued, and the burden of further social welfare should be taken up by family and community. This was his version of a "kinder and gentler nation," but it was one to be achieved by voluntarism—the "thousand points of light" he would evoke again in his inauguration and many other times.

In some respects, this proposal simply updated Prescott Bush's old New England emphasis on charitable and educational activity. In 1964, the *Texas Observer* had commented that Senate candidate Bush "admits to having normal human feelings for the poor and the dispossessed, although he does not let these feelings interfere, in any way, with his steadfast convictions against the issues."[61] In fact, in charitable matters, George H. W. Bush had a record to match his father's. After leaving government in 1977, he chaired the American Heart Fund; became cochair of Yale's 1978 fund drive; and joined the boards of two Texas universities, Baylor and Trinity (San Antonio), and that of the Phillips Academy Andover.[62]

Politically the "points of light" approach also served as a tactical counter to activist, high-cost government involvement in education and welfare. The meddling side of government was a much bigger issue in 1988 than it had been in his father's day, especially in the South and other racially tense areas. Moreover, as the money-managing Bushes knew full well, most of the thousand points of light qualified for the all-important tax deductibility of contributions under section 501(c) (3) of the U.S. Internal Revenue Code. Compassion was more easily accepted as a deduction to income taxes than as an add-on.

On one hand, no one can doubt that Bush longed for a "kinder, gentler" political and cultural climate than the Texas conservative milieu that had bedeviled him for three decades. On the other hand, the very harshness of social conditions in Texas suggested that in policy terms, the "points of light" were more likely to be expressed as "points of lite." If charitable commitment hadn't been able to keep friendly and hospitable but low-spending Texans from having the nation's highest levels of cancer risk or child inequality in the 1990s, it was hardly going to serve as a practical alternative to federal, state, and local social welfare and regulatory activity.

Not that any of these positions sparked much of a debate. By the time

George H. W. Bush came up for reelection in 1992, his rhetoric about "points of light" and "education" and "environmental" presidencies had dissolved under the pressure of the real-world issues of high deficits and hard times. Worse, his triumphalism in early 1991, after the Gulf War victory had boosted his job approval to 89 percent, had lulled him into downplaying any domestic agenda and taking for granted political leaders and constituencies that had been troublesome before the Mideast fighting. When their doubts resumed in 1992, he had to court them with ad hoc attention—more meetings with preachers and a prime-time slot for Patrick Buchanan's "culture wars" speech at the GOP convention—that left many on the Right still unconvinced and many in the middle disenchanted.

These paternal travails were instructive to George W., who had faced some of the same during his own, much briefer, transformational years. When he ran for Congress in West Texas in 1978, one Bush television ad, quickly pulled, showed him jogging. The conservative Democrat who beat him, Kent Hance, found it naively eastern; in Muleshoe, joked Hance, the only people who jogged were running away from something or somebody. Other effective radio spots belabored Bush dynastic ambitions and bragged that Hance had gone to Dimmit High School while Bush was back east at prep school.[63] In the immediate disappointment of his defeat, Bush blamed local "provincialism." Then he shrewdly realized that he had learned an important lesson; friends said he vowed never to be out-Texaned again—and he never was.

George W. Bush and the Economics of Evangelical Protestantism

Where his father had always had one foot in Midland and Houston and the other in Connecticut and Manhattan's United Nations Plaza, George W. planted himself firmly in Texas and evolved a temperament to match. When in the 1990s he took up the same "compassionate conservatism" slogan he had recommended to his father in 1988, his version had different nuances, bolder religious connections, and stronger regional roots. It also had more emotion—and more brass. The civic duty and noblesse oblige that were the foundation of his father's "kinder and gentler" approach were old Puritan, Yankee stuff. The religion that increasingly infused the son's rhetoric, a far cry from the traditional Protestantism of Massachusetts and

Connecticut, was the enthusiastic, evangelical Christianity of the nineteenth-century South and border states. Instead of a New England communitarianism that embraced activist government, the southern vision emphasized free will, personal salvation, hostility to interfering officialdom, and rejection of "blame society" excuses for personal failure.

The accompanying "compassion" did not fit many northern definitions of the term. Although too little data exist to correlate precisely the state-by-state geography of evangelical and fundamentalist Protestantism with the state-by-state weakness of social services, literacy, and child welfare, enough is available to support a tentative conclusion: that leaving compassion to private services and charity below the Mason-Dixon line (and above it) usually did less for the recipients than for the upper brackets, who saved large amounts in state and local taxes. This is an old and familiar side of southern culture.

In the early nineteenth century, the coming together of Yankees and southern "butternuts"—so named from the color they dyed their home-spun clothing—in states from Ohio west to Iowa produced very different cultural landscapes. The Yankee immigrants were given to building townships around schools, libraries, neat churches, well-attended town meetings, and well-kept farms, and these communities produced scholars and inventive mechanical entrepreneurs. The butternuts, critics said, often settled for rural subsistence farming, camp meetings, and adult baptism. European travelers often noted the striking contrast between the two groups.

Obviously, this depth of division was long gone by the Bush era. However, as late as 1972, the respected elections analyst Samuel Lubell flagged an unsung but powerful new political force in Dixie, the coming-of-age of America's Southern Baptists:

> Little attention has been paid to the one ethnic element that is currently having the most explosive impact on the country—the white Southern Baptists. The traits which characterize Baptists [are] an ingrained individualism, suspicion of government and a resentment of taxes. Childhood memories of poverty have also given them a hungry drive for material gain—often both husbands and wives work—and scornful contempt for blacks on welfare. Some of these traits are shared by white Southerners generally; still, much of the ingrained individualism reflects their Baptist upbringing. . . . Baptists generally do not hold society responsible for man's

failings, but believe that each man must find personal salvation by mastering his own inner soul and coming to know Jesus personally. They seem less concerned with changing society than with changing oneself.[64]

Written in the wake of Richard Nixon's record-setting majorities among Southern Baptists, Lubell's expectation of their political importance was doubly prescient. Baptist membership was about to explode—outside the South as well as within. Between 1950 and 1990, while most mainstream denominations were losing members, the Southern Baptist Convention more than doubled its size, from 7,080,000 to 15,044,000.[65]

At this point, it is necessary briefly to divide our analysis of George W. Bush's "compassionate conservatism" and its outreach. The core element, to which we will return, is his all-important appeal to religious white Protestants. The second aspect, more peripheral and concerned with hoopla or political organization, is his approach to blacks and Hispanics.

In campaigning, Prescott Bush often cited his fund-raising for the United Negro College Fund. To appeal to black voters during his 1966 Houston congressional campaign, George H. W. Bush, the ex–Yale first baseman, had put a few hundred dollars into creating the "George Bush All-Stars," a local black girls' baseball team. After becoming president in 1989, he sought to supersede the memory of his campaign tactics by meeting with African American Republicans and praising the memory of Martin Luther King. Blacks got symbolism and lip service but not a lot more.

George W. Bush, by contrast, developed the use of minority imagery into a calculated routine. In 1999, as he went from million-dollar fundraiser to million-dollar fund-raiser, his cavalcade regularly stopped for photo opportunities in black and Hispanic schools and community centers. In the words of New York Times reporter Frank Bruni, "He prayed in black churches. He went to Central High School in Little Rock, site of one of the most famous battles in the South to integrate schools. He embraced no past president as tightly as Abraham Lincoln, who put an end to slavery. The apotheosis of this trend eventually came in the Republican National Convention in late July, where the stage featured nearly as many black performers and speakers as the Apollo Theater in a good month."[66] When visiting cities like Chicago, Milwaukee, or Philadelphia, in pivotal states, he would drop in at Hispanic festivals and parties, sometimes joining in singing "The Star-Spangled Banner" in Spanish, sometimes partying with a "Viva Bush" mariachi band flown in from Texas.

The Republican convention itself featured speeches by Colin Powell, Condoleezza Rice, and half-Hispanic nephew George P. Bush; blind mountain climber Erik Weihenmayer leading the convention in the Pledge of Allegiance; words from Nancy Goodman Brinker, founder of the Susan G. Komen Breast Cancer Clinic; and a first-night theme of "Opportunity with a Purpose: Leave No Child Behind." Cynics bemoaned what they saw as new heights of orchestration-cum-artificiality, and the mere 8 percent of the national black vote that Bush received in 2000—down from Dole's 14 percent in 1996 and his father's 12 percent in 1992—suggested that the happy talk and camera focus on advisers Powell and Rice counted for very little with the constituency at which it was directed.

The 31 percent Bush won among Hispanics represented more of a breakthrough. Helpful factors included his ethnic outreach in Texas, and his close relations with Mexican president Vicente Fox and their serious conversations about amnesty for illegal Mexican immigrants (a plan Bush would abandon after 9/11). In addition, both Bush brothers, as governors of Texas and Florida, spoke Spanish and had been building Hispanic appointees and elected officials into their state Republican machines. Blacks were not strategically vital; Hispanics were. Here was realpolitik at work. There was nothing particularly Hispanic or Catholic about the religious and cultural tenor of George W. Bush's "compassionate conservatism"; the religious part of that message was essentially Protestant.

In fact, his appeals to Catholics lacked sophistication or sensitivity. In a commencement address at Notre Dame in May 2001, Bush invoked "God's special concern for the poor" and cited what "the late Dorothy Day [a Catholic social activist] called the 'weapons of the spirit.'" He had misspoken, because in identifying these "weapons," Day had been referring to a voluntary renunciation of possessions. She had also insisted upon "just distribution of wealth [as] a central point in Catholic social doctrine."[67] Day's daughter and granddaughter subsequently accused White House speechwriters of distorting her words in "their arsenal of deceit."[68]

In practical, which is to say electoral, terms, "compassionate conservatism" was oriented toward white Protestants and directed at a national audience, although most appreciated in the South. By underscoring the importance of a compassion that did not come from the government, George W. reached far beyond the charitable-donation constituency so important to previous Bush generations. To the realigning Southern Baptists, fundamentalists and evangelicals in particular, the social welfare programs implemented by government—and also unpopular judicial rulings on racial integration, religion, and abortion—had by the 1980s become resented as *undercutters* of personal responsibility, not upholders. This occurred, conservative theorists argued, because the liberal sociology suffusing the social programs launched in the 1960s had promoted welfarism and weakened commitment to self-help on the part of the poor and uneducated.

In such circumstances, self-identified evangelicals were far more likely than other voters to reject government programs and to insist that free will gave everyone equal opportunity to make something of him- or herself. If blacks or welfare mothers did not take advantage of the opportunity or if the rich did too well, those outcomes were individual, not structural.[69] Government, to be helpful, should uphold personal religion and morality. In response, as the Southern Baptist Convention passed under conservative (and Republican) leadership in the 1990s, yearly resolutions that had once addressed structural problems of society—hunger, help for the poor, welfare, or support for family farms—now gave way to "personal responsibility" resolutions disapproving of abortion, homosexuality, television or movie content, and the moral quality of Bill Clinton's presidency.[70]

For George W. Bush, this change in focus presented a multiple opportunity. During his 1994 campaign for the Texas statehouse, he swung the redesigned welfare issue as the political broadsword his father never had—a style that allowed him to be both tough and caring, reflective yet aggressive, by urging Texans to turn to God (in the form of "faith-based programs") rather than rely on government.[71] By 1997, preparing for a presidential campaign, he grasped how the same welfare and personal-responsibility theme could be enlarged to defuse discussions of his own potentially embarrassing pre-1986 wastrel period. He would run as a compassionate conservative, rooting his ideology in his own mid-1980s rescue by religion and religiously imbued personal responsibility. By the winter of 1999–2000, the press had picked up on the new phrase book: ". . . compassionate conservative; if I knew the law that could make people love each other, I'd sign it right now."[72] His inauguration further expanded the lexicon: "Compassion is the work of a nation, not just a government; every day we are called to do small things with great love."

Among more secular electorates, principally in the North, rhetoric about personal responsibility and a conservatism that would deliver compassion through faith-based organizations struck less of a chord. To many, it seemed profoundly hypocritical. The new president's ideological offensive in the spring of 2001, proposing legislation that abolished the inheritance tax, cut income tax brackets, slammed organized labor, further deregulated the electricity industry, weakened occupational safety, and reversed election-year pledges to curb carbon dioxide emissions, seemed on its face to be the very opposite of compassionate governance.

Not surprisingly, as Bush poised himself against an international "Axis of Evil" in addition to Al Qaeda terrorism, even his domestic rhetoric became more religious and biblical. His January 2001 inaugural address had included ten religious references in a fifteen-minute speech.[73] By the early months of 2003, *Newsweek* ventured a chart identifying the religious and gospel messages in recent Bush speeches. Analyses in the *New York Times* and the *Washington Post* saw the president, to an unprecedented extent, casting "the full range of his agenda—foreign, domestic and economic—in spiritual terms."[74] His core Christian conservative constituency was delighted.

The Rise of Mayberry Machiavellianism

The same media spotlight, however, also focused on apparent contradictions in the messages. Many of the president's actions seemed surprisingly at odds with his promises. Some commentators suggested that Bush was acquiescing to congressional GOP abandonment of his supposed "compassion agenda." Still others assailed the fact that the federal budget for the 2004 fiscal year doomed compassion by building up deficits in order to fund upper-bracket tax cuts. By 2003, the president was also being flayed for his unwillingness to help the dozens of states being forced to slash educational, health, medical, and law enforcement outlays in the face of what was becoming the worst state fiscal crisis since World War II.

Two thousand two became the year in which commentators began to switch their attention from George W. Bush's flow of verbal gaffes—the fluffs about "misunderestimating" and trying to conduct "a winning victory," the mangled syntax of "Is our children learning?"—to his administration's repeated patterns of deceiving statements in its speechmaking. So insistently, for example, did he cloak his October 2001 economic "stimulus" proposals in terms of supposed job creation that when poll takers told focus groups about some of the actual components—nearly $700 million in tax rebates for General Electric and $250 million for Enron—many startled citizens simply refused to believe the actual facts.[75]

Bush strategists had borrowed "Leave no child behind," the catchphrase of the Children's Defense Fund, as a slogan for the 2000 GOP convention. Slightly rearranged, that phrase also became the official title of the president's education program. The fund, however, countered with an analysis demonstrating that the Bush tax cuts soaked up so many hundreds of billions that little would be left for education. Its president, Marian Wright Edelman, summed up: "The Bush Administration's words say 'Leave no child behind.' The Bush Administration's deeds say 'Leave no millionaire behind.' "[76]

In December 2002, White House press secretary Ari Fleischer disclosed that George W. Bush saw "education as the next civil rights movement." However, his education bill had already dropped the small school-voucher provision that he had promised in election year speeches to blacks.[77] When Congress passed a measure expanding support for nurse training, Labor Secretary Elaine Chao announced that "the Bush Administration has issued what I call 'a call to care.' " But the spending bills left out the funds, prompting cynics to scoff that "it's all just rhetoric."[78]

The centerpiece of Bush's faith-based proposal, mobilizing "Armies of Compassion" among religious and community service organizations, had begun with a huge $90 billion promise of giving charitable deductions to those who did not itemize tax returns. This was cut to $6 billion in late 2002 by an agreement between the White House and the Republican leadership of the House. Professor Robert Putnam of Harvard University, consulted by the White House, commented, "They talked a really good game, but in the end, the compassionate part of compassionate conservatism got omitted from the final calculation."[79] Even religious constituencies started to discern the deception that left pledges unfulfilled.

At the end of 2002, an examination by the *Washington Post* found that only one out of six "compassionate conservative" priorities had achieved meaningful success in Congress—the No Child Left Behind education legislation signed in January 2002. However, even that was put in some doubt by underfunding, as we have seen, and by federal budget director Mitchell Daniels's criticism of excessive education outlays. Meanwhile, state-level plans to rein in education spending were especially notable in the two Bush political bailiwicks. In Texas, a 2003 funding crisis pushed the state share of school financing to a fifty-year low, forcing major cutbacks. In Florida, which likewise ranked near the national bottom in per capita education spending, graduation rates, and SAT scores, Governor Jeb Bush was working to thwart an expensive school class-size reduction mandate passed by the voters in 2002.[80]

Increasingly aware of the disconnect between compassionate rhetoric and real-world action or funding, portions of the press corps took particular issue with Bush's 2003 State of the Union and budget messages, employing descriptions that ranged from "gulf of credibility" and "artful misdirection" to "surreal" and "bald-faced lie." David Broder, columnist for the *Washington Post,* marveled at the administration's commitment to $726 billion worth of upper-bracket-tilted tax cuts over ten years in the face of the education, mental health, scholarship, and law enforcement cuts taking shape as states prepared to deal with an estimated $80 billion revenue shortfall for the 2004 fiscal year. He concluded that "that nonchalance— the brush-off to nitpicking questions about the massive debt being handed to our children and grandchildren—is what makes the atmosphere in Washington so mind-boggling these days."[81]

The magazine *The American Prospect* trod harder in an article entitled "All the President's Lies," which, after listing examples, deplored the public's passivity in response to them. Comparing him to Johnson, Nixon, and Clinton, regarded by many as the principal fibbers of the last half century, the authors concluded that "George W. Bush is in a class by himself when it comes to prevarication. It is no exaggeration to say that lying has become Bush's signature as president."[82]

Untruthfulness, of course, was calculating rather than Christian, deceptive rather than doctrinal. In 2003, Wayne Slater, who had watched Governor Bush in Austin for the *Dallas Morning News,* published a book that, among other things, gave credit to political guru Karl Rove for one of the apparent guiding principles of Bush governance: namely, that "perception is reality." Rove was a great reader of Machiavelli, who was quoted as follows: "The great majority of mankind is satisfied with appearances, as though they were realities."[83]

In fact, Machiavelli was even harsher, calling deception and disguise essential to rulers. In *The Prince,* his most famous work, he lauded the success and effectiveness of the Borgia pope Alexander VI, "who did nothing else but deceive men."[84] He advised that "a prince must take great care that nothing goes out of his mouth which is not full of the above-named five qualities, and, to see and hear him, he should seem to be all mercy, faith, integrity, humanity and religion."[85] However, because "everybody sees what you appear to be, few feel what you are," a ruler can ignore the mob and devote himself to the interests of the ruling class, gulling the inert majority who constitute the ruled.[86] Borgia references aside, twenty-first-century American readers of *The Prince* may feel that they have stumbled on a thinly disguised Bush White House political memo.

Comparatively speaking, too few have measured the second Bush presidency alongside the first. *Time* writers Goodgame and Duffy, in their 1992 study of the George H. W. Bush administration, identified him in the very first paragraph as "remorselessly deceitful when it served his purpose."[87] They also found his domestic policy, as his son's would be, in thrall to political convenience: "What was remarkable about the Bush White House, however, was the rigor, clear-eyed cynicism and political self-interest that drove their domestic policy. . . . All of domestic policy was subordinated to the goal of Bush's re-election and almost everything that didn't fit was thrown overboard."[88] This may partly have reflected the influence of George H. W. Bush's chief political adviser, Lee Atwater; Rove, a friend, later recalled Atwater's saying that he reread *The Prince* every year.[89] A decade later, University of Pennsylvania professor John J. DiIulio, director of the White House Office of Faith-Based and Community Initiatives, resigned with a similar evaluation of the George W. Bush administration. He deplored "the reign of the Mayberry Machiavellis, in which everything— and I mean everything—[is] being run by the political arm. . . . There is no precedent in any modern White House for what is going on in this one: a complete lack of a policy apparatus."[90]

Alas, the reality is that there is all too much precedent: dynasties, by their very nature, tend toward inheritance and continuity. Despite the new overlay of evangelical Protestantism, the economic record of the forty-third president essentially extended the practice of the forty-first: favoring the small group of rich Americans while systematically misleading a much larger portion of the population.

CHAPTER 5

The Enron-Halliburton Administration

The Enron failure is the biggest political scandal in American history. Teapot Dome—a scandal about pay-offs to Secretary of the Interior Albert Fall by a couple of greedy oilmen—was memorable but involved very few people. The Watergate scandal was bigger and more pernicious, but it, too, involved relatively few people. . . . Enron was different. By the time of its bankruptcy, Enron owned—or perhaps was just renting—politicians in the White House, Congress, state courts, state legislatures, and bureaucrats at every level.

Robert Bryce, *Pipe Dreams,* 2002

Oil is high-profile stuff. Oil fuels military powers, national treasuries, and international politics. It is no longer a commodity to be bought and sold within the confines of traditional energy supply and demand balances. Rather it has been transformed into a determinant of well-being, of national security, and of international power.

Robert Ebel, Center for Strategic and International Studies, 2003

It is clear that everywhere there is oil there is Brown and Root [Halliburton]. But increasingly, everywhere there is war or insurrection there is Brown and Root also. From Bosnia and Kosovo, to Chechnya, to Rwanda, to Burma, to Pakistan, to Laos, to Vietnam, to Indonesia, to Iran to Libya to Mexico to Colombia, Brown and Root's traditional operations have expanded from heavy construction to include the provision of logistical support for the U.S. military.

Michael C. Ruppert, *From the Wilderness,* 2000

To the global energy industry and those who lobbied for it in Washington, the election of George W. Bush in 2000 brought a new set of dominant corporations, power alignments, and overseas entanglements. In an unprecedented pairing, both the president and the vice president of the United States were former energy company executives, products of upbringings in oil-centered cities like Houston, Midland, and Casper, Wyoming, and former heads of Texas-based oil services companies with ties to Bahrain, Kuwait, and shadowy Saudi Arabian families.

With their accession, national policymaking became more energy-centered, as did national security calculations and criteria. The overlap between oil services and military support activities expanded. The sole previous U.S. chief executive to have come from the oil or energy business had been the new president's father. But by the time George H. W. Bush reached the White House in 1989, his active participation in the industry was twenty-two years in the past. The Bush-Cheney pairing was fresher from industry and more intensely involved in the issues. In addition, 2001 also brought the first White House national security adviser, Condoleezza Rice, with a specialty in what had been Soviet Central Asia and a particularly strong oil industry background. A former Chevron director, Rice even had a company oil tanker named after her—a red-hulled, 129,000-ton, Bahamas-registered Suezmax behemoth.

For some eight months after the 2001 inauguration, two major Texas companies—Halliburton, run by Cheney since 1995, and Enron, closely linked to the latest two generations of Bushes—loomed especially large in capital calculations. Lobbyists expected the two firms' interests to both influence and signal administration policy. Focal points included fuller deregulation of U.S. energy markets, repeal of the Public Utility Holding Company Act, commoditization of both natural gas and electricity marketing, closer U.S.-Russian oil collaboration, intensified commitment to U.S. control of Iraqi and Caspian oil supplies, and large-scale privatization of support functions hitherto performed by the U.S. military (ranging from energy procurement to war-zone logistics). There was also an ambitious, even imperial, trade agenda aimed at empowering the World Trade Organization to regulate the global trade in energy and utility services. Within the Washington-based Coalition of Service Industries, Enron and Halliburton had been the driving U.S. proponents, anxious to pry open foreign markets for U.S. utility, pipeline, construction, and oil-field-service providers.

The collapse of Enron dashed short-term industry hopes for further deregulation and privatization, much as the administration's ability to take the point on Enron's behalf had ended in November 2001 as the noose of probable bankruptcy began to tighten. Halliburton's own agenda became controversial soon thereafter, moving to center stage in 2003 with the debate over government plans to award contracts to rebuild war- and sanctions-ravaged Iraq. At no time in recent memory had Washington faced an ethical conundrum over the influence generated by the recent corporate alliances and connections of both a president and a vice president.

The Bush Family and the Coming-of-Age of the U.S. Energy Industry

From a business standpoint, the energy industry involvements of George Herbert Walker, Samuel Bush, and Prescott Bush provided an important early backdrop for the two Bush presidents. High-level Walker-Bush family involvement in energy actually dates back four generations.

Samuel Bush, in his pre–World War I positions as president of Buckeye Steel Castings and as director of several Ohio and Pennsylvania railroads, had worked closely with the Rockefellers' Ohio-bred Standard Oil. The latter held a large minority interest in Buckeye, and insisted that all the railroads hauling Standard's large oil shipments purchase their couplers and related equipment from Buckeye. Well managed and with powerful friends, the Bush-run firm prospered and became the most up-to-date steel mill of its type in the United States.[1] More than most businessmen who were his contemporaries, Samuel Bush understood the extent to which oil was a rapidly accelerating force in U.S industrial development.

George Herbert Walker, through his own St. Louis firm, had bought and resold the Missouri-based Laclede Gas Company in the first decade of the twentieth century. Then, between 1919 and 1930, as president of New York–based W. A. Harriman and Company, Walker served as a director of Petroleum Bond and Share and, more important, was closely involved with Harriman's Russian oil investment company, the major postwar redeveloper of the war- and revolution-torn Baku oil fields in the Soviet Caucasus.

This was the Barnsdall Corporation, which was jointly owned by Harriman and Company, Boston-based Lee Higginson, and the Guaranty Trust.[2] In the early and mid-1920s, it rebuilt and modernized the Baku fields— which as recently as 1900 had made Russia the world's top oil producer— in close alliance with the American International Corporation. The latter, formed in 1915, had influence in Bolshevik Russia through its status as an overseas investment and political relations vehicle of the New York financial community, and is a subject to which we will return in chapter 6.

Walker served for some years as a director of both Barnsdall and the American International Corporation.[3] In the mid-1920s, the president of American International, Matthew C. Brush, was simultaneously the president of Barnsdall and of Georgian Manganese, Averell Harriman's other mineral enterprise in the Soviet Caucasus. He was also a director of W. A. Harriman Securities and chairman of its finance committee.[4]

Besides Barnsdall, the Harriman firm's other major between-the-wars venture into the world of petroleum came through oil services, via its 1929 purchase and reorganization of Dresser Manufacturing (the future Dresser Industries), at that point still headquartered in Bradford, near the original U.S. oil district in northwestern Pennsylvania. From 1930 to 1952, Brown Brothers Harriman's supervision of Dresser was handled by its managing partner Prescott Bush, working through his Yale classmate, Neil Mallon, installed as Dresser's president. Bush would later describe his role as a board member thus: "I was Neil Mallon's chief adviser and consultant in connection with every move that he made."[5]

During the 1930s, Bush's challenge didn't go much beyond helping Dresser dig out of the Depression. There was none of the glamour his father-in-law had found in 1920s Europe and Russia. That was confined to the international oil companies, whose quasi-governmental role was described by Anthony Sampson in *The Seven Sisters*: "To radical critics, it looked as if the State Department had simply abdicated the whole process of oil diplomacy to the oilmen. The government, however much they might distrust the oilmen, were not prepared to set up their own organization. They preferred to use the oil companies, at a discreet distance, as the instruments of national security and foreign policy."[6]

As we will see, World War II finished what World War I had begun in underscoring the national security importance of the availability of oil supplies. New pipelines were built from Texas to the East Coast to avoid having to ship fuel through coastal waters menaced by enemy submarines. In 1943, as FDR allocated Lend-Lease funds to shore up the Persian Gulf, he got a five-decade jump on two gulf wars by proclaiming, "I hereby find that the defense of Saudi Arabia is vital to the defense of the United States."[7] When the war was over, major international oil companies like Esso, Mobil, Texaco, and Gulf, still New York– or Pittsburgh-based at midcentury, would become even closer to Washington policymakers and intelligence agencies than they had been in the 1930s.

As the world went to war in 1939, Dresser prospered, and the term "oil services" soon became too narrow to describe what the company actually did. Under Mallon and Bush (whose closeness to Mallon continued after he went to the U.S. Senate), Dresser provided the Defense Department and a number of other federal agencies with highly specialized and highly classified products: pumps for gaseous diffusion used in developing the atomic bomb, M69X incendiary bombs dropped on Tokyo, radar towers for the postwar DEW (distant early warning) line across Canada and Alaska, spiraxial compressors for nuclear submarines, launcher buildings for BOMARC missiles, and radioactivity monitors for nuclear attack missile-tracking systems.[8] Under Mallon-Bush guidance, Dresser, relatively small as it was, could properly be considered a component of the "national security–industrial complex."

Not surprisingly, this World War II and cold war stage of the energy industry's deepening connections to national security, aerospace, government services, and overseas construction contracts brought Prescott Bush's New York and Washington influence to the fore. He was doubtless a millionaire, probably worth $5 million to $10 million when he died. However, oil as a commodity had not been a principal contributor to his wealth; his vocation lay more with oil's interface with national security. George H. W. Bush, following his father's lead, likewise seems to have most enjoyed the financial and international side of the energy business—consider Zapata Offshore, for example, with its deep-sea rigs, international subsidiaries and tax angles, and tropical breezes of foreign intrigue off Cuban and Arabian shores.

Nevertheless, George H. W. declined to return to the oil business after leaving the CIA and government service in 1977. On becoming vice president in 1981, he had a net worth of only $2.1 million.[9] In 1962–63, just short of age forty, he had yielded to the greater lure of politics and international affairs. Partly in consequence, when he took up the vice presidency, he was not a major force in the oil industry, either in Texas or nationally.

For Texans, petrodollars have usually been *the* yardstick of success. Back in the 1930s, most of the nation's large oil-related fortunes were a generation old, eastern-held, and amassed from oil fields in Pennsylvania and Ohio, the Texas Gulf Coast, and Oklahoma. That profile changed when the oil price increases of 1973–81 propelled a handful of oil-rich Texas families to even higher levels of affluence. In 1982, following several years of sky-high oil prices, the upper tier of U.S. wealth, as profiled in the first annual survey of the Forbes 400 richest Americans, was top-heavy enough with oil money, much of it Texan, to constitute a virtual Petroleum Club of the United States.

Just below the leading oil fortunes of the Rockefellers (Standard Oil) and Mellons (Gulf) came the richest of the Texas-California operators: the Gettys, Hunts, Basses, and Cullens. Down a bit, Philip Anschutz, Marvin Davis, and the Koch family crowded around the billion-dollar mark. Cyril Wagner and Jack Brown had about $500 million. The oil-holding Texans whom George H. W. Bush knew best—Robert Mosbacher, William S. Farish III, Hugh Liedtke, et al.—were rich but considerably further down the rankings. The Bushes themselves had no particular oil industry, as opposed to political, stature.

Upon his inauguration as vice president in 1981, George H. W. set out to change that. Tentatively the Republican heir apparent to Reagan, he began burnishing his oil industry credentials. In the early 1950s, Prescott Bush had made friends along the Gulf Coast—and perhaps even a future client or two for his son's 1950s and 1960s offshore drilling rig business—by Washington politicking. As a senator, he had backed the sovereignty of states like Texas, Louisiana, and Mississippi over the submerged offshore oil deposits of the continental shelf against the competing claims of the federal government. The policy focus chosen by George H. W. Bush in the 1980s would turn out to be even more timely and opportune: *energy deregulation.*

Helped by his chairmanship of Reagan administration task forces on deregulation and regulatory relief, the vice president from Houston turned this topic into a two-decade political framework. Through it, both Bushes, during multiple terms in the White House and six years in the Texas statehouse, recast their political and financial relationship with the energy industry. Simultaneously, deregulation meant enormous change for the energy sector itself. In the end, which side did more for the other—the dynasty or the industry—is hard to determine. This is partly because so many political, regulatory, and financial details have been lost or remain unobtainable.

Another Houston resident who had likewise set his sights on the commercial opportunities to come in the wake of energy deregulation was Kenneth Lay. After spending time in Republican Washington in the 1970s on the staff of the Federal Power Commission and then in the Interior Department as a deputy undersecretary for energy, Lay moved on to a series of increasingly senior jobs at Florida Gas, Transco Energy, and then Houston Natural Gas, where he became president. InterNorth, an Omaha-based pipeline company, bought the Houston concern in 1985 in an arranged, friendly acquisition. Within a year, the combined businesses had a new name, Enron—and a new chief executive, Ken Lay.

In 1986 and 1987, from their respective corporate and governmental perches, Lay and George H. W. Bush were considering essentially similar subject matter: the early implications (and complications) of the piecemeal 1984–86 federal deregulation of the natural gas industry, the rewarding improvements that might be made, and, further out, a prospective bold deregulation of the larger $250 billion annual U.S. market for electricity. The deregulation and commoditization of natural gas and electricity was on a par with perhaps only one other policy venture—the hot pursuit of Iraqi or Caspian oil reserves—and was bound to reshape the U.S. energy sector. With a presidential election coming up, it was logical enough that politics and deregulation should be drawn together.

The Bush Dynasty and the Rise of Enron

Enron and George H. W. Bush were hardly the first corporation and president to find advantage in each other. Richard Nixon was close to Pepsico, which he had represented as a lawyer. Atlanta-based Coca-Cola had good access to Jimmy Carter's White House. And one biographer noted of Lyndon Johnson that "if Lyndon was Brown & Root's kept politician, Brown & Root was Lyndon's kept corporation."[10]

On its own, George H. W. Bush's connection to Enron would not nearly have matched Johnson's to Brown and Root. What makes the Bush-Enron connection more significant is its dynastic aspect—the mutual support over two decades, two generations, and two presidencies.

George H. W. Bush and Ken Lay seem to have first met in 1980. After being introduced by mutual friends in the energy business, Lay contributed to Bush's quest for the presidential nomination.[11] During the early and mid-1980s, Lay came to Washington frequently on natural-gas-related issues and occasionally met with Vice President Bush.[12] In 1984, Lay served as the Harris County (Houston) chairman of a one-thousand-dollar-a-plate Reagan-Bush fund-raiser, and by 1985–86, perhaps not surprisingly, the company that was metamorphosing into Enron had established some minor oil and gas business ties to Spectrum 7, the firm run by George W. Bush.

It is not clear whether either principal, George W. Bush or Lay, would have known of these small partnership interests. However, the younger Bush would later be disingenuous when he claimed that he first came to know Lay in 1994. By March 2002, White House communications director Dan Bartlett admitted to the *Chicago Tribune* that George W.'s relationship with Lay probably started in 1987 and 1988, when Bush was in Washington working on his father's presidential campaign, but it could have been earlier.[13]

What seems obvious is that by election day of 1988, the relationship between Ken Lay and the Bush family was more than cordial. In that year's presidential campaign, Lay had been a Bush donor, but not a top one—not a member of Team 100. The stronger bond may have been between Lay and George W. Bush, who were closer in age and appear to have had by then some commercial relationship. The *Tribune's* research into Bush's personal oil and gas holdings and royalties at the time of his gubernatorial inauguration in 1995 turned up an interesting pair of wells in a Sonora, Texas, field. Although the wells were imprecisely described in Bush's ethics filing, it appears that their gas production was being sold to Enron.[14] In any event, back in 1988–89, Lay had been looking for Washington assistance in his pursuit of grand objectives both at home and abroad.

His ambitions to make Enron into the first great international utility, pipeline, and energy-trading company involved three initial objectives: (1) negotiating for and then constructing a huge electricity cogeneration plant in England (Teesside), where the Conservative government of Margaret Thatcher was deregulating gas and electricity; (2) arranging chemical and pipeline contracts in Argentina; and (3) opening up access to loans and insurance from the World Bank, the U.S. Export-Import Bank, and the Overseas Private Investment Corporation (OPIC). The imprimatur of federal financing would be critical for Lay to achieve his global dreams. In several of these areas, the Bushes were able to lend their assistance.

Just weeks after the 1988 election, it was George W. Bush who called Rodolfo Terragno, Argentina's minister of public works, the official overseeing the bidding for a major gas pipeline. "He told me he had recently returned from a campaign tour with his father," Terragno later recalled to reporter Lou Dubose. Awarding the pipeline deal to Enron, Bush reportedly said, "would be very favorable for Argentina and its relations with the United States."[15] The Argentine government changed in 1989, however, and Enron did not get its stake in the Argentine pipeline system until 1992. What the company did get in 1989, however, was its vital stamp of approval from OPIC, which provided $56 million in loans and insurance for a chemical plant in Argentina. Ratification of a project by OPIC's board of directors—in confidential deliberations not subject to the Freedom of Information Act—sent an important signal to the private-sector financial markets: Enron had government backing. (It would in fact become one of OPIC's biggest clients.) Access to the Export-Import Bank and Inter-American Development Bank would soon follow.

The White House also gave Lay two other internationally helpful nods of approbation: In mid-1990, Bush chose the Enron chief to organize that year's G-7 Economic Summit in Houston, and later that same year he named him to the President's Export Council. Whether or not these were decisive factors, in November 1990, following two years of spadework, Enron secured British government approval for the $1.6 billion Teesside project. It became the first independent plant approved in the United Kingdom, and John Wakeham, Britain's secretary of state for energy, later became an Enron board member.[16]

Completed in 1993, the Teesside plant made Enron's name in the international power business, and many other projects would follow. One of them, to which we will return, was the $2.9 billion Dabhol power plant near Bombay, India, assented to by the Maharashtra State Electricity Board in July 1992. Nine years later, Dabhol's growing unpopularity in India would be among the straws that helped to break Enron's corporate back.

Lay was no less involved domestically. In 1992, he lauded the elder Bush as "the energy president," recalling that "just six months after George Bush became president, he directed Energy Secretary James Watkins to lead the development of a new energy strategy," which eventually grew into the Energy Act of 1992.[17] Well might Lay exult. This act, which mandated the deregulation of electricity at the wholesale level, also obliged utilities to carry privately marketed electricity (like Enron's) on their wires and permitted states to deregulate retail electricity. Transmission lines, in short, became common carriers. It was one of several breakthroughs that made possible Enron's exponential growth during the 1990s.

As could be expected, Enron and its executives labored mightily for George H. W. Bush's reelection in 1992. Lay, this time around a major donor, was named cochairman of the Bush reelection committee, as well as chairman of that summer's Republican National Convention (to which Enron also contributed $250,000). After Bush lost, Lay and George W. Bush spent some time unsuccessfully trying to get the George H. W. Bush presidential library to locate in Houston. In the meantime, Enron needed another favor in Washington—and quickly.

Under legislation already on the books, the Commodity Futures Trading Commission (CFTC) was empowered to regulate exchange-traded futures contracts and exempt ordinary commercial futures. In the arcane world of energy trading, however, differentiation between the two was becoming more complicated. What Enron wanted—and on November 16, 1992, requested by petition—was a ruling that defined energy derivative contracts and interest rate swaps, two prime trading vehicles, in a way that *excluded* them from CFTC oversight.

Normally, this sort of reformulation would have involved a lengthy process and been unlikely to succeed. But with two of the five seats on the commission temporarily vacant, CFTC chairwoman Wendy Gramm— wife of Enron-friendly Texas Republican U.S. senator Phil Gramm—was in a position to initiate the rule-making process, cut short the usual yearlong examination, and speed the decision through before Bill Clinton was inaugurated and new appointees were named. This she did, and on January 14, 1993, the commission voted 2–1 to grant Enron's request. A week later, Wendy Gramm resigned from the CFTC, and roughly a month afterward she was named to Enron's board of directors. For this, her compensation between 1993 and 2001 was calculated by Public Citizen at between $915,000 and $1,853,000.[18]

In a nutshell—a very fat, rich nutshell—the CFTC exemption allowed Enron to set up its own, unfettered in-house derivatives exchange without being regulated like a Wall Street firm or complying with the requirements of the New York Mercantile Exchange or the Chicago Board of Trade. This side of Enron's business quickly expanded, rising 30 percent in 1993 and ballooning by the decade's end.

Mrs. Gramm was not the only former Bush administration official to be signed up by Enron. In February 1993, Lay announced that outgoing secretary of state James Baker and outgoing secretary of commerce Robert Mosbacher had agreed "to join us in the development of natural gas projects around the world," a business-seeking odyssey that would sweep from the Persian Gulf to China, from Latin America to Turkmenistan. Under a joint consulting and investing arrangement, Baker and Mosbacher (who had earlier been an Enron director) were to participate financially in the deals they arranged. Although Enron never disclosed any figures, each must have banked millions—perhaps many millions.

On one trip that Baker and former president Bush took to Kuwait in 1993, two of George H. W.'s sons, Marvin and Neil, tagged along as lobbyists. According to reporter Seymour Hersh, Neil tried to sell the Kuwaitis not only on Enron's bid to rebuild the Ushaiba power plant, which was damaged in the first Gulf War, but on a management contract that, after various corporate twists and turns, would yield proceeds to a company in which the young Bush had an interest.[19]

During the Clinton years, to be sure, Enron steered almost $2 million to Democratic causes, partly so that Lay and other executives could participate in business-seeking junkets run by the Clinton Commerce Department under Secretary Ron Brown and, more important, to maintain the firm's warm welcome at the Export-Import Bank and the Overseas Private Investment Corporation, where it secured several billions of dollars of loans and insurance.[20] However, Enron retained its GOP bias, favoring the Republicans by three to one in congressional contributions for the 1990s. On the presidential level, Lay's own commitment was firmly Republican. During the contest for the 1996 GOP nomination, he served as a regional chairman for Texas's own Senator Phil Gramm, who was also endorsed by Governor George W. Bush.

In the meantime, close Bush relations with Chairman Lay had resumed as the 1994 Texas gubernatorial race approached. When George W. asked the Enron chief to be his top Houston fund-raiser, Lay turned that responsibility over to Richard Kinder, his president and chief operating officer. Lay, Kinder, and other Enron executives ultimately donated $146,500 to Bush, almost seven times what they gave to incumbent Democrat Ann Richards.[21]

When Bush won, Lay immediately began lobbying him on state issues ranging from taxes and tort reform to deregulation. In December of 1994, he asked the governor-elect to name Patrick Wood, a supporter of deregulating electric utilities, to head the Texas Public Utility Commission, which Bush did once inaugurated. In other areas, too, policymaking seemed to have returned to the happy Washington collaboration of 1988 to 1992. As governor, Bush no longer telephoned Latin American public works ministers on Enron's behalf, but he did receive occasional visitors at Lay's request, including one from Uzbekistan after Enron had opened an office in Tashkent and was negotiating a joint venture.[22]

In formulating his major overhaul of Texas state taxes, Bush seems to have been very much influenced by Enron. Company president Richard Kinder served on the seventeen-member committee that recommended a $3 billion program easing taxes on capital-intensive industries (like natural gas and petrochemicals) and making up the revenue in part by shifting the burden onto services and professionals.

Other important early guidance on tax policy seems to have come from former deputy treasury secretary Charls Walker, an old friend of Lay's. Walker's brother Pinkney, an economist and former member of the Federal Power Commission, had been the Enron chief's original Washington mentor. Charls Walker, himself a longtime Enron director and lobbyist, doubled as the chairman of the American Council for Capital Formation, a Washington group funded by capital-intensive industries, including Texaco, Shell, Exxon, and Enron. Although Bush's tax package failed in the legislature in 1997, it followed the Enron-Walker outline, and one reporter noted that "his willingness to advocate Walker's position indicates the kind of consideration Bush gave to Enron's point of view."[23]

On the international front, meanwhile, the Dabhol plant project—far and away the biggest foreign investment India had ever allowed—had been followed by a dozen other ventures, making Enron the closest thing to a global utility and energy-trading firm. Besides building a natural gas and electricity market in Europe, Enron also owned all or portions of power plants in Latin America (Brazil, the Dominican Republic, Guatemala, Nicaragua, and Panama), as well as in India, China, the Philippines, Guam, and Turkey; natural gas pipelines in Argentina, Bolivia, Brazil, and Colombia; and the Elektro electric utility and transmission grid in Brazil.[24]

The speed and success of this huge agglomeration can be explained in two words: crony capitalism. Over the course of a single decade, government agencies, both American and foreign, gave Enron $7.2 billion in publicly funded financing for thirty-eight projects in twenty-nine countries. The World Bank provided $760 million but also aided Enron's cause by pressuring third-world countries to privatize their economies. In the words of one report, "The World Bank would issue loans for the privatization of the energy or the power sector in a developing country and make this a condition of further loans, and Enron would be among the first, and often the most successful, bidders to enter the country's newly privatized or deregulated energy markets." The U.S. Export-Import Bank and Overseas Private Investment Corporation together funded twenty-five Enron power projects with $3.7 billion in loans and insurance. The Inter-American Development Bank loaned $751 million, and the Asian Development Bank, $26 million. Nations, development banks, and agencies elsewhere in the world produced an additional $1.9 billion to support Enron expansion.[25]

Domestically, Enron's sales and profits appeared to be doubling every few years during the mid-nineties as energy and futures deregulation opened novel opportunities for trading, marketing, and speculation. At the end of 1993, there were only 11 power-marketing companies or "merchants" in the United States; by early 1995, there were 60; and by early 1997, there were 284—and Enron was the biggest. Wholesale-type marketing of power to industrial customers got the commercial ball rolling, after which retail deregulation at the state level speeded evolution in the marketplace.

California was the first to open its electricity market, in early 1998, and six more states followed by early 1999. By late 2000, the tally had grown to twenty-four states.[26] The volume of electricity traded nationally climbed slowly in 1995 and 1996, followed in 1997 by a surge that somewhat paralleled the speculative bubbling of the NASDAQ stock market index. One can reasonably hypothesize, in somewhat similar terms, a turn-of-the-century energy marketing and trading bubble.

Besides trumpeting Enron-modeled electricity deregulation in Texas, George W. threw his support behind the company's nationwide lobbying campaign to restructure and open up as many other states as possible. In 1997, Bush telephoned Pennsylvania governor Tom Ridge to convince him that the state would benefit by letting Enron and the marketers in. Shortly thereafter, Pennsylvania deregulated. In Texas, where some officials did not agree with the Enron blueprint, Lay himself got involved. According to Enron lobbyist George Strong, "We'd call Houston and ask Lay to call the governor and explain our position." Other corporate executives had access to Bush, Strong said, "but from the Houston standpoint, Lay had better access to Bush than just about anybody."[27] The legislature eventually passed electricity deregulation in 1999.

By the end of the 1990s, the Houston firm had become a major political power in Texas and Washington alike. Beginning in 1993, Enron climbed to the top of the list of corporate federal campaign contributors in the energy–natural resource sector, giving a total of $5.3 million to federal candidates from 1993 to 2001—40 percent more than the number two company on the list.[28] In 1999 and 2000, Enron's in-house lobbyists spent $3.4 million promoting a deregulation agenda in Congress, and the salaries of those registered came to nearly $1.6 million.[29] At its peak, the company's Washington office staff was over one hundred strong, including former aides to House majority leader Dick Armey and the wife of House majority whip Tom DeLay. When this kind of money spoke, national and state legislators listened.

Enron also poured money into home-state politics. During the 1997–98 and 1999–2000 election cycles, the firm moved $1,003,273 to Texas political action committees and state politics, as well as spending $4.8 million on eighty-nine Texas lobby contracts.[30] Of the money spent on state candidates, George W. Bush got $238,000; Lieutenant Governor Rick Perry, $187,000; and Attorney General John Cornyn, $158,000. Texas also elects judges, and justices of the Texas Supreme Court received $134,058 from Enron between 1993 and 2000, making it the court's single largest corporate donor.[31] The bulk of these outlays, virtually all to Republicans, came in 1996, the year that the justices would reverse a lower court decision, thereby slashing $15 million off the inventory taxes that Enron owed to the Spring, Texas, school district.[32]

During the 1997–2000 election cycles, Enron, like other power merchants, maximized its contributions to local candidates in states where statewide electricity deregulation was in the forefront of debate. The industry totals for the two cycles were roughly $20 million. No comprehensive nationwide total was released for Enron alone, but the National Institute on Money in State Politics found that in the 1999–2000 cycle, the firm gave more than $419,000 to local candidates in nineteen states. The spigot was especially wide open in three: California ($142,880) and Texas ($107,650), states that had enacted deregulation; and Florida ($67,000), which was studying the idea.[33]

By 2000, federal issues were once again on Enron's front burner. Trouble was brewing in India, where Lay needed assistance from Washington to pressure the Indian government to pay for a Dabhol project that, after Enron outlays of $900 million, had worn out its welcome. There were multiple reasons for the plant's failure: alleged company human rights violations; electricity production that was so expensive the Indians stopped paying; the bankruptcy of the local state utility board; and refusal by the World Bank to support Enron. Without help and luck, the project could well be a write-off.

In California, where electricity deregulation was off to a rocky start, a supportive Federal Energy Regulatory Commission might soon be vital in upholding the practices of Enron and the other power merchants. On the dicey futures-trading front, Lay was pushing for a full federal deregulation that would exclude companies like Enron from both the Commodity Exchange Act and the not-always-clear jurisdiction of the Commodity Futures Trading Commission. Last but hardly least, hundreds of the hidden subsidiaries and partnerships set up to camouflage Enron's debt and inflate its profits—soon-to-be-famous entities like Chewco, Osprey, and LJM Cayman L.P.—were based in the Cayman Islands, a prominent overseas tax haven. This secrecy was threatened by the Clinton administration's proposal to apply economic sanctions to tax havens that did not reform their disclosure procedures before July 2001.

For all these reasons, Enron made its biggest-ever effort on behalf of a White House candidacy. Lay and Enron combined would provide George W. Bush's biggest contribution, with Vinson and Elkins, Enron's Houston law firm, not too far behind. Enron aircraft were placed at Bush's disposal, although the cost of their use had to be reimbursed by his campaign. Lay became one of Bush's early "Pioneers"—fund-raisers who had raised $100,000 or more—and Enron and its executives also gave $713,200 to the Republican National Committee.[34]

Indeed, the fruits of the larger reach of Enron influence—donations to George W. Bush in 2000 by the Texas energy firm's bankers, investors, insurers, and accountants—were also juicy, although these contributors had other reasons for giving. A subsequent study of U.S. donations in the 2000 campaign compiled in Enron-loathing India found that fully half of Bush's twenty largest donors had major ties to Enron.[35]

When the election wound up in the courts, Lay doubtless breathed a sigh of relief as the Bushes called in the A-Team: James A. Baker III, the ex–secretary of state who had traveled the world for Enron, and his long-time lieutenant, Robert Zoellick, also an Enron adviser. Baker and Zoellick, sometimes called "Baker's Second Brain," earned their pay, and it was later revealed that Enron had been a major contributor to funding the Republican support team in the Florida recount.

In Texas, Enron had provided $50,000 for the 1995 Bush gubernatorial inaugural and a second $50,000 for the 1999 follow-up. For the 2001 festivities in Washington, Ken Lay's apparent money machine produced $300,000. When the ceremonies were over and the Bush White House opened for business on Tuesday morning, Enron may have had more influence than any single company had previously commanded in a new administration. The surprise was that it turned out not to be enough.

Bush II and the Collapse of Enron

The hubris at Enron during the winter of 2000–2001 involved much more than high expectations of White House helpfulness. The company itself was tracing a cometlike path across the business rankings in publications like *Fortune, Forbes,* and *Business Week.* Between 1998 and 2000, Enron's annual sales jumped from $31 billion to $101 billion, and then reached $139 billion during just the first nine months of 2001. That put it fifth on the Fo tune 500 list for 2001, trailing only Wal-Mart, ExxonMobil, General Motors, and Ford. At the same time several other energy merchants—American Electric Power, El Paso, and Duke—also jumped into the top twenty. The transactions involved in achieving this success were not quite like sales as understood at other companies, but that was a quibble. In 2000, Enron president Jeffrey Skilling had suggested that before long, his company would be number one in the United States and in the world.

As George W. Bush announced his new appointments in the first few months of 2001, three departmental and agency clusters would have been of most interest to Enron. Energy regulatory positions led the list. Lay himself was one of five Bush Pioneers from the energy industry who were named to the Energy Department transition team. Including Lay, three of the five were Texans. Vice President Cheney, Texas-based since 1995, was picked to head the administration's energy policy task force.

Patrick Wood, Lay's handpicked chairman of the Texas Public Utilities Commission, was appointed to the Federal Energy Regulatory Commission in May, becoming chairman in August—the federal-level equivalent of his Texas position. Once again, Lay was his sponsor. Nora Mead Brownell, a Pennsylvania regulator who had supported Enron in that state's deregulation brouhaha, was also named as a FERC commissioner. Lay's third request, also granted, was the appointment of Glenn L. McCullough to be chairman of the Tennessee Valley Authority (TVA), an important agency in the Southeast. With more than two dozen hydroelectric dams and power plants under its jurisdiction, the TVA was reported to have "a terrible relationship with Enron due to a dispute over huge electricity contracts Enron did not want to fulfill."[36]

Appointments relating to international commerce and trade were a second focal point. As with the Energy Department, Enron enjoyed representation in the Commerce Department transition team. Donald Evans, the new secretary, was a Texas oilman and old friend of the president, and well aware of the company's place in the Bush universe. Theodore Kassinger, the department's new general counsel, was a former Enron adviser from the Houston law firm of Vinson and Elkins. More important, the new U.S. trade representative, the man who would have to get global energy services into the World Trade Organization framework so that Lay and his associates could push into more overseas markets, was Robert Zoellick. In the previous Bush administration he had been undersecretary of state for economic affairs; more recently he had been on Enron's Advisory Board and a research scholar at Harvard's Enron-aided Belfer Center for Science and International Affairs. Zoellick, too, understood the stakes.

The third arena of Enron's federal ambition was privatization—the expanding list of services and functions that government was considering contracting out. The military was privatizing some functions, one of which was providing for the services' energy needs. For secretary of the army, Bush nominated former army brigadier general Thomas White, who in his most recent incarnation had been vice chairman of Enron Energy Services.

Appointments to the board of the Commodity Futures Trading Commission became less of a priority a month before the inauguration, thanks largely to the legislative skill of Texas senator Phil Gramm, whose wife had displayed so much kindred regulatory collaboration eight years earlier. In December 2000, Gramm spearheaded a successful effort to implement a new round of commodity deregulation—this time of the *trading* of energy futures, not just the futures themselves—in a rushed-through appropriations bill, where the provision avoided scrutiny. The benefits to Enron—and the drawbacks for consumers—were quickly felt, foes claimed, because the company was able to enlarge its speculative presence in the electricity markets. These additional distortions helped to plunge deregulated California into a monthlong stretch of rolling blackouts.[37]

The critical locus of Enron support, of course, was in the White House itself, beginning with the president and vice president and extending to the chief political adviser and the chief economic adviser. The latter, Lawrence Lindsay, had been on the Enron Advisory Board for a year, absorbing the scripture of energy deregulation as preached by Baptist missionary Lay. Karl Rove, the political adviser, had a sizable block of company stock in his portfolio, but more to the point, he had a relationship with Enron not unlike Lyndon Johnson's with Brown and Root. According to former Texas Republican state chairman Tom Pauken, an old foe, the Austin-based Rove had been able to tell Enron who in Republican politics and opinion molding should get Enron money and who shouldn't. "The whole time I was chair," Pauken later recalled, "we didn't get any Enron money because Karl was close to those people and dissuaded them."[38] Elsewhere in the GOP, Marc Racicot, a former Montana governor and Bush friend turned Enron lobbyist, was chosen as Republican national chairman in 2001, replacing Jim Nicholson.

And in the new administration, if it wasn't Enron suasion, it was likely to be that of El Paso, Reliant, or Dynegy, three other firms with a large merchant business. White House personnel director Clay Johnson was a substantial El Paso shareholder; National Security Adviser Rice had been a director of Chevron, which owned 29 percent of Dynegy. Two successive chairmen of Houston-based Reliant, Don Jordan and Steve Ledbetter, were both Bush Pioneers, and the ubiquitous James Baker was a Reliant board member. What suited Enron in most cases also suited El Paso, Reliant, and Dynegy.

All these companies had been involved in the energy tremors and price spikes that followed California's deregulation of electricity in 1998, although Enron's role in shaping the legislation had been particularly visible. Deregulation had first triggered problems in the Midwest in 1998, when a heat wave brought price surges, which were aggravated when several merchant companies defaulted on their power contracts. National trading volume in electricity had just started to soar the previous year, and *Newsweek*'s Allan Sloan caught the Triassic ethos: Electric companies used to be "as exciting as watching cows graze. The herd members were ultra polite. They traded power back and forth, but no one gouged, because the guy you gouged today might be in a position to gouge you tomorrow. But since deregulation began in the electric biz a few years ago, a whole new bestiary has emerged. Bye bye cows. Hello, independent electricity traders: sharp-toothed velociraptors willing to bite, slash and maim to make a buck."[39]

A month after the 1998 Midwest episode, California prices also spiked, and Southern California Edison blamed two merchant companies, the AES Corporation, and Houston Industries, for trying to game the system to raise prices.[40] Moody's Investment Service warned that fragile finances could lead to more contract breaches by power traders.[41] By the winter of

2000–2001, Californians, facing a series of blackouts and price spikes up to fifty times normal, were seething. Deregulation advocates blamed environmental laws and the fact that the state's electricity market had been only partly deregulated. One member of Congress countered that "the model for full deregulation, Great Britain, has been plagued by price spikes, consumer gouging, service complaints and reliability problems as well. Even the British government has had to partially re-regulate to stem market manipulation and other abuses."[42]

Political strategists at Enron had been correct, by their lights, to want friends in charge at FERC to resist state demands for price caps. Besides this support from FERC officials, the president and vice president also insisted, through May and early June, that California prices would not be capped and that there would be no investigation of market manipulation. Not until June 18, after rolling blackouts and near blackouts had put the state in an uproar and forced Pacific Gas and Electric into bankruptcy, did FERC approve limited price caps, which quickly calmed the roiled markets.

While this wasn't quite the beginning of the end for Enron, it was at least the end of a spectacular beginning. For four years in a row, *Fortune* had picked Enron as America's most innovative company. Price caps, however, cut profits, which further reduced a cash flow already gutted by high debt and the swollen capital costs required to maintain liquidity in such varied trading markets. Problems with finished and unfinished foreign plants and pipelines also took their toll. Enron stock, which top executives were already quietly starting to unload, turned out to have hit its 2001 peak at around $80 shortly after Bush's inauguration; by June, it had fallen to $50. Earlier in the spring, a handful of increasingly skeptical Wall Street analysts had started to ask what really made Enron tick financially. Senior executives had their own silent worry: that the tick might be that of a time bomb.

How much the many Enron-wise officials in the administration—former Enron executives, advisers, consultants, attorneys, and investors by the dozen—grasped about what was developing is impossible to say. Clearly, Bush and Cheney followed Ken Lay's urgent pleas not to cap prices for as long as they could: about five months, despite the howls from California. Ultimately, it turned out that several power companies had indeed been manipulating the market, in Enron's case through strategies with provocative names like Death Star, Get Shorty, Fat Boy, and Ricochet.

In mid-May, Cheney's task force, the National Energy Policy Develop-

ment Group, released a legislative blueprint including a number of proposals in line with Enron recommendations: the creation of a national
electricity grid, the greater use of eminent domain to speed up construction of new electric power lines, the expediting of gas pipeline permits, the
creation of a market-based program for trading pollution credits, and a
recommendation that "the President direct the Secretaries of State and Energy to work with India's Ministry of Petroleum and Natural Gas to help
India maximize its domestic oil and gas production." This last was added
by the White House as a platform for a dialogue with India about Dabhol.
Before long, the input that Cheney's task force had received from Ken Lay
would be an issue in its own right.

Indeed, once California prices were capped in June, at least some of the
administration's attention turned to Dabhol, where the threat to Enron
was growing. Beginning that month, officials at Condoleezza Rice's National Security Council launched an effort to pressure the Indian government to make good on at least portions of its agreement. Documents
collected by the *Washington Post* showed that the NSC coordinated a campaign that included the State Department, the vice president's office, the
Overseas Private Investment Corporation, and others.[43] What made the
situation even more perilous was Enron's still-unsuspected cash flow crisis.

With Enron's future and $700 million of Ex-Im Bank loans and OPIC
guarantees at stake, administration officials swung into action. The vice
president talked to Indian leaders, as did the assistant secretary of state for
South Asia on a visit to New Delhi, followed by the American ambassador,
who in August warned businessmen in Bombay that the Enron dispute was
causing U.S. companies to rethink investments in India. That same month,
Lay himself, possibly remembering all the former Enron lawyers and advisers in the Commerce Department and U.S. trade representative's office,
told the *Financial Times,* "There are U.S. laws that could prevent the U.S.
government from providing any aid or assistance to India going forward if,
in fact, they expropriate property of U.S. companies."[44]

While "expropriate" was an overstatement, Lay had compelling reasons
to make such threats. As Enron's credibility shrank, its stock price fell below $20 in October. By then George W. Bush himself was being briefed to
make Enron's case as part of a meeting with Indian prime minister Atal Bi-
hari Vajpayee on November 9 in Washington.

As the date of the meeting approached, though, the planned discussion
of Dabhol was scrubbed at the last minute. Enron was now less than four

weeks away from being forced into bankruptcy, and press references to a potential financial implosion of the company were beginning to appear. Commerce Secretary Donald Evans and others let it be known that they had declined to intervene to help Enron maintain its ratings with the major national credit-grading concerns—Standard and Poor's, Moody's, and Fitch.

The administration's insistence that it refused to bail out Enron, however, is disingenuous. There were so many executive-branch connections to Enron about to make the front pages of America's leading newspapers as November turned to December that any attempt at an overt rescue would have been a prime target. In any event, there was no obvious form that a full-fledged bailout could take: The company was on the verge of imploding. Moreover, in addition to the drawn-out Bush-Cheney refusal to cap electricity prices in California—a respite Enron and the merchants could not have been granted by any other administration—and the efforts to pressure India to pay Enron, two other administration moves have been cited for less obvious pro-Enron rescue designs. One was Treasury Secretary Paul O'Neill's February 17 decision to review and thus delay Clinton's proposed crackdown on offshore tax havens. The second was the inclusion in the post–September 11 "stimulus" package, proposed by the president in October, of a provision giving three large corporations—General Motors, IBM, and Enron—huge tax rebates for supposed overpayment of the federal alternative minimum tax. While Enron's rebate would have been a whopping $254 million, the Democratic Senate never seriously considered the proposal.

Critics had a field day dissecting O'Neill's February shuffling of Clinton's planned crackdown on offshore tax havens to take effect in July. This was followed by the treasury secretary's lackadaisical November agreement with the Cayman Islands that no bank-law tightening needed to be undertaken until 2004. Still, it seems improbable that in February O'Neill would have known anything about Chewco or Osprey; more likely his delaying tactic was just a courtesy to the nation's upper-income-tax minimizers.

On the other hand, the insistence by the president and his supporters that the Enron debacle, with all of its ramifications, was "a business scandal, not a political scandal," smacks of farce. No mere marketplace nurtured Enron from a company with $6.4 billion revenues in 1992 to one boasting $20 billion in 1997, $40 billion in 1999, and $101 billion in 2000. That degree of growth required four or five episodes of political engineering to turn the trick: the two-decade-long dynastic collaboration of the Bushes; the bipartisan crony capitalism represented by OPIC and the Export-Import Bank, without which Enron never could have expanded globally; the venality of the Clinton Commerce Department under corporation-cultivating secretary Ron Brown; the legislative and regulatory chicanery of Senator and Mrs. Gramm (described by *Barron's*, the financial weekly, as "Mr. and Mrs. Enron"), which created a black hole for run-amok energy futures trading; and the huge 1997–2000 flood of pro-deregulation Enron money into federal and state-level politics and lobbying. The politics involved on so many fronts had no twentieth-century precedent.

As to whether the Enron scandal exceeded its closest historical precedent, the Teapot Dome mess of the Harding years, the answer has to be yes. The Teapot Dome outcome did not affect hundreds of thousands, even millions, of pension holders and investors as did Enron. Teapot Dome likewise had no dynastic connection; President Harding's own personal involvement was minor and mostly permissive. While the comment made in June 2000 by Ken Lay that "no member of the Bush family has ever been on the Enron payroll" is almost certainly true, it is also irrelevant. Much larger amounts of money than ever changed hands in Teapot Dome reached the Bush family and their close political associates through multiple nonpayroll routes: hard-dollar political campaign contributions, soft-dollar party contributions, consulting fees, joint investing agreements, funding for presidential libraries, lucrative speech payments, contributions to the cost of inaugurals, hypothesized Enron purchases of Bush-owned gas production, oil-well partnerships, and possibly even some of those off-the-books arrangements scattered around the world's many tax havens.

One maverick, politically experienced Washington investment banker, Catherine Austin Fitts, concluded that the Bush administration did manage a late 2001 Enron bailout of sorts by failing to seize control of all the documents in the case, in effect allowing extensive shredding by Enron and accountants Arthur Andersen alike, and permitting the January 2002 sale of EnronOnline, the company's trading vehicle, to the Union Bank of Switzerland, a major Enron creditor. That sale may have caused the information needed to explain key portions of what happened to pass under restrictive Swiss law.[45] Lack of EnronOnline, bank, and accountancy records may have made it impossible to prove who did what and where the money went.

Cheney and Halliburton

While Enron and Halliburton were not in the same business during the 1990s, they did share a fundamental corporate approach: putting politics, lobbying, and Washington connections ahead of hymns to laissez-faire. After Richard Cheney took over at Dallas-based Halliburton in 1995, the company's levels of federal political contributions, lobbying outlays, government contracts, Export-Import Bank loans, and OPIC guarantees mounted almost as rapidly as those of Enron a few hundred miles away in Houston.

In 1992, as secretary of defense, Cheney had hired Halliburton's Brown and Root Services unit to conduct a major classified study detailing how private companies—Brown and Root prominently among them—could provide logistics for U.S. military forces in potential war zones around the world. That same year, Brown and Root—having since become Kellogg, Brown and Root—received the first big five-year logistics contract from the U.S. Army to support U.S. soldiers in places like Zaire, Haiti, Somalia, the Balkans, and Saudi Arabia. Awarded contract dollars rose in the late nineties after Cheney became chief executive officer. However, in a statement issued in 2002, the company asserted that Cheney had "steadfastly refused" to market Halliburton/Kellogg, Brown and Root services to the U.S. government during his five years as chief executive.[46]

Luckily, Chairman Steadfast had a trusted lieutenant available. David Gribbin, his boyhood friend, administrative assistant in the House of Representatives, and chief of staff in the Defense Department, followed him to Dallas and, as a Halliburton senior vice president, handled these contacts as well as Ex-Im Bank and OPIC-connected lobbying. When Cheney and Gribbin left the company in 2000, the latter was replaced by former admiral Joseph Lopez, who had been Cheney's military aide at the Pentagon in the early nineties.[47] By 2000, oil-related work had fallen to roughly 70 percent of Halliburton's business. Military-related activity, by contrast, climbed steadily.

Under Cheney, Halliburton also broadened the political geography of its Ex-Im Bank and OPIC-assisted overseas oil- and gas-related projects. The attention that had originally been concentrated on Algeria was expanded to include Russia, Angola, Mexico, and Bangladesh. Between 1995 and 2000, according to the Center for Public Integrity, Halliburton and its subsidiaries had "undertaken foreign projects in which Ex-Im and its sister

U.S. bank, the Overseas Private Investment Corp., have guaranteed or made direct loans totaling $1.5 billion, mostly over the last two years. That compares with a total of about $100 million the government banks insured and loaned in the five years before Cheney joined the company."[48] As we will see, several of these projects, notably one to refurbish the massive Siberian fields owned by Russia's Tyumen Oil Company, became extremely controversial.

Federal government contracts with Halliburton and its subsidiaries also expanded, jumping from roughly $300 million in 1995 to $800 million in 1999 and higher under Bush after 2000. During Cheney's five years as CEO the total awarded was $2.3 billion, up from $1.2 billion for the five preceding years.[49] In 2002, explaining that Halliburton stock had lost two-thirds of its value because of an array of accounting and business issues, the *New York Times* pointed out the timely influx of profits from the war against terrorism:

> From building cells for detainees at Guantanamo Bay in Cuba to feeding troops in Uzbekistan, the Pentagon is increasingly relying on a unit of Halliburton called KBR, sometimes referred to as Kellogg, Brown and Root. Although the unit has been building projects all over the world for the federal government for decades, the attacks of Sept. 11 have led to significant additional business. KBR is the exclusive logistics supplier for both the Navy and the Army, providing services like cooking, construction, power generation and fuel transportation. The contract recently won with the Army is for ten years and has no lid on costs, the only logistical arrangement by the Army without an estimated cost.[50]

According to a survey by the Center for Public Integrity and the International Consortium of Investigative Journalists, Halliburton is first and foremost among the two dozen or so U.S. firms that fit the new category of "private military companies" (PMCs)—primarily service providers of high-tech warfare, including communications and intelligence, logistical support, and battlefield training and planning.[51] Since 1994, the Defense Department has entered into just over 3,000 contracts with PMCs, valued at more than $300 billion; 2,700 of them were held by just two companies: Kellogg, Brown and Root, the Halliburton subsidiary, and the Virginia-based management and technology consulting firm Booz, Allen and Hamilton.[52] After George Bush and Richard Cheney took office, Kellogg, Brown and Root—looking more than ever like a quasi agency of the U.S. government—also received an unusual number of foreign military contracts, including one from Russia to eliminate liquid-fueled intercontinental ballistic missiles and their silos and one from the British army to support a fleet of large new tank transporters.[53]

The employees of PMCs ran a considerable gamut, from cooks and bottle washers to retired generals, with wide variations in their duties and proximity to combat. At least one PMC, Oregon-based ICI, had no restriction about using weapons in combat situations. As for Kellogg, Brown and Root, under the ten-year agreement signed in 2001, the bases to which its employees were assigned included ones in Afghanistan, Uzbekistan, and Kyrgyzstan. Critics and supporters alike found questionable implications in contracting out such work. Privatizing military functions circumvented accountability to Congress, while effectively militarizing confrontations in which the Pentagon might otherwise be reluctant to send uniformed troops. In addition, by using for-profit "soldiers," the executive branch could evade congressional limitations on troop strength.

The post-1992 privatization of functions hitherto handled by the uniformed military—a procedure similar to the CIA's delegation of contract work to an array of firms in nearby Northern Virginia—involved ever-larger billions. It also empowered calculated amorality. As vice president of the United States, Cheney participated in describing democracy and liberation as the raison d'être of the U.S. 2003 intervention in Iraq. As chairman of Halliburton, he had argued against the imposition of international and U.S. sanctions, usually human rights related, on countries with which Halliburton wanted to do business.

In 1996, Cheney lobbied to lift sanctions under the U.S. Freedom Support Act against aid to Azerbaijan (the oil-rich former Soviet republic in the Caucasus), which had beeen motivated by concern over Azerbaijani ethnic cleansing of the Abkhazians. Cheney claimed that the sanctions were largely the result of biased lobbying by Armenian Americans, but in 1997 Brown and Root bid on a major Caspian project from the Azerbaijan International Operating Company.[54] On a related front, Halliburton supported overturning the Massachusetts "Burma Law," which discouraged the state government from awarding contracts to companies doing business in repressive Burma (Myanmar). The complicity of Halliburton's

Burmese operations in major human rights violations had been asserted in a 2000 report by EarthRights International.[55]

Similarly, Cheney lobbied heavily against the U.S. Iran-Libya Sanction Act of 1995, trying to secure an exemption so that Halliburton could participate in the development of Iran's offshore oil fields, as well as in the construction of proposed pipelines to carry Caspian Sea oil to the Persian Gulf. Once the sanctions were in place, Cheney was charged with ignoring them.[56] As for the sanctions against Iraq, Cheney both supported and, in a sense, evaded them. Detailed investigative reports by the *Financial Times* and the *International Herald Tribune* indicated that Halliburton, through two subsidiaries, did $23.8 million worth of business with the country, repairing some of the Iraqi infrastructure that Cheney, as defense secretary, had helped to damage in 1991. Cheney's company did such transactions through European subsidiaries "to avoid straining relations with Washington and jeopardizing their ties with President Saddam Hussein's government."[57]

Although Cheney's stewardship of Halliburton also raised some questions of domestic business ethics—overcharging the government, fraudulent accounting practices, and the like—the more important issues concerned two larger topics: (1) Halliburton's growing role as something of a U.S. "private military adjunct"; and (2) the extent to which this emergence drew upon Cheney's positions as secretary of defense and then vice president of the United States. As noted, Cheney launched the Defense Department's privatization effort in 1992, took advantage of it as CEO of Halliburton from 1995 to 2000, and then helped to extend and entrench the "private army" aspect as vice president.

Following the award of Halliburton's ten-year contract of 2001 with no lid on costs, critics took up watch—and many renewed their suspicions in March 2003, when the Pentagon revealed hiring the company's Kellogg, Brown and Root subsidiary, on a multiyear contract without competitive bidding, to help contain any Iraqi oil well fires started in response to a U.S. attack. Lack of competitive bidding was justified, officials claimed, because the war plans were still secret at the time, and Halliburton was the only company with the necessary qualifications.[58] Revealingly, the contract also provided that KBR would "provide for the continuity of operations of the Iraqi oil infrastructure," which included "operation of facilities and distribution of products." By early May, the company was pumping 125,000 barrels of oil per day, a circumstance that one Democratic congressman found "at odds with the administration's repeated assurances that the Iraqi oil belongs to the Iraqi people."[59]

Overall, Halliburton's commercial position at the intersection of oil services, petro-diplomacy, and military support, backstopped by the omnipresence of its former CEO within the executive branch, had arguably built it into a private-sector amalgam of oil industry, corps of engineers, and intelligence agency. As such, the firm has taken up some of the delegated role and governmental influence Anthony Sampson attributed to oil companies in the simpler years of the 1930s, 1940s, and 1950s. Halliburton's and Cheney's 2000 role in convincing the State Department to set aside CIA arguments and decide in favor of a project with Tyumen, a Russian oil company controversial for its KGB and mob links, was a case in point.

The Tyumen deal, a linchpin of Cheney's plans to involve Halliburton (and the U.S. energy sector) in Russian oil and gas production, had bogged down because of information compiled by BP-Amoco and the CIA that documented the Russian firm's roots in what the Center for Public Integrity later described as "a legacy of KGB and Communist Party corruption, as well as drug trafficking and organized crime funds."[60] In late 1999, the State Department had initially decided that the deal would run counter to the national interest, but Halliburton had a $292 million contract stake in Tyumen's success in obtaining a $489 million loan guarantee from the Export-Import Bank.

Oil-sector Washington well understood that Tyumen's Republican connections went beyond Cheney. The company's lead attorney, James C. Langdon, a managing partner at Washington's Akin, Gump law firm, was one of George W. Bush's elite fund-raising Pioneers and had helped coordinate a $2.2 million Bush dinner largely attended by lawyers and lobbyists. So when Cheney came to the capital in February 2000 to argue Tyumen's merits with Alan Larson, Clinton's undersecretary of state for economic affairs, he miraculously succeeded. Two months later, the State Department withdrew its objections, and Tyumen and Halliburton got their Export-Import Bank financing; and in early 2001, Larson became the only senior Democratic official in the State Department to retain his position in the Bush-Cheney administration. Tyumen's fortunes likewise flourished, and in October 2002, Tyumen became the first Russian firm to send oil to the U.S. Strategic Petroleum Reserve, shipping it 285,000 barrels.[61]

No vice president—not even George Herbert Walker Bush in the transformational 1980s, the closest precedent—has positioned himself so firmly at the meeting point of energy strategy, military decision making, and intelligence planning and operations.

Oil, Military Privatization, and the Redefinition of National Security

The election of a president and a vice president who were both conservatives from the oil industry obviously intensified and accelerated two important trends: the prioritization of energy issues and geopolitics, and the privatization of military functions. Had Enron survived to reach $300 billion to $400 billion in sales, dominate global energy trading markets, and leap to the head of the Fortune 500, a bolder paragraph could have been penned here about a new U.S. global energy strategy and diplomacy, supported by what might have been described as a military–energy–national security–industrial complex. As matters developed, part of that potential complex self-destructed, leaving a sour global legacy—uncompleted power plants, angry regulators, and some three thousand secret partnerships, from Luxembourg to the Caymans, many presumably milked like a prize Wisconsin dairy herd within months of the company's bankruptcy filing. In the absence of Enron, only a smaller-scale military–energy–national security–industrial complex can be identified, but even so, Halliburton has become an important part of its global transmission system.

Setting aside concerns about business corruption and armaments excess—most wars have featured both—the notion of energy-specializing military units seems all too plausible. As chapter 8 will amplify, World Wars I and II had major oil-strategy components on each side. The contemporary, even more pronounced geopolitical focus on the Persian Gulf, Caucasus, and Transcaspia exudes petro-military déjà vu and recalls the *Drang nach Osten,* "Great Game," and heartland theory of a century ago. Whatever the timing, name, or magnitude of World War III, resource questions seem bound to stand out as a primary motivating force. To the extent that fighting takes place near oil fields, gas fields, pipelines, or offshore rigs, private armies may play important combat-zone roles. Halliburton uniforms may have their own insignia and service stripes.

However, before turning to the four horsemen of twenty-first-century Middle Eastern confrontation—oil, armaments, religious fundamentalism, and terror—it is necessary to go back to the early years of the previous century, when cavalry rode horses; Germany, Russia, Austria-Hungary, and Turkey were still empires; and Americans were just beginning to pay attention to overseas possessions. An essential story remains to be told about the rise of the U.S. military-industrial complex and national security (intelligence) community and about the climb of the Walker and Bush families through their corridors of power, paths of emolument, and labyrinthine values systems.

CHAPTER 6

Armaments and Men:
The Bush Dynasty and the
National Security State

We should constantly keep in mind how recent the military ascendancy is. During World War One, the military entered the highest economic and political circles only temporarily, for the "emergency"; it was not until World War Two that they intervened in a truly decisive way. Given the nature of modern warfare, they had to do so whether they wanted to or not, just as they had to invite men of economic power into the military. For unless the military sat in on corporate decisions, they could not be sure that their programs would be carried out; and unless the corporation chieftains knew something of the war plans, they could not plan war production. Thus, generals advised corporation presidents and corporation presidents advised generals.

C. Wright Mills, *The Power Elite,* 1957

This conjunction [circa 1961] of an immense Military Establishment and a large arms industry is new in the American experience. . . . We recognize the imperative need for this development. Yet we must not fail to comprehend its grave implications.

President Dwight D. Eisenhower, farewell address, 1961

Despite his World War I position as head of the small-arms, ordnance, and ammunition section of the U.S. War Industries Board, Samuel Bush probably never met Sir Basil Zaharoff, the famous chairman of the British armaments firm of Vickers-Armstrong, described as "the mystery man of Europe" because of his own shadowy career in that era and his reputed holdings in Krupp, Skoda, and other Continental munitions makers. Nor is it likely that George Herbert Walker, who had fingers in many European pies, ever personally routed rifles to German extremists of the early 1930s. Neither name, Bush or Walker, appears in the popular literature on the so-called Merchants of Death hearings begun in 1934 before rapt crowds by the U.S. Senate's Nye committee.

But Bush and Walker did know some of the reviled merchants—the World War I–era munitions makers, "armor trust" members and arms manufacturers being investigated during the early New Deal years. Both men knew Samuel Frazier Pryor, the former president of Remington Arms, whose firm was queried by the Nye committee about the clandestine flow of American-made weaponry to Germany through Holland in the early 1930s. Walker was not investigated by the committee, but the American Ship and Commerce Corporation's partial ownership and influence over the German Hamburg-Amerika line may have helped Remington fire-arms reach right-wing political factions in the early 1930s. The guns were probably illicitly transferred—without inconvenient police inspection—to German-bound river barges in Holland's Schelde estuaries.

George Herbert Walker and Samuel Frazier Pryor had several things in common. They were of the same generation; they had kindred business backgrounds before the war in St. Louis; and they also shared a taste for guns and financial buccaneering. Both were on the periphery of a frequently collaborative group of moneymen—Averell Harriman, Percy Rockefeller at National City Bank, and others at Guaranty Trust—who had large international plans. In 1915, a number of these business and financial leaders had helped to set up the American International Corporation as a private vehicle for U.S. ambitions and investments in Europe and Russia. A collateral objective was to abet any Bolshevik-inspired upheaval in Germany that might end German participation in the war.[1]

In 1916, the American International Corporation (AIC) bought New York Shipbuilding, a major navy contractor, which by 1918 owned the world's biggest shipyard.[2] More than a year earlier, some of the same New York interests, centered on National City Bank, had reorganized the principal U.S. small-arms and munition producer, hundred-year-old Remington, installing Pryor as general manager and later president, to meet what became an avalanche of wartime demand. Ultimately, as company publications boasted, Remington produced 69 percent of all rifles manufactured for U.S. troops during the First World War, as well as over 50 percent of all the small-arms ammunition for the United States and the Allies.[3]

After the war's end, Remington officials wondered about their next markets. Russia wouldn't be among them, because in 1917 the new revolutionary government had voided Remington's multimillion-dollar arms contract with the czar's regime—and some of those rifles instead armed White Russian troops to fight the Bolsheviks. Nor could meaningful sales volume be achieved by arming countries like Paraguay and Bolivia for the 1933 Chaco War. In consequence, Remington executives had to look to other major markets—for example, Germany.

Meanwhile, in 1919, National City Bank had also joined in setting up the new W. A. Harriman and Company, soon to be under George Walker's presidency. Like Harriman and Walker, National City would do a lot of 1920s business in Germany. Percy Rockefeller of National City, a moving force in the Remington reorganization—and a director there as well as at AIC—also became a W. A. Harriman director.[4]

Remington's Samuel Pryor was part of this cabal, and took a role in the first big Harriman-Walker international gambit: the arrangement of a major participation in Germany's once great Hamburg-Amerika steamship line. Harriman and Walker held their Hamburg-Amerika shares through another mutual framework, the American Ship and Commerce Corporation. Pryor was named one of AS&C's directors.

In 1924, when Harriman and Walker set up the Union Banking Corporation in New York on behalf of the politically active German steel baron Fritz Thyssen, control of UBC was held by a Dutch entity, the Rotterdam-based Bank voor Handel en Scheepvart. This Dutch bank, in turn, was owned by Berlin's August Thyssen Bank. The Rotterdam bank, it has been proven, handled some of Thyssen's 1920s contributions to the fledgling Nazi Party—for some reason, Samuel Pryor of Remington was named an original director of UBC. He seems to have been a tight third side of the Harriman-German triangle. Indeed, after he died in 1934, his son became a director of Harriman Securities Corporation, joining the two Harriman brothers, Averell and Roland.[5] This does make one wonder about Remington-made arms going to Thyssen—or Thyssen's friends.

The Special Senate Committee on the Investigation of the Munitions Industry—perhaps unfairly nicknamed the "Merchants of Death" investigation—never got too deeply into the major 1933–34 surge of U.S. military exports to Hitler's Germany. Although the committee chairman cited figures that exports to Germany by United Aircraft (Boeing Aircraft, Chance-Vought, and Pratt and Whitney) had increased by 500 percent between 1933 and 1934, the State Department leaned on committee members to make no reference to secret reports about German rearmament.[6] At any rate, no documentation exists for how many Remington-made weapons reached Germany through Dutch barge routes or Thyssen transport.

Indeed, by 1933 Remington was losing enough money that it had to let Du Pont, the nation's leading munitions maker, acquire a controlling interest.[7] War was not far off, of course, and once again the company became the principal U.S. small-arms and ammunition supplier, its payrolls rising from under 4,000 in 1939 to 82,500 at the peak of production in 1943.[8]

Exactly how much time Walker spent in Europe during the 1920s, especially at the Harriman firm's Berlin office, is an enigma. However, if he did not himself know men like Feliks Dzerzhinski, Joseph Stalin, Leon Trotsky, Fritz Thyssen, Heinrich Himmler, and Hjalmar Schacht, he certainly had plenty of friends who did—Averell Harriman; the 1916–19 U.S. ambassador to Russia, David Francis; and the Dulles brothers. After AIC's incorporation in 1915 by leading New York financiers, researchers have pointed out, it maintained ties to both Bolshevik and imperial German organizations and espionage over the next few years.[9] Its prime goals seem to have been to gather intelligence, seek influence, and pursue investment opportunity. Gordon Auchincloss, the number two man in the State Department's World War I intelligence unit, became an AIC director for four years in the early 1930s. The actual record of George H. Walker's activity is minimal.

During the mid-1920s and early 1930s, the peak years of Harriman and Walker commercial activity in Germany and the Soviet Union, Walker was intermittently one of AIC's directors. Matthew Brush, who served as president of AIC for many years, was at various times a director of Harriman Securities.[10] Chapter 5 has already mentioned Brush's role in Harriman's Russian oil and manganese interests. Although few books about the period have discussed AIC—Antony Sutton's *Wall Street and the Bolshevik Revolution* is the conspicuous exception—its financial role in post-1917 Russia, along with its corporate links discoverable through the *New York City Directory of Directors,* reflect its considerable clout and connection to a network of internationally oriented companies in which Rockefeller, Harriman, Brush, Walker, and Pryor held interlocking directorships. (See appendix A.)

In different roles, both Samuel Bush and George H. Walker were present at the creation of the U.S. military-industrial complex and its intelligence-gathering adjunct, albeit as members of the supporting cast, in the years surrounding World War I. From the thirties to the early sixties, Prescott Bush would play his own substantial but unheralded role. Then the next two generations of Bushes would operate at the top, reaching out from the Central Intelligence Agency and the executive offices at 1600 Pennsylvania Avenue to script arms sales, launch missile strikes, and order invasions from Panama to the Persian Gulf.

It is an extraordinary record. If there are other families who have more fully epitomized and risen alongside the hundred-year emergence of the U.S. military-industrial complex, the post-1945 national security state, and the twenty-first-century imperium, no one has identified them. Certainly no other established a presidential dynasty.

It is important to note that while becoming the center of global military technology and power, the United States had by the 1980s turned itself into by far the largest arms dealer in the world, once the collapse of the USSR ended Soviet competition. The two Bush presidents, in turn, served as chief executive officers of weapons complexes and commanded nuclear, biological, and chemical arsenals that even Sir Basil Zaharoff—to say nothing of their own dynasty's founding generation—would have found utterly unbelievable. This penchant for armaments and arms deals is rarely highlighted in biographies of either president. On the dynasty's résumé it is a recurring entry, as we will see—and sometimes to the detriment of regional and world peace.

World War I and the Bush Family

The War Industries Board of 1917–18, run by South Carolinian Bernard Baruch, brought to wartime Washington a considerable crop of border state and midwestern Democrats, among them Samuel Bush, the president of Ohio-based Buckeye Steel Castings. His background in steel and railroading did not make him a natural choice to head the board's small-arms, ammunition, and ordnance section, which procured rifles, pistols, machine guns, ammunition, and artillery. However, he knew forgings and castings, railroads and Rockefellers, and he had been involved in government relations activities at the National Association of Manufacturers and the U.S. Chamber of Commerce before 1917.

In 1918, Baruch made Samuel Bush director of the WIB facilities division, charged with strategic coordination of manufacturing output and railroad transportation capacity. When the war ended, Bush was already mulling subjects like peacetime conversion and a framework of antitrust revision to allow companies to collaborate within individual industries and through trade associations. When some WIB functions were transferred to the Commerce Department, he migrated to that department's advisory board. Before long, however, the Commerce board's support for government planning and collaborative price fixing to cushion postwar deflation displeased President Wilson as overly interventionist, and the effort was abandoned.[11]

Samuel Bush's background and wartime responsibilities had brought wide acquaintance—first, with railroad-connected Harrimans and Rockefellers; second, with influential board officials like Clarence Dillon, Robert Brookings, Judge Robert S. Lovett (and perhaps their friend George H. Walker); and third, through his brief involvement in small arms and ordnance, with top executives of firms like Du Pont, Remington, Winchester, and Colt Arms. Paul Koistinen, the principal historian of the political economy of American warfare, found that in contrast to the Spanish-American War, the 1917–18 challenge drew industrial, military, and business together into the lasting relationships that would dominate the twentieth-century political economy. Despite the hiatus in the twenties and thirties, this marked "a major and seemingly irrevocable step in the direction of [the United States'] becoming a warfare or national security state."[12]

How much Samuel Bush drew on his experience and connections to advance the career of son Prescott during the 1920s and 1930s is a gap in the various Bush biographies and memoirs. For good reason, the arms connection is not one the family has wanted to see pursued. Still, it is striking how clearly Prescott Bush's employment after his demobilization in 1919 related to areas that had been within WIB's purview.

He got his first job in St. Louis with Simmons, a railroad-equipment manufacturer, through its president, Wallace Simmons. Simmons was a Skull and Bones alumnus, and also a wartime planning colleague of Samuel Bush. Samuel Pryor had also worked for Simmons before the war. One of the younger Bush's assignments at Simmons involved selling a wartime saddlery plant in Kingsport, Tennessee, to Winchester Arms. After his mother's death left his father disconsolate, Prescott came back to Columbus in 1921 with his new wife to help run a small rubber enterprise in which Samuel Bush had an investment. Already a growth industry of the automobile era, rubber had been much regulated in the last year of the war, leaving postwar circumstances uncertain. When his father's small Ohio rubber business was bought by a New England firm, Prescott Bush moved to Massachusetts, and in 1924 he left to work for U.S. Rubber in New York. This was a Harriman-connected company, so that patronage was presumably his entrée. Two years later, at the age of thirty-one, he became a vice president of W. A. Harriman and Company.

Prescott Bush, by this time, sat in the middle of three overlapping circles that would play a huge role in directing his future. One was made up of his friends and classmates from Yale and especially Skull and Bones (E. Roland Harriman, Neil Mallon, Ellery James, Robert A. Lovett, R. Knight Woolley, et al.). All of them eventually wound up at W. A. Harriman or a Harriman-controlled company or came together under one roof through the Brown Brothers Harriman merger in 1931. The clubbiness must have been keen.

A second group centered on his father-in-law, George H. Walker, president of W. A. Harriman and Company; his brother-in-law, George H. Walker Jr., entering his senior year at Yale (and Skull and Bones); and Walker associates including the AIC and National City people. A third ring was made up of his father's old acquaintances from the War Industries Board (including Bernard Baruch, Edward Stettinius Sr., Clarence Dillon, and others). It was quite a clutch of influence wielders, and all had already provided Prescott with work and connections.

As the twenties became the thirties and another world war gathered, Brown Brothers Harriman and Skull and Bones each boasted extraordinary numbers of persons who would become private or public leaders of the future military-industrial complex and its intelligence auxiliaries. Averell Harriman was also dabbling in the aviation business, studying imaginative new airplane designs and helping to finance fellow Bonesman Juan Trippe's Pan American Airways. Henry Stimson took time away from presiding over the Andover Board of Trustees to serve as secretary of state under Hoover (1929–32) and then join the Roosevelt administration as secretary of war in 1940. David Ingalls, a pillar of the World War I Yale Flying Unit who had briefly flown Sopwith Camels for the British, became assistant secretary of the navy for aviation (1929–32). F. Trubee Davison, another Bonesman in the Yale Flying Unit, became head of the Civil Aeronautics Board and assistant secretary of war for air under George H. Walker's good friend and fellow Missourian, Secretary of War Dwight Davis (1925–29).*

---

*Indeed, George H. Walker had something of a rivalry with Davis. The latter had founded the well-known Davis Cup in tennis, so Walker followed suit with golf's equally reputed Walker Cup.

On the Brown Brothers Harriman side, David K. E. Bruce, son-in-law of banker Paul Mellon, was a partner before spending World War II running the London office of the OSS and moving up to undersecretary of state. Artemus Gates, at the firm in the 1930s, went on to become assistant secretary of the navy for air under Stimson during World War II.

Quite literally, Prescott Bush spent the first two decades of his financial career in the company of people whose actions and ideas would shape the War Department, the OSS, the CIA, and other pivots of the emerging U.S. national security complex. A British writer, Godfrey Hodgson, has pointed out that "the War Department was directed by a tiny clique of wealthy Republicans, and one that was almost as narrowly based, in social and educational terms, as a traditional British Tory Cabinet."[13] The importance of these connections is almost as neglected as the family links to the arms trade.

World War II and the Painful Emergence of a U.S. National Security Complex

War is among the most underestimated of political forces. It has been a powerful factor in the rise of the English-speaking nations to world hegemony, and the great armed conflicts within the United States have had deep political consequences. Over the last decade, I have published two books touching on these forces. *The Cousins' Wars* (1999) examined the catalytic and formative roles of the English Civil War, the American Revolution, and the U.S. Civil War in the interrelated evolution of the two great nations. *Wealth and Democracy* (2002), as one of its subthemes, assessed the importance of the American Revolution, the War of 1812, the Civil War, the two world wars, and the war in Vietnam in precipitating political upheaval, abetting the rise of new U.S. wealth elites, and sometimes doing both.

The American Revolution, for example, rearranged the lists of greatest wealth to begin with wartime financiers (like Robert Morris and William Duer), merchants and commissaries who supplied the U.S. and French forces, and shipowners (Elias Derby and William Bingham) whose privateers took many British vessels as prizes. The U.S. Civil War economy of 1861–65 was also a realigning force, creating hundreds of nouveau riche war profiteers and elevating a remarkable generation of young Yankee businessmen who avoided military service and took rapid wartime steps up the economic ladder: John D. Rockefeller, Andrew Carnegie, J. Pierpont

Morgan, Jay Gould, Collis Huntington, Philip Armour, Jay Cooke, Marshall Field, and others.

The First World War entered more new names to the ranks of the wealthiest—warhogs Charles Schwab of Bethlehem Steel and Pierre du Pont, the Delaware munitions maker. However, most observers have overlooked its role as the seedbed of a new elite, focusing their attention principally on the opportunities from the Second World War. They've thus missed seeing the *connection* between the two wars: how so many 1917–18 officials and Washington-involved businessmen and financiers (or their sons) rose higher still in 1941–45. Likewise they have overlooked the extent to which businessmen, financiers, and lawyers commercially involved with the Germans and Russians during the 1920s and 1930s wound up in the inner circles of U.S. intelligence operations during World War II. In both cases, the makeup of the post-1945 eastern establishment was noticeably affected by activities and relationships from the first war as well as the second.

From an economic standpoint, 1939–41 was not the gold mine for U.S. manufacturers and financiers that war production for Britain, France, and Russia had been in 1915–17. Besides prohibiting most U.S. exports to any belligerents, the Neutrality Acts of 1935, 1936, and 1937 had also blocked U.S. private lending to them. The Nye hearings had left Congress concerned about how investment bankers and armaments makers seemed to encourage wars. The rapid military collapse of France in June 1940, in just two months of fighting following the seven-month "Phony War," ended French demand for war matériel and also stirred widespread doubt about whether Britain by herself could stand off Hitler.

All of these circumstances permitted many corporations to hold to "America First" thinking, elaborated in some cases by pro-German economic commitments. In the 1920s, Germany had been by far the most important international market for recycling the new private U.S. capital created by the war. Most of this U.S. investment, which approached $2 billion, took the form of loans to German industry, direct investment in German companies, loans to German municipalities, and endless dollars of Dawes Plan credits. Christopher Simpson, in *The Splendid Blond Beast*, listed the principal U.S. firms that bought or began establishing major German subsidiaries or joint ventures during the 1920s: ITT, General Motors, Ford, Standard Oil of New Jersey, and General Electric.[14] All were among America's dozen largest companies.

U.S. overseas investment didn't end with Hitler's accession to power. Capital continued to move to Germany during the 1930s under the Third Reich. Reports by the U.S. Commerce Department showed the U.S. investment in Germany increased by 48.5 percent between 1929 and 1940, while declining almost everywhere else in continental Europe.[15]

By 1939, many of these various units—manufacturing engines, armored chassis, and artificial rubber—were mainstays of the German war machine. As pricey, immobile assets that could not be repatriated, the large German subsidiaries were also important props of the valuations of many of the biggest U.S. companies. Instead of the obvious pro-Allied economic self-interest of 1917, many major corporations faced a very different conundrum in 1939–41. Top executives and investment bankers uncertain about what they ought to do—or how they ought to take cover—hired lawyers like John Foster and Allen Dulles.

As for the U.S. economy emerging from the Great Depression and the 1937–38 recession, it grew moderately in 1939 and 1940. Congress did not vote large military outlays until spring 1940, following the German breakthroughs in France and the Low Countries. Production for military purposes really took off in the first six months of 1942, when procurement officers placed orders for $100 billion worth of equipment, more than the U.S. economy had ever produced in a single year. Its momentum matched escalating U.S. defense outlays: from $2 billion in 1940 to $14 billion in 1941 and $52 billion in 1942.

Virtually all of Prescott Bush's Yale friends had been pro-British back in the 1914–17 period before the United States declared war. Several had been in the Yale Flying Unit, serving in Britain before the United States joined in. By contrast, however, the twenty-five months of European war before Pearl Harbor produced somewhat more sentiment for U.S. neutrality. Although pro-British sentiment predominated, writers, educators, and civic leaders, not businessmen and financiers, were the leading voices in prointervention groups in 1940 and 1941. Some businessmen, including Bush friends like Sears Roebuck chairman Robert Wood, became prominent in the America First movement.

When war began in Europe in 1939, 82 percent of Americans expected the Allies to win, according to polls. By mid-May, when blitzkrieg had sped German panzers into France, only 55 percent did; and by June, when Paris fell, just 30 percent.[16] After Hitler's triumph, Roosevelt sought to rally American opinion molders behind a "Government of National Unity," broadening his outreach by appointing pro-British Republicans Henry Stimson and Frank Knox as secretaries of the War and Navy Departments, respectively. He also appointed a business-dominated National Defense Advisory Commission to coordinate industrial mobilization.[17] "Dr. New Deal," Roosevelt eventually admitted, would be replaced for the duration by "Dr. Win-the-War."

However, as victory grew uncertain from mid-1940 on, considerable segments of conservative opinion in both Britain and the United States thought it might be necessary to negotiate some kind of peace with the Germans. The greatest peril ended in September 1940, when the Royal Air Force, by winning the Battle of Britain, staved off Hitler's cross-Channel invasion. Joseph P. Kennedy, stepping down that December as Roosevelt's ambassador to the Court of St. James's, remained among those who were unimpressed by the British efforts. For several months into 1941, he thought that Britain would be beaten, and even in early 1943, he favored a negotiated peace with Germany to end the war.[18]

The whole underpinning of the Roosevelt effort was shifting, with broad consequences in the areas of interest to the Bush family—especially, eventually, intelligence. Gregory Hooks, in *Forging the Military Industrial Complex* (1991), argued plausibly that the Left-liberal domestic reform-minded New Deal was displaced during the 1941–43 period by a Washington-led economic mobilization effort. Activist government was further enlarged, but for different purposes and under a more conservative set of business, financial, and military elites. The War and Navy Departments did share some of their influence with a succession of new boards and agencies: the War Resources Board (1939), the National Defense Advisory Commission (1940) timed with the Stimson and Knox appointments, the Office of Production Management (1941), the War Production Board (1942), the Office of War Mobilization (1943), and then the Office of War Mobilization and Reconversion (1945). But although the names of these organizations sounded like more New Deal alphabet soup, they were run by businessmen—for business's goals.

The consequences would be long term, lasting well beyond 1945. World War I had also brought business, financial, and military elites into more power and prominence, but their influence waned after Versailles and 1920s disarmament measures. After World War II, as the cold war froze relations between the United States and the Soviet Union, the military-industrial complex was left largely intact. This chill piled a new post-1946 layer of conservative-leaning politics on top of a similar 1941–43 mood, bred by fifteen to eighteen months of war gloom and rightward reaction that followed Pearl Harbor.

In the early phases of World War II, given the uncertainty and ambivalence of 1941–43, the interaction of business, politics, and government had a conservative tone. Part of this conservatism was due to lingering prewar isolationism, with conservative Republicans speaking openly of "Mr. Roosevelt's War." Both elites and the broader electorate reacted to the apparent rout of the domestic New Deal, as well as the numerous naval and military defeats experienced by the United States during 1942, from losses to Japan in the Pacific to embarrassment at German hands in Tunisia and the devastation wrought by U-boats in the sea lanes off the U.S. East Coast. Together, they brought large and unexpected Republican congressional gains in that year's midterm elections. The House of Representatives, in particular, became strongly conservative.

Roosevelt also faced dissension in the military and intelligence communities. Not a few senior officers, especially in the navy, disagreed with the White House priority on supporting Britain against Germany. They urged greater attention to the Pacific theater and war against Japan. Some intelligence officials, in turn, were ambiguous about favoring the Soviet Union over Germany, maintaining quiet connections through Switzerland with non-Nazi Germans and some Nazi officials. During the winter of 1942, the Swiss-based Allen Dulles discussed with emissaries, at least half seriously, a settlement in which Germany would keep Austria and some other new territory, SS chief Heinrich Himmler would replace Hitler, and Eastern Europe would be made into a cordon sanitaire against Communism.[19] By way of backdrop, Missouri senator Harry Truman had argued in 1941 that as between the warring Russians and Germans, "if we see that Germany is winning we ought to help Russia, and if Russia is winning we ought to help Germany and in that way, let them kill as many as possible."[20] It was not a sentiment that got Truman in trouble.

For a while, Hitler's armies did little but advance. In August 1942, hard-driving German troops planted the swastika flag on top of snow-clad, eighteen-thousand-foot Mount Elbrus in the Russian Caucasus, halting a month later only 300 miles from both Iran and the Soviet Baku oil fields. In July, Field Marshal Erwin Rommel's Afrika Korps had driven within 150 miles of Cairo. A year earlier, British troops had suppressed pro-Axis forces in Iran and Iraq, the latter supported by Vichy French Syria and a few German planes. Joseph Kennedy was hardly the only American dubious about the outcome. The turning points of mid-1942—victories at Midway and El Alamein—were more emphatic in retrospect than entirely assuring at the time.

It was in this context of political and military uncertainty that the Roosevelt Justice Department, acting under the Alien Property Act, was obliged to move against German-connected corporations, including the half dozen noted in chapter 1 that counted Averell Harriman, George H. Walker, or Prescott Bush as officers or directors. Aware of press reports and government concern about his corporate ties to Germany, Bush had elevated his patriotic profile in February 1942 by becoming chairman of the United Service Organization (USO) annual fund drive, which raised $33 million that year to entertain soldiers and sailors. He was in no way a political target of government prosecutors—unlike William S. Farish, the publicly pilloried chairman of Standard Oil of New Jersey.

During that embattled spring and summer of 1942, Franklin D. Roosevelt was hardly well positioned to pick a fight with important elites of the same U.S. business community he needed to mobilize for a war—one that some disgruntled industrial leaders believed the president had courted. Grousing was especially widespread in the strategic oil and chemical industries, in which a number of important companies either had cartel and patent-sharing relationships with German firms like I. G. Farben or had set up subsidiaries in Germany. Two other much-affected industries were automobiles (General Motors and Ford) and electrical equipment (General Electric and ITT). For the government to single out Farish's flagrant withholding of processes for making artificial rubber was one thing; to tangle with the Rockefellers, the du Ponts, and half of America's largest corporations was something else.

In March 1942, Secretary of War Stimson had made the argument for caution: pursuing and conceivably litigating controversial corporate practices, he said, would only inhibit a united war effort. Oil executives hinted that too much interference with their particular industry could jeopardize wartime petroleum supplies. Allen Dulles and others in the intelligence community made that same point. Given the political climate, restraint carried the day. Here it is well to underscore oil's strategic role, as described by Daniel Yergin:

America's entry into the war would be followed, in 1942 and 1943, by a wholesale redefinition of the importance of the Middle East, based on a new outlook that completely gripped Washington, if not always the oil companies. Oil was recognized as the critical strategic commodity for the war and was essential for national power and international predominance. If there was a single resource that was shaping the strategy of the Axis powers, it was oil. If there was a single resource that could defeat them, that, too, was oil.[21]

Former Justice Department prosecutor John Loftus, author of several books on the period, has argued that politics required FDR to play a double game, evidenced by some of his own German-connected choices for sensitive jobs—Ambassador Kennedy in London, Allen Dulles as a ranking intelligence official, and James Forrestal as a special assistant to the president in 1939, then undersecretary and ultimately secretary in the wartime Navy Department. Loftus's thesis has FDR choosing to bring these men (and others) inside the tent, confident that any Kennedy or Dulles missteps would be picked up by British intelligence wiretaps and passed along to him.[22]

In a related vein, journalist Burton Hersh, in his book *The Old Boys: The American Elite and the Origins of the CIA,* pointed out that the Alien Property Office, far from being a nest of New Deal liberals, was itself tied to the German-connected Schroeder Bank and the Dulles faction: "The Alien Property Custodian, Leo Crowley, was actually on the payroll of the New York J. Henry Schroeder Bank, General Aniline's depository, where Foster and Allen Dulles both sat as board members. Foster arranged an appointment for himself as special legal counsel for the Alien Property Custodian while simultaneously representing [another Farben subsidiary] against the Custodian."[23] By this interpretation, the Alien Property Office itself was part of a cabal inclined to rock as few large corporate boats as possible. At the very least, it reflected powerful crosscurrents.

British intelligence, despite the plethora of soft-on-Germany viewpoints in the United Kingdom, which included some of the royal family, often scoffed at the U.S. government's indulgence. However, MI6 did not condescend to Prescott Bush and his blue-chip clients. Brown Brothers, the investment bank with which W. A. Harriman and Company had merged in 1931, had longstanding British as well as American connections. Montagu Norman, the embarrassingly pro-German governor of the Bank of England, was a former Brown Brothers partner in London. Many of the accounts Prescott Bush handled after the 1931 merger were British, some invested on the German side of the Rhine. Based on unnamed intelligence sources, Loftus contended that Prescott Bush was close to "C"—the British Secret Service chief, Sir Stewart Menzies—"who knew that there were too many British investors in Brown Brothers Harriman to make an issue out of their aid to Nazi Germany."[24]

Unfortunately, we have no reliable way of knowing exactly why, after 1933, men like Averell Harriman, George Walker, and Prescott Bush, the Dulles brothers, James Forrestal, Henry Ford, and several Rockefellers maintained investment relationships with Hitler's Germany, in a few cases up to (and even after) Pearl Harbor. The reasons may not have been sinister altogether—in some cases, but hardly all, the Germans these Americans kept in touch with were old-line conservatives who from time to time did favor negotiations with the Allies, the overthrow of Hitler, or a new alliance against the Soviets. Given the pressures and possible peace negotiations of 1941 and 1942, many of the German-connected American businessmen and financiers must have appeared worth more to U.S. intelligence officials as sources of information and expertise. Disciplined or prosecuted, many would only have led to other, even more embarrassing and grander captains of industry and titans of finance, who had kept subsidiaries operating in, or lines open to, wartime Germany.

In his postwar book, *Germany's Underground,* Allen Dulles sought to portray his stable of Third Reich contacts in a better light. Relatively few had dissented from Hitler's early objectives—reoccupying the Rhineland, annexing Austria, or carving up Czechoslovakia or Poland—so they were not Western-type moderates. What they did represent, however, were information–cum–secret negotiation channels and fault lines in a less-than-monolithic Germany. Besides the old-line aristocrats, military officers, and diplomats—products of the kaiser's Germany, not Hitler's—some of whom proved open to exchanges or the possibilities of negotiated peace or anti-Soviet alliances, others represented different economic and cultural fault lines.

Financiers with Western European and North American exposures like Hjalmar Schacht, Baron Kurt von Schroeder, and others were not entirely trusted by Hitler. The Cologne-based Schroeder, for instance, had in 1919 and 1923 helped fund and lead movements to take the Rhineland out of Germany and put it under French protection.[25] Industrialist Fritz Thyssen had given money to Hitler years earlier, but after war-related disagreements, his German citizenship was taken away in February 1940, and he spent much of the wartime period in Switzerland, in flight, or under loose house arrest in Germany. Eduard Schulte, who managed the (Harriman-connected) George Giesche mining operations in Silesia near the German-Polish border, was pro-Western enough to provide early (1942) reports on Hitler's plan for a murderous "Final Solution" of Europe's Jewish population.[26] Schulte fled to Switzerland in 1943.

Many of the Germans who ran I. G. Farben or the high-powered German subsidiaries of U.S. firms like Ford, General Motors, ITT, General Electric, and Standard Oil contributed to a "Keppler Leadership Circle" that funded SS chief Himmler and his resident schemer–cum–intelligence chief, Walter Schellenberg.[27] I. G. Farben's American-connected chairman, although a Nazi, had opposed 1939–41 German discussions of war with the United States. Although the moral distinction between Hitler and Himmler was negligible, the latter kept up an off-and-on indirect dialogue with Allen Dulles and MI6 about the separate peace that might be possible in U.S. eyes only if another German regime replaced Hitler.[28] Despite their huge contribution to the German war effort (and in some cases, help in maintaining concentration camps), these U.S.-affiliated firms—some of them keeping in touch with the United States through Sweden or Switzerland—assumed that transatlantic parent companies and cartel mates would help ease their way back into a postwar American orbit. For spymasters like Dulles, it would have been an important nuance.

That same view would also shape the postwar intelligence world. Most of the American businessmen, investment bankers, and lawyers who had the greatest acquaintance with German politics and commerce wound up in the U.S. war effort, usually in intelligence work. A small group, especially the Yale and Skull and Bones people, must have been loose assets of the intelligence community all along. International business ethics were lax enough that anything that wasn't actually illegal was more or less acceptable.

Lawyers have always been privileged to represent skunks without being deemed odorous, and in business the pressure of World War II seems to have pushed conflict-of-interest standards back to the laxity of the twenties or even the Gilded Age. When business executives joined Washington's wartime planning agencies, instead of being required to take inadequate government salaries, they were "permitted to retain their positions, salaries and career trajectories in private firms while nominally serving the government. Paid just one dollar per year or not compensated at all, they became known as 'dollar a year' men." While conflict of interest was not quite out the window, the biggest constraint was that dollar-a-year men could not make decisions "directly affecting the affairs of their own company."[29] As for senior officials, Averell Harriman maintained his partnership in Brown Brothers Harriman, along with his Russian bonds and securities, as he carried out his duties as ambassador in London and Moscow. He even negotiated with the Soviets over the bonds and certificates he had received on liquidating his Russian manganese concessions in 1928.[30]

Such minimalist ethics would have aided acceptance of the actions before (and even after) Pearl Harbor by corporate executives whose assets and German subsidiaries required them to deal with—realistically, to get along with—the Third Reich. Within a few years after the German surrender, prosperity was blurring any embarrassment at Ford or ITT.

By 1950, one could see the superstructure of the military-industrial complex and the national security establishment that would still be visible a half century later. The combined Defense Department had ingested the old War and Navy Departments, and the $40 billion defense budget of 1950 was two-thirds as big as the military bottom line for 1945. The inner or E-Ring of the Pentagon had more generals than ever. The aerospace business was huge and growing. The military applications of high technology were becoming a regular boardroom preoccupation. The CIA had been agreed upon in 1946 with the help of a secret blueprint prepared by Robert A. Lovett, Prescott Bush's partner at Brown Brothers Harriman. The National Security Agency—already called the Taj Mahal of global eavesdropping—would emerge in 1952 from the former Armed Forces Security Agency.

The speed with which postwar U.S. military and intelligence officers welcomed anti-Soviet Germans who had worn Hitler's insignia throughout the war reflected the historical preference for practicality over morality. Considerable portions of the German Abwehr and wartime Reinhard Gehlen organization—Fremde Heere Ost, the army intelligence group monitoring Eastern Europe and Russia—had shifted to the employ of the United States by 1950, implementing the anti-Soviet alliance scores of Germans had discussed with Stewart Menzies and Allen Dulles in other days and other uniforms. Hans Gisevius, the agent sent by Admiral Wilhelm Canaris and German intelligence to meet with Allen Dulles in wartime Switzerland, was about to begin a new cold war role: carrying messages and

ideas from Neil Mallon at Dresser Industries to the same Allen Dulles, soon
to head the CIA.

In 1950, Robert A. Lovett himself was deputy secretary of defense and
about to become secretary; Averell Harriman was the president's national
security adviser; Prescott Bush was about to run for the U.S. Senate from
Connecticut; Allen Dulles was deputy director of the CIA; and John Foster
Dulles was waiting for the next Republican president to appoint him to the
post of secretary of state earlier held by his grandfather and his uncle.
Whatever these men and their investment banks and law firms had or hadn't
done for I. G. Farben, Fritz Thyssen, and the Union Banking Corporation,
in terms of broad politics, at least, they had picked the right side—the
camp that became the U.S. national security establishment.

Prescott Bush: National Security Gray Eminence?

When the short post–World War II economic downturn in 1946 yielded to
the vigor of a new arms race, the public began to understand that something was different. Peacetime was no longer all that peaceful. The gargan-
tuan size and budgetary appetite of the new military–national security–
industrial complex also meant a transformed economy. The statistics were
awesome, and so was the technology and military power. Corporate profits blossomed in the sunshine.

Simply put, World War II made government, business, and the military
larger, more permanent, and more powerful—and also obliged each to pay
more attention to the other elements. Politically, this favored a conservative-
leaning centrism—one that admitted the need of an active government but
also promoted business interests. As government military contracts went
disproportionately to big companies during the declared or hot war of
1941–45 and then continued to do so during the undeclared cold war,
America's largest companies kept expanding. From owning 38 percent of
all manufacturing assets in 1941 and 1947, the top one hundred firms grew
to control 40 percent in 1953, 45 percent by 1959, and nearly 49 percent by
1968.[31] The national security state, in short, concentrated economic power
and favored business.

Federal purchasing clout was especially felt in durable-goods manufacturing. In 1970, the Pentagon consumed 77 percent of ordnance output, 72
percent of aeronautics production, 39 percent of radio and TV communications equipment, 34 percent of electronic components, and 26 percent of

transportation equipment, especially ships.[32] The military role in the economy, and especially in developing technology, raised questions: Was the new national security state shortchanging or feeding the nonmilitary side of the economy? Was overall national economic growth being crimped—or did national security outlays support it?

No one ever answered those questions, but either way, military officers and businessmen could not ignore their new interdependence. The army chief of ordnance had an advisory group including the chairmen of Johns-Manville, Chrysler, and U.S. Steel. Sociologist C. Wright Mills, in his 1956 book *The Power Elite,* also listed the corporations that had signed on retired military officers as chairmen: Continental Can (General Lucius Clay), Bulova (General Omar Bradley), Remington Rand (General Douglas MacArthur), Jones and Laughlin Steel (Admiral Ben Moreell), and Koppers (General Brehon Somervell).[33]

Although the federal government had provided much of the investment capital needed for plants during the war, private finance had regained the high ground by the 1950s boom. Historian Arthur Schlesinger, writing in 1965, noted, "The New York financial and legal community was [still] the heart of the American establishment. Its household deities were Henry L. Stimson and Elihu Root; its present leaders, Robert A. Lovett and John J. McCloy; its front organizations, the Rockefeller, Ford and Carnegie foundations and the Council on Foreign Relations."[34] The essential subtext, however, is that Root, Stimson, and Lovett were all former secretaries of war or defense, while McCloy was a senior assistant secretary who had gone on to become U.S. high commissioner in postwar Germany. During the quarter century after the war, the overlap between the national establishment and the military–national security–industrial complex was substantial and increasing, as provable in midtown Manhattan as in California.

Prescott Bush was no Stimson or Lovett. However, he was a reasonably senior establishment figure, well known to both men, and like both, he was deeply tied into both the military and intelligence communities. When Connecticut sent him to the U.S. Senate in 1952, he wound up on the Armed Services Committee. The personal matched the political; his most frequent golfing companions from the executive branch were President Eisenhower and the White House national security adviser, Gordon Gray. Vice President Richard Nixon was another.

Bush also kept up with the Dulles brothers. In 1946, almost as soon as

Allen Dulles was back in New York, Bush had him to lunch. In 1961, when Dulles was pushed from his CIA director's aerie because of the Bay of Pigs foul-up, he made it a point, on the day before his successor, John McCone, was named, to bring McCone along to a dinner with Prescott Bush.[35]

In 1962, as Bush was about to leave the Senate, he helped to launch the new National Strategy Information Center, to be run by Frank Barnett, a Right-tilting expert on political warfare and covert operations who had previously directed research at North Carolina's CIA-linked Smith Richardson Foundation. Bush knew well those involved, because during the early 1950s, at the request of H. Smith Richardson and his son-in-law Eugene Stetson, a Bonesman and former Brown Brothers Harriman colleague of Bush's, he had given the Richardsons advice and supportive counsel on setting up *their* foundation.

Which brings us to what, in the television quiz show parlance of that very era, was called "the $64,000 Question": Who—and what—was Prescott Bush in the U.S. intelligence community? And did he leave a legacy to his son?

The senior Bush was not *of* the intelligence community, in the sense of having been the director or an official of the OSS or CIA; but he was indisputably close to it, probably as a confidant, "asset," or high-level counselor, much as Juan Trippe of Pan American Airways and William S. Paley of CBS were widely thought to have been. Indeed, Prescott Bush was a long-serving member of both Trippe's and Paley's corporate boards. He was also a wartime board member of two companies—the Vanadium Corporation of America and Dresser Industries—that provided uranium ore and uranium gaseous diffusion pumps, respectively, for the Manhattan Project and subsequent atomic bomb development.[36]

Dresser's CIA connections probably matched those of CBS and Pan American. Researcher Bruce Adamson has obtained copies of 1953–54 correspondence between Dresser chief Neil Mallon and CIA director Allen Dulles. The meetings arranged between the two men sometimes also included Senator Prescott Bush, ex–German agent Hans Gisevius, or Defense Secretary Charles Wilson.[37] Several of the letters cited plans, notably a pilot project in the Caribbean, that had been thought up by Gisevius—hardly your everyday Dallas executive—now working for Dresser and Mallon.

The intrigued researcher, connecting these dots and many others, starts to assume that Prescott Bush of Yale, Skull and Bones, and Brown Brothers

Harriman was an off-the-books éminence grise, a Man Who Could Be Trusted, perhaps even a shadow CIA director. How he might have gotten there is even more murky. His uniformed service in World War I was in the artillery, not (apparently) military intelligence. Yale could have been an entry point, of course. Skull and Bones was an especially powerful initiation into the etiquette of keeping secrets and declining to discuss one's activities with outsiders. The New Haven milieu has been captured by one of the most descriptive paragraphs in Robin Winks's Yale-focused book *Cloak and Gown:*

> When, in March of 1945, Professor Norman Holmes Pearson of Yale's Department of English, on leave of absence as chief of the London branch of X-2, the counterintelligence operation of the OSS, rose to address fifty Yale alumni assembled at the Allies Club, he recognized almost no one, so quickly had the war changed the university, but he and all present (even two soldiers whom Pearson had flunked in his course) rose at the end of the talk. Out across Pall Mall floated the words, first of Yale's nearly official anthem, "Bright College Years," sung a bit incongruously to the air of the German anthem of World War I, "Die Wacht am Rhein," with its closing lines, "Oh, let these words our watch-cry be, / Where'er upon life's sea we sail—For God, for Country and for Yale!" And then, of course, all linked arms and serenaded Pearson with the "Whiffenpoof Song."[38]

Author John Loftus, with his compendia of anonymous intelligence interviews, put the finger on London's Whitehall, which hardly excluded New Haven: "Prescott himself had served in military intelligence during World War One, liaising with the British. According to our sources, he was trained by Stewart Menzies, later head of the British secret service during World War Two."[39] It is not implausible; the principal U.S. intelligence-coordinating body of 1914–18, the State Department's U-1 bureau, was run by two Yale Anglophiles, Frank Polk and Gordon Auchincloss, who were sometimes manipulated by the old hands of British intelligence.[40]

The Skull and Bones entente at Brown Brothers Harriman—Bush, both Harrimans, Robert A. Lovett, Ray Morris, Ellery James, and R. Knight Woolley—could also have drawn Bush in. Several besides him must have had intelligence connections. Moreover, it is hard to imagine that these men, including several future high-ranking national officials, didn't frequently discuss, in their Skull and Bones vein of confidentiality, the firm's more precarious involvements in Germany and elsewhere. With respect to the case of the German-linked Union Banking Corporation managed by Brown Brothers Harriman, several besides Bush shared legal responsibility. By the early 1940s, they had probably perceived UBC less as a profitable entity than as a poisonous snake to be watched closely. Whom they might have reported to, conceivably including Allen Dulles or Stewart Menzies, is not a matter of record.

Although no record remains of its dealings, there is little reason to believe that the Union Banking Corporation sat inertly and uneventfully through the tumultuous 1920s and 1930s. Even before the United States became involved in World War II, the bank's role in the Hitlerite scheme of things was a matter of keen speculation. The *New York Herald-Tribune,* a pillar of the state's Republican establishment, ran a front-page story on July 30, 1941, entitled "Thyssen Has $3,000,000 Cash in New York Vault."

Still, the notion cherished in some lurid publications and on Internet sites that the bank had post–Pearl Harbor significance or distributed cash to either Prescott Bush or George H. Walker seems fanciful. Indeed, the *Herald-Tribune* noted that one of Bush's Brown Brothers Harriman partners had contacted the New York State Banking Department in 1941 to inquire whether, with U.S. war involvement possibly imminent, he and his colleagues should leave the Union Banking Corporation board. State banking superintendent William R. White replied that while his office wouldn't try to stop them from stepping down, it would "be gratified if these gentlemen could find it possible to remain on the board during this period of uncertainty."[41] Eventually, the U.S. Justice Department took the money, and the UBC shares outstanding were canceled.[42]

One conclusion can reasonably be drawn: that the men who managed most of the high-level financial and corporate relations between the United States and Nazi Germany in the period from 1933 to 1941 developed an unusual kind of information and expertise that made them important to the war effort in general and the U.S. intelligence community in particular. As a result, after World War II was over, with the Soviet Union soon becoming an enemy and Germany being transformed into a U.S. ally, the new American national security state formed around a new establishment in which Prescott Bush and many of his friends were prominent and honored members.

George H. W. Bush:
Man in the Brooks Brothers Trench Coat?

It might even have started when the forty-first president was a boy. Phillips Andover, perhaps more than any other mid-twentieth-century American preparatory school, had its own ties to the Central Intelligence Agency— and not just because so many of its graduates wound up at Yale. Arthur Burr Darling, George H. W. Bush's history teacher at Andover, was a known intelligence community asset, obviously of considerable standing, who was chosen during the immediate post–World War II period to organize the historical files of the new Central Intelligence Agency and put together the agency's own official (but until 1989, altogether secret) account of its formation and early years. Its title: *The Central Intelligence Agency: An Instrument of Government to 1950.*

In the spring of 1942, it is unlikely that Darling was doing any OSS recruiting among the school's seventeen- and eighteen-year-olds. Ironically, though, as part of the curiosity many people have had about George H. W. Bush's hypothesized intelligence background, it has been suggested that after graduating from Andover in June, he could have been directly commissioned that year into the extremely flexible OSS as a way of easing him into navy flight school. Being only eighteen and fresh from Andover, he could not satisfy the normal flight-school entry requirement of two years of college.

Stranger things have happened. Still, most of the speculation-cum-analysis has assumed that if George H. W. Bush was one of the many, many mid-twentieth-century Ivy Leaguers to develop some kind of relationship with the CIA, it would have happened at Yale, or through his father's kaleidoscope of friends and intelligence community connections, or through his entry into the offshore oil rig business just at the time (1954) when U.S. intelligence activity in the Caribbean was escalating. This is where the probabilities start to mount.

The relationship between Yale and the CIA is hard to overstate. America's first spy, Nathan Hale, was Yale, class of 1773. Washington's later spymaster, dragoon major Benjamin Tallmadge, had been Hale's roommate. The statue of Hale in front of the CIA was cast from the original that stands in front of Yale's Connecticut Hall. Whereas other intelligence headquarters were called the fort, base, post, or station, the CIA's setup at Langley, Virginia, was named "the campus." In *Cloak and Gown*, Robin Winks described how the OSS and the CIA took from the Ivy League not just elitism or a penchant for academic studies but a sense of prankishness: "Put itching powder into safes, soon to be delivered to the Germans, so that file clerks would be discomfited? Parachute drop thousands of pornographic pamphlets onto the grounds at Berchtesgarten so that Hitler might be driven mad with sexual desire? . . . Invent exploding donkey turds that could be mixed with the real thing on the roads of Morocco?"[43]

Social standing could count as much as political dexterity. Yaleman and *Harper's* editor Lewis Lapham, whose brother served as CIA general counsel under George H. W. Bush, has told of his own interview for the CIA in the late 1950s, staged by interlocutors steeped in the mentality of Yale's Fence Club. Instead of being asked to

> discuss the treaties of Brest-Litovsk or name the four roads through the forest of the Ardennes, I was asked three questions bearing on my social qualifications for what the young men across the table clearly regarded as the best fraternity on the campus of the freedom-loving world:
>
> 1. When standing on the thirteenth tee at the National Golf Links in Southampton, which club does one take from the bag?
> 2. On sailing into Hay Harbor on Fishers Island, what is the direction of the prevailing wind?
> 3. Does Muffy Hamilton wear a slip?

Lapham, who got two out of three, decided he could pass up the career opportunity.[44]

Because George Bush attended Yale from 1946 to 1948 as a married man and new father, he missed some aspects of campus life, including living in the residential colleges, which were known as places for CIA recruiting efforts. On the other hand, as Professor Winks makes clear, Yalemen from schools like Andover were particularly attractive to the CIA. So were members of the secret societies and the major sports teams, especially the crew. He described this mood during Bush's own era in New Haven:

> The laying on of hands, quietly and effectively, in the college and the classroom, at the master's tea and in the seminar, over a cup at Mory's and during a break in crew practice, had by the 1950s become so accepted, as John Downey, a graduate of 1951, remarked, that it was taken for granted that one would serve the nation in some way; for him the choice lay between the CIA and fighting in Korea.[45]

From Yale's class of 1943 alone, at least forty-two young men entered the intelligence services.

Researcher Loftus, drawing on various intelligence sources, suggests that "there is reason to believe that George Bush's first association with intelligence operations came through his own circle of friends, not his father's. The Skull and Bones club was one of the principal recruiting sources for Dulles's Office of Policy Coordination [soon renamed the Office of Strategic Services] and later the CIA. Two of the thirteen members of George Bush's Skull and Bones class joined Dulles's intelligence fronts."[46]

On the other hand, Anthony Kimery, in *Covert Action Information Bulletin* (summer 1992), offers a different view: "The CIA's full-time headhunter at Yale was crew coach Allen 'Skip' Waltz, a former naval intelligence officer who had a good view of Bush. As a member of Yale's Undergraduate Athletic Association and Undergraduate Board of Deacons, Bush had to have worked closely with Waltz on the university's athletic programs from which the coach picked most of the men he steered to the CIA. It is inconceivable that Waltz didn't try to recruit Bush, say former Agency officials recruited at Yale." To Kimery, this suggested that Bush had *already* been recruited into intelligence, presumably during his military service.[47]

The influences of Prescott Bush's milieu must have been significant. But we should not forget George H. Walker's role. We've explored Prescott Bush's own circle and its wide connections. As for Walker, no one can know what, in those summer walks and hours out on the old man's boat in the 1930s and 1940s, he told the grandson who carried his name. However, Walker had derring-do to spare, plus strong interests in the Caribbean, where the political and covert action was soon to heat up. In addition to his European ventures, he had longstanding ties to Cuba and served as a director of seven related companies during the mid- and late 1920s and early 1930s: the Cuba Company, the Cuban Railroad, Cuban-Dominican Sugar, Barahona Sugar, Cuba Distilling, Sugar Estates of Oriente, and Atlantic Fruit and Sugar.[48] Prominent New York investment bankers did not undertake such commitments lightly; Walker was centrally involved with the island through three major industries: sugar, (rum) distilling, and a major railroad that served these enterprises (and became a symbol of *yanqui* power).

In the 1930s and early 1940s, young Bush's favorite uncle, Herbie—George Herbert Walker Jr.—took over directorships of several of these Cuban-Dominican sugar companies, which ultimately merged into West

Indies Sugar in 1942.[49] It is not hard to imagine the young George H. W. Bush picking up from grandfather and uncle alike a romantic sugar-plantation, rum, and palm-trees image of the heavily policed, old-regime Cuba of Fulgencio Batista. The island was much liked by a visiting generation of middle- and upper-class Americans.

His uncle would have been angry in 1959, when the new leftist Castro regime announced that it would nationalize the holdings of the U.S. sugar companies. Castro had launched his revolution several years earlier in eastern Cuba's sugar- and rum-centered Oriente Province, and some of the American owners of sugar mills and estates had contributed funds in the hope of moderating his movement.[50] Oriente-based West Indies Sugar had been a particular target of rebel levies and depredations.[51] Coincidentally, 1959 was the year when Uncle Herbie helped to finance the reorganization of Zapata by which the offshore drilling rigs—at least one operating near Cuba—became independent under Walker-Bush control. George H. Walker Jr. must have been even angrier in 1960 when Castro nationalized the West Indies Sugar Company, of which he had been a director until 1959. Infuriated by Castro's sugar estate seizures, the U.S. government withdrew its recognition of Cuba and launched an economic embargo in January 1961. Three months later came the Bay of Pigs invasion.

Grandfather Walker had died in 1953, but Prescott Bush, too, had a considerable psychological involvement with Cuba, its politics, and its importance to the United States. The events of the late 1950s and early 1960s would make the commitments of both Prescott and George H. W. Bush stand out in bold relief. Cuba's fate would be a personal as well as professional preoccupation. Old Batista-era loyalties would linger (even into the twenty-first century, when Florida governor Jeb Bush would nominate Batista's grandson, Raul Cantero, to the state supreme court).

George H. W. Bush's intelligence connections may have affected when and why he went to Texas. Working for Ray Kravis in Tulsa might not have been relevant; working for Neil Mallon, as Dresser shifted its focus and headquarters from Ohio to Texas and turned global, would have been more so. Dresser had top secret clearances during the 1941–45 war years for various projects, and after Mallon relocated to Dallas in 1950, the company's greatest growth came from overseas activity, conceivably including some covert projects.

The international side of the oil business, whether in the Middle East or the Caribbean, lent itself to close involvement with the CIA and U.S. intelligence, as numerous chroniclers have elaborated. Although George Bush left Dresser in 1951, he maintained close relations with Mallon and other friends there. They referred clients to him after he joined up with the Liedtke brothers in 1953 to form Zapata Petroleum, which decided to branch out into deep-sea drilling with Zapata Offshore in 1954. This happened to be the year that the CIA under Allen Dulles stepped up its own Caribbean activity with the overthrow of the Left-leaning government of Jacobo Arbenz Guzmán in Guatemala. Bruce Adamson, who assembled the Dresser-Dulles correspondence, wondered about a possible connection between the Bush-Liedtke Zapata Offshore enterprise and the Caribbean project that Dresser chief Mallon and former German intelligence officer Hans Gisevius had discussed a little earlier with Dulles.[52]

Here analysis has to rely on implication and common sense. Adamson, Loftus, *The Nation* magazine, and the U.S. journalism effort named Project Censored all posited some direct George H. W. Bush–CIA connection emerging between 1954 and 1963. Related hints of a Mexican-connected Bush initiation also came from reporter Jonathan Kwitny in his 1988 *Barron's* article "The Mexican Connection."[53] The implications are considerable; concrete proof is minimal.

In 1988, during Bush's presidential campaign, Kwitny revealed that back in 1960, Bush and Zapata Offshore, together with Jorge Diaz Serrano, a Mexican oilman recommended by Dresser, had set up a new Mexican company called Permargo. The latter, under the authority of Pemex, the Mexican oil monopoly, was to do deep-sea drilling off the Mexican coast for Pan American Petroleum, a firm run by U.S. oilman Ed Pauley. Pemex and Pauley were both known for CIA connections.

Bush, however, was already drilling for Pauley under a Zapata Offshore contract. Details about Zapata's Permargo involvement didn't check out, and Kwitny smelled a rat or two, especially when it emerged that in 1981, shortly after Bush had been elected vice president, the SEC "inadvertently destroyed" the Zapata Offshore SEC filings for 1960 to 1966.[54] Some years later Loftus wrote, "The 'old spies' say Bush lost his virginity in the oil business to Ed Pauley."[55] He added that "the Zapata-Permargo deal also caught the attention of Allen Dulles who, the 'old spies' report, was the man who recruited Bush's company as a part-time purchasing front for the CIA. Zapata provided commercial supplies for one of Dulles' most notorious operations: the Bay of Pigs invasion."[56]

Biographers have found more Zapata details in the papers of former

U.S. senator Ralph Yarborough, whom Bush unsuccessfully opposed in the 1964 election. That year, Yarborough, who liked to call Bush "a Connecticut carpetbagger," had arranged for a supporter named Allan Mandel to do some campaign research on Bush's company. What Mandel turned up—his report still exists among the senator's papers in Austin—was a description of Zapata Offshore's unusual and complex business structure: a half-dozen subsidiaries ranging from Zapata International, Seacat Zapata, and Zapata de Mexico to the Zapata Overseas Corporation.[57] Tax advantages were one explanation; handling covert funds could have been another.

As for CIA ties, Permargo obviously had some; in addition, note has been made of the published correspondence that connected Dresser with the CIA and Allen Dulles. We will also see shortly that the Liedtkes and Zapata-turned-Pennzoil were tied with Pemex to a 1972 CIA money-laundering chain related to the Watergate break-in. Bruce Adamson added that "George Bush and Edwin Pauley (both CIA) were both listed in 1954–55 in (CIA asset) George de Mohrenschildt's personal address book, which I obtained a copy [of] from the West Palm Beach Sheriff's office in 1992."[58] In 1988, Project Censored, a journalistic consortium based in California, chose the probability of George H. W. Bush being a CIA asset in 1963, when he ran Zapata Offshore, as one of the "top 10 censored" stories that year.[59]

Earlier in 1988, *The Nation* magazine had weighed in by reporting a November 29, 1963, FBI memo that "Mr. George Bush of the Central Intelligence Agency" was briefed by the Bureau about the reaction of the Cuban exile community in Miami to the Kennedy assassination.[60] In response, the CIA contended that the Bush involved was actually an agent named George William Bush. The magazine then tracked down George William Bush and found out that in 1963 he was only a junior analyst of the contours of coastlines.[61] *The Nation* added that a "source with close connections to the intelligence community confirms that Bush started working for the agency in 1960 or 1961, using his oil business as a cover for clandestine activities."[62]

The motive for Bush's intense feeling about Cuba—still throbbing in his 1964 Senate campaign, when he called for a U.S. invasion—becomes more understandable when one thinks about the Cuban rebels' treatment of family-connected sugar and distilling interests. No details exist on Walker-Bush holdings, but between 1957 and 1960, the assets of West Indies Sugar shrank from a value of $53 million to almost nothing, as the

Castro regime seized the company's lands, mills, and machinery.[63] George H. Walker Jr., who had arranged the funding for his nephew's Zapata Offshore enterprise, might well have warmed to his own covert action. Besides his presumed anger over the West Indian Sugar seizure, Walker was Skull and Bones, like his brother-in-law Prescott and his nephews George and Prescott junior. Things clandestine were part of their culture.

Yaleman Ron Rosenbaum, who wrote about Skull and Bones in the *New York Observer* and elsewhere, came up with a chilling angle in his attempts to trace the shell corporation—the Russell Trust Association—that had funded the society's year-to-year existence. A check with the Connecticut secretary of state's office in 2000 found no such corporation, which seemed to leave a dead end. But then a researcher's careful follow-up found out that years earlier the association had been abolished, then reestablished under the name RTA Incorporated.

Let Rosenbaum tell his own tale of discovery:

> The new papers of reincorporation that erased the century-old Russell Trust Association were filed at 10:15 A.M. on April 14, 1961. Two hours later, at noon on that day, the orders went out to begin the Bay of Pigs operations—the covert CIA-financed invasion of Castro's Cuba, a bloody fiasco that still haunts us four decades later. Coincidence? Probably. But then it's also true that one of the CIA's masterminds for the Bay of Pigs operation was a man named Richard Drain, Skull and Bones '43. And the White House planner of the Bay of Pigs operation was McGeorge Bundy, Skull and Bones '40. And the State Department liaison for the Bay of Pigs Operation was his brother William P. Bundy, Skull and Bones '39. And the man who filed the reincorporation papers that erased the Russell Trust Association from existence on the day of the Bay of Pigs was Howard Weaver, Skull and Bones '45W (George Bush's class), who retired from the CIA in 1959. All of which might lead one to suspect that the Skull and Bones corporate shell had been used as a clandestine conduit for the Bay of Pigs, and then erased from existence to cover up the connection as the invasion got under way.[64]

Yes, it must be a coincidence; it has to be a coincidence.

It is fair to say that by December 1975, when White House chief of staff Donald Rumsfeld was working to derail George H. W. Bush's presidential ambitions by slotting him as CIA director, three generations of the Bush and Walker families already had some six decades of intelligence-related activity and experience under their belts. However, there is still one more connection to mention: the Pemex-Pennzoil-CIA money line coincidentally or otherwise exposed in 1972 after funds it provided through Mexican banks were found in the hands of the Watergate burglars. Of those men, a solid majority—Howard Hunt, Frank Sturgis, Eugenio Martinez, Virgilio Gonzalez, and Bernard Barker—had been involved in the abortive Bay of Pigs episode.

Nixon and his senior advisers knew that the money had come through Mexican banks from "the Texans": regional Nixon finance chief William Liedtke, Robert Mosbacher, and other Bush friends. Apparently they were not sure what that meant—what kind of a CIA pipeline was involved or what kind of usage was under way. Author Loftus says that George H. W. Bush's subsequent high standing with the intelligence community came not from his Bay of Pigs involvement but from "when he told Nixon that he could not shift the blame for the Mexican slush fund to the CIA without wrecking the intelligence community."[65]

There is no proof that Bush conveyed any such warning. Moreover, Nixon's White House chief of staff, H. R. Haldeman, gave a different view in his 1978 book *The Ends of Power:* "If the Mexican bank connection was actually a CIA operation all along, unknown to Nixon, and Nixon was destroyed for asking the FBI to stop investigating the bank because it might uncover a CIA operation (which the Helms memo seems to indicate it actually was all along), the multiple layers of deception by the CIA are astounding."[66]

At any rate, the national security state was only slightly wounded in the sixties and seventies, rebounding to thrive in the eighties and nineties despite a few bumps after the breakup of the Soviet Union, when the CIA briefly feared for its future. More to the point, two men named George Bush would be CIA director, vice president, or president of the United States for seventeen of the twenty-eight years between 1976 and 2004. In a very real but little understood sense, the Bush dynasty was already getting under way in 1980–81 when George Bush went from the CIA director's job to the vice presidency, a jump no one had ever managed before and one that brought a new and unfamiliar mind-set to the elected executive office.

In 1981, because of Bush's CIA experience—and perhaps also because of the influence of the White House chief of staff, James A. Baker III, who had managed the Texan's 1980 nomination campaign—President Reagan issued National Security Directive 3, naming the vice president to head a Special Situation Group to identify national security crises and plan for them. A new era of clandestine arms sales, massive armaments buildups, secret diplomacy, and covert actions, perhaps as much Bush's doing as Reagan's, was about to unfold in the Middle East generally and in Iran, Iraq, and Afghanistan specifically. With it, the seeds of two Persian Gulf wars and hundreds of terrorist strikes would be fertilized and watered.

PART III

Religion, Oil,
Armaments,
and War

CHAPTER 7

The American Presidency and the Rise of the Religious Right

"Fundamentalism" is one of the most significant political phenomena of our time. Since the Iranian Revolution, purported fundamentalist movements have risen to the highest levels of power in five countries—in Iran in 1979, in the Sudan in 1993, in Turkey, Afghanistan and India in 1996, and again in India in 1998 and 1999. There have been even more frequent penetrations by fundamentalist movements into the parliaments, assemblies and political parties of such countries as Jordan, Israel, Egypt, Morocco, Pakistan and the United States.

Gabriel Almond, R. Scott Appleby, and Emmanuel Sivan, *Strong Religion,* 2003

Bush believes in God's will—and in winning elections with the backing of those who agree with him. As a subaltern in his father's 1988 campaign, George Bush the Younger assembled his career through contacts with ministers of the then-emerging evangelical movement in political life. Now they form the core of the Republican Party, which controls all of the capital for the first time in a half century. Bible-believing Christians are Bush's strongest backers.

Newsweek, March 10, 2003

Geor ge W. Bush's early emergence in national politics, between 1986 and 1994, tapped religious forces akin to those promoting Ariel Sharon and Benjamin Netanyahu in Israel and fueling the rise of Islamic parties in Pakistan, Turkey, and elsewhere. The consequences of this late-twentieth-century upheaval may not be clear until well into the twenty-first.

This is not a daring statement. These years saw conservative religion on a roll from Texarkana to Tashkent. Several dozen religious scholars assembled by the Fundamentalism Project of the American Academy of Arts and Sciences concluded that significant populations in several dozen countries—the United States prominent among them—shared in a deep-seated countermovement against secular trends and measures ascendant during the 1960s and 1970s.[1]

The "family resemblance" the Fundamentalism Project perceived among movements did not mean they were identical. Yet each of the movements displayed "a discernible pattern of religious militance by which self-styled 'true believers' attempt to arrest the erosion of religious identity, fortify the borders of the religious community, and create viable alternatives to secular institutions and behaviors."[2] That kind of militance bred most easily within religions that allowed congregations autonomy: Protestantism, Islam, and Judaism. Roman Catholicism was not as fertile a ground, being more centralized. Beyond indignation over secularization, other circumstances nurturing fundamentalism included high ratios of uprooted persons, unstable politics or civil war, large-scale migration, economic distress, loss of territory, defeat by foreigners, or "imperialist" subjection.[3]

Militant white Protestants in the southern United States met the project's criteria, as did radical minorities of Israeli Jews; many movements in Islam; Hindus and Sikhs in India; Buddhists in Myanmar, Thailand, and Sri Lanka; Confucians in East Asia; and Pentecostals in portions of Latin America.[4] Signs of fundamentalist behavior were clear in most of these places by the 1970s and 1980s.

The Making of a Fundamentalist Politician

Besides the larger trends affecting the nation, George W. Bush had a personal vulnerability. After growing up in the shadow of a successful family, disdaining Ivy League elites at both Yale and Harvard Business School, then wandering around the Sun Belt in a series of National Guard assignments and unsuccessful jobs and enterprises, by the late 1970s he *personally* fit several of the Fundamentalism Project's "frustration" criteria. He would fit one more by the mid-1980s as collapsing oil prices crippled yet another Bush business.

By 1985–86, evangelist Billy Graham had, in Bush's own words, "planted a mustard seed" of salvation in his soul. The message apparently caught hold during a summer weekend in 1985 when Graham was visiting George and Barbara Bush at their summer house in Kennebunkport, Maine. Before long, son George W. was studying the Bible, giving up liquor (in 1986), and preparing to put his new "born-again" faith to the test by assuming responsibility for liaison with the Religious Right in the 1988 presidential campaign, which his father was assembling. As this liaison role unfolded, many in the Washington press corps paid little attention. Some thought George W. was not much more than a loyalty enforcer and a contact within the campaign for the family and its friends. His public role was so small that in 1989, when two long-established and respected Washington reporters, Jack Germond and Jules Witcover, published a full-length campaign chronicle entitled *Whose Broad Stripes and Bright Stars? The Trivial Pursuit of the Presidency, 1988,* they did not discuss the part played by George W. Bush. The campaign's successful courtship of the Religious Right was barely noted. The name of the Republican nominee's eldest son did not appear in the index.

A decade later, however, as George W. Bush prepared for his 2000 presidential race, Texas-based biographer Bill Minutaglio of the *Dallas Morning News* devoted a dozen revealing pages in his book to the "First Son"'s frontline baptism in the 1988 campaign: serving as his father's ambassador to the suspicious but ever-growing Religious Right.[5] Being the prodigal son redeemed by Billy Graham was a helpful credential. The younger Bush also had the services of Doug Wead, an Assemblies of God minister for two decades, formerly associated with Amway, singer Pat Boone, and televangelists Jim and Tammy Faye Bakker.

The son was not the only family member listening to the Religious Right. Campaign officials who shrugged off George W.'s influence on his father were ignoring the transformation of George and Barbara Bush. By the end of the summer of 1986, they had invited Jim and Tammy Faye Bakker for a visit, telling them how much they enjoyed watching *The P.T.L. Club* on television. The vice president also appeared at Jerry Falwell's Liberty University, and discussed his own born-again "life-changing experiences" in a video that was shown to evangelical leaders.[6]

As for George W.'s own evolution from 1986 to 1988, biographer Minutaglio summed up:

> He plowed through receiving lines, acting as his father's surrogate at swings through the southern states; glad-handing evangelicals at the Washington campaign headquarters and being the family spokesman in the intense and often uncomfortable mating ritual between Team Bush and the Christian Right. . . . Throughout the spring and into late summer [of 1987],

he was conferring with Wead about how to seal Team Bush ties to [Paul] Weyrich and the unflinching Christian right wing—how to do it the way that Reagan had done it—and they were also talking about the book he was helping oversee with Doug Wead that would serve as one of the "authorized" Bush campaign publications. Aimed at evangelicals and right-leaning conservatives, it would be entitled *Man of Integrity* . . . and it catalogued the Bush family's relationships with [Billy Graham and] several other religious leaders, including "dear friend" Jerry Falwell.[7]

After the election, several senior GOP strategists recalled how they had met this or that religious leader for the first time in George W.'s office during the campaign. Wead and the younger Bush swept a broad net, bringing religious leaders into the political fold. In the race for the 1988 nomination, the ostensible Religious Right candidate, televangelist Pat Robertson, had scored early successes by inundating party caucuses in the Midwest and West with his highly motivated Pentecostal supporters. However, when the broader and decisive southern GOP primaries rolled around in March, the elder George Bush, an Episcopalian hitherto distrusted by the Religious Right, reaped the profits of his team's—and his son's—early backstage alliance-building. He crushed Robertson by 47 percent to 29 percent even among white Dixie born-again Christians.[8] Afterward, Bush strategists brought Robertson and his backers into the national campaign, both harnessing and silencing them. Meanwhile, they borrowed several Robertson themes—deploring secular opposition to the Pledge of Allegiance, belaboring alleged American Civil Liberties Union hostility to religion—that proved effective against Democratic nominee Michael Dukakis, an ACLU member, in the general election.[9]

November brought George H. W. Bush 70 percent of the evangelical vote, just 5 points below Reagan's 1984 landslide share. Political scientists James Guth of Furman University and John C. Green of the Ray Bliss Institute at the University of Akron collected a dozen revealing analyses in their book *The Bible and the Ballot Box: Religion in the 1988 Election*. While these analyses rarely pointed to individual strategists, they documented an efficient and highly successful Republican campaign so far as the Religious Right was concerned. Green and Guth saw politics in the United States "moving toward a more European pattern, in which conservative parties draw heavily from religious groups and leaders, while parties of the left are supported by more secular forces."[10]

That would soon be an understatement. Six years later, as George W. Bush launched his 1994 Texas gubernatorial bid, a survey by the Washington magazine *Campaigns and Elections* found that of the eleven southern states, nine had state Republican parties that were controlled or substantially influenced by the Religious Right. As we have seen, the convention that nominated him for governor that year began with a Grand Old Prayer Breakfast; there, old-line country-club Republicans found themselves outnumbered by Christian tabernacle-goers.

In critical ways, George W. was the reverse of his father. Whereas George H. W. Bush so lacked underlying credibility that between 1985 and 1988 (and again in 1992) he had to fawn on the Religious Right, his son's personal ties and connections to evangelicals were strong and believable. From 1994 to 2000, his overt religiosity, penchant for biblical phraseology, and careful cultivation of the "parachurch" network—viewers of religious broadcasting, key ministers, activists, and coalition members—eliminated any need for counterproductive public kowtowing.[11]

On election day in 2000, George W. Bush won only 48 percent of the nationwide popular vote, but his backing from high-commitment evangelicals (84 percent) exceeded Reagan's in 1984 or his father's in 1988. In a related development, support for the GOP presidential nominee correlated with the intensity of individual churchgoing and religiosity among Protestants, Catholics, and Jews alike. Nevertheless, for the first time, a Republican presidential victory rested on a religious, conservative, southern-centered coalition led by a bloc of white Protestant fundamentalists and evangelicals numerous enough to cast 40 percent of the total ballots amassed by its presidential nominee.[12]

Two decades earlier, as we will see, Ronald Reagan had talked of how world events seemed to signal Armageddon. By 2000, some 46 percent of U.S. Christians told poll takers of their own Armageddon belief. What few in the press had pursued, though, was just how much similar fundamentalism George W. Bush and his advisers had absorbed from their own biblical readings. If the extent was unclear, its relevance was increasing. Despite important differences, Christian, Jewish, and Muslim prophecies converged in anticipating a great confrontation in the Middle East.

Within each faith, important minorities thought the hour might be approaching: doctrinal Christians looked for signs of the end times, Jews for the tenth red heifer that would signal the messiah, and the apocalyptic segment of Muslims for a rising tempo of wars, corruption, and fighting over

Jerusalem. Meanwhile, in the United States, Israel, and more than half of the Islamic world, national government was controlled by parties or coalitions that depended on true believers for vital support.

This meant that after the World Trade Center was destroyed in September 2001, the Islamic fundamentalists-cum-terrorists of the Al Qaeda movement faced a U.S. president interested in more than cold-blooded retribution. Having been chosen disproportionately by America's own doctrinal believers, he responded with overtly biblical attacks on evil and "evil ones." He confided to friends that he felt chosen by God to lead the nation in its response. He would even, in an excess of candor, describe the U.S. response to 9/11 as a "crusade."

The Bush Family and the Rise of the Religious Right

Two of the forty-third president's four great-grandfathers, George H. Walker and Samuel Bush, were Episcopalians. So were his grandfather and his father. However, while few have ever doubted the sincerity of George W. Bush's conversion from the staid church of New England to the emotional church of evangelical Texas, that conversion does provide a vivid metaphor for the cultural and political transformation of U.S. Protestantism during the last decades of the twentieth century.

In 2003, Professors Gabriel Almond, R. Scott Appleby, and Emmanuel Sivan, drawing on the Fundamentalism Project's interdisciplinary research into "antimodernist, antisecular militant religious movements of five continents," included latter-day U.S. Protestant fundamentalism prominently among them. The term "fundamentalism" had first been used in the United States in 1920 to describe a combat to uphold religious fundamentals against the teaching of evolution and other forms of modernism.[13] It would apply again to the aggressive U.S. Protestantism of the late twentieth century, shouldering aside the easygoing mainline denominations.

Between 1960 and 2000, the membership of the evangelical Southern Baptist Convention jumped from 10 million to 17 million, while the Pentecostal churches soared from under 2 million to almost 12 million. Mormons and Seventh-Day Adventists likewise gained. On the more sedate side of the ledger, the mainline Episcopalians dropped from 3.5 million to 2 million, and the United Methodists slumped from more than 10 million to under 8 million.[14] The meaning of these changes deepened when one compared the religious intensity, ideology, and party preference of the different clergies. Strict fundamentalist-type churches gained; doctrinally loose mainline churches—the Coolidge- and Eisenhower-era pillars of the old Protestant Republican establishment—shrank.

The allegro movement of this realignment was swelling in the mid- to late 1980s, precisely when a born-again George W. Bush walked onto the national political stage. Liberal religion was being routed. Surveys taken for the 1988 election captured the extraordinary theological and public policy divisions between the clergy of the Pentecostal Assemblies of God and the Southern Baptists and the mainline (then still unmerged) Presbyterians. Political party preference mirrored the ideological chasm.

On the theological right, 97 percent of the Assemblies of God (AOG) clergy and 88 percent of the Southern Baptist Convention preachers agreed that Jesus was the only way to salvation; 95 percent of the AOG and 79 percent of the SBC clergy insisted that the devil actually existed; 83 percent of the AOG and 54 percent of the SBC shepherds expressed belief in the church's "rapture." Conversely, among the Presbyterian clergy—mainline Episcopalians and Congregationalists would not have been too different— only 30 percent identified Jesus as the only way to salvation, just 18 percent believed in the devil, and a tiny 5 percent expected the rapture.[15]

Abortion, pornography, and gay rights topped the concerns of the Pentecostal clergy. Presbyterian ministers, by contrast, prioritized hunger and poverty, civil rights, and the environment. In 1988 voting, 99 percent of the Assemblies of God clergy and 83 percent of the Southern Baptist Convention preachers backed Republican George H. W. Bush for president, while 63 percent of the Presbyterian sample cast votes for Democrat Michael Dukakis. Between then and 2000, the gap between the Pentecostals and evangelicals and the mainline denominations would continue to widen, but without the sudden momentum of the seventies and eighties.[16]

A further and important family resemblance between the fundamentalists in the United States and those in the Islamic world, Israel, and elsewhere lay in the urgent events in their separate countries. According to Fundamentalism Project scholars, dissonance had swelled in Israel after the disappointments and territorial concessions that followed the 1973 Yom Kippur War. Unrest across Islam in the 1960s and 1970s grew not just over Israel but in response to the Westernization and secularization promoted by governments in Egypt, Iran, and elsewhere. The New Christian Right in the United States found roots in a sense of "U.S. society spinning out of control in the sixties."[17]

In the United States, the alienation defined itself more quickly in politics than in theology. In 1969, I published a book called *The Emerging Republican Majority,* the analyses of which had been used in the Republican presidential campaign of 1968. Its premise was that antiliberal cultural resentments arising out of the 1960s were realigning U.S. politics and would give the Republican Party a generation of national supremacy based on the South, the Midwest, and the West once Dixie abandoned the third-party racial politics of George Wallace. All this came to pass in 1972 when the Democrats settled on the very liberal George McGovern as their presidential nominee. Religious explanations also began to appear.

Two researchers, Gerald Strober and Lowell Streiker, published *Religion and the New Majority: Billy Graham, Middle America, and the Politics of the 1970s.* The Democrats could not win in 1972, the two said, without a centrist nominee whose appeal had "some relation to the theological and social positions of Billy Graham."[18] Dean Kelley of the National Council of Churches added a compelling 1972 presentment, *Why Conservative Churches Are Growing.* "Strong" or high-commitment, absolutist churches, he explained, were overpowering the weak and doctrinally permissive mainline Protestant denominations. Samuel Lubell, the voting-patterns expert, brought out *The Future While It Happened* in 1973, including his shrewd analysis of the coming pivotal role of the Southern Baptists, cited in chapter 4.

The political mobilization of a full-fledged Religious Right, however, was still years away. The early antiliberal countertrends were cultural and political, much in evidence from 1967 to 1970 as racially related riots and antiwar demonstrations ripped cities and campuses. Political liberalism buckled in 1968 as Richard Nixon and George Wallace got 57 percent of the total presidential vote. Cultural strands emanating from white rural America, meanwhile, were writ large in the craze for country music—full-time country radio stations exploded from 208 in 1965 to 650 by 1970—which often voiced populist and patriotic themes, like Merle Haggard's "Okie from Muskogee." A second display came in the proliferation of white ethnic neighborhood groups, folk festivals, and heritage studies.[19]

By 1972, these currents, swelled by voter dislike of George McGovern's identification with campus liberalism and notions of an Age of Aquarius dawning over America, enabled Nixon to carry every county in Oklahoma and all but one in both Missouri and West Virginia. This was an unprecedented GOP sweep of old Jeffersonian rural areas steeped in border-state history and small-town, church and flag values—even in Eisenhower's 1956 landslide, thirty-eight counties in Oklahoma, fifty-nine in Missouri, and seventeen in West Virginia had gone Democratic. The brief liberal reformation of the sixties had unleashed a counterreformation, and even Watergate in 1973–74 would only delay, not abort it.

The seventies brought an open religious backlash against what conservatives distastefully called "secular humanism." In 1971, the U.S. Supreme Court in *Lemon v. Kurtzman* narrowed what federal and state statutes could permissibly do to support religion, increasing churchgoers' unhappiness prompted by the Court's 1962 *Engel v. Vitale* prohibition of even nondenominational school prayers. Additional provocation came in 1973 as Congress sent the Equal Rights Amendment to the Constitution to the states for ratification, and the Supreme Court ruled in *Roe v. Wade* that laws restricting abortion during the first six months of pregnancy were unconstitutional. In 1977, parental concern about nudity, profanity, and violence on televison and in the movies spurred Donald Wildmon, a Methodist minister from Tupelo, Mississippi, to launch the Coalition for Better Television, a national movement to purify the airwaves.

The first major organizations of the political Religious Right were born in 1979, when Washington conservative strategist Paul Weyrich and Virginia minister Jerry Falwell established the Moral Majority to combat the spread of secular humanism; Tennessee evangelical activist Edward McAteer launched the Religious Roundtable to conjoin political and religious conservatives; and Californians set up Christian Voice to grade the Christian morality of officeholders on issues from sex education to school prayer and abortion.

Nineteen eighty brought the election of the first president to be supported by—and more or less publicly allied with—the Religious Right: Ronald Reagan. Although he delivered more rhetoric than tangible rollbacks of secularism, his pronouncements made him a hero to many traditionalist Democrats of Catholic, Southern Baptist, and Pentecostal beliefs. Winning landslide reelection in 1984, he sometimes regained and in a few cases exceeded Nixon's 1972 levels among these groups.

Such was the tenor of the era as George W. Bush stepped into national politics. Reagan's landslide reelection confirmed Nixon's prior cultural and religious breakthroughs—80 percent support from fundamentalists and evangelicals and roughly 70 percent from Baptists—which opinion molders had chosen to dismiss following Watergate and the Republican loss of the White House.[20] For several years, the 1976 victory of Jimmy Carter, a born-again peanut farmer from rural Georgia backed by about 58 percent of his Baptist co-religionists, was taken to reaffirm Democratic access to the fundamentalist and evangelical electorate. However, when Carter's share of the Baptists slipped to 40 percent or so in his 1980 loss to Reagan, the Republican tidal flow became a topic again—and Reagan's 1984 landslide set up a template.

In 1988, George H. W. Bush came through with flying colors so far as maintaining the loyalty of the Christian Right. If Nixon and Reagan had shown that the fundamentalists could be won by huge majorities under favorable circumstances, the elder Bush demonstrated that with serious preparation, most could be held for a less appealing candidate in a difficult year. It helped, to be sure, that Michael Dukakis was a prim and colorless Massachusetts governor, described by Garry Wills as the "first truly secular candidate" for president in U.S. history.[21]

In 1989, after his father's inauguration, George W. Bush returned to Texas, locating in Dallas, where he ran the Texas Rangers baseball team. With his sponsor gone, Doug Wead did not last long in the Bush White House. Moreover, as George H. W. Bush became overconfident about reelection in the wake of the Gulf War, his relations with the Christian Right deteriorated. Among the many factors in his 1992 reelection defeat was that, as his reelection support dropped, he attempted to make up for this by openly pandering to right-wing preachers, a tactic that is usually a net loser in the court of public opinion.

Jimmy Carter's victory in 1976 had been taken as restoring the Democratic Party's opportunity with evangelical voters; Bill Clinton's election in 1992 was not. Sixteen years earlier, Carter had carried most of the South. In 1992, even in defeat, George H. W. Bush won seven of the eleven ex-Confederate states, his largest bloc of electoral votes. Clinton stirred a deep and widespread animosity—and fundamentalist, Pentecostal, and evangelical voters took front rank because of their moral indignation. The Republican capture of Congress in 1994 topped a year in which the Religious Right was acknowledged to have played a starring anti-Clinton role. Both Bush brothers, George W. and Jeb, enjoyed its strong backing in their Texas and Florida gubernatorial races. Of the two, Jeb Bush took the harder line, writing off the black vote and selecting the Christian Coalition's Legislator of the Year, Tom Mooney, as his lieutenant gubernatorial running mate. This tactical rigidity probably helped to bring about his narrow loss to Democrat Lawton Chiles.

In Texas, though, George W. Bush also had the state's deeper religiosity on his side. In the words of one political study, "It is an understatement to say that religion holds a paramount position in Texas society. . . . Fully 92% of Texans believe that religion is 'important' in their lives. Most, some 70%, routinely attend religious services. Eighty-six percent pray at home at least once a week. . . . A majority proclaim a traditional commitment to their religion, while one-fifth characterize their religious fervor as fundamentalist, evangelistic, or charismatic. . . . More than seven of every ten adult Texans believe that the Bible is God's word and that all its prophecies will transpire."[22] Not surprisingly, a culture so steeped in religion encouraged the Christian Right of the 1990s to eschew third-party activities, preferring a degree of control over the Texas GOP. In the Lone Star State, church and preacher influence was not easily impugned.

No state, in short, could have been better at preparing a born-again Republican governor to pursue a similar coalition—business being the second pillar—at the national level. By the 1990s, established GOP candidates did not have to pander to preachers at election time. Homilies about compassion and "the wounded traveler on the road to Jericho" confused northern journalists more than experienced Texans, who knew that the Scripture a politician might read from wasn't necessarily his or her weekday text in the state legislature.

In 1998 and 1999, as George W. Bush prepared for his White House run, he periodically took pains to cloak himself in his father's old moderate themes—words like "education," "reading," "literacy," and "children" dotted his speeches and press conferences. Constituencies in the Religious Right locked up during his 1998 Texas reelection drive wouldn't be offended or jeopardized, and in any event, the back door to the governor's mansion was kept open to their emissaries.

The Christian Right's embarrassment in the 1998 elections over its excesses in promoting Clinton's impeachment—Democrats turned preacher prominence into a late-hour issue—sent a further cautionary message to Bush strategists: Secure the religious leaders and power centers privately, then convince them to keep a low profile. In explaining that year's results, the University of Akron's John Green, now a leading national expert on religious politics, concluded that "the 1998 election can only be described as a defeat for the Christian Right. Several of its most prominent supporters were retired by the voters, many allies lost close contests, and the movement was a liability in some high-profile races. However, the 1998 election was not a debacle for the Christian Right. Many of its key supporters were re-elected, some new allies gained office, and the movement was an asset in some important races. . . . The Republicans actually won the congressional election, posting the highest popular vote margin since 1946."[23]

For George W. Bush, the Religious Right's sense of rebuff was a tactical blessing, much like the discomfiture of the Robertson forces in 1988 following their fumbles and negative portrayal by the press. Chastened, the Robertson forces had let themselves be pulled into the Republican Party organizationally. In 1999, embarrassed Christian Right impeachment leaders by and large made the same choice: to accept the tactical critiques being circulated, seek a low profile, and back party favorite Bush rather than Gary Bauer, the little-known Christian Right leader planning his own 2000 presidential race.

Bauer withdrew in early February, never having gained traction. In the end, the only significant Religious Right sightings in the 2000 campaign came at George W. Bush's own request, in urgent need: in South Carolina, where their loyal legions enabled him to win that state's February 19 Republican primary, thereby derailing the bandwagon started by John McCain's New Hampshire primary landslide on February 1. The negatives came in the general election, when he paid the cost of three incidents: visiting controversial right-wing Bob Jones University, seeking praise from Robertson and Falwell, and tangling with McCain over the role of theocracy in the GOP. Together these hurt Bush among middle-of-the-road voters.

In January 2001, at a Washington panel called "Evangelicals in Civil Life: How the Faithful Voted," some conservative activists pointed out that evangelical turnout was lower in 2000 than in 1994 and 1996. However, greater attention focused on another query: "Isn't there an untold story here how Bush got Christian Right leaders to keep a low profile during the campaign?"[24] John Green agreed: "I was absolutely amazed that those leaders actually worked quite hard for the Republican ticket and didn't make the type of headlines they have typically made that would disillusion other voters. Yes, there is a good untold story there."[25]

The President of the United States as the Leader of the Christian Right

To understand George W. Bush, it is crucial to understand how the president of the United States could simultaneously be the leader of the nation's Christian Right. Serious discussion of that once improbable identification intensified after 9/11, but it actually began, backstage, during the 2000 politicking.

One indispensable ingredient was the contrast between Bush and the Right's leading bogeyman. "Bill Clinton's moral bankruptcy created the essential need to replace him with someone who would be closer to them," said Georgetown University political scientist Clyde Wilcox.[26] Bush's commitment to prayer and born-again testimony attracted conservative Christians, who backed him hoping that his religious beliefs would lead to policy changes that favored faith. The confrontation in South Carolina may have alienated some moderates; it also galvanized religious conservative voters *for* Bush.

The idea that religion itself was imperiled had been a Religious Right theme for a quarter of a century, and now had a political payoff. Denominations that hitherto had sniped at one another or split hairs were working together. After the 2000 election, as we have seen, polling data upheld a startling breakthrough. In each religious category, evangelical and Pentecostal, mainline Protestant and Catholic, the more observant who attended church at least once a week gave the highest backing to Bush. Religious intensity was becoming more important than denomination.

Thirty or forty years before, middle-class and more secularized Catholics had been most inclined to the Republicans, with old-line, churchgoing ethnic Catholics remaining Democratic. In 2000, this had reversed. Observant Catholics supported Bush by at least three to two, depending on which poll was cited. Within the Jewish community, nominal and secular Jews were the strong Democrats. But among New York City's Orthodox Jews, some of them ideological cousins of Israel's own Religious Right, Democratic presidential candidates had been losing for decades. Albert Gore drew only 25 to 30 percent in Brooklyn's Orthodox and Hasidic strongholds. More than a million Muslims voted in the United States in 2000, and according to a sampling in Florida, they went heavily for Bush.[27] Whether or not religiosity itself made them more Republican was not probed; perhaps they were countermobilized by the Gore-Lieberman ticket.

As the Republicans became the party of the godly, the Democrats edged toward representation of secular America. Each trend seemed to reinforce the other. Overall, Americans fell away from organized religion between 1960 and 2000, as the proportion of voters who said they attended services every week dropped from 38 percent to 25 percent.[28] Thus, even as the percentages of churchgoers who were evangelicals or fundamentalists grew, the "secular" share of the total U.S. population—persons never going to religious services—jumped from 11 percent of the population in 1972 to 33 percent in 2000. As these nonchurchgoing ratios rose, so did their relative importance to the Democratic Party. In the 2000 election, secular voters went lopsidedly for Gore and cast an important percentage of his total vote.[29]

The terrorist attacks of 9/11 cut two ways. To the faithful, Bush's invocation of good versus evil and his assumption of an almost biblical leadership role not only resonated but increased his Christian stature. Secular voters, despite doubt about some of Bush's language, accepted it at least as a clarion amid crisis. Most also supported his harsh military response to the Taliban clerics in Afghanistan. In the near term, both reactions were boons to Bush, strengthening what previously had been an insecure presidency with no particular national mandate.

Not that favor was unanimous. Some mainline Protestant leaders worried about misusing religious language and breaching the wall between church and state. And on the day before Christmas, 2001, the *Washington Post,* based on interviews with Christian political activists, reported an extraordinary development: "Pat Robertson's resignation this month as President of the Christian Coalition confirmed the ascendance of a new leader of the religious right in America: George W. Bush."[30]

"I think that Robertson stepped down because the position has already been filled," said Gary Bauer, the religious stalwart who challenged Bush in the GOP primaries. The president "is that leader right now. There was already a great deal of identification with the president before 9-11 in the world of the Christian Right, and the nature of this war is such that it has heightened the sense that a man of God is in the White House."[31] Ralph Reed, the Christian Coalition's former president, added, "I've heard a lot of 'God knew something we didn't.' In the evangelical mind, the notion of an omniscient God is central to their theology. He had a knowledge nobody else had: He knew George Bush had the ability to lead in this compelling way."[32]

In fact, the willingness of the Religious Right to keep quiet to help Bush win had already taken its own leaders out of the spotlight in 2000, subordinating movement causes to Bush's success. "He is the leader of the Christian right," said another former Christian Coalition activist, Marshall Wittman. "As their institutions peel away, he can go over the heads" of religious conservative leaders.[33] Some journalists took these postelection circumstances as acknowledgment of a weakened Religious Right.

A different way of looking at Bush's support might be that fundamentalists, evangelicals, and Pentecostals had decided they had more to gain by consolidating their influence—already considerable from casting 40 percent of the president's 2000 popular vote—*within* his administration and party. This new relationship rested on three principal pillars.

First, Bush's personal religiosity was conspicuous. An adviser described him as "our first modern president who is born again not only in his heart and mind but in his actions," an implied contrast to the secular political behavior of Jimmy Carter. According to religious broadcaster Janet Parshall, "He's so unhesitatingly unembarrassed by his faith. He works it into his verbiage, his public policy, his comportment. . . . His faith so totally defines him."[34]

Second, belief in the "power of prayer" was a bulwark. Bush told one California assemblage how he knew the American people were praying for him: "I can just feel it. I can't describe it very well, but I feel comforted by the prayer." He asked that Americans pray for "God's protection . . . a spiritual shield that protects the country."[35]

Finally, if prayer also did duty in gathering true believers, Bush's day-to-day language was a veritable biblical message center. Besides the ever-present references to "evil" and "evil ones," chief White House speechwriter Mark Gerson, a onetime college theology major, filled George W. Bush's delivery system with phrases that, while inoffensive to secular voters, directed more specific religious messages to the faithful. Examples cited in the popular press included "whirlwind" (a medium for the voice of God in the Books of Job and Ezekiel), a "work of mercy" (a reference to Catholic theology's "seven corporal works of mercy"), and phrases like "safely home" and "wonder-working power," taken from hymns and gospel songs.

Biblical scholar Bruce Lincoln's line-by-line analysis of Bush's October 7, 2001, address to the nation announcing the U.S. attack on Afghanistan identified a half dozen veiled borrowings from the Book of Revelation, Isaiah, Job, Matthew, and Jeremiah. He concluded that for those with ears to hear a biblical subtext, "by the [speech's] end America's adversaries have

been redefined as enemies of God and current events have been constituted as confirmation of scripture." Through "strategies of double coding,"
George W. Bush could relay one message to secular listeners and another to
the faithful awaiting their reassurance.[36]

Occasional presidential use of phrases popular with preachers like Falwell and Robertson could be used to give them quiet recognition. A top
campaign operative told *Newsweek* that during the critical 2000 primary in
South Carolina, sending Bush to ultrafundamentalist Bob Jones University
had been a calculated appeal to Christian Right voters: "We had to send a
message—fast—and sending him there was the only way to do it."[37]

Bush's religious allies also responded to the large number of top personnel and policymaking jobs given to Christian Right appointees, especially where they would deal with hot-button subject matter: church-state
relations, federal aid to religion, women's rights, birth control, abortion-
related drugs, family aid, and federal volunteer programs.

As head of the Office of Personnel Management, in charge of federal
workforce support, Bush chose conservative activist Kay Coles James, formerly dean of the Robertson School of Government at Pat Robertson–
founded Regent University. David Caprara, made head of AmeriCorps
VISTA, the federal community volunteers group, had directed the American Family Coalition, a faith-based affiliate of Sun Myung Moon's Unification Church. By some accounts, Caprara was one of Moon's top grassroots
organizers.[38]

At the Justice Department, Attorney General John Ashcroft was a lay
activist in the Pentecostal Assemblies of God, pious enough that before being sworn in he had himself anointed with cooking oil in the biblical manner of King David. Ashcroft chose Carl Esbeck, who had directed the
Center for Law and Religious Freedom run by the conservative Virginia-
based Christian Legal Society, as the first chief of the department's faith-
based office. He named Eric Treene, former litigation director at the
conservative Becket Fund for Religious Liberty, as special counsel for religious discrimination, a new position in the Justice Departmen.[39] Added as
an adviser to the department's Office of Legal Education was Jay Sekulow,
chief counsel at the American Center for Law and Justice, affiliated with
the School of Law at Regent University. Sekulow and other conservatives
also helped draft a somewhat more permissive set of school prayer guidelines released by the federal Department of Education in 2003.

J. Robert Brame III, a Bush nominee for the National Labor Relations

Board, was forced to withdraw in 2001. It emerged that he had been a board member of Atlanta-based American Vision, which favored putting the United States under biblical law and opposed women's rights. Also obliged to step aside was Jerry Thacker, proposed for the Presidential Advisory Committee on HIV and AIDS. A conservative evangelical, Thacker had called AIDS the "gay plague."[40]

Bush's selections for related positions at the U.S. State Department and Department of Health and Human Services dealing with abortion, family planning, and reproductive rights were mostly staunch conservatives who opposed federal funding of any family planning. None had Christian Right identifications; several, however, were supporters of faith-based "abstinence" movements.

Bush stirred a hornet's nest with his choice of Kentucky obstetrician-gynecologist W. David Hager to chair the Food and Drug Administration's eleven-member Reproductive Health Drugs Advisory Committee. Hager, author of the book *As Jesus Cared for Women: Restoring Women Then and Now,* was also the author, with his wife, Linda, of *Stress and the Woman's Body.* Their book put "an emphasis on the restorative power of Jesus Christ in one's life" and recommended specific scriptural readings and prayers for headaches and premenstrual syndrome.[41] Unsuccessful opponents of Hager's appointment had emphasized how he would direct the committee's study of hormone-replacement therapy for menopausal women and might be able to get the committee to reconsider its 1996 recommendation of the abortion pill RU-486.

In a kindred example of choosing a proven foe to help supervise a federal program, Bush named Nancy Pfotenhauer, president of the Independent Women's Forum, to the National Advisory Committee on Violence Against Women, the panel that advised the federal government on implementing the Violence Against Women Act. The forum had opposed the VAWA and supported a lawsuit challenging it.[42]

Defenders of these appointments were correct in saying they stretched no further to the right than some in prior Democratic administrations had to the left. By previous GOP standards, however, they represented an enormous bow to the Christian Right.

This, too, was a striking transformation. Voters who had hoped the Republican presidential nominee would use his policies and appointments to advance faith must have shared in the post-9/11 satisfaction of movement leaders. George W. Bush, willing to tread where Ronald Reagan was not, had become the leader of the Religious Right by dint of his religiosity, patronage, and faith-based activism in desecularizing the American presidency.

Radical Fundamentalism and Global Conflict

Scholars anxious to document the turn-of-the-century importance of fundamentalism frequently found themselves confronting the underlying skepticism of modern secular elites: persistent doubt that such movements could really achieve or exercise power. Fanatics, extremists, and terrorists are a problem, cosmopolitans acknowledge. But the idea that 20 to 25 percent of a modern national electorate might support returning to rule by biblical (or Koranic or Torah) law—or at least be willing to join true believers in a political coalition—was rarely taken seriously.

Several layers of disbelief vanished in the aftermath of 9/11: "As a result of the attacks," said the authors of *Strong Religion*, "the United States and Great Britain, among other nations of the West, finally and fully came to grips with the fact of religious violence in the fundamentalist mode. Now manifested on a truly global scale, the astonishing power of religious fundamentalism became undeniable, even within the policymaking circles accustomed to formulating secular explanations for a range of acts and operations that have been engineered and enacted by self-styled true believers."[43]

Not entirely. Even after 9/11, there was little evidence that most Americans aroused by Islamic radicalism simultaneously understood that religious fundamentalism had gone global, that partially related behavior played a major role in the United States and commanded significant support from Northern Ireland to East Asia.

Israeli political scientist Ehud Sprinzak had taken aim at a similar myopia in his 1991 book *The Ascendance of Israel's Radical Right:* "Perhaps because of this [Holocaust] history, few observers, whether Israeli or not, are willing to recognize the magnitude of the new Israeli radical right and its impact on national politics. When faced with the attitudes and activities of this camp they argue that its members are the lunatic fringe. As disturbing as these activities are, so run the arguments, the radical right has usually no say in the government and its impact on critical national decisions is minimal at best."[44] The Jerusalem professor scoffed at such pretense.

Author Ian Lustick, in *For Land and the Lord: Jewish Fundamentalism in*

Israel, found self-deception rife in both the United States and Israel. He began his preface with a lament: "In recent years, Americans have become accustomed to the idea that Muslim fundamentalism can impel masses of believers to employ war, revolution and terrorism to meet their religious and political obligations. What still seems strange to most Americans is that the same fundamentalism phenomenon—defined here as political action to radically transform society according to cosmically ordained imperatives—exists among Jews and is a key element on the Israeli side of the Middle Eastern equation."[45]

The American and Israeli authors of *Strong Religion,* utilizing research by the Fundamentalism Project, pointed out a recurring fallacy among sophisticates: failing to realize that the idea of progress, so prevalent among elites, had actually been thwarted twice before. It happened first through the revolutionary, bloody-guillotine contradiction of the eighteenth-century Enlightenment, then again through the displacement of pre-1914 internationalism by Left and Right totalitarianism. As a result, "what we call fundamentalism is the third rebuff that history has administered to modernization and secularization. . . . What is remarkable about the third rebuff is that it is being administered after the great scientific revolutions of the twentieth century—after the unlocking of nuclear power, the development of molecular biology, the replacement of Newtonian cosmology by relativity and the quantum theory."[46]

Given this history, the late-twentieth-century momentum of desecularization, together with desecularization's politically radical counterreactions, constitutes a necessary lens through which to consider fundamentalism in the United States, Israel, and the Islamic world. We are not concerned here with similar behavior among Sikh radicals in India, Sinhalese Buddhists, and others, because they have limited effects beyond their own countries' borders. By contrast, the U.S., Israeli, and Islamic cultures represented the expansive variety of fundamentalism and thus stirred conflict. Each sought to add or reclaim territory or take up a new world role, drawing on religion-based interpretations. Unfortunately, the competition involved much of the same territory. Not a few Bush administration officials sought to remake the culture of the Middle East.

By the millennium, rank-and-file U.S. Protestant fundamentalists displayed an emphatic worldview—more proactive than a secular layman might expect from rural Oklahoma or the South Carolina Piedmont. In this, they were like Oliver Cromwell's seventeenth-century Puritans, who knew more about the geography of the Holy Land than about the English terrain two counties away. The comparable Bush-era influence of American evangelicals and fundamentalists, and of their churches, movements, and ministries, on U.S. Mideast policy must ultimately elicit scores of twenty-first-century doctoral theses.

Tom DeLay, the second-ranking Republican leader in the House of Representatives—Houston's answer to mid-seventeenth-century London's Anabaptist parliamentarian Praisegod Barebones—determined to call the Palestinian territories by their biblical names "Judaea and Samaria," flatly assigning them to Israel. DeLay confidently assured a Texas Baptist audience that God had made Bush president "to promote a biblical worldview."[47]

Prominent right-wing U.S. clergy, according to the *Economist* magazine, also were "spoiling for a clash of civilizations. Jerry Falwell has called the Prophet Mohammed a 'terrorist.' He has since apologized, but Pat Robertson, who called him a 'wild-eyed fanatic,' a 'robber' and a 'brigand,' has not. Franklin Graham, son of Billy, has branded Islam 'evil.' "[48] Falwell also replied to criticism of former Southern Baptist Convention president Jerry Vines, who called Muhammad a "demon-possessed pedophile." For his part, Ed McAteer of the Religious Roundtable dismissed Arabs and Muslims as tracing back to Ishmael, the unfavored son of Abraham, who was never satisfied with his lands.[49]

Other theologians took issue with this truculence. Richard Mouw, the president of Fuller Theological Seminary in Pasadena, California, worried about "Iraq as Babylon—I've been hearing that a lot lately. The two prominent images are the glorious city of Jerusalem and the wicked city of Babylon . . . and there's no question [that] the fact Iraq is the site of ancient Babylon is a motif that influences evangelicals."[50] Rabbi Eric Yoffie, the head of the Union of American Hebrew Congregations, deplored how evangelicals and their preachers "see any concession as a threat to Israel, and in this way they strengthen the hardliners in Israel and the United States. That may make it difficult for the peace process to go forward."[51]

A few American preachers and their flocks embraced especially provocative tactics in Israel—strategies designed to speed up the biblical tempo. In *The End of Days: Fundamentalism and the Struggle for the Temple Mount*, Gershom Gorenberg of the Center for Millennial Studies profiled "The Cattlemen of the Apocalypse," American livestock breeders shipping herds to the Holy Land to breed the red heifer that would signal Israelis to rebuild the Temple.[52] Of the 145 supposedly illegal Israeli settlements in the Palestinian territories, funds from American evangelicals were said to support a third.[53]

Evangelical members of the U.S. Christian Zionist movement funded the California-based Jerusalem Temple Foundation to develop plans and conduct geophysical research for Israel's hoped-for temple, but theirs was not patient capital. One expenditure was for hiring lawyers to defend the twenty-nine Israelis arrested in 1983 for planning to blow up Jerusalem's Al-Aqsa Mosque—the Muslim holy place that must come down before any new temple can go up.[54] End-times theologian Hilton Sutton, president of the Christian Evangelical Zionist Congress of America and the National Christian Leadership Conference for Israel, was one of the foundation's organizers.

On September 14, 2001, George W. Bush initially responded to the terrorist destruction of the World Trade Center by promising a "crusade . . . against a new kind of evil." Four days later, however, adverse reaction to terminology evoking Christian holy war forced him to back off.[55] By 2003, as Muslim anger focused on U.S. war plans and the much-publicized rhetoric of Falwell, Graham, Robertson, and others, perception of the United States lofting the old Crusader banner increased again.

Clive Calver of World Relief, the humanitarian arm of the National Association of Evangelicals, remarked that Franklin Graham's remarks about Islam being "a very evil and wicked religion" had been circulated widely throughout the Middle East and "used to indict all Christians."[56] Two dozen Southern Baptist missionaries in Asia, the Middle East, and Africa urged their home-front brethren to stop insulting Islam and Muhammad: "Comments by Christians in the West about Islam and Mohammed can and do receive much attention on local radio, television and print sources. These types of comments . . . can further the already heightened animosity towards Christians."[57]

Five years earlier, evangelicals had been mobilized—in a way, pointed toward a minicrusade—by books like Paul Marshall's *Their Blood Cries Out: The Growing Worldwide Persecution of Christians* and Nina Shea's *In the Lions' Den: Persecuted Christians and What the Western Church Can Do About It.* The anti-Christian practices were blatant and bloody. In the Sudan, half a million Nubian Christians were killed during the nineties; in China, home to over 40 million Christians, thousands were sentenced to "re-education camps" for attending prayer meetings or Bible lessons; in

Egypt, Christian Copts numbering over 5 million became second-class citizens frequently set upon by Islamic militants. Some 240 million Christians lived in nations where they were vulnerable.

"We are not talking about mere discrimination," said Shea, "but real persecution—torture, enslavement, rape, imprisonment, forcible separation of children from parents." Marshall called abuse of Christians "the largest pattern of persecution in the world."[58] The Christian Coalition and other activists had worked hard to secure passage of the International Religious Freedom Act of 1998, and when Bush took office, evangelicals tried to mobilize the administration on behalf of embattled Christian communities from Nigeria to Bangladesh, but with little result. After 9/11 crystallized Bush's good-versus-evil rhetoric and unleashed the anti-Muslim language of Christian Right clerics, prospects for amelioration, which may never have been very bright, clouded further.

To begin with, realpolitik inclined Washington policymakers to ignore religious persecution by countries cooperating with the United States against terrorism or casting swing votes at the United Nations. Aroused Muslim nations, in turn, behaved more harshly toward local, mostly poor Christian populations—black in the Sudan, brown in Bangladesh, or Copts in Egypt—now more than ever likely to be seen as dissidents, political subversives, or potential fifth columnists.

As 2003 spurred war discussions, attention to the controversial theologies of the Christian Right led some analysts to query the ideas influencing the president. Although George W. Bush never held a candid interview or press conference to discuss the views of the clerics from whom he sought advice, several men—in addition to Falwell and Graham *père et fils*—began to draw attention. Bush had picked the Reverend Jack Hayford, a California charismatic, to give the benediction at the Fifty-fourth Inaugural Prayer Service at the National Cathedral. Involved in the founding of the Promise Keepers men's revival group, Hayford was a supporter of Christian Reconstruction or Dominionism.

Anthony T. Evans of Dallas, who likewise preached a worldview based on the Bible, was a speaker at the preinaugural Washington Prayer Luncheon in January 2001 sponsored by Sun Myung Moon and choreographed by former Bush assistant Doug Wead. Identified in 2001 by the *New York Times* as a friend and confidant from whom Bush often sought spiritual guidance, Evans told a British journalist that for Bush in Texas, "one of the impetuses for his considering running for president was biblical teaching. He feels God is talking to him."[59]

What Hayford and Evans had in common, other preachers said, was a shared adherence to "Kingdom Now"or Dominionist theology. Loosely put, it called for seizure of earthly power by "the people of God" as the only way by which the world could be rescued. Prayer and evangelism were not enough; a Christian-led political and social reformation was necessary because Christ will not return to earth until a revived church has set the scene. Evans, in particular, had written several books on prophecy and the future. A president convinced that God was speaking to him, some pundits surmised, might through Dominionism start to view himself as an agent called by the Almighty to restore the earth to godly control.

Author Bob Woodward, in his book *Bush at War*, had already perceived a sweeping assumption of mission in the president's September 14 response to Al Qaeda and Osama bin Laden: "Our responsibility to history is already clear: To answer these attacks and rid the world of evil." To Woodward, "the president was casting his vision and that of the country in the grand vision of God's master plan."[60]

In 1999, before the campaign began in earnest, George W. Bush had assembled pastors for a "laying on of hands" and told them he had been "called" to higher office.[61] A year after 9/11, David Gergen, a longtime adviser to presidents, told the *New York Times* that Bush "has made it clear he feels that Providence intervened to save his life, and now he is somehow an instrument of Providence."[62] After an analysis of presidential rhetoric, Baptist minister and Interfaith Alliance leader Welton Gaddy concluded, "You see a growing feeling he [believes] he is, in fact, a divinely chosen leader in this moment of history. It's as if he discovered the power of religion late in life and thinks the nation needs to [do the same]."[63]

If true believers were thrilled, the nation's secular citizens were not. Before Bush, even the most religious of U.S. presidents had perused the Bible for notes of grace, not strategic mandates. Woodrow Wilson did not ponder the battlefield at Megiddo before deciding to send troops to France in 1917. Nor did William McKinley, in contemplating war with the Spanish Empire, consult the Book of Revelation. For a president to interweave international geopolitics and the Bible—to submerge realpolitik in New and Old Testament eschatology—had no American precedent.

Beyond Dominionism and hints of divine guidance, a further Bush controversy lay in making belief in Jesus fit alongside collaboration with Sun Myung Moon—a self-proclaimed messiah—and his international Unification Church. This controversial association began with the elder Bush. During 1995 and 1996, two years after leaving the White House, he made at least nine paid appearances in Buenos Aires, Montevideo, Tokyo, Washington, and elsewhere on behalf of Moon. The Korean businessman and evangelist, who dismissed Jesus as a failure and styled himself "the Lord of the Second Advent," was said to be paying the former president $100,000 per speech. The Argentine newspaper *La Nacion* also reported rumors that Bush and Moon might do business together in South America.[64]

The forty-first president, who told Argentine president Carlos Menem that he had joined Moon in Buenos Aires for the money, had actually known the Korean reasonably well for decades. Their relationship went back to the overlap between Bush's one-year tenure as CIA director (1976) and the arrival in Washington of Moon, whose Unification Church was widely reported to be a front group for the South Korean Central Intelligence Agency.[65] Within Washington councils, Bush was a powerful voice against any unnecessary crackdown on the U.S. activities of allied intelligence services. In the eighties, Moon and his newspaper, the *Washington Times,* prominently supported Reagan-Bush Iran-Contra activities and Republican causes.

George H. W. Bush's praise for Moon and the conservative newspapers he ran, including the influential *Times,* surprised the press in Buenos Aires. The Reuters story filed on November 25, 1996, was headlined "Bush Praises Sun Myung Moon as 'Man of Vision.'" It also reminded readers that "Argentina's influential Catholic Church takes issue with Moon's portrayal of himself as an incarnation of God fulfilling the mission of Christ. Critics say he brainwashes the vulnerable into joining him, and some countries, such as Germany, consider him a threat to public order and refuse him an entry visa."

Four years later, President-elect George W. Bush allowed his onetime religious aide, Doug Wead, to arrange a Moon-sponsored Inaugural Prayer Luncheon on January 19, 2001, a Washington event that drew over 1,700 public officials, ministers, and conservative activists. Some attendees felt deceived by not having been told of Moon's role in the event. One was Morris Chapman, the chief executive of the 18-million-member Southern

Baptist Convention. "I was shocked," he said, "to see that Sun Myung Moon was on the program and, in essence, the host. I was even more surprised on the way out to be given a propaganda book on the Unification Church." Chapman added that the event "will serve to remind evangelical Christians that the world increasingly is filled with wolves in sheep's clothing."[66]

That Bush aides would collaborate with a group described as "wolves" by the Southern Baptist Convention worried some conservatives. Steve Hassan, a journalist who followed religious cults, had for years found Moon's Washington acceptance just as puzzling: "Here's a man [Moon] who says he wants to take over the world, where all religions will be abolished except Unificationism, all languages will be abolished except Korean, all governments will be abolished except his one-world theocracy, yet he's wined and dined very powerful people and convinced them that he's benign."[67]

Whatever the explanation, radical religion had been wielding ever more political power around the world. The Mutawwa'in, the Saudi religious police, had searched out hidden church services among the millions of Filipinos, Koreans, and other foreign workers, sometimes imposing death sentences. But the Saudis were too important for Washington to criticize. Israeli prime minister Ariel Sharon, another close U.S. ally, doubtless greeted hundreds of religious extremists during his tenure in office. However, like the Saudis—and like the Bushes fraternizing with end-times preachers and Sun Myung Moon—Sharon walked away largely unscathed.

In the United States after 9/11, only Muslim fanatics and religious extremists were generally so identified. U.S. citizens working to bring on Armageddon were not. Most Americans were too angry to care that Africans, Latin Americans, and Asians saw hypocrisy in this—and that such inconsistencies seriously damaged U.S. standing abroad. In June 2003, Washington's Pew Research Center for the People and the Press released new spring poll results updating its huge mid-2002 sampling of what people in forty-four nations around the world thought of the United States. Few such negative measurements of American war policy–cum–diplomacy had ever been recorded.

In the 2002 Pew Survey, negative attitudes toward the United States had on the whole been confined to the Middle East and Pakistan. Following Bush's announcement of the close of the war with Iraq, survey takers reported that U.S. unpopularity had spread to Africa and to Indonesia, the world's most populous Muslim nation. Some 83 percent of Indonesians had a negative view of America, up from 36 percent a year earlier. "Dislike of the United States had really deepened and spread throughout the Muslim world," said Andrew Kohut, the Pew Center director. Majorities of those sampled in seven of eight predominantly Muslim nations worried that their nation would be *attacked* by the United States. In all but four of the nations polled in the spring of 2003, however, respondents said that the problem in the United States was "mostly Bush" rather than "Americans in general."[68]

Americans, however, continued to assume that the extremists and terrorists loose in the world were mostly Islamic—Hamas, leftover mujahideen, Taliban, Hezbollah, and, of course, Al Qaeda. These were the names that became synonymous with death and murder. Ironically, Bruce Lincoln, a professor of divinity at the University of Chicago, studied Osama bin Laden's words taped in early October following the destruction of the World Trade Center and found him constructing "a Manichean struggle, where Sons of Light confront sons of darkness, and all must enlist on one side or the other."

To his followers and the world, bin Laden said: "I tell them [the Americans] that these events have divided the world into two camps, the camp of the faithful and the camp of infidels. May God shield us and you from them."[69] He exulted that America would now feel what the West had done to Islam.

The second Manichaean view came from Washington. Professor Lincoln explained how George W. Bush, in his October 7, 2001, address to the American people, approached the confrontation in a similar way but with the sides reversed: "Every nation has a choice to make in this conflict," said Bush. "There is no neutral ground. If any government sponsors the outlaws and killers of innocents, they have become outlaws and murderers themselves. And they will take that lonely path at their own peril."[70]

Richard Neuhaus, a theologian allied with the Bush administration, nevertheless acknowledged "the hard reality of religion in defining, more and more, the lines of conflict in politics among nations. The war against terrorism is—more than it is politic for world leaders to say in public— also a war of religion."[71] History, though, does not usually explain religious wars—the eleventh-to-fourteenth-century Crusades, for example—as good versus evil.

If Islam and the United States both have Manichaean attitudes and various species of extremists, Israel watchers Sprinzak and Lustick added that nation to the list. "The rise of religious fundamentalism, extreme nationalism and aggressive anti-Arab sentiment in Israel since 1984," said Sprinzak, "reveals a significant political and cultural process that has neither been fully recognized nor named for what it is—the emergence of the Israeli Radical Right."[72] Moreover, its resemblance was not to the European radical Right but to the U.S. model—in which "most rightwing American extremists believe that the desired American revolution has already taken place but that it has been betrayed by modern pluralist democracy and central government." The Israeli version is also "ultranationalist, extralegal, hostile to pluralist democracy, with movements and parties of this camp earnestly believing that they are exclusively the true Israelis and the genuine Zionists."[73]

While Israel's hard-core radical Right counted only 5, 6, or 7 percent of voters, the radicalism of the Gush Emunim (territorial expansionists), the National Religious Party, and others had so penetrated the ruling Likud Party of Ariel Sharon that about a quarter of its leaders and members looked at the world "through the symbolic prism of the radical right."[74] Sprinzak estimated that "these attitudes are shared by about 20–25% of the Jewish citizens of Israel." If this approximated the equally loosely defined U.S. Christian Right, he saw another parallel in symptoms of theocracy and manifest cultural nostalgia: "Like the American radical right who constantly hark back to the founding fathers, the Constitution, rugged (pre-FDR) individualism, and the 'American Way of Life,' the Israeli radicals yearn for the old days of the *Yishuv*—the Jewish community in Palestine."[75] Small wonder the academicians guiding the Fundamentalism Project used the term "family resemblance."

Lustick's observations, although more territorially based, largely dovetailed with the project's findings. Since the 1970s, the extreme views of Gush Emunim and the fundamentalists had pulled Israel relentlessly rightward. In 1986, they launched a national campaign able to gather over three hundred thousand signatures supporting amnesty for the Jewish terrorists who had tried to blow up Jerusalem's Al-Aqsa Mosque. Although the Israeli parliament rejected amnesty legislation, most of the prisoners were soon freed. By Lustick's poll analysis, roughly 20 percent of the Israeli Jewish population went along with destroying Muslim shrines and forming Jewish terrorist groups to strike at local Arabs, while 30 to 35 percent backed the expulsion of Israel's Arab population.[76]

Decades before George W. Bush and the Pentagon announced the doctrine in 2002, Israel's embattled citizenry had developed a theology of preemptive war, drawing on the Old Testament words of the Book of Esther. According to Lustick, the king declared that Jews might do unto their enemies before their enemies did unto them—in the words of Esther 8:11, "to stand up for themselves, to destroy, to slay and to annihilate any armed force of any people or province that might assault them, with their little ones and women."[77] That, of course, was also the old American frontier ethic.

Still another U.S. commonality with Israel is that for many Americans, especially the early Bible-centered Protestant settlers, the British North American colonies and then the thirteen uniting states were to be the new Israel, a concept that huge numbers of twenty-first-century Protestants continued to espouse. In both countries, many of the religious radicals have—literally—read from the same book.

Not that religious radicalism in either the United States or Israel matched Islamic intensity. As noted in this chapter's opening epigraph, within the universe of late-twentieth-century fundamentalism only Muslim and Hindu extremism had captured entire national governments: in Iran, Turkey, the Sudan, Afghanistan, and India. Another critical distinction—Muslim willingness to die in suicide attacks against infidels—had plagued U.S. military forces occupying the southern islands of the Philippines in the early twentieth century. However disconcerting, it was an old characteristic.

On the other hand, more than intensely observant Islam, the religious Rights of the United States and Israel (and the politicians they sway) have been drawn toward a unique incitement: a web of prophecies that sometimes appear to overlap uncannily with current events. In the dreams of the Cattlemen of the Apocalypse, fulfillment is only a pure red heifer away.

Armageddon, Prophecy, and Politics

The historiography of American presidential reference to Armageddon is limited but instructive. Theodore Roosevelt's famous 1912 comment about standing with the Lord at Armageddon was merely dramatics. The possible events in the Holy Land were not a discussion point. Britain had yet to capture Palestine, and Foreign Secretary Arthur Balfour had yet to promise it to Zionists as a Jewish homeland. The purported ultimate battlefield itself—at the ancient ruins of Megiddo, north of Jerusalem—was still a half century removed from parking lots crowded with tourist buses.

Even Jimmy Carter, whose election in 1976 attuned Americans to born-again Christians, left Armageddon alone. He never provoked the kind of debate that ballooned in the early 1980s over Ronald Reagan's view that war in the Middle East might bring in the Soviets, trigger nuclear holocaust, and fulfill the biblical prophecies. In the second presidential debate of 1984 between Reagan and Democrat Walter Mondale, journalists asked the president what he meant. He replied, "No one knows whether those prophecies mean that Armageddon is a thousand years away or the day after tomorrow. So I have never seriously said we must plan according to Armageddon."[78]

Reagan's preoccupation was with the Soviet Union—the "Evil Empire," he called it—and how Russia appeared to fit the biblical reference to the invasion of Israel by "Gog," a power to the north. His support for the "Star Wars" missile defense system, some critics thought, was tied to fear of a nuclear Armageddon, a Klaxon already being sounded by preachers like Jerry Falwell. The end of the cold war and the breakup of the Soviet Union cooled the great-power-confrontation aspect, and George H. W. Bush as president said nothing about Armageddon. Nor did Clinton, the next born-again Baptist in the White House. Like Carter, he avoided dire biblical prophecies. His only reference was to an Armageddon *avoided*—the nuclear confrontation narrowly averted between Pakistan and India in 1999.

Publicly, George W. Bush also chose to shun discussion of Armageddon, though the Dominionist preachers he openly admired had produced a small shelf of volumes, pamphlets, and videotapes on the turmoil to come. The events of 9/11 drew further attention to Armageddon theology, and several religious publications called on the president to set out his views: In March 2003, the editors of *Christian Century* insisted that "the American people have a right to know how the president's faith is informing his public policies, not least his design on Iraq."[79]

More than Bush's earlier religious phraseology, his Scripture-flavored preparation for war against Iraq—the latter-day Babylon of biblical notoriety—stirred scrutiny. Those who followed Bush's religiosity had seen a change, in one pundit's words, "from talking about a Wesleyan theology of 'personal transformation' to describing a Calvinist 'divine plan' laid out by a sovereign God for the country and himself. At the National Prayer Breakfast Feb. 6, for instance, Bush said, 'We can be confident in the ways of Providence. . . . Behind all of life and all of history, there's a dedication and purpose set by the hand of a just and faithful God.' "[80]

Leaders of George W. Bush's own Methodist denomination certainly thought he was edging away. Robin Lovin, professor of religion and political thought at Southern Methodist University, commented that "all sorts of warning signals ought to go off when a sense of personal chosen-ness and calling gets translated into a sense of calling and mission for a nation."[81] Bishop Melvin Talbert, the United Methodists' top ecumenical official, argued that "it's clear to us that he is not following the teachings of his own church or the teachings of churches that believe in a 'just war' theory."[82]

Indeed, not all the religious community was eager to follow the president onto the battlefield. As war approached in 2003, portions of the clergy began to register blunt dissent. The president of the Interfaith Alliance, Baptist minister Welton Gaddy, while lauding Bush's respect for faith, admitted to "grave concerns about how he incorporates the vocabulary of that faith into presidential addresses that significantly impact both the domestic and foreign policies of this nation."[83] Martin Marty, the Lutheran minister and historian, commented that "after September 11 and the president's decision to attack Iraq, the talk that other nations found mildly amusing or merely arrogant has taken on international and historical significance."[84]

The president's turn from Wesleyanism toward Calvinism, some thought, reflected his 2001 reorientation toward a view of a God with a master plan—a God who had chosen him to be in the White House and carry out an attack on Iraq that, he declared, "would be in the highest moral traditions of our country." The God of Methodism didn't operate that way, but theocratic John Calvin's God could be said to. Calvinist tenets were also supportive in two other important ways. Dominionists committed to the political action necessary to restore the earth to God's control generally embraced a version of Calvinism. In addition, the French-Swiss theologian Calvin—unlike Luther, Zwingli, and the rest—was the only major sixteenth-century Protestant reformer to accept apocalyptic millennialism and the Bible's Book of Revelation.

Talking about such things was far from the norm of U.S. political debate. Only war in the Middle East could push this kind of issue to the forefront. However, the argument that Bush had let his eschatology—his religious view of the end times or Second Coming—shape the calculus of military intervention in the region touched a rare combination of possibilities.

The millennial year of 2000 had sharpened the public's focus on explosive prophecy. Law enforcement discussions, for example, had already crystallized mistaken judgments. Police in Israel and experts worldwide assumed that Armageddon zealots would be extremist Jews or Christians trying to blow up a Muslim holy site, probably the Al-Aqsa Mosque on Jerusalem's Temple Mount. Several major attacks on Al-Aqsa had already been attempted, and another Muslim holy site had been attacked in 1994 when Baruch Goldstein, an American immigrant to Israel, killed twenty-nine Muslims in the midst of Ramadan prayers at the Tomb of the Patriarchs in Hebron.

The chance of World War III's trigger being pulled in Jerusalem had produced many fearful predictions. In 2001, Carmi Gillon, the former chief of Shin Bet, Israel's internal secret service, warned that the bombing of the Temple Mount by a Jewish group "would likely lead to all-out war and unleash destructive forces that would imperil Israel's existence."[85] According to another expert, "A simulated war game at Harvard concluded that conservatively it [bombing the Temple Mount] would have caused a new phase in the Middle East conflict, a crisis broader, deeper and longer lasting than anything in the past. A less conservative estimation suggested the scheme could have triggered a third world war."[86]

What few had considered beforehand was that "Armageddon" might be hinted or precipitated by a strike against New York and Washington, designed and carried out by self-fancied Islamic liberators—people who, in Osama bin Laden's words, wanted America to taste "what our Islamic nation has been tasting . . . for more than eighty years of humiliation and disgrace, its sons killed and their blood spilled, its sanctities desecrated."[87] Bin Laden himself openly sought a larger war.

Far from being cowed by 9/11, American fundamentalists and evangelicals, in particular, all but took up the helms, swords, and banners of neo-Crusaders. Survey after survey showed them applauding retaliation against the Taliban in Afghanistan and then giving overwhelming support to George W. Bush's plan for a preemptive attack on Iraq. Baghdad, it must be remembered, is the evil Babylon of the Bible, "the seat of idolatry and persecution." The Bible (Jer. 50:8–20) says that "the mercy promised to the Israel of God shall not only accompany but arise from the destruction of Babylon." That would have been enough for ardent fundamentalists, even absent weapons of mass destruction.

Back in 1999, on the cusp of the millennium, *Newsweek* had polled Americans regarding the so-called end times—Armageddon and the Second Coming of Christ. Fully 45 percent of U.S. Christians saw the world ending with an Armageddon battle between Jesus and the Antichrist. Of those believers, large majorities thought that natural disasters, epidemics, and shootings pointed to its happening soon. The *Newsweek* pollsters did not simultaneously query George W. Bush, but the implied political coalitions were startling.[88]

Among the 90 percent of Americans at least nominally Christian, 71 percent of evangelical Protestants believed in Armageddon, but only 28 percent of nonevangelical Protestants and 18 percent of Catholics. Reapplying the religious voting preferences of the 2000 elections, in which committed churchgoers were lopsidedly Republican, one can estimate that roughly 55 percent of Bush voters were Armageddon believers. Almost two-thirds of that 55 percent were evangelical white Protestants, just under a fifth were mainline white Protestants, and not quite a tenth were white Catholics. Intensity of religion and Armageddon belief would have a significant correlation, at least among Protestants.

Could 75 to 80 percent of the believers in Armageddon have voted for Bush? So it appeared. Churchgoing black Protestants, overwhelmingly Democratic, would have been the only major pool of Armageddon awaiters to prefer Gore. Moreover, hypothesizing the Bush coalition as a narrowly Armageddon-believing electorate—probably the first in recent Republican presidential history—helps to explain Bush's biblical rhetoric and overt pursuit of war in the Middle East. The commitment of his supporters was insufficiently particularized. For about half of his constituency, war in and around the Holy Land was not about battle per se. It was about the Second Coming of Jesus Christ.

In turn, Ariel Sharon's Israeli governing coalition may have been 40 to 50 percent dependent on messianic or expansionist Jewish voters ready to expel Arabs from Eretz Yisrael, with its biblical boundaries that included Palestine and even a portion of Iraq. This follows from Sprinzak's view that 20 to 25 percent of all Jewish Israelis shared something of a radical Right worldview.

Gershom Gorenberg, an American Jew who moved to Israel and wrote *The End of Days: Fundamentalism and the Struggle for the Temple Mount*, explained the stakes:

> If there is any place in the world where belief in the End is a powerful force in real-life events, it's the Holy Land. The territory today shared and contested by Jews and Palestinians is the stage of myth in Christianity, Judaism and even Islam. . . . The impact of such belief on a complex national

and religious struggle has received too little attention. It underlies the apoc-alyptic foreign policy promoted by many on the American religious right: support for Israel based on certainty that the Jewish state plays a crucial role in a fundamentalist Christian script for the End. In Israel, belief in final re-demption has driven the most dedicated opponents of peace agreements. Among Muslims, expectation of the final Hour helps feed exaggerated fears about Israel's actions in Jerusalem. Belief in the approaching End has influ-enced crucial events in the Arab-Israeli conflict. Time and again, it has been the rationale behind apparently irrational bloodshed.[89]

The "high" Islam of the established scholars assigned little space to apocalypse, according to Gorenberg. However, it thrived in less official tra-ditions attributed to Muhammad, usually taking the form of a Jewish An-tichrist—*al-masih al-dajjal*—who will be defeated by Jesus in the name of Islam, in some versions accompanied by a redeeming figure called the Mahdi.[90] Beginning in the 1980s, a new genre comprising hundreds of Is-lamic books in this vein—of Jewish and American Christian–led aggres-sion in the Holy Land and against Jerusalem's Al-Aqsa Mosque heralding the Last Days—became best-sellers in the bookstalls from Cairo and Pales-tine to the Gulf.[91]

R. Scott Appleby, the former codirector of the Fundamentalism Project, amplified the motivation of the Muslim radicals who took up arms and terrorism to end the eighty-year "corruption" of the Islamic world by West-ern rule and influence, abetted by "traitor" elites like the Egyptian ruling class, the Saudi royal family, and the oil sheikhs of the Persian Gulf. "The reason why the Islamic fundamentalists have a much better chance of re-cruiting than fundamentalists in other traditions," he said, "is that Islam remains . . . a very literal and supernaturally oriented religion in its prac-tice. It has not undergone a kind of church/state separation process, or an enlightenment that would differentiate religion from other realms of life, and so it is a very strong religion, in that sense, in terms of holding its people under a canopy of belief that is genuinely Islamic."[92] Shiite and Sunni Muslim radicals showed signs of collaborating because they have "a common enemy—the global markets, the United States of America, and so forth."[93]

In the chronicles of America going to war, meanwhile, much has de-pended on the president's wishes, if not quite on his whim. Thus the pointed references of dissenters in the history books to Mr. Madison's War (1812),

Mr. Lincoln's War (1861), Mr. Wilson's War (1917), and Mr. Roosevelt's War (1941). The apparent early-twenty-first-century convergence of three religions' prophecies in one shared Holy Land gave the president's personal yardsticks in the Middle East—secular caution or biblical fulfillment—an unprecedented and unnerving importance.

Nevertheless, before wrapping a religious banner around the events stretching from North Africa to Indonesia or raising a crusader's standard over U.S. military intervention, it is necessary to consider a second, essentially secular, group of circumstances: how the century-old drive for oil, the emergence of a new geopolitics, and the huge late-twentieth-century global arms buildup wound up agitating and spotlighting essentially the same region. In such councils, the concern has been about petroleum geology, nuclear missiles, and Eurasia as hinge, not about fundamentalists dedicated to blowing up the Dome of the Rock.

CHAPTER 8

Indiana Bush and the Axis of Evil

With the arrival of Bush Junior in the White House, it was immediately plain that secret intelligence would receive a high status and more money. While the CIA may have been the creation of a Democratic president (Harry Truman), it now seemed to be strongly favored by Republicans, notably conservative Republicans and especially the Bushes. Alarm bells began to ring for those who remembered past CIA excesses and who for years had campaigned for restrictions, oversight and even abolition. But these sounds were soon drowned out by the deafening roar of 9/11.

Rhodri Jeffreys-Jones, *The CIA and American Democracy,* 2003

In many cases, the United States has been busy arming opponents in ongoing conflicts—Iran and Iraq, Greece and Turkey, Saudi Arabia and Israel, and China and Taiwan. Saddam Hussein, the number one "rogue" leader of the 1990s, was during the 1980s simply an outstanding customer with an almost limitless line of credit because of his country's oil reserves. Often the purchasing country makes its purchases conditional on the transfer of technology so that it can ultimately manufacture the item for itself and others. The result is the proliferation around the world not just of weapons but of new weapons industries.

Chalmers Johnson, *Blowback,* 2000

Despite the millennial fears of security experts over how World War III could start with terrorists blowing up Jerusalem's Al-Aqsa Mosque, before 9/11 defense and foreign policy experts generally had secular agendas and explanations. Religious wars, the historians agreed, had ended in the seventeenth century. Few questions about Sinhalese Buddhism, the Koran, or even militant Christianity were asked on the U.S. Foreign Service examination.

We now turn to this familiar language of international affairs, which since the end of the cold war has focused on oil, geopolitics, shaky alliances, U.S. unilateralism, and—more recently—the rise of terrorism. Defense and foreign policy intellectuals, triumphal in the 1990s after the Soviet collapse, developed grand theories of Pax Americana, preemptive warfare, and even the prospect that U.S. control of the Middle East might nurture full-blown regional democracy. During a period of eruptions in Pakistan or Indonesia, to be sure, Washington officials might quietly ponder the blowback effect of decades of U.S. arms shipments, air strikes, and covert operations.

The Walker and Bush family financial and business agendas over the course of eighty years—agendas that both Bush presidents brought with them to the Oval Office—had been secular, indeed Machiavellian: global oil ventures, national security, sophisticated investments, arms deals, the Skull and Bones chic of covert operations, and committed support of established business interests. Until George W. Bush, religious impulses and motivations had not been a factor.

The urbane, rich, and cosmopolitan within the Republican Party understood that the new fundamentalist, evangelical, and Pentecostal South required the younger Bush as president occasionally to address that constituency with resonance and biblical imagery. Culture, not traditional economics, kept the small-town South in the Republican national coalition. In this context, Bush's provocative 2002 State of the Union speech decrying Iraq, Iran, and North Korea as an "Axis of Evil" could be understood as a bow to his believing voters, not a religious reinterpretation of the case for preemptive war.

Throughout history, wars have rarely been undertaken for the reasons politicians use to sell them. In retrospect, simple explanations typically broaden into complex ones. Even in the fullness of time, experts invariably disagree. Besides, wise strategists have understood that wars serve as Rorschach blots for politicians, historians, and multihued coalitions alike. If constituency A appreciated one explanation, constituency B preferred another. World War I was a case study. By the 1920s, the initial U.S. optimism about "a war to end war" and "to make the world safe for democracy" had curdled, with such naïveté being dismissed by academicians and intellectuals like Charles Beard, Carl Becker, and Harry Elmer Barnes as "the Sunday School theory."[1] War profiteers, bankers, and munitions makers had played too much of a role.

In the last chapter, we discussed the cultural and political mobilization of Protestant, Jewish, and Islamic fundamentalists. This chapter examines economic self-interest and realpolitik: oil as a lens and organizing principle to explain twentieth-century war. We will also look at imperialism, the penchant for covert operations, and the historical necromancy of arms dealing. The next chapter will add the Texas backdrop: bravado, deceit, and inept geopolitics over a post-1963 span of three wars.

National self-interest has been a powerful force in the history of U.S. international relations. Talk about making the world safe for democracy or human rights has usually been half to three-quarters political window dressing—recurring insistences of a particularly Anglo-Saxon sort, like the aforementioned Wilsonian dialogue later ridiculed by revisionists. George W. Bush's recent Texas cowboy imagery, condemnation of global "evildoers," and call for building a democratic Middle East fit neatly—perhaps too neatly—alongside his tendency to cast issues in the black-and-white simplicity of his own 1986 religious redemption.

Moral rhetoric notwithstanding, petroleum needs and armaments buildups have been important factors and motivators in two world wars; not incidentally, they have also been pillars of Bush family advancement. Oil, in particular, has long been a linchpin for defense and national security elites. After eight decades of Bush family private experience, even the born-again George W. Bush of the late 1980s was happy to take investment dollars from oil sheikhs.

Important as oil has been, great-power geopolitics has had a glamour and historical momentum beyond economics. Intellectuals in U.S. defense agencies, for their part—especially those denied their own military surfeit as youths—became caught up in what pundits called a latter-day version of the "Great Game" played out a century ago in south-central Asia. Indeed, imperial motivations have led to an outsized share of military conflicts.

None of the Bushes has ever been a serious intellectual in defense or foreign policy matters. For them, physical activity—especially sports such as golf or speedboating—has been more appealing than long evenings devoted to abstract thought. The effect has been to leave George W. Bush, like previous Texan wartime president Lyndon Johnson, at the mercy of second-rate defense intellectuals, this time ones who had changed the gray pinstripes of neoconservative think tanks for Pentagon togas of neoimperialism.

Meanwhile, the massive global armaments flow since the 1970s, with the United States as its chief sales office, had poured huge amounts of weaponry into precisely the regions menaced by religious and resource conflicts—and had done so on a scale unseen since the decades leading up to 1914. The blowback, or backlash, in Iran, Afghanistan, the Palestinian territories, Iraq, and even Turkey and Saudi Arabia has helped to complete the image of a region on the cusp of chaos.

Facing such circumstances and multiple convergences, even Indiana Jones, the fictional American basher of evildoers from the crude, triumphalist movie sets of the 1980s, might have hesitated before jumping into his attack vehicle. Understandably aroused by the horrors of September 2001, "Indiana Bush" did not.

World Wars, the Middle East, and Oil

Few Americans have realized the extent to which both world wars dripped petroleum concern. Save for the bloody 1942–45 island-hopping in the Pacific, we usually picture both world wars in European terms. Peripheries like North Africa were just that—sideshows. Ship convoys were maritime adjuncts.

What we have especially neglected is the role of the Middle East and oil in the two wars. Twice, the Germans and their allies pursued both. Important in the first conflict, petroleum became absolutely central between 1939 and 1945. Sixteen years before the guns of August 1914, the sultan of Turkey—Abdülhamid II, often called "the Damned"—received a secret-service report about clandestine German exploration in what is now Iraq but then was Ottoman Mesopotamia. The kaiser's state visit to Constantinople, his grandiose profession of Muslim sympathies, his pursuit of a Turkish alliance, and his dream of a railroad from Berlin to Baghdad had a further, dark and seeping motivation. According to British historian Peter Hopkirk, "German geologists posing as archaeologists were at that very moment prospecting for oil around Mosul, in northern Mesopotamia. In fact, or so his spies informed him, they had already found it, for an intercepted German report spoke of the region offering 'even greater opportunities for profit than the rich oilfields of the Caucasus.'"[2] Those fields had made Russia the Ottoman Empire's great rival, the world's top turn-of-the-century producer.

The oil era was just beginning. After war broke out in 1914, the battlefield presence of automobiles, trucks, and aircraft, as well as the British navy's reliance on oil rather than coal power, made petroleum an ever more important war resource. Luckily, large new oil fields in the United States and British development of Persia, together with Russian production still accounting for 15 percent of world output, gave the Allies a leg up in dominating petroleum geography.[3] After Germany, despite its advantages in coal, iron, and rail transport, failed to win a quick victory advancing into France in 1914, the war moved into the trenches. Motor transport and aircraft use mushroomed, and Germany's lack of oil became perilous.

Through 1916, German war managers got some oil from overseas but relied mainly on supplies from neutral Romania, Europe's second-largest producer. Although the kaiser had completed his railroad from Berlin to Baghdad, commercial oil and gas development was not yet under way in Mesopotamia—despite conspicuous natural gas vents and oil seepage widely commented upon since the days of Nebuchadnezzar, king of Babylon.

Alas for Berlin, little came of the Turco-German "holy war" designed to stir 1914–15 Muslim revolution in the Russian Caucasus and against British authority in Persia and India. Although the sultan, as caliph of Islam, proclaimed jihad, no serious rising took place.[4] Turkish troops in the north did little more than mass near the Russian border. In the south, they threatened but did not attack the Anglo-Persian oil refinery in Abadan, just across the border in neutral Persia. The limited success came in 1915, when local tribesmen agitated by German agents and the Turks damaged the Anglo-Persian pipeline from the oil fields to Abadan, greatly reducing its flow for five months.[5] Ironically, Winston Churchill, as first lord of the admiralty in 1914, had despaired of Britain's ability to defend the Persian oil fields and refinery: "There is little likelihood of any troops being available for this purpose. We shall have to buy our oil from somewhere else."[6]

Each side put a high priority on constricting the other side's oil supply. Germany responded to Britain's naval blockade and control of surface waters with a submarine campaign that decimated British shipping, not least oil tankers. In early 1917, adoption of unrestricted submarine warfare against Allied shipping doubled the tonnage sunk from a year earlier, reducing the Royal Navy's oil supply to a level that threatened paralysis.[7]

On the other side, when neutral Romania joined the Allies in late 1916, the Germans responded by capturing the Romanian oil fields around Ploesti, but they were partly thwarted by a group of British destruction teams led by Colonel John "Empire Jack" Norton-Griffiths. Given reluctant permission by the Romanian government, they wrecked derricks and pipelines, set the wells ablaze, and left such destruction that production could not be resumed until spring. Output by the Germans for all of 1917 was only one-third that of 1916. After the war, General Ludendorff acknowledged the dire effects.[8]

After the kaiser's Islamic holy war had fizzled, Britain, France, and Russia turned their thoughts to a postwar division of the crumbling Ottoman Empire. As set out in the Sykes-Picot Agreement of 1916, Russia's postwar sphere of influence would include the Bosporus and part of Anatolia; France's would comprise Lebanon, Syria, and oil-rich Mosul. Britain would hold sway in Arabia, Palestine, and most of Mesopotamia, including Baghdad. Sir Maurice Hankey, secretary of the war cabinet, explained: "Oil in the next war will occupy the place of coal in the present war. . . . The only big supply we can get under British control is the Persian and Mesopotamian supply. [Therefore,] control over these supplies becomes a first-class British war aim."[9] Revolution cost Russia its place at the postwar table, so Britain and France alone divided the Middle East pie.

Besides guiding a tribal revolt in Arabia, British troops also prevailed in Palestine and Mesopotamia. From a base in Basra near the Persian border, between 1915 and 1917 they drove up the valleys of the Tigris and Euphrates to seize Baghdad. Some of the same towns and battlefields—Shaiba, Al 'Amara, Nasiriya—would be revisited in the Anglo-American invasion of Iraq in 2003.

One other petroleum-driven campaign took place before the armistice. When revolution-racked Russia left the war in 1917, Germans and Turks took aim at the scarcely defended Russian oil fields in Baku, just north of Turkey and Persia. Before German diplomacy could work, a Turkish army put Baku under siege in the summer of 1918. However, a small British relief force arrived, delayed the oil center's capture, and then slipped away. Turkish troops did not take the city until September, too late for desperately needed oil to help Germany, which was forced to surrender on November 11.[10]

Insufficient oil turned out to be disastrous for the Germans. But even the Allies, filling three-quarters of their needs from America—the United States then controlled two-thirds of world production—had come to understand the petroleum thirst of a mechanized military. From a few hundred warplanes in 1914, nearly 250,000 had been built by 1918. Tanks, nonexistent in 1914, numbered seven thousand in 1918. Trucks, staff cars, and motorcycles were everywhere. The British and Americans together had one hundred thousand in France.

Just after the armistice, Lord Curzon, chairman of the Inter-Allied Petroleum Conference, observed that "one of the most astonishing things [in France] was the tremendous army of motor lorries. The Allied cause had floated to victory upon a wave of oil."[11] The French concurred. "Oil," said Premier Georges Clemenceau, "is as necessary as blood."[12] Henri Bérenger, the director of France's Comité Général de Pétrole, said that "Germany had boasted too much of its superiority in iron and coal, but it had not taken sufficient account of our superiority of oil."[13] Because Americans had oil, Europeans were the ones obliged to scramble. Britain and France, Anthony Sampson observed, hoped to make the Middle East into their own Texas but were obliged to cut in the Americans.[14]

This, we must keep in mind, is the cutthroat context into which Averell Harriman, George H. Walker, and their New York financial allies jumped in 1922 when—against the wishes of the U.S. government—they contracted to refurbish the once lucrative oil fields of the Russian Caucasus. The bold venture failed in part because of political unrest in the Baku region. Foreign concessions, like that at the Barnsdall Corporation, were withdrawn by 1925.[15] Since Baku is not far from the northern border of modern-day Iraq, pursuit by the Bush family of this region's petroleum can be said to go back four generations.

In Germany, Adolf Hitler, who took power in 1933, had seen the perils of insufficient oil during his own wartime military service. As chancellor, besides ensuring supplies from Romania, he launched a hugely successful program of producing synthetic fuels through the German-invented hydrogenation process. According to oil economist Daniel Yergin, Hitler prided himself in knowing more about economics than his generals did:

> "In the economic field," one historian has written, "Hitler's obsession was oil." To Hitler, it was the vital commodity of the industrial age and for economic power. He read about it, he talked about it, he knew the history of the world's oilfields. If the oil of the Caucasus—along with the "black earth," the farmlands of the Ukraine—could be brought into the German empire, then Hitler's New Order would have within its borders the resources to make it invulnerable. In that conception, there was a striking similarity to the Japanese drive to encapsulate the resources of the East Indies and Southeast Asia within its empire, an ambition also powered by the belief that such a resource base would make it impregnable. Albert Speer, the German Minister for Armaments and War Production, said at his interrogation in May

1945, "the need for oil certainly was a prime motive" in the decision to invade Russia.[16]

Petroleum was just as important at the Asian end of the Axis. Japan was even less well endowed, producing only 7 percent of the oil it consumed. Having to import most of the rest from the United States (80 percent) and the Dutch East Indies (10 percent) put Tokyo officialdom in a bind. For Japan to invade more than Korea, Manchuria, and coastal China would require getting oil from someplace besides the United States, which would not assent. Seizing the most plausible substitute oil—in Indochina, Borneo, and the Dutch East Indies—would also mean war with the United States or at least an oil embargo. Both possibilities mounted in mid-1940 as Japan began to import unusual quantities of oil and gasoline and signed the Tripartite Pact with Hitler and Italy's Benito Mussolini.

The insight of Yergin's 1991 book *The Prize: The Epic Quest for Oil, Money, and Power* lay in his detailed depiction of World War II as a conflict that was both oil-related and effectively oil-decided. His narrative of 1939–45—the war as a chessboard of pivotal U.S. oil supplies, irreplaceable sunken tankers, and battles lost by fuel shortages—leaves a reader in very little doubt about subsequent U.S. motivations in the Persian Gulf, or the lessons an oil-focused clan like the Bushes would have learned.

In mid-1942, lack of gasoline helped to cripple German field marshal Erwin Rommel's drive on Cairo. Until then, Rommel had believed the Egyptian capital only a way station for a campaign that would cross Palestine, Iraq, and Iran and meet up with other German forces in Baku and the Caucasus oil fields. Seeing the same jeopardy, British and American oilmen in Saudi Arabia, Kuwait, and Iran plugged oil wells with cement to keep them from being destroyed by possible bombing. Late that summer, the six-hundred-mile German advance on the Caucasus had stalled—partly because of mountainous terrain, partly because of sturdy Russian resistance, and partly because tanks and trucks had outrun gasoline supplies (their engines couldn't use Russian diesel fuel). A manic Hitler still refused to shift Caucasus-bound troops to rescue the embattled German Sixth Army at Stalingrad, telling Field Marshal von Mannstein, "Unless we get the Baku oil, the war is lost." Alternative histories of how the Germans could have won usually script Rommel taking Cairo and moving east while the panzer corps of Generals Guderian and Kleist capture Baku and Tabriz and head south into Iran. Such confections tend to skip the vital fuel-gauge factor.[17]

While the German army aimed for Baku and Iran, German submariners took their own aim at the tankers carrying oil to Britain. By July 1941, Britain was down to only two months of fuel for the Royal Navy, seven months being the rock bottom for safety. Nineteen forty-two saw the United States lose a quarter of its total tanker tonnage, and British naval fuel supplies hovered just above empty. The nadir came in early 1943, after U-boats had sunk 108 ships in March. "The Germans," concluded the British Admiralty, "never came so near to disrupting communication between the New World and the Old as in the first twenty days of March, 1943."[18]

Fuel concerns also dominated Pacific strategy. By Yergin's calculus, shrinking oil inventories forced the attack on Pearl Harbor in December 1941 "to safeguard the Japanese invasion of the Indies and the rest of Southeast Asia by incapacitating the American fleet and, thereafter, to protect the sea lanes, particularly the tanker routes for Sumatra and Borneo to the home islands." Retreating U.S., British, and Dutch personnel tried to destroy the East Indies oil fields but were only partially successful. Production in 1942 was only 40 percent of the 1940 level, but by 1943 the Japanese had regained 75 percent.[19]

In both the Pacific and the Atlantic, mid-1943 marked a turning point. By late 1944, after U.S. bombers had smashed Hitler's synthetic-fuels production, German aircraft—including potentially decisive jet fighters just becoming operational—lacked fuel because Luftwaffe aviation gasoline had shrunk to just 10 percent of what was needed. In the Pacific, the U.S. naval strategy of denying the enemy oil sank so many tankers that by late 1944, Japan lacked fuel for its ships and aircraft, using them only for desperate maneuvers. The Japanese turned to wood turpentine and pine roots for fuel—and to suicide missions that pilots flew with gas tanks only half filled.[20]

After 1943, U.S. tankers fed an almost insatiable demand. At peak consumption, American forces in Europe used one hundred times more gasoline in the Second World War than in the First. Petroleum accounted for roughly half of the total tonnage shipped from U.S. ports. The United States, in sum, was not just the "Arsenal of Democracy," it was also the "Oil Field of Democracy"—and the tanker fleet to boot. The United States had established a global hegemony based on oil. Between 1914 and 1917, the U.S. share of world oil output grew from 65 to 67 percent of a much larger production. Between 1940 and 1945, it rose from 63 percent to some two-thirds of a nearly doubled world output at war's end. The Middle East, by contrast, produced less than 5 percent in 1940 and not much more in 1945.[21]

Well before Germany and Japan surrendered in 1945, however, U.S. petroleum geologists had brought Washington policymakers unwelcome news: The Middle East had huge reserves and future production capacity that far surpassed those of the United States, where reserves were being depleted. Prescott Bush was attuned better than most, because, through his long service on the board of Dresser Industries, he knew Texan Everett de Golyer, who headed the U.S. geological team. Mindful that the lopsided U.S. petroleum edge that had won two world wars would end in several decades, Dresser stepped up the globalization of its operations through the 1950s. Oil and defense experts in Washington had their own new strategic thinking to do.

Adjustment came in fits and starts. The 1950s saw Saudi Arabia, Iran, and Iraq integrated—in the broadest terms—into the Western alliance, but with few U.S. military or support personnel on hand until the 1970s. Economic relations were badly jolted when, with inflation and frustration rising after the 1973 Arab-Israeli War, the Arabs quadrupled the price of oil and cut off deliveries to the United States. By 1975, oil was becoming a critical factor to the CIA, where George H. W. Bush took over in December (his appointment was confirmed by the Senate in January 1976). A few months earlier, Secretary of State Henry Kissinger had made it clear that the United States would go to war to prevent any strangulation of U.S. and world oil supplies, a pledge later restated by the White House in the so-called Carter Doctrine of 1979. By this point America had come to depend on the Middle East for about one-quarter of its oil, and U.S. strategists began to look for more diversity in supply, increasing purchases from Mexico, Venezuela, and Nigeria.

The geography of world oil production (and U.S. oil import dependence) was shifting decisively. By 1980, the United States produced under 20 percent of world petroleum output and had to import 30 percent of its needs. By 2000, the U.S. share of production had shrunk further and 50 percent of U.S. consumption had to be imported. For all that scientists talked about new fuel sources, notably hydrogen, few policymakers ex-

Indiana Bush and the Axis of Evil

pected a real alternative to oil before 2020, or more likely 2030. The crunch would come between 2000 and 2020, when world oil consumption was predicted to increase by almost 50 percent, spurred by development in Asia—a virtual doubling of demand by China, India, and the Middle East.[22]

By this point, the oil industry was lopsidedly Republican—or, more precisely, the GOP White House was now filled with oilmen—and the new Bush-Cheney regime made concern about the United States' losing further ground in the global oil competition a top priority. Within months of George W. Bush's 2001 inauguration, Cheney's energy task force predicted that domestic oil production would decline 12 percent by 2020, compelling the United States to import fully two-thirds of its oil. Leverage would continue to swing to the Middle East, with Gulf producers alone expected to provide 54 to 67 percent of world oil exports in 2020. Next to Saudi Arabia's 262 billion barrels of proven reserves, Iraq was second with 120 billion—and possible but unproven Iraqi reserves could carry the total a lot higher.[23] A careful listener could almost hear the war drums.

Indeed, Cheney and his chief of staff, Lewis Libby, had already participated in drafting a 2000 report for the Project for a New American Century that called for taking over Iraq—this well before 9/11—as part of a larger, oil-minded Pax Americana.[24] Thus emerged the early inklings of the military strategy needed to implement the later energy task-force findings.

The Germans and Japanese had been the desperate oil seekers of 1941–42; now, Russian, Chinese, and American eyes were fixed on the Middle East and adjacent Central Asia. In 2001, resource-war theoretician Michael Klare foresaw armed confrontation: "The likelihood of future combat over oil is suggested, first of all, by the growing build-up of military forces in the Middle East and other oil-producing areas. Until recently, the greatest concentration of military power was to be found along the East-West divide in Europe and at other sites of superpower competition. Since 1990, however, these concentrations have largely disappeared, while troop levels in the major oil zones have been increased."[25]

The March 2003 invasion of Iraq substantially reflected these pressures. At U.S. Central Command headquarters, biblical wisecracks about the second fall of Babylon were as infrequent as battlefield signs giving mileage and directions to Armageddon. However, until someone responded to the unwise symbolism, two big U.S. gasoline dumps on the road to Baghdad were given highly ironic nicknames: Exxon and Mobil.

Great Games I and II

Since the late eighteenth century, Western imperialists had swashed and buckled their way across Asia, creating a colorful mythology of expansion to match the exotic landscape. As the British Empire spread and consolidated in India, the Russian Empire did likewise in Central Asia, and on the margins the two plotted and competed. This rivalry became the so-called Great Game of spies and intelligence organizations. Grand geopolitical theory also danced attendance, from Germany's *Drang nach Osten* (push to the East) to British geographer Sir Halford Mackinder's "Heartland" thesis, which argued that the cockpit where Asia met Europe represented the hinge of world politics.

In the 1980s and 1990s, intensifying U.S. military and covert involvement with Iran, Afghanistan, and Iraq set similar cook pots boiling, further heated by the 1991 breakup of the Soviet Union and the creation of eight new republics in the Caucasus and Transcaspia. Splitting into latter-day khanates, Circassian mountain republics, and bristling encampments of missile-bearing Tatars, Eurasia was once again in play. The second Bush administration had piles of grand stratagems mounting even before taking office in 2001. If God was speaking to George W. Bush, neoimperialists like Paul Wolfowitz and Richard Perle also had occasional conversations.

So arose the opportunity for a new Great Game, this time for control of the Caucasian and Transcaspian oil fields. In 1993, Boris Rumer of Harvard's Davis Center for Russian and Eurasian Studies, argued that "this new Great Game in the heart of Asia is unfolding not so much among the old colonial powers as among their former minions"—the Caspian and Caucasian states from the old Soviet Union, as well as Afghanistan, Pakistan, and India from the British sphere.[26] In a 1996 article titled "Central Asia: A New Great Game," Lieutenant Colonel Dianne Smith of the U.S. Army War College's Strategic Studies Institute identified Iran, Pakistan, India, China, and Russia as the players. The interest of the United States, she said, was not in being a direct participant but in avoiding conflagration.[27]

In the three years before the attack on the World Trade Center, the emphasis turned to great-power oil and gas rivalry. A section in Klare's *Resource Wars* was headed "The Great Game II: U.S.-Russian Competition in the Caspian."[28] In these terms, the United States under Clinton had clearly started to play. So had a number of Bush allies, with Dick Cheney, James Baker, former White House chief of staff John Sununu, and former national security adviser Brent Scowcroft all signed up to counsel the Azerbaijan International Operating Company (a consortium 40 percent owned by Amoco, Pennzoil, Unocal, McDermott, and Exxon). George W. Bush's future national security adviser, Condoleezza Rice, as a Chevron board member, advised the company on its Tenghiz-Chevroil joint venture in Kazakhstan.

Although the events of 9/11 buried references to a U.S.-Russian petroleum competition, oil and its political economics remained a hereditary preoccupation of any Bush chief executive. Several analysts have argued that George H. W. Bush, as vice president and president, invariably had oil-related motives not just in the 1991 Gulf War but in other U.S. involvements in the Middle East. The first was the Iran-Contra affair—arms for Iran might prolong the Iran-Iraq War, reduce Persian Gulf output, and raise prices for U.S. oil producers. The second was the late-1992 intervention in Somalia, just across the Red Sea from Saudi Arabia, where potentially important U.S. oil concessions were at stake.[29]

According to Klare, the resource-war theorist, a Greater Game guided George W. Bush in 2003: "Controlling Iraq is about oil as power, rather than oil as fuel. Control over the Persian Gulf translates into control over Europe, Japan and China. It's having our hand on the spigot."[30]

Yet the old game also had a second facet, clandestine rather than imperial, which has also shown early-twenty-first-century relevance. Overambition in the region has been common, because locales from the Caucasus to the Khyber Pass have exerted an extraordinary pull on Western adventurers, "soldier sahibs," intelligence chiefs, and secret agents. They have been romanticized and glorified since 1901, when Rudyard Kipling's *Kim,* set in what was then India's North-West Frontier Province, evoked Pashtun horse traders, Russian spies, and the general mystique of the clandestine world.

So influential was Kipling's novel that two well-known early-twentieth-century agents took its title as a nickname. One was Kermit "Kim" Roosevelt, an American Arabist who served in the World War II OSS and directed the 1953 coup that restored the young shah Mohammad Reza Pahlavi to power in Iran.[31] As a young man in 1920, Kim Roosevelt had served briefly as secretary of the Averell Harriman–George H. Walker American Ship and Commerce entity, before resigning with a complaint about excessive German influence—"the doubtful allegiance of some new element in the American Ship and Commerce Corporation."[32] The second

Kim, of course, was H. A. R. "Kim" Philby—the post–World War II British archtraitor.

American spymaster Allen Dulles, born too late for the Great Game, thrilled to its memory. In 1914, sailing to India to spend a year teaching at a missionary school, he read Kipling's book for the first time. Its imprint was so indelible, said his biographer, that *Kim* was at Dulles's bedside when he died in 1969.[33] From his 1924 post as director of the Near Eastern Bureau of the U.S. State Department, in which he helped to get Standard Oil of New Jersey a Mesopotamian oil concession, to his 1953 role as CIA director in restoring the shah to power in Iran, Dulles enjoyed playing on Kipling's turf. In the 1980s, on visiting CIA headquarters in Langley, Virginia, John Keegan, the British military historian, perceived a resemblance to British India's Political and Secret Service of yore. "It [the CIA] has assumed the mantle once worn by Kim's masters," he wrote.[34]

Although George H. W. Bush never nicknamed a son, nephew, or grandson Kim, no major American leader remotely matched his 1976–92 record of pouring weaponry into Afghanistan, co-opting Pakistani intelligence, liaising with the shah's Iranian police, making secret arms deals with Shiite ayatollahs, becoming near family to Saudi princes, rescuing undemocratic Kuwait, and helping to transform Peshawar—Kipling's mountain gateway to the Khyber Pass—into a CIA station and munitions dump. Son George W. Bush, who frequently invoked the difference between his father's Greenwich Country Day School years and his own San Jacinto Junior High School experience, was the product of a less sophisticated arms-bearing culture. His baseball team, of course, was the Texas Rangers; his favorite television program, he would tell reporters, was *Walker, Texas Ranger*. His game was good-versus-evil, God fearing, confrontational, and Texan.

The distinction between the Bush generations is telling. Like the British a century earlier, Americans have draped their bid for empire in the utter conviction that they represent modernity and, in the words of British prime minister William Gladstone in 1894, "the noblest example yet known to mankind of free, adaptable, just government."[35] Kipling's white man's burden has become the obligation of American democracy. However, there was a uniquely American hue to the insistence of 2003, led by neoconservatives clustered in the Defense Department, that U.S. troops were liberating Iraq to begin a process of reverse dominoes—the establishment of a democratic example that would inspire neighboring Islamic states to throw off strongmen and fundamentalist clerics.

Imperial Britain left uplift to religious missionaries, being politically content to divide and rule. Imperial America has invariably deployed clichés of Wilsonian democracy, improbabilities that leave cynical analyses barely contradicted, in the process creating a huge hypocrisy gap. Experts like former White House national security adviser Zbigniew Brzezinski, Paul Wihbey of the Institute for Advanced Strategic and Political Studies, and Ilan Berman of the American Foreign Policy Council have also echoed Mackinder and romanticized Eurasia, but their conceptual veneers have attracted little public interest.[36]

Instead, foreign and U.S. attention has correctly concentrated on the neo-conservatives' Wilsonian pretense and anti-European rashness, a familiar and recurrent American attitude presumed to reflect the thinking of George W. Bush. Administrations enjoying strong foreign policy leadership from a skilled president or a dominant secretary of state rarely put on such displays. But in a regime where a fundamentalist chief executive sought to play Texas Ranger captain to the world—as we will see, Vice President Cheney proudly accepted the word "cowboy"—simplistic observations emanating from the White House contributed to shaping a negative U.S. global image.

In this contemporary imperial mix, though, is a new and hazardous ingredient: the vast arsenals, ammunition dumps, and airfields with supplies and weaponry shipped over three decades by the United States and other marketers to shaky or despotic Middle Eastern regimes, some of them eventually mired in large-scale corruption or drug trafficking. Significantly more than its Kipling-era predecessor, the twenty-first-century Great Game is rife with blowback and backlash.

"Merchants of Engines of Destruction"

Back in 1934, the lurid title of a book called *Merchants of Death*, which blamed munitions makers for the First World War, quickly became a popular phrase. FDR himself soon coined the very similar term "merchants of engines of destruction" in the same year. It was his hedged, more precise way of explaining—as he did several times in related discussions—how "the grave menace to the peace of the world is due in no small measure to the uncontrolled activities of the manufacturers and merchants of engines of destruction."[37]

The "merchants of death" label is also remembered as an ultimately crippling nickname attached to the hearings of the Senate Special Committee on the Investigation of the Munitions Industry, which also began in 1934. At that time, the weapons industry, with which the Bush and Walker families had both been involved, was in disrepute. But by 1939, the coming of war had reframed the argument, so that antimunitions sentiments were criticized for having hindered Franklin D. Roosevelt's mobilization against fascism and for having abetted the Neutrality Acts of 1935, 1936, and 1937.

This change in public mood did more than rebut disdain for munitions makers and encourage patriotic support for "war industries." It also undercut the 1920s and early 1930s consensus that arms races and merchants did indeed help to stir up wars—a contention that remained unfashionable in U.S. establishment circles through most of the twentieth century, save for the late Vietnam years and the subsequent Carter-era disenchantment. Through most of the cold war period, defense contractors were almost automatically "good guys." As a political strategy, centrist internationalists avoided attacking munitions makers and shunned any associations with the old "isolationist" rhetoric.

When the Senate special committee started its hearings in 1934, the new president was sympathetic. As assistant secretary of the navy from 1913 to 1920, he had seen contractor abuses firsthand. He was also a politician. FDR especially looked forward to the discomfort of his political enemies the du Ponts, whose munitions empire included E. I. du Pont de Nemours, Atlas Powder, Hercules Powder, Remington Arms, and a major interest in General Motors. The du Ponts had contributed some 60 percent of the funding for the bitterly anti-Roosevelt Liberty League just formed to oppose the New Deal. Members of the Senate committee obliged the Du Pont company's executives to admit that its common stock paid out a whopping 458 percent of its original value in dividends during the war. However, when Missouri senator Bennett Clark brought out evidence of a meeting between Felix du Pont and a representative of the Nazi Germany military staff, the secretaries of state and commerce met with committee members to squelch public discussion of secret reports on German rearmament. The Commerce Department likewise prevented testimony from the U.S. commercial attaché in Berlin.[38]

Indeed, when the Senate special committee had finished with Du Pont executives and began to display an equal willingness to embarrass government officials, FDR's attitude chilled. From early 1935, he favored other venues and a more moderate approach to the regulatory and war profits issues. Meanwhile, as hearings continued into 1936, some committee mem-

bers, especially Chairman Gerald Nye of North Dakota, became more stri-
dent. Through press comments and radio broadcasts, he played to his
home state's strong isolationism, and his political rhetoric tainted the investigation's image.[39]

In the long run, the armaments industry profited in three ways from
the committee's being discredited. First, the Nye embarrassment took attention away from the role that banks and armament makers had played in
the run-up to and unfolding of the First World War. Second, the crippled
committee failed to expose how "merchants of what FDR had called the
engines of destruction" might be helping to bring about *another* world war
(as the engines and equipment wound up in Heinkels, Messerschmitts, and
Tiger tanks). Third, by the late twentieth century, as arms sales got out of
hand again, few were inclined to mount a similar investigation—and possibly suffer the same ignominy. By 2000, we had as a nation suppressed our
memory of earlier abuses by arms makers.

When we look back, the actual reports of the Senate special committee
were quite restrained, as Texas historian Matthew Coulter reported in his
1997 book *The Senate Munitions Inquiry of the 1930s: Beyond the Merchants
of Death.* David Eisenhower, writing in 1992 about his grandfather's 1961
farewell address warning about the military-industrial complex, explained
how the future president had been impressed by the munitions hearings.[40]
Back in 1970, Paul Koistinen, the principal historian of the U.S. war economy, had also given the senators a favorable nod. Despite overblown rhetoric, he said, the committee had avoided conspiracy allegations, while its
"most impressive reports" detailed a large array of companies and connections that foreshadowed the "full-blown 'industrial military complex' of
World War Two and the Cold War Years."[41]

The committee had struck another useful chord in attaching culpability to American firms busy arming the future aggressors—Germany, Japan,
and Italy. As Coulter summarized, "Many U.S. munitions firms did substantial business in Germany during the 1930s, and some experienced huge
increases in orders after Hitler took power. For the munitions committee,
it was 'apparent that those who stood to profit by the rearming of Germany
were (a) those who sold her the arms, and (b) those who would profit from
the scare of a rearmed Germany, which would have tremendous repercus-
sions on the armament program of the other continental countries.'"[42]

Unfortunately, this part of the committee's analysis was thin and incomplete. For one thing, it ended in 1936; for another, the Departments of

State, War, and Commerce had worked to suppress confidential reports on German rearmament. Only later did it become clear how significant the U.S. role had been in building up the German war machine Hitler would rely on.

As discussed earlier, 1920s Germany was the part of Europe into which the United States pumped the largest share (nearly $2 billion) of its new wealth from 1914 to 1918. True, millions of dollars were wasted on loans to German municipalities that later defaulted. But other large sums were raised by major American investment firms to refinance and retool companies—Thyssen Steel, I. G. Farben, Siemens Electric—that became central pillars of Hitler's war effort. Additional funds poured into new German subsidiaries of major U.S. companies—General Motors, Ford, ITT, and Standard Oil—that wound up building trucks for the Wehrmacht, tanks for panzer divisions, and Focke-Wulf aircraft for the Luftwaffe, as well as pumping oil for Nazi U-boats.

Hitler's Germany was the European country in which U.S. investment grew most rapidly during the 1930s even while it declined on the Continent as a whole. Rearmament was the growth sector and the high-profit stock ticket. National City Bank and Brown Brothers Harriman, according to several chroniclers, during the late 1930s used an agent named Henry Mann—well enough connected to meet several times with Hitler—to bring Third Reich deals back for New York decision makers.[43] Dillon Read, as we have seen, had a busy subsidiary handling investments in Germany.

Alternative outcomes make for interesting contemplation: Would Hitler have been able to take power without the U.S. arms said to have reached him in the early 1930s through the Hamburg-Amerika Line or Thyssen's assistance? Probably. Would he have remilitarized the Rhineland in 1936 if National City Bank, Dillon Read, and Brown Brothers Harriman had promptly shut down investments, loans, and deal making after he started rearming in 1935? This is hard to say. Would he have been prepared to fight in 1939 if ITT, General Motors, Ford, and General Electric had shut down the subsidiaries that wound up producing for the Nazi war effort? Probably not, which makes the "engines of destruction" thesis relevant to both world wars—and also sets our scene to examine the late-twentieth-century arms buildup.

For most of the half century before the Second World War, Britain, not the United States, was the world's number one arms exporter. The United States had led only during the 1914–18 period. Longtime Vickers-Armstrong clients like the shah of Persia, the king of Siam, and the emir of Afghanistan stayed loyal. But after 1945, the United States, as the wartime "Arsenal of Democracy," went on to become the cold war arsenal of anticommunism.

During the 1950s, annual U.S. foreign military sales had totaled only several hundred million dollars, and most of the weaponry went to NATO allies, Australia, and Japan, not to the third world. As the U.S. balance-of-payments surplus shrank in the early 1960s, the Kennedy administration cited this as a reason to encourage arms exports. In 1968, U.S. foreign military sales crossed the $1 billion level for the first time, but the big jump came after the 1970s OPEC crisis, when Washington policymakers unofficially decided that high-priced arms sales to Saudi Arabia and Iran, in particular, could retrieve some of the dollars the oil producers were banking from soaring prices. The official explanation, less candid, had Saudi Arabia and Iran assuming new roles as U.S. "surrogates" in Middle Eastern regional defense.

As the oil zone of the Middle East became the jewel in the Lockheed-Boeing-Northrop crown, U.S. foreign military sales jumped from $1.6 billion in 1972 to $10 billion in 1975. The balance-of-payments benefit was considerable. Weapons had become one of the most profitable U.S. exports.

Then in 1979, when the shah was overthrown, the new revolutionary government canceled $8 billion to $10 billion of orders, some already begun by U.S. contractors.[44] The Carter administration—after having earlier pledged to curb arms exports—now scrambled to find takers for the orders just repudiated. Israel and Egypt moved up the ladder. Saudi Arabia was willing to buy more advanced weaponry and systems, but the U.S. Congress, under Israeli pressure, blocked several arrangements. As a result, early 1980s sales to the Saudis declined markedly. The United States slipped to fourth place behind Britain, France, and even China.[45]

The regional concentration of weapons deliveries was notably lopsided. Between 1970 and 1979, Middle Eastern countries accounted for $57 billion in new foreign military sales orders, close to two-thirds of the U.S. total for those years. Because Soviet arms sales were not far behind, the research institutes doing the monitoring affirmed that "the Middle East has become the world's premier weapons market, accounting for approximately half of all arms transfers to the Third World between 1976 and 1980."[46] As CIA director in 1976, George H. W. Bush had been closely involved in the peak period of U.S. arms sales to the shah.

As Congress blocked high-technology sales to Saudi Arabia and the aya-tollahs held on to power in Iran, U.S. arms exports in the early 1980s sagged to the Saudis and ended to the Iranians, at least on an official basis. The Reagan administration, favorable to arms exports as a matter of both economics and philosophy, countered by further reducing the restrictions on what advanced technology could be sold to which buyer. James Buckley, the undersecretary of state for security assistance, told the Aerospace In-dustries Association in 1981 that the administration flatly rejected the no-tion that military sales are "inherently evil or morally reprehensible." "This Administration," he argued, "believes that arms transfers, judiciously ap-plied, can complement and supplement our own defense efforts and serve as a vital and constructive instrument of our foreign policy."[47]

Although U.S. outlays for arms in the Middle East declined somewhat from 1980 to 1989, the region echoed with the loud staccato of armed vio-lence. The United States steadily raised its funding through the CIA—from $30 million in 1984 to $634 million in 1987—for the mujahideen rebels fighting the Russians in Afghanistan, sums that were matched by the Saudis.[48] With Vice President George H. W. Bush taking a lead role, the United States also began clandestinely supplying Iraq in its 1980–88 war with Iran. James Adams, defense correspondent of the *Sunday Times* of London, reported "an extraordinary feeding frenzy by the sharks of the arms business. Fifty countries sold arms to the protagonists in the war. Of these fifty, four countries sold only to Iraq, eighteen to Iran and twenty-eight, including France, China, Italy, South Africa, Britain, the United States and West Germany, sold weapons to both sides."[49]

Swollen by Iraqi and Iranian war demand, the Persian Gulf nations ac-counted for 30 percent of all arms deliveries to the third world in 1984–88, according to the Stockholm International Peace Research Institute. The Middle East in its entirety took 48 percent.[50] The various international or-ganizations tracking arms sales did not use identical criteria, but the region maintained roughly the same primacy in deliveries it had a decade earlier. More arms-producing nations were competing for export markets, though. The Iraq-Iran War involved large enough orders over a long enough time to nourish the weapons industries of Brazil, China, South Africa, and North Korea.[51]

In 1990, after Saddam Hussein's partially U.S.-equipped forces invaded Kuwait, George H. W. Bush successfully organized a coalition to expel him, which further enlarged the U.S. military presence in the Persian Gulf—and with it the regional arms buildup. Although the cost of the first Gulf War in 1991 was mostly borne by allied nations, the United States quickly thereafter sold the member states of the Gulf Cooperation Council (GCC)—Bahrain, Kuwait, Oman, Qatar, Saudi Arabia, and the United Arab Emirates—the advanced weaponry and basing facilities needed to support any follow-up rapid U.S. deployment. "Between 1990 and 1997 alone," noted one expert, "the United States provided these countries with arms and ammunition worth over \$42 billion—the largest and mostly costly transfer to any region in the world by any single supplier in recent history."[52]

From a military standpoint, the strategy of arming the Gulf Cooperation Council worked well enough into 2003. But the larger effects of a four-decade influx of U.S. weaponry, money, support personnel, and covert operations could not be ignored: The Middle East and southern Eurasia were turning into an Islamic Dodge City. This was the core of what Chalmers Johnson called "blowback"—"the unintended consequences of policies that were kept secret from the American people."[53]

Country after country reaped bitter rewards. In *The Arms Bazaar: From Lebanon to Lockheed* (1977), Anthony Sampson described the eighteen-month Christian-Muslim civil war that ripped Lebanon, gutted Beirut, and killed forty thousand to sixty thousand people, more than the combined casualties of all four Arab-Israeli wars:

> The great city of Beirut, which had been the hub of Middle East commerce, had become a ruined shell, its gutted skyscrapers staring out, with blank holes instead of windows, across the desolate port. It had become a lethal laboratory of the world arms trade. Beirut was always unique in the Middle East for its cosmopolitanism and free trade: it was the city where everything was for sale. It was appropriate that it should become the center for the free trade in weapons, flowing in from all corners of the world. Money could be quickly transmuted into guns; and the most prosperous city in the Middle East had become the most deadly.[54]

Kindred laments have been penned for Kabul, Peshawar, Baghdad, and Bethlehem. For all of Afghanistan, Human Rights Watch reported at the end of 2000 that the nation "has been at war for more than twenty years. Some 1.5 million people are estimated to have died as a direct result of the conflict. Another five million fled as refugees to India and Pakistan."[55]

Excluding the U.S. arms for Israel and Egypt, both major recipients of

U.S. aid and weaponry, the nations inundated by waves of American arms, military forces, and trainers since the oil-price shocks read like a directory of regional trauma wards: *Saudi Arabia* (a first wave of arms and trainers in the 1970s, followed by a flood of U.S. servicemen and -women, and installations, during and after the Gulf War of 1990–91); *Iran* (a huge flow of weaponry under the shah in the 1970s; a second, smaller covert supply during the 1980s through the October Surprise and related Iran-Contra machinations); *Afghanistan* (huge 1980s shipments—given the small population—to rebels fighting the Russians); *Pakistan* (large-scale military and weapons assistance since the 1970s, plus the nation's 1980s experience as a U.S. weapons and insurgency pipeline to Afghanistan); *Iraq* (large-scale U.S. military and dual-use equipment assistance during its 1980s war with Iran, followed by the devastation of intermittent bombing, sanctions, and two wars); and the *Gulf oil sheikhdoms* (a tidal wave of U.S. weaponry and facilities during the 1990s and a lesser one in 2002–3). Some might add Turkey to the list because of its large-scale U.S. military support, although membership in NATO put it in a different category.

Although the United States greatly increased its military facilities and predominance in the Middle East, four other, interrelated effects could be summarized by 2003:

1. a regional upsurge in corruption promoted by the influx of oil money, armaments, covert operations, and arms-dealer commissions, accompanied in Afghanistan and Pakistan by a ballooning business in drugs;
2. the broad regional alienation of Muslim religious leaders and the rise of Islamic fundamentalism;
3. the political nurturing and success of Islamic revolutionary movements (the overthrow of the shah in Iran, the ascent of the Taliban in Afghanistan, Saudi support for Al Qaeda, the success of Pakistani religious parties in the frontier provinces, and the Islamic victories in nearby Turkey); and
4. the increasing dependence of the United States on alliances with the Saudi royal family and the oil-rich, nondemocratic Gulf sheikhdoms, all fearful of being overthrown by the popular and fundamentalist forces unleashed.

Often, the more intensive the United States presence, the greater the problem. Members of the U.S. Defense Science Board underscored just this in a 1997 report: "Historical data show a strong correlation between U.S. involvement in international situations and an increase in terrorist attacks against the United States. In addition, the military asymmetry that denies nation-states the ability to engage in overt attacks against the United States drives the use of transnational actors [terrorists from one country attacking in another]."[56]

Some strategists and any number of suspicious liberals justified, at least privately, the U.S. invasion of Iraq in 2003 by the need to secure new oil supplies and to obtain territory to which the United States could shift its forces from a fundamentalist-imperiled Saudi Arabia next door. None of these arguments could be made publicly, and the official Washington insistence on the need to build democracy in Iraq left world opinion unswayed.

The political economics of the Bush dynasty over four generations, two of them presidential, suggested no such nation-building commitment. Indeed, their taste for covert operations and transactions suggests the reverse. As good a case could be made that their exercise of power has been biased toward destabilization: in Central America, Chile, Afghanistan, and Iraq. The family's ties were to wealthy U.S. and foreign elites—from Cuban sugar plantation owners to Persian Gulf sheikhs—as well as to the intelligence and national security establishment, the oil business, "crony" capitalism, and related foreign policy specialists. Ground-level popular democracy has more often been something to subvert rather than something to promote.

Going back four generations, armaments production and arms dealings have made repeated appearances. Samuel Bush's Ohio steel business temporarily produced gun forgings in 1917–18, even while Bush himself was in Washington regulating ordnance, among other things, for the War Industries Board. However, this did not really put him in the arms business, despite his exposure and contacts. His ethics were high, and at war's end he returned to making railroad equipment and aiding local charities in Columbus, Ohio.

The ghost of George Herbert Walker, queried about covert operations and his own predilection for armaments, would probably just chuckle. The interwar corporate crony structure that he helped to develop—American International Corporation, Remington Arms, National City Bank, W. A. Harriman and Company, Georgian Manganese, American Ship and Commerce, and the Union Banking Corporation, with their partial interlocking directorates (Harriman, Walker, Rockefeller, Pryor, Brush, et al.)—teamed builders and manufacturers of arms, ships, and munitions with liquid capital, offering the corporate capacities to equip a war in South America, re-furbish Soviet mines and oil fields, or sneak rifles through Dutch backwaters into Germany circa 1932. Few clear sets of Walker's international finger-prints exist, because little government regulation required paperwork or scrutiny, and the man seems to have put the *c* in covert.

Prescott Bush, who died in 1972, never had to discuss publicly his role in the Union Banking Corporation, Brown Brothers Harriman's invest-ment dealings with Nazi Germany or the purposes of that complicated sex-tet of German-connected companies discussed in chapters 1 and 6. During World War II, two of his corporate directorships may have put him on the periphery of U.S. atomic bomb development. A committed Castrophobe, he favored covert operations against post-1960 Cuba, proposed giving refugee Cubans the weapons to establish their own blockade of the island, and supported the relentless destabilization of Castro's regime ever after.[57] As we have seen, rumor tied him to earlier service in military intelligence. Nation building was not what he did.

George H. W. Bush's introduction to the great American gun culture probably came in the 1930s, when he and his brothers visited their grand-father Walker's South Carolina hunting preserve. As chapter 6 noted, some accounts have tied George H. W. to support work in the CIA's 1961 Bay of Pigs invasion, and in the years to come his record of clandestine arms deals and shipments as CIA director and then vice president would involve countries from Cuba and Nicaragua to Iran, Iraq, Israel, Pakistan, and Afghanistan. If any vice president in U.S. history could fairly be known as "the secret-arms-deal vice president," he would be the one.

As president, Bush senior gloried in the Gulf War and the 1989 invasion of Panama, both cast as strikes for democracy—even if the dictators at-tacked were former friends. Over a decade, as chapter 9 will detail, his web of covert international relationships prompted charges of his participating in and covering up in three actual or alleged illegalities: the Republican Party's "October Surprise" negotiations with Iran in 1980, supposedly un-dertaken to ensure that no hostages taken in Iran would be released before the election; the Iran-Contra scandal; and "Iraqgate," secretly arming Iraq from 1984 to 1990 before hurriedly changing course after Saddam Hussein took Kuwait. Two catchphrases recur in the family résumé: "arms deals" and "clandestine operations." A third recurring association would be "cover-up."

George W. Bush was a willing recipient of this inheritance—witness the CIA and BCCI ties of some who financed him, from Arbusto to Harken Energy a decade later. For example, James Bath, who invested fifty thousand dollars in the 1979 and 1980 Arbusto partnerships, probably did so as U.S. business representative for rich Saudi investors Salem bin Laden and Khalid bin Mahfouz (Osama bin Laden's brother-in-law). Both men were involved with the Bank of Credit and Commerce International, the rogue bank and occasional CIA front known for financing arms deals—indeed, bin Mahfouz owned 20 percent of its stock. Bath, who made his fortune investing for the two Saudis, was a colorful Texan—and then some. According to former *Houston Post* reporter Pete Brewton, Bath was "an asset of the CIA, reportedly recruited by George Bush himself" in 1976 to keep the Agency up to date on Saudi activities.[58]

A decade later, Harken Energy, the company willing to handsomely buy out George W.'s crumbling oil and gas business, had its own CIA connections. Chairman Alan Quasha was the son of a Philippine lawyer connected to the Nugan Hand Bank, a notorious Australian bank closely linked to the CIA. Equally to the point, 17.6 percent of Harken's stock was owned by Abdullah Bakhsh, another Saudi magnate reported by some to be representing Khalid bin Mahfouz.

A U.S. Senate subcommittee investigating BCCI in 1992 reported on how the bank bought friendship and favors from politicians around the world; details of the investigation were published in two books: *False Profits: The Inside Story of BCCI, the World's Most Corrupt Financial Empire*, by Peter Truell and Larry Gurwin, and *The Outlaw Bank: A Wild Ride into the Secret Heart of BCCI*, by Jonathan Beaty and S. C. Gwynne. According to the latter, the story of the Bush involvement in the BCCI scandal involved "trails that branched, crossed one another or came to unexpected dead ends." It was like a "three dimensional chess game."[59] The *Wall Street Journal* added, "The mosaic of BCCI connections surrounding Harken Energy may prove nothing more than how ubiquitous the rogue bank's ties were. But the number of BCCI-connected people who had dealings with Harken—all since George W. Bush came on board—likewise raises the question of whether they mask an effort to cozy up to a presidential son."[60]

In *The Outlaw Bank,* Beaty and Gwynne had this to say about BCCI: "It was a conspiratorialist's conspiracy, a plot so byzantine, so thoroughly corrupt, so exquisitely private, reaching so deeply into the political and intelligence establishments of so many countries, that it seemed to have its only precedent in the more hallucinogenic fiction of Ian Fleming, Kurt Vonnegut or Thomas Pynchon."[61] Not that the Bush brothers seemed to care.

As we have seen, Jeb Bush began his business career in Miami collaborating with Cubans tied to the CIA or to kindred intelligence agencies in pre-Castro Cuba. He socialized with Adbur Sakhia, BCCI's Miami branch manager and later its top U.S. official.[62] Jeb Bush's partners and early associates included a number of Cuban émigrés with CIA, Nicaraguan Contra, or Batista-era Cuban intelligence connections.

To say that armaments, clandestine operations, and money-laundering banks recur in the history of the Walker-Bush family is no exaggeration at all. No other presidents have been so caught up in this kind of foreign policy. And the Bushes' preoccupations are not clear until you consider the whole dynasty. It is the dynastic aspect that truly reveals the pattern—the clandestine behavior over multiple generations.

The Axis of Evil— and the Web of War Profits

Wars, profits, and new wealth have historically been closely linked in the United States, as in the rest of the world. Supplying armies and navies paid well. So did government-licensed looting. Even in the early nineteenth century, many of the richest men in Britain, France, and the United States— Nathan Rothschild, Gabriel-Julien Ouvrard, John Jacob Astor, and Stephen Girard—owed much of their primacy to the fruits of wartime finance. The phrase "fortunes of war" has been a notable double entendre.

In the United States, at least, the politics of obtaining weath through war has not had a particular party label. New Englanders and Philadelphians of future Federalist politics finished the American Revolution as the new nation's richest men thanks to war dealings and the fat proceeds of their privateer vessels' captures of British merchant ships. Jeffersonian-connected financiers like Astor and Girard did best in the War of 1812, but Republican bankers, contractors, and industrialists controlled the huge Civil War pot. During World War II, labor unions and working-class America split the proceeds with industry. Each war had its profiteers, but there was no regional, party, or ideological continuity.

By the end of the twentieth century, however, what began three generations earlier as a new U.S. military-industrial complex had achieved glossy permanence. Unlike the mass barracks for servicemen and the mass production lines for ships, ordnance, and aircraft central to World War II and the 1950–53 Korean War, the millennial version was more selective. It involved fewer unskilled infantry and their heavy-industry equivalents and much greater reliance on intelligence gathering and technology. While many mid-twentieth-century plants had been built by government funds—from 1940 to 1943, a peak 67 percent of industrial financing was federal—private capital totally dominated the last quarter of the twentieth century.[63]

Military preparedness increasingly became a for-profit activity. By 2003, through an initiative launched by Defense Secretary Richard Cheney in 1992, many government-run military support activities were being replaced by privatization and national security entrepreneurs—the private military corporations (PMCs) that did everything from train police in Croatia to handle Alabama airbase logistics or restore captured oil fields. Northern industrial labor unions and military draftees circa 1950 had long since given way to Sun Belt bases, nonunionized high-tech workforces, de facto private armies, and every kind of subcontractor imaginable.

In addition to these rightward-pushing forces, the Sun Belt was the nation's most promilitary region, stamped by the traditional military caste of the South. Its evangelical, fundamentalist, and Pentecostal churches were the most applauding of the new Middle East–centered U.S. military commitment. So long as actual U.S. war casualties—the stuff of evening news reports—remained minimal, the public could be counted on to cheer the "cruise missile diplomacy" and clandestine operations that had superseded the old gunboat diplomacy of U.S. Marines pouring ashore to restore order in Santo Domingo or Nicaragua. Conservative Congresses, run by Republicans from South Carolina, Georgia, Mississippi, and Texas, were happy to appropriate what the president wanted for the military, and add some more.

If these functions collectively commanded a somewhat lower share of national gross domestic product in 2004 than they had during the Eisenhower years, the opportunities for private enterprise were greater. The much increased share of money going to Pentagon functions, information systems, high technology, homeland security, the CIA and other intelligence services, "black operations," and PMC contracts avoided the highly unionized workforces of yesteryear, creating a higher ratio of commercial niches. In the Eisenhower era, aerospace companies earned only a 2 to 3 percent return on assets, half that of manufacturing corporations overall.[64]

By the Bush-Cheney years, military contractors could expect two or three times that return.

Indeed, the basic 2004 U.S. military budget of $400 billion a year was more than twice as much as the combined outlays of past and potential foes like Russia, China, Iraq, Syria, Iran, North Korea, Libya, and Cuba. The Axis of Evil was also the Axis of Reduced Military Resources. The U.S. outlay was twice that of all the NATO nations combined, and in 2002 the United States had accounted for 45.5 percent of all global conventional weapons deals and 48.6 percent of those concluded with developing nations.[65] As weaponry became the most successful U.S. manufactured export, markets became economic drivers. Preparedness itself was not simply a necessary posture but a giant interest group.

Private military enterprises, rare to unthinkable in Eisenhower's day, were becoming important governmental auxiliaries. Senior military officers liked how PMCs could edge into a difficult overseas situation without officially committing the United States or technically violating U.S. neutrality laws. They could also sidestep public attention and congressional oversight. In the winter of 2002–3, *Parameters,* the quarterly of the U.S. Army War College, published "The New Condottieri and U.S. Policy: The Privatization of Conflict and Its Implications." Its thesis was that in the post–cold war climate of instability and failed and failing states, the increasing importance of so-called niche wars or military operations other than war (MOOTW) demanded a wide range of PMCs to support U.S. objectives.[66]

The downside was that the PMCs aroused their own resentment, some of it fierce. One of the best known, the Vinnell Corporation—a specialist in training and advising police and military units in the Balkans and the Middle East (and a CIA cover)—became especially disliked during its quarter century of operations training internal security forces in Saudi Arabia, where its personnel reached several thousand. Its Riyadh facilities were car-bombed in 1995, killing five Americans.[67] They were attacked again by a suicide bomber in May 2003 after the second Iraq war, when nine employees were killed. In 1991, after the first Iraq war, when Turkish security forces trained by Vinnell turned back thousands of Iraqi Kurdish refugees to certain death, gunmen shot up the company's Ankara, Turkey, offices. They killed a retired U.S. Air Force chief master sergeant.[68]

The Carlyle Group, founded in 1987 as a merchant bank focused on political influence and defense-sector investments, became famous for turning its impressive portfolio of national-security-related companies—United Defense, BDM, Vinnell, U.S. Investigations Services, Composite Structures, EG&G, Federal Data Corporation, Lear Siegler, and Vought Aircraft—into winners for Carlyle's operation or profitable resale. This was achieved through the acumen and rainmaking of high-powered former officeholders in its employ, people ranging from George H. W. Bush, former secretary of state James Baker, and former defense secretary Frank Carlucci down to dozens of lesser cabinet, subcabinet, and senior regulatory agency officials.

Thirty to 40 percent yearly gains were common, but from the early days of the second Bush administration, so were conflict-of-interest charges. Carlyle's preoccupation was with companies that could profit from its Washington connections. One newspaper called Carlyle "the thread which indirectly links American military policy in Afghanistan to the personal financial fortunes of its celebrity employees, not least the President's father."[69]

"It should be a deep cause for concern that a closely held company like Carlyle can simultaneously have directors and advisers that are doing business and making money and also advising the president of the United States," said Peter Eisner, managing director of the Center for Public Integrity. "The problem comes when private business and public policy blend together. What hat is former president Bush wearing when he tells Crown Prince Abdullah not to worry about U.S. policy in the Middle East?"[70]

Richard Perle, the neoconservative stalwart who chaired the Pentagon's Defense Policy Board, was simultaneously an investor in Middle East war preparations. As described by Seymour Hersh in *The New Yorker*, "Perle is also a managing partner in a venture-capital company called Trireme Partners, L.P., which was registered in November, 2001, in Delaware. Trireme's main business, according to a two-page letter that one of its representatives sent to [Saudi financier Adnan] Khashoggi last November, is to invest in companies that are of value to homeland security and defense."[71]

Carlyle was not the only Pentagon-connected gold mine. In the weak, bubble-shocked U.S. investment-banking climate of 2001–3, which reduced initial public offerings to a trickle, defense-sector IPOs reached their highest levels since the Reagan arms buildup of the 1980s.[72] The defense business, soon fleshed out by companies providing homeland security services, was one of the few to flourish through the bear market.

Homeland security became a cornucopia as the new Homeland Security Department's annual budget hit $40 billion, and hundreds of Secretary Tom Ridge's former aides and other insiders registered to lobby for companies seeking a slice of the pie. "Homeland Security appears to be viewed by the lobbying firms as a huge honeypot," complained Fred Wertheimer, president of the public interest group Democracy 21.[73]

Those better connected than former Ridge aides had found the pot of gold within months of 9/11. Marvin Bush, the brother of George W. Bush, was a large shareholder—through his Winston Partners investment firm— in Sybase, which marketed a "Sybase PATRIOT Compliance Solution" to put companies and banks in compliance with the anti-money-laundering provisions of the 2001 USA Patriot Act. Clients included the People's Bank of China and Sumitomo Mitsubishi Bank.[74] Former CIA director James Woolsey, a leading neoconservative, was a principal of the Paladin Capital Group, a private firm investing in companies that defended against terrorist attacks; Richard Perle had a stake in the Autonomy Corporation, a supplier of eavesdropping equipment to intelligence agencies.[75]

L. Paul Bremer III, the antiterrorist expert named by Bush to govern Iraq in May 2003, was profiled this way by The Nation a month later: "On October 11, 2001, just one month after the terror attacks in New York and Washington, [Bremer,] once Ronald Reagan's Ambassador at Large for counter-terrorism, launched a company designed to capitalize on the new atmosphere of fear in U.S. corporate boardrooms. Crisis Consulting Practice, a division of insurance giant Marsh and McLennan, specializes in helping multinationals come up with 'integrated and comprehensive crisis solutions' for everything from terror attacks to accounting fraud."[76]

Another group of firms, concentrated in and around Washington, D.C., profited from the CIA subcontractor market. Although the combined intelligence budgets were not only secret but tunneled like Swiss cheese by so-called black ops, estimates for the early 2000s put the total at some $35 billion a year. From this exchequer came tens of billions of dollars in annual contracts, most pouring into the so-called intelligence-industrial complex that surrounded the CIA's Northern Virginia headquarters. So loosely administered were some of these accounts that a 1996 congressional investigation "revealed that the National Reconnaissance Office (NRO), a super-secret agency whose existence was publicly acknowledged only a few years ago, lost track of a $2 billion slush fund because it was so highly classified even top officials had no control over it."[77] The world of CIA largesse was grand enough that "the CIA's own 4,000 intelligence analysts are dwarfed by the more than 40,000 analysts who work for private companies that have government intelligence contracts."[78]

A second controversial aspect of CIA wealth and influence involved the Agency's frequent, if unofficial, assertion of a modern version of benefit of clergy. If a CIA asset (as opposed to a mere salaried clerk or researcher) was indicted or arrested, the CIA often intervened—with frequent success—to talk the local law enforcement agency, the FBI, or the U.S. attorney's office out of prosecuting. Leave matters to us, the CIA said. This has been a virtual "get out of jail free" card enabling many CIA-connected operatives to avoid prosecution for various styles of moneymaking: drug running or, back during the eighties, milking federally insured mortgage programs or federally insured savings and loan associations.

One of Florida governor Jeb Bush's former Miami business associates, real estate operator Camilo Padreda, a pre-Castro Cuban counterintelligence officer, ducked an S&L indictment in Texas when the CIA helped.[79] Miguel Recarey, who had CIA connections and used his Miami-based International Medical Centers to help treat wounded Nicaraguan contras, was the business associate who had paid Jeb Bush a $75,000 real estate fee. When Recarey was indicted for large-scale Medicare fraud, his connections got him an expedited $2.2 million IRS refund that allowed him to flee to Venezuela.[80]

This is neither traditional Republicanism nor traditional conservatism, but a perverse mutation of the intelligence business. As we have seen, in January 1961, on leaving the presidency, Dwight Eisenhower, a conservative-minded Republican and former five-star general, made headlines with a farewell speech that has been his most quoted—and that specifically warned of the hazard of such associations. In its central paragraphs, he said: "In the councils of government, we must guard against the acquisition of unwarranted influence, whether sought or unsought, by the military-industrial complex. The potential for the disastrous rise of misplaced power exists and will persist. We must never let the weight of this combination endanger our liberties or democratic processes. We should take nothing for granted. Only an alert and knowledgeable citizenry can compel the proper meshing of the huge industrial and military machinery of defense . . . so that security and liberty may prosper together."

A canny prophecy, and over the years former advisers and Eisenhower family members have been asked to amplify on its origins and underpinning concerns. One friend with whom Eisenhower discussed the speech

ten days earlier, Ellis Slater, recalled that "the boss commented that Du
Pont years ago was always accused of fomenting wars," and "now that point
of view has subsided with respect to that particular company, but he is dis-
turbed because of the inter-relation of the economy with real disarmament. . . . The more successful we are in effecting disarmament, the more
disastrous the effect will be in many directions from the standpoint of the
economy."[81]

David Eisenhower, himself a respected historian of those years, commented in 1992 that his grandfather "was concerned that an unnecessary
growth of large organizational systems such as the integration of military
and business interests had evolved to the point that they could cause or
perpetuate international conflict. His work in the 1930s with Congressional hearings investigating the impact of munitions manufacturers on
policy in World War One helped to shape this opinion, as did his experiences as a general and a president."[82]

How much the military-industrial complex or the CIA drew the United
States into the imbroglio of Vietnam was unclear, but the Bay of Pigs, Vietnam, and Watergate threw both power networks into temporary disrepute,
stalling for a time the "unwarranted influence" that President Eisenhower
had seen growing. Yet, the countertide was brief. The revitalized national
security state that resurged in the 1980s, and then again after 2001, tran-
scended Eisenhower's definition of the military-industrial complex, which
had not mentioned the intelligence agencies. What took shape in later
years was not just his feared "integration of military and business interests"
but a new complex of technology, arms exports, internal security, and
clandestine operations, with its particular concentration in the crossroads
of world oil production and religious prophecy.

The participation in military-connected business of the president's
"family"—blood relations and close political associates alike—recalled the
eighteenth-century in its openness. These were practices I discussed in detail in *Wealth and Democracy: A Political History of the American Rich* (2002).
As noted, during the American Revolution, dozens of Patriot leaders got
rich off commissary fees, privateering rewards, and banking and trading
opportunities. The ethics of that era allowed as much.

Under Bush and Cheney, relatives, allies, and their own former companies have also done well—consider the favoritism to Cheney's Halliburton;
former president George H. W. Bush's very prominent role on behalf of the
Carlyle Group, especially in Saudi Arabia; and Marvin Bush's connection

to Stratasec, an electronic security firm.[83] Eighteenth-century standards seemed to be returning.

The family relationship to Carlyle and the CIA raised the largest, but also least-focused, question: Just what are the conflict-of-interest rules for dynasties? Can the old ruler, no longer on the throne but advising his son, do as he wishes commercially, especially when his business trips for an influence-dealing company take him to hot spots like Saudi Arabia and Korea? To put matters differently, can dynasts truly be private citizens? More specifically, what about dynasties with a four-generation relationship to the intelligence community and a three-generation tie to the CIA? When CIA power and domestic reach expand under such a dynasty, what does that bespeak—and suppose it should be proved that the enthusiastically pro-Bush CIA took a hand in the "October Surprise" operation in the 1980 election?

However, we are straying. By the end of the 1980s, the first U.S. mobilization against Saddam Hussein and Iraq was only months away. President George H. W. Bush was busy ensuring $1 billion in U.S. loan guarantees for Iraq and Saddam Hussein, declining to cut off the Iraqis from shared U.S. intelligence data, and disregarding Commerce Department advice to stop the flow of advanced equipment to Baghdad.[84] A decade of covert involvement—and more than a little misjudgment—was about to come home to roost.

CHAPTER 9

The Wars of the Texas Succession

Observers have faulted our intervention in Vietnam as evidence of American arrogance of power—attempts by the United States to be the World's Policeman. But there is another dimension to American arrogance, the international version of our domestic Great Society programs where we presumed that we knew what was best for the world in terms of social, political, and economic development and saw it as our duty to force the world into the American mold—to act not so much the World's Policeman as the World's Nanny. It is difficult today to recall the depth of our arrogance.

Colonel Harry Summers, *On Strategy: A Critical Analysis of the Vietnam War*, 1982

If, however, President Bush succeeds in bringing about regime change in Iraq, he will set a historic precedent—for Iraq, which could become the first Arab democracy; for the United States, which will demonstrate to all the compatibility of its interests and ideals; and for the world, which America will have made a safer and more just place.

Neoconservative commentators William Kristol and Lawrence Kaplan,
"America's Mission, After Baghdad," 2003

By 1990 and 2000, the overseas preoccupation of the Bushes, no longer with Germany, Mexico, or Cuba, had settled around the Middle East, especially the Arabian Peninsula, Iraq, and the Persian Gulf. The implications can hardly be overstated. Through four vice presidential and presidential terms, two emblematic wars with Iraq, and an unknown number of covert operations, the fortunes of the United States in the world's principal cockpit of diplomacy and religious fervor would be significantly swayed by a single family's entanglements, mistakes, financial alliances, and commitments.

The groundwork went back generations. The youthful George H. W. Bush would have heard his father and grandfather discussing the Harriman firm's 1920s Russian Central Asian manganese and oil adventures, the financial proceeds of which were administered through the 1930s in U.S. corporations named Georgian Manganese, Barnsdall, and Russian Finance and Construction. We must remember that Soviet Georgia, on the Black Sea, with its huge deposits of manganese, needed for weapons-grade steel, was a mere four hundred miles from Iraq. The Baku oil fields were about the same distance. For Averell Harriman, George H. Walker, and Prescott Bush, the Eurasian Great Game of the 1920s and 1930s was economic—liquidating assets, repatriating capital from the Caucasus and Baku, and collecting payments of interest and principal on Soviet bonds.

George H. W. Bush's Zapata Offshore drilling company, formed in the 1950s—the firm is said to have scouted for the CIA in pre–Bay of Pigs surveillance of Cuba—had some intelligence-connected British investors, friends of the family, with helpful access to Kuwaiti officialdom. Zapata Offshore organized a subsidiary to carry out Kuwait's first deep-sea oil drilling in 1961. When the young Republican oilman challenged Democratic U.S. senator Ralph Yarborough in 1964, the old populist brought up the "sheikh of Kuwait and his four wives and 100 concubines," dismissing Bush as "a carpetbagger from Connecticut who is drilling oil for the sheikh of Kuwait to help keep that harem going."[1] When Bush left government for several years in 1977 and became chairman of the executive committee of both Dallas's First International Bancshares and its London merchant banking subsidiary, he renewed some of those old ties.

Texas residence imbued its own Middle Eastern focus. Oil-fixated Houston and Midland were much closer psychologically to Saudi Arabia and the Persian Gulf than other parts of the United States were. At the postwar center of the global petroleum industry, Texas had already begun luring Arabs and Iranians during the 1960s. As the 1973–74 oil-price hikes rearranged the world power balance and bestowed fortunes from Qom to Qatar, the Gulf's new rich began flooding into Houston. By the 1980s, greater Houston had a Muslim population of twenty-five thousand. Scores bought homes in River Oaks and adjacent upscale neighborhoods. Some of the city's rich bankers and money managers had names like Tom, Dick, and Harry; others answered to Tayat, Abdullah, and Fayez.

Running the CIA for a year gave George H. W. Bush national motivations as well as petroleum-sector and hometown ones to monitor the oil-flush Middle East bankers and power brokers. As we have seen, this is when he supposedly recruited as a CIA asset James Bath, the Houston representative of two rich Saudis, Salem bin Laden and Khalid bin Mahfouz. The latter owned 20 percent of Abu Dhabi–based BCCI, already beginning to spread its tentacles through the international financial and intelligence communities. Journalists Peter Truell and Larry Gurwin, in their revealing BCCI book *False Profits* (1992), noted that during Bush's 1977–79 stint with First International Bancshares following his CIA tenure, "he traveled on the bank's behalf and sometimes marketed to international banks in London, including several Middle Eastern institutions. Some speculate that he met with BCCI officers at this time."[2]

Indeed, it would be accurate to say that by the 1980s the Bush family's overseas focus was increasingly Middle Eastern, but through bank and intelligence community lenses as well as through oil industry economics and geopolitics. These connections kept building.

When son George W. Bush organized his first oil venture, the 1979 Arbusto partnership, Bath had invested Saudi money. Far more overt was the prominence of former CIA agents in the senior Bush's emerging 1980 presidential campaign, where they eventually clustered like White Russian émigrés in 1920s Shanghai. The *Washington Post* noted that "simply put, no presidential campaign in recent memory—perhaps ever—has attracted so much support from the intelligence community as the campaign of former CIA director George Bush."[3] David Keene, a Republican consultant briefly employed by Bush, joked that at Bush's candidacy announcement, "half the audience was wearing raincoats."[4]

Team Trench Coat reflected more than ordinary political enthusiasm. During his tenure as CIA director, Bush's intra-Agency appointments had advanced covert operations practitioners: William Wells to deputy director for operations, Theodore Shackley to associate deputy director for operations, John Waller to inspector general. In late 1976, Bush had also protected wayward or hot-triggered Agency operatives—veterans of everything from Chilean assassinations to Vietnam's Phoenix Program and improper domestic surveillance—from indictment by President Ford's Justice Department. In the eyes of Attorney General Edward Levi and his aides, Bush's actions verged on obstructing Justice Department investigations.[5] Not least, Bush had been insistent in protecting former CIA director Richard Helms—aptly named by his biographer "the Man Who Kept the Secrets"—

who was ultimately let off with a fine and suspended sentence for lying to Congress. Never had an "outside" director of Central Intelligence, especially one so briefly in office, been such a staunch institutional defender.

The 1980 presidential campaign, from the early primaries to the November finale, became the first in which a surprised American public—and an almost equally surprised CIA—found their eyes fixed on the Middle East and its borderlands. Popular anger focused on Iran's newly fledged Islamic republic, run by ayatollahs, which had seized the U.S. embassy staff as hostages in November 1979. Afghanistan, invaded by Russia in 1979, also commanded attention. To a lesser extent, so did Iraq, which launched an invasion of Iran in September 1980. Bringing the hostages home led the list of concerns.

Voters now attached increasing importance to skill and toughness in foreign policy. After the U.S. Marines' helicopter mission to rescue the hostages held in Tehran failed in April 1980, President Carter began to slide in the polls, dropping to 20 to 30 percent approval levels during the summer. To win reelection, aides concluded, he had to get the hostages back by November.

When July's Republican convention ratified Bush as Reagan's vice presidential running mate, it made him the first former CIA director ever slated. Given the international stakes, however, the choice may have been shrewd. Bill Casey, the Reagan campaign manager named in February, was another old intelligence hand. The doubling up was utterly unprecedented. A senior OSS officer during World War II, Casey had also been an acquaintance of Prescott Bush's. In 1962, the two had worked together in launching the National Strategy Information Center, which advocated U.S. use of political and covert operations. The NSIC's obsession led some to assume that it was a CIA front.

In any event, the summer and autumn of 1980 saw the CIA offices at Langley bloom with pro-Bush political escutcheons—typically the torn-off Bush half of an official Reagan-Bush campaign poster. Langley's old-boy network had a new mission, and its outcome, possibly vital to 1980 GOP victory, would help to embroil the next three Republican presidents in Persian Gulf crosscurrents and war.

The 1980 "October Surprise": Historical Hinge or Hoax?

In a milestone of naive politics, most of the CIA covert operations stalwarts vulnerable to indictments during the last year of the Ford administration, along with many others, were abruptly discharged in 1977 by the Carter administration—some eight hundred in covert operations were sacked out of a total of four thousand.[6] Intelligence services elsewhere in the West were stunned.

Dozens of those fired eventually joined the 1980 Bush campaign. By that point, the potential Washington reempowerment of secrecy defenders like George H. W. Bush and Bill Casey must have seemed like political and vocational deliverance. They focused above all on the Iranian hostage crisis as Carter's weak point and their prime opportunity. By midsummer, two principal fears remained: the possibilities that Carter could (1) mount a second, successful military hostage-rescue mission despite the first failure; or (2) work out a deal so that the Iranians themselves would return the hostages before the election. The countermove by the GOP—apparently in harness with portions of the CIA's old-boy network—was to predict, and organize to cope with, either variety of "October Surprise" that Carterites might arrange.

Most persons familiar with the 1980 election will recall its outcome as lopsided—an easy win for the Reagan-Bush ticket. But that was not apparent from the start. For much of the year, in the spring and then again in September and October, polls showed a close race. The actual GOP victory by 10 percentage points on November 4, 1980, reflected an extraordinary bit of fortune: how election day fell on the bitter anniversary of November 4, 1979, the very day Iranians had taken the U.S. embassy staff as hostages. In-depth coverage by the U.S. print and broadcast media on November 3 and 4—a collective lament that after a whole year, fifty-two Americans remained captive—cost Carter several last-minute percentage points of national support.

From the start, the hostages had represented the election's X factor, although initially to Carter's great benefit. Before the seizure, his job approval in the Gallup poll had been a debilitating 30 percent. But by early December, in one of those rally-round-the-president surges that domestic and foreign crises occasionally trigger, his performance rating doubled to 61 percent. Politically, that inoculated the shaky incumbent against his intraparty renomination challenger, Senator Edward M. Kennedy, who since 1978 had led him by roughly two to one in trial heats. By the New Year, the president was taking the lead.

Remaining in the White House through January and February to display his preoccupation with Iran and the hostages—he nevertheless managed to spend evenings telephoning activists in Iowa and New Hampshire—Carter beat Kennedy in the Iowa caucuses by two to one and in the New Hampshire primary by 47 percent to 37 percent. By late March, as the hostage situation dragged out, some thought Kennedy was resurging in the Wisconsin primary. On the morning of the April 1 voting, Carter got up early to announce that he expected good news from Iran.[7] He carried Wisconsin handily.

But when two rescue helicopters crashed on April 28, so did Carter's political strategy. By June, challenger Kennedy was beating the president in the final-stage primaries—California, New Jersey, New Mexico, Rhode Island, and South Dakota—and Reagan had pulled ahead of the incumbent in the Gallup poll's November trial heats.

At one point or another, several poll takers, including the Reagan camp's Richard Wirthlin, hypothesized that the return of the hostages might provide an all-important 6- to 10-point swing. If Carter brought them home before the election, he would get the surge; if he didn't, fence-sitting voters would jump to Reagan. Data from mid-September to the end of October generally put the Republican ahead, but within range of a hostage-return halo effect. Carter's campaign manager, Hamilton Jordan, later recalled his end-of-October hope: "If something dramatic happened Monday [November 3]—like the release of the hostages—it would probably allow us to nose Reagan out; a bad signal from the Iranian Parliament Sunday would probably mean Reagan's election."[8]

Because U.S. national elections are in November, so-called October Surprises are a recurring rumor and gambit—and occasionally a major November force. In the quarter century after World War II, favorable events had produced substantial benefits for the incumbent party. Republican Eisenhower, respected for his international experience, got a 1956 reelection spike from late October's short-lived Hungarian revolt and a nearly simultaneous Anglo-French-Israeli invasion of Egypt. In 1962, John Kennedy's Democrats profited from the late-October Cuban missile crisis. In October 1968, Democratic presidential nominee Hubert Humphrey got a boost from retiring president Lyndon Johnson's carefully timed Vietnam peace negotiations; then in 1972 a quick-learning Richard Nixon reprised with his own late-hour peace negotiations. Against this backdrop, the 1980 election might also swing on an Iranian hinge. Both sides, Democrat and Republican, had reason to distrust and watch the other.

The enigma of 1980—the ultimate test of whether it was a hoax or a great historical hinge—is what the Republicans did or did not do with the unique group of skills they had put together. It can hardly be overemphasized that their vice presidential nominee was an ex-CIA director, that the party's national campaign manager was a man whose covert operations and contacts went back to World War II, when he served as chief of the OSS secretariat in the Europe theater.

At the staff level, the Republican campaign structure overflowed with ex-CIA people, not a few of them 007 wanna-bes who had worked at the CIA under George H. W. Bush and been exiled by Carter's CIA director, Admiral Stansfield Turner, in 1977. This kind of major intelligence community presence in a presidential campaign organizational structure was altogether new. The key to success was the GOP's overall ability to penetrate the CIA and the Carter-controlled National Security Council, as well as liaise with foreign intelligence agencies, in order to extract both information and cooperation.

Nine years later, Richard Allen, the Reagan campaign foreign policy chief who went on to serve briefly as White House national security adviser, recalled that in 1980 "a plane-load of former CIA officers" had moved into Reagan-Bush campaign headquarters in Arlington, Virginia, where they were "playing cops and robbers." Because of these "nutballs," said Allen, he preferred to work out of his own downtown Washington office.[9]

One such campaign recruit was Theodore Shackley, the famous "blond ghost" who had been Miami station chief during the Bay of Pigs buildup and had been made the CIA's associate deputy director for operations by Bush, only to be dropped by the Carterites. On October 27, 1980, a week before election day, Allen made handwritten notes that George H. W. Bush, in a telephone call, had asked him to follow up on a rumor about the Iranian hostages and to report his findings to Bush through none other than Shackley.[10]

The extent to which the Republican campaign harnessed informants and collaborators still serving with the CIA and NSC—and with what legal and political ramifications—remains conjecture. Leaks were plentiful, and collusion highly likely. Speculation most often attached to Donald Gregg, a

Middle East expert who served during 1980 as the National Security Council's intelligence liaison and coordinator, and Robert Gates, another rising CIA official on assignment to the National Security Council. There was also the adventuresome trio of Major General Richard Secord, Major (soon to be Lieutenant Colonel) Oliver North, and Albert Hakkim. These last three were part—Secord, in fact, was chief planner—of the Carter-launched April hostage rescue mission, inauspiciously named Operation Eagle Claw. All would emerge as prominent Bush operatives by the mid-1980s. Carter, after leaving the White House, specifically implied that Gregg might have betrayed key security items to Bush during the 1980 campaign.[11]

A few writers, including former Reagan campaign and White House aide Barbara Honegger, author of an early (1989) October Surprise exposé, thought Secord might have helped to botch Eagle Claw.[12] But Honegger was a low-level employee whose musings could be dismissed.

That was not true of Gary Sick, the ex–Navy captain and 1979–81 Iran desk officer on Jimmy Carter's National Security Council. In April 1991, he weighed in with a similar and more substantial book, entitled *October Surprise: America's Hostages in Iran and the Election of Ronald Reagan.*

For purposes of hypothesis, not any broad affirmation, the general framework of what Sick and others believed happened in 1980 is as follows. Campaign manager Casey supposedly opened relations with the Iranians in March 1980, just weeks after taking his top post. However, that first brief Washington meeting was exploratory—to open up hostage-related discussions with the Khomeini government through Jamshid Hashemi, a well-connected Iranian visiting the capital, and his brother Cyrus, a New York banker. The two Hashemis were already working with the Carter administration, but they decided to play both sides of the street. Eventually, a late-July meeting in Spain was arranged between Casey and a Tehran leader, the Ayatollah Karrubi. Tentative arrangements were to be made there.

Casey was said to have made the critical side trip to Spain while he was attending a July 27–30 London conference on the history of the Second World War. In Spain, he met with Iranian representatives. Early insistences that his schedule would not have permitted the trip turned out to be unfounded. The Republican National Convention (July 14–17) had just nominated Reagan and Bush, and postconvention polls gave the GOP ticket a 10- to 20-point lead. Casey, by this point presumed by Tehran to represent the next U.S. government, supposedly wound up with the basis of an agreement: Iran would not release any hostages before Reagan became president in January 1981. As a quid pro quo, the Reagan administration on taking office would release a large portion of the $12 billion in blocked Iranian assets held in the United States and provide further covert arms shipments. Meanwhile, Casey would see to the September or October delivery to Iran of needed U.S. armaments and vital spare parts for existing Iranian aircraft through Israeli third parties. The agreement would be finalized at an October meeting in Paris that also included Israeli representatives, and this supposedly occurred between October 18 and October 22.

A weakness, in Sick's case, though, was that he hadn't reached his final, harsh conclusion about GOP tactics until 1988–89. Most of his sources had insisted on remaining anonymous, and the handful identified in the book were not impressive. Skepticism remained widespread, fanned by dismissive late-1991 articles in *Newsweek* and *The New Republic*. The former NSC man also suffered from unfortunate timing; his book came out just weeks after the initial U.S. victory in the first Iraq war. With Bush basking in 80 to 90 percent job approval, critics were not anxious to hop on a dissident bandwagon.

By June 1992, that had changed. An embattled George H. W. Bush—his high approval ratings gone and facing a threatening three-way presidential election—had become agitated about the Sick thesis. Without ever giving official testimony or submitting a sworn statement, he used comments at a press conference to demand that an investigating task force of the House of Representatives clear him of the undocumented charge that he had secretly flown to Paris in October 1980 to cement a postponed hostage-release arrangement with the Iranians. He never did testify, then or afterward. However, task force chairman Lee Hamilton obliged with the clearance. By January 1993, when Bush had already been defeated for reelection, the House investigation had closed down, saying it hadn't really found anything.

Thus was history's first, semiofficial verdict framed: The Sick account, if not an intended hoax, was a gullible misreading of complicated international negotiations. Washington pundits joined in the exculpatory conclusion: No twisted or stolen election, *case closed.*

But not quite. Between 1992 and the end of the decade, contrary evidence accumulated. Important portions came from testimony and analyses given to the House investigators, but ignored or discarded by them. The evidence was recovered in 1994 from a dusty subbasement office of the

Rayburn House Office Building. The finder was Robert Parry, a former Associated Press, *Newsweek,* and PBS/*Frontline* reporter for whom the October Surprise case had become a near fixation.

Corroboration from French intelligence sources who had agreed to and arranged the autumn 1980 meeting in Paris first emerged in December 1992. David Andelman, the former *New York Times* and CBS News reporter who ghostwrote the memoirs of Count Alexandre de Marenches, the head of the Service de Documentation Extérieur et de Contre-Espionnage, testified that month to House investigators that the French intelligence chief admitted setting up the October 1980 meeting for Casey.[13]

In 1996, longtime ABC News Paris bureau chief Pierre Salinger, in memoirs published in France, described asking Andelman to get more detail from Marenches, and "Andelman came back to me [in 1992] and said that Marenches had finally agreed [that] he organized the meeting, under the request of an old friend, William Casey. . . . Marenches and Casey had known each other well during the days of World War Two. Marenches added that while he prepared the meeting, he did not attend it."[14] Count de Marenches, a stalwart conservative, paid one late-1980 visit to President-elect Reagan and another in 1981, when he counseled Reagan on U.S. strategy in Afghanistan.[15] The new president had reason to be welcoming.

Salinger recounted other corroboration: "In the mid-'80s, I had a long and important meeting with a top official in French intelligence. He confirmed to me that the U.S.-Iranian meeting did take place on October 18 and 19 and he knew that Marenches had written a report on it, which was in intelligence files. Unfortunately, he told me that the file had disappeared." The paragraphs in question were not published in the English-language version of Salinger's memoirs.[16]

In January 1993, in newly friendly Russia, the Committee on Defense and Security Issues of the Supreme Soviet, which had pored over intelligence files in Moscow at the request of U.S. congressional investigators, reported back that it had indeed found documents showing that Casey had come to Europe in 1980 to meet with Iranians. At the Paris meeting in October, "R[obert] Gates . . . and former CIA director George Bush also took part," said the report drafted by Sergei V. Stepashin, later to become Russia's prime minister.[17]

The six-page Russian report, sent in response to a query by task force chairman Hamilton, was not seriously pursued because the task force was within days of closing up shop when it arrived. Yet it was an extraordinary document, not least for its implicit accusations. As summarized by Parry, the document "stated, as fact, that Casey, George Bush and other Republicans had met secretly with Iranian officials in Europe during the 1980 presidential campaign. The Russians depicted the hostage negotiations that year as a two-way competition between the Carter White House and the Reagan campaign to outbid one another for Iran's cooperation on the hostages. The Russians asserted that the Reagan team had disrupted Carter's hostage negotiations after all, the exact opposite of the [House] task force conclusion."[18] What the Russians described was a large-scale violation of U.S. law.

Kindred bubbles of explanation surfaced in the Middle East. In 1991, Israeli agent Ari Ben-Menashe published his story in a book called *Profits of War*. He claimed to have been part of a team that worked with the French to arrange secret meetings between George Bush, Casey, and the Iranians.[19] In a May 1993 videotaped interview in Tel Aviv, former Israeli prime minister Yitzhak Shamir replied, "Of course, it was," when asked, "Was there an October Surprise?"[20] In 1996, during a meeting in Gaza, Palestinian leader Yasir Arafat personally told ex-president Carter, "You should know that in 1980 the Republicans approached me with an arms deal if I could arrange to keep the hostages in Iran until after the elections."[21]

While the ayatollahs did not speak, other Iranian factions did. In 1985, Abolhassan Bani-Sadr, Iran's president during the crisis, had said that George Bush might personally have flown to Paris for the crucial meeting to convince Khomeini representatives "that the hostages should not be released during the Carter administration."[22] In 1988, former president Carter publicly recollected that "former Iranian president Bani-Sadr gave several interviews stating that such an agreement was made involving Bud McFarlane, George Bush and perhaps Bill Casey."[23]

In a December 1992 letter to the U.S. House investigators, Bani-Sadr affirmed that he first learned of the GOP initiative in July 1980, when a Khomeini nephew returned from a meeting with Cyrus Hashemi. This account was rediscovered in 1994 by journalist Parry, who summarized: "Bani-Sadr said the message from the Khomeini emissary was clear: the Republicans were in league with the CIA in an effort to undermine Carter and were demanding Iran's help. Bani-Sadr said the 'emissary told me that if I do not accept this proposal, they [the Republicans] would make the same offer to my [Iranian political] rivals.' The emissary added that 'the Republicans have enormous influence in the CIA.' "[24]

Mansur Rafizadeh, a CIA agent of sorts who had previously been the chief of SAVAK, the Iranian secret police under the shah, told a U.S. public radio documentary that during 1980, when he had checked with "powerful" sources in Iran to see how the U.S. government was pressing for release of the hostages, he was told, "You are wrong. American government doesn't want the hostages released, or possibly there's a government inside of the government."[25]

These disclosures oozed potential political significance. Whether the events described were hoax or history still undergoing tortuous clarification remained unclear even a quarter century later. Still, the issues looked to persist as twenty-first-century Americans pursued explanations of (1) the rise of the nation's first real presidential dynasty; (2) the paralysis of U.S. political morality; and (3) the fateful genesis of two U.S. wars in the Persian Gulf. Although 2001–3 debate was almost nonexistent in the major media, easy Internet accessibility enabled a competitive dialogue—a buzzing wasp's nest in cyberspace. From it, the amateur historian might frame disturbing possibilities:

- Would the Iranians, Israelis, Russians, and French have been likely to make up more or less the same damning explanations?

- Could—and did—the 1980 Republican presidential campaign partially merge with a dissident element of the CIA?

- Did the Reagan-Bush campaign actually negotiate a deal with the Iranian government in a way that would have violated federal law?

- Was this a precondition to the victory of the Reagan-Bush ticket in 1980 and thus to the emergence of the Bush dynasty?

- Could any involvement by George H. W. Bush be tied to his and his family's prior intelligence and covert-operations relationships?

- Was the subsequent Iran-Contra scandal, likewise involving arms, hostages, and many of the same players, an extension and thus confirmation of the October Surprise?

- Was "Iraqgate," George H. W. Bush's clandestine 1984–90 arms buildup of Iraq so vital to Saddam Hussein's war machine, still another product of the 1979–81 contretemps with Iran?

Had the elder Bush's defeat in 1992 led to the end of the Bush family's role in national politics, the allegations of 1980 would have mattered much less. They would have withered on the vine of convenience. One can easily see why the House task force wanted to walk away from them in 1993. However, with George W. Bush's subsequent election, the events regained historical significance, somewhat like the English debate down through the centuries over who killed the young princes in the Tower of London in the mid-1480s. If it wasn't their mean uncle, Richard III, might it have been the founder of the new Tudor dynasty, Henry VII? Many thousands of trees have died to produce the paper for the hundreds of cult books on this enduring mystery.

Having read hundreds of pages of October Surprise material, fascinating in evidentiary potential yet appalling in implication, I can imagine that book catalogs in 2050 may list many such whodunits. This, however, will not be one of them. These few pages must suffice. Bill Casey—a born schemer and true buccaneer—and his associates probably were involved in machinations akin to those Sick alleged. However, the mentions of Bush having flown to Paris hint of the sort of red herring sometimes dragged across a true trail to confuse it. Vice presidential nominee Bush reviewing plans over dinner with Casey at Washington's elite Alibi Club—where the two did in fact meet and dine right after Casey came back from Europe in midsummer 1980—has a greater ring of plausibility.[26]

Indeed, the 1980s played out much the way Sick's scenario would have suggested. The CIA budget soared; the Middle East became a veritable Covertistan. Whatever other geopolitical hand George Bush might have preferred, his cards for 1981 to 1992 had essentially been dealt: crisis management, covert operations, and a reindulged CIA; multibillion-dollar guerrilla warfare in Afghanistan; the byzantine Iran-Israel relationship and the bitter Iraq-Iran War; the clandestine but flagrant U.S. arming of Saddam Hussein; the transformation of parts of the Middle East into insect colonies of arms dealers, corrupt banks, and drug dealers; and a gathering blowback against U.S. policies and activities from Palestine to Peshawar. On top of this came the near fatal Iran-Contra scandal, to which we will shortly return.

That son George W. Bush would be drawn into much the same regional and interest-group context when he ran for president and was chosen in 2000 followed logically enough. The younger Bush's own ties to the Middle East and oil were substantial. As chapter 1 discussed, much of his life, aside from his middle-aged conversion to fundamentalism, had been spent trying to imitate his father. Part of the spur to his 1994 Texas campaign and his 2000 presidential bid was revenging his father against the liberals—from Governor Ann Richards to Bill Clinton and Albert Gore—who had ejected Bush senior from the White House in 1992.

The pattern of revenge, cronyism, and dynastic pride also carried into broader Middle Eastern relations, particularly dealings with Saudi Arabia and Iraq. With Saddam Hussein remaining family enemy number one, the plans being made by conservative hard-liners for regime change in Iraq intensified during the late 1990s as George W. Bush's nomination prospects solidified. Once he was elected, officials who had helped his father cover up in Iran-Contra and other scandals received new jobs in Bush II.

Also shaping Middle Eastern relations was the fact that the family had cemented unique business and personal ties to the royal families of Saudi Arabia, Kuwait, and the emirates. After he left the White House in 1993, George H. W. Bush made a number of visits. His relationships with the Saudis, in particular, remained so close that the Saudi ambassador in Washington, Prince Bandar, and his wife considered the Bushes "almost family."[27]

As president, Bush senior had occasionally dissembled about these relationships. His claim in one 1991 press conference that he didn't know Saudi (and BCCI) power broker Kamal Adham, a former Saudi intelligence chief, was a glaring instance. It produced this description by *Time* correspondents Jonathan Beaty and S. C. Gwynne in their book *The Outlaw Bank:*

> The reporters were incredulous. Adham had been the director of Saudi Arabia's equivalent of the CIA in 1976, when George Bush headed the CIA. The American agency had been helping to modernize Saudi intelligence during Bush's tenure, and Kamal had been Saudi Arabia's main liaison with the CIA. Even without that connection, the chances were slim to none that George Bush, who was known throughout the Middle East as "the Saudi Vice President" and had more first-hand knowledge of the Middle East than any previous U.S. president, didn't know the Sheikh.[28]

If BCCI was an embarrassment that the elder Bush tried to keep at arm's length, the Carlyle Group was not, for all that the dollar sum of his personal stake was closely guarded. Despite the conflict-of-interest issues noted in chapter 8, Bush served on Carlyle's Asian Advisory Board, made highly compensated speeches and trips on its behalf—most frequently to Saudi Arabia and the Persian Gulf—and helped the group procure well-heeled investors. Twelve rich Saudi individuals and families signed up (including the bin Laden family prior to 9/11), as well as the investment offices of Kuwait and Abu Dhabi. The *Washington Post* reported in 2002 that "Saudis close to Prince Sultan, the Saudi defense minister, were encouraged to put money into Carlyle as a favor to the elder Bush."[29] By some accounts, Carlyle acted as a gatekeeper for would-be U.S. investors in Saudi Arabia.

Watchers also noted that the new U.S. ambassador to Saudi Arabia named in 2001 by George W. Bush—Texas lawyer Robert Jordan—was the lawyer who had defended the younger Bush in the 1990 probe of possible insider trading in the sale of his Harken stock, as well as a partner in Baker and Botts, the attorneys for the Carlyle Group.[30] He would respect the Bush family's interests and close relationships.

George W. Bush had gotten his slice of Middle Eastern pie earlier through the help of the Saudis, Kuwaitis, and Bahrainis in financing Arbusto and Harken (as well as the Bahrain drilling contract awarded to Harken). In 1993, two of his brothers, Neil and Marvin, had visited Kuwait.[31] A consulting arrangement proposed by Neil fell through, but Marvin did better. That year he became a major shareholder, along with Mishal Yousef Saud al-Sabah, a member of the Kuwaiti royal family, in the Kuwait-American Corporation, which had holdings in several small U.S. defense, aviation, and industrial-security companies.[32] In 1998, Marvin Bush also became a director of Fresh Del Monte, the giant fruit company owned by Kuwait's Abu-Ghazaleh family. By 2000, he was no longer on any of the Kuwait-controlled boards.[33]

In January 2002, Neil Bush, now an educational-software entrepreneur, made his fourth trip to the Middle East since his brother had become president. Besides meeting with members of the Saudi royal family, he pursued joint ventures with computer software firms in Dubai and contracts with the United Arab Emirates' Ministry of Education.[34]

Rarely, if ever, has a U.S. president's family been so involved, both in commerce and in high-level connections, in such a strife-ridden, high-stakes part of the world. As we will see, some believe that these involvements helped to make the United States a target for Islamic radicals in 2001.

Texan Macho and the Vietnam-Iraq Continuum

Not only have Texas values been more hawkish than those of the United States as a whole, but since the 1960s, the critical military initiation or escalation of the three principal U.S. wars has occurred under the three Texan presidents.

Part of what dynasties in Europe upheld was continuity, tradition, shared belief, tribalism, and sometimes war making and nationalism. Most stood for something—a religious faith, war-making prowess, identifiable commitments, familiar biases, undying grudges. In 2000, George W. Bush sought to stand for upright family values, moral probity, and the Christianity of the old rugged cross. However, because of his father's unfinished confrontation with Iraq, to many voters he also stood for action and the resolution of unrequited national frustration in the Persian Gulf—and that sensitivity, in turn, related back to the earlier frustrations fed into the U.S. psyche by defeat in Vietnam.

Through the history of Britain, at least, dynasties usually had a particular military, diplomatic, or territorial focus extending beyond national borders. Often, these were controversial. The medieval Plantagenet kings—including alleged Bush ancestor Henry III (son of the Prince John who chased Robin Hood)—were always crossing to France to assert their control of Aquitaine and to press their claims to the French crown. The Tudors—Henry VII and Henry VIII, at least—kept their eye on their ancestral Wales, knitting it into the English kingdom. The Stuart kings shared a tendency for secret arrangements with Catholic authorities in France, Ireland, and Rome. The first two Hanoverian monarchs—George I and George II—insisted on using British power to support the interests of Hanover, the northern German state from which they hailed.

Thus, it became an American dynastic confirmation that the record and ambition of the Bushes had their own geography—recurring ties to the oil fields, banks, and Bible lands of the Middle East, as well as adjacent south central Asia and the regions of the Caucasus and the Caspian. In addition to multigenerational grudges being part of the warp and woof of dynasty, the Republicans under the House of Bush also became the new imperial party, despite brief contrary sentiments in the Balkans a few years earlier.

After the election of 2000, son George II followed the Iraq warpath of George I, even attacking similarly near the midpoint of his term. Arguably more parentally motivated in his foreign wars than England's restored Charles II, George W. Bush was demonstrably more Bourbon in vengeful recollection than France's Louis XVIII. This is based on his reappointment of officials charged, indicted, or tarred in his father's best-known scandal (Iran-Contra): Elliott Abrams, John Poindexter, John Negroponte, et al. The younger Bush also promoted the 1989–92 Bush warhawks most eager for a follow-up with Iraq—Paul Wolfowitz and Douglas Feith—and likewise selected his father's Gulf War defense secretary, Richard Cheney, as vice president.

Planning for the second invasion of Iraq seems to have begun well before election day in the Washington meeting rooms of the Project for a New American Century, the neoconservative think tank for which Cheney, Rumsfeld, Wolfowitz, Florida governor Jeb Bush, and Lewis Libby, Cheney's chief of staff, completed a detailed but unreleased Pax Americana blueprint in September 2000. In one section it stated that "the United States has for decades sought to play a more permanent role in Gulf regional security. While the unresolved conflict with Iraq provides the immediate justification, the need for a substantial American force presence in the Gulf transcends the issue of the regime of Saddam Hussein."[35]

No such intentions were announced or debated during the 2000 campaign. However, George W. Bush was known to feel strongly about allegations that Saddam Hussein had tried to assassinate his father in 1993 during the ex-president's visit to Kuwait. In September 2002, at a Republican fund-raiser in Houston, the younger Bush referred to Saddam Hussein as "the guy who tried to kill my dad," which in his eyes made the conflict with Baghdad "an American issue, a uniquely American issue."[36] Bush quickly broadened his reference, but he may have provided a window into his innermost thinking. The relentless efforts to kill Saddam Hussein and his family in 2003 made a similar point.

Upholding his family, its honor, and its causes clearly resonated among staunch supporters. However, before moving on to the first and second Bush presidential confrontations with Saddam Hussein, we must return to the influence of Texas, which by the 1980s was displacing California as the breeding ground of Republican presidents. Lone Star State culture was an important, but also confusing, contributor to the emerging late-twentieth-century war milieu.

From the Gulf of Tonkin Resolution in 1964 to the 2003 attack, all three of the nation's major offensive overseas combats—the first in Indochina, the second and third with Iraq—were begun or critically escalated by chief executives from the Lone Star State. Besides the Persian Gulf relevance of Texas's oil and gas preoccupation, the state's large military presence, Alamo tradition, belief in U.S. manifest destiny, barely inhibited gun culture, and male bravado all served up related encouragement.

It also made sense that in a war involving the Bible lands of the Middle East, Texas would be unusually supportive. The widespread belief of Texans in biblical scripture was set out in chapter 7, and in bygone days, preachers sometimes commanded Texas Ranger units. More recently, Texas stockmen were among those trying to breed a red heifer to fulfill biblical prophecy, and in 1998, John Hagee, minister of the Cornerstone Church in San Antonio, announced that his congregation would give over $1 million to Israel for the resettlement of Jews from the former Soviet Union in supposed Palestinian territory in the West Bank and Jerusalem. Even the Waco-based Branch Davidians had a biblical name.

Texas psychologies are as much southwestern as southern. Some of the state's psychological distinctiveness has arisen out of a unique crucible: winning independence from Mexico on its own in 1836, and then during its nine years as a republic (and afterward) attracting a particularly tough and combative bunch of migrants from North America and elsewhere, gritty folk ready to man its battlements and outposts against Mexicans, Comanches, and Kiowas. Its most influential southern cultures were both fierce: Scotch-Irish Appalachian uplanders from Virginia and Tennessee (epitomized by Sam Houston and Davy Crockett) and proud Cotton Belt South Carolinians (William Barrett Travis and James B. Bonham, both killed at the Alamo).

It is a staple of local historians that Texans inherited the ferocity of the Scotch-Irish, who two centuries earlier had held northern Irish Ulster for the English Crown against dispossessed and warring Catholics. Moreover, much of the emigrant stream that wound up in Texas had a multiple "border" ancestry. Before moving to seventeenth-century Ireland, some Scotch-Irish had been "border reivers" on the equally bloody Anglo-Scottish border of Elizabethan times. Latter-day "Cowboy Celtic" ballad singers have shown the descent of the tunes of Texas herd drivers on the likes of the Old Chisholm Trail from the music of the sixteenth-century Scottish herdsmen.

In eighteenth-century America, the Crown favored—and in several cases planted—fierce Scotch-Irish borderers along the colonial New Hampshire and Pennsylvania frontiers. The first contingent became the French and Indian War mainstay of Rogers' Rangers, and those on the Pennsylvania frontier fought off Senecas and Shawnees from fortified stone "bastles" like those they had built in Derry or Tyrone.

Subsequently, much of western Virginia and North Carolina, and then Kentucky, Tennessee, and Missouri, was settled by Scotch-Irish from Pennsylvania pouring south and west through the mountain valleys and passes. The Tennesseans and Kentuckians who wound up in Texas—the Crocketts, Houstons, Fannins, and many more—shared these origins. Before coming, many had also served with another Scotch-Irishman, Andrew Jackson, defeating the Cherokees and Creeks. By the time they reached Austin, Goliad, and Washington-on-the-Brazos in the 1830s, 1840s, and 1850s, the heritage of these multiborderers put them among the "fightingest" people in the world. Antonio López de Santa Anna, the ill-fated Mexican president and general, probably had no comprehension of who faced him.

The prideful Texas that became a state in 1846 was the only one to have spent a decade as an independent republic before entering the Union. It had its own military shrine: the Alamo. Nineteenth-century legislators periodically proposed incorporating the Code Duelo into state law. The new state even retained a paramilitary force, the Texas Rangers. George W. Bush, a particular admirer, bought a ranch near Waco, the home of the Texas Rangers Hall of Fame. There, in a reconstruction of old Fort Fisher at the crossing of the Brazos, young and old can revisit the legends of Rangers like Frank Hamer and Deaf Smith and see sketches of Ranger companies preparing for preemptive strikes against the Mexicans and Kiowas. Talking tough is part of Texas culture.

The Texas writer Michael Lind hypothesized a Texan-Israeli parallel to offset the ties between Texas and Middle East oil producers. "The gun-toting, Bible-thumping Anglo-Celtic Texan in former Mexican and Indian territories, with his admiration for the Hebrew patriarchs and professed devotion to the Ten Commandments, is remarkably similar to the gun-toting, Torah-thumping Israeli settler in the occupied Arab territories. The 'sabra' ideal of a certain strain of Zionism—macho, militaristic, pious—is a cousin of the Southern/Western 'redneck' or 'cowboy,' down to the contempt for the disposable 'Canaanites'—blacks and Mexican-Americans in Texas and Arabs in Israel."[37] This was not unlike the point made by Israeli political scientist Ehud Sprinzak that the Israeli radical Right followed the American, not the European, model in its bent for religious leaders, frontier toughness, and a recapture of the lost values of the founding fathers.

Even more than the rest of the South, Texas has been the buckle on the U.S. Gun Belt. According to historian David Hackett Fisher, "From the quasi war with France [in 1798] to the Vietnam War, the two southern cultures [Appalachian and low country] strongly supported every American war no matter what it was about or who it was against. Southern ideas of honor and the warrior ethic combined to create regional war fevers of great intensity in 1798, 1812, 1846, 1861, 1898, 1917, 1941, 1950 and 1965."[38] Although Texas and the South have been given a larger economic stake since World War II by the massive regional growth in military bases and aerospace, defense, and high-technology contractors, this history suggests that local war support has been more a matter of culture. Texans, in particular, have had an extra hawkish chromosome or two, likewise caring little whether the rest of the world agreed or disagreed.

More popular in Texas than in most other states, the war in Vietnam drew on this hawkishness. However, the strategic sophistication of Texan presidents has not matched their strut. If anything, the gap between the two has brought problems. The embarrassment Americans suffered in Southeast Asia helped to set the scene for U.S. involvement in Iraq. And because the Vietnam War got its principal definition from a Texan, President Lyndon Baines Johnson, and the resultant "Vietnam syndrome" later served as a goad to the Texan Bushes, the continuities are important.

Johnson, the first Texan in the White House, was hardly a cool apostle of realpolitik. Nor had he ever displayed any serious interest in military strategy. What drove his 1963–68 presidency, in addition to escaping the shadow of the Kennedys, was a mixture of latter-day U.S. manifest destiny and a personal compulsion to match Franklin D. Roosevelt's New Deal in the usual Texas style—with something bigger. The result was not just domino theory but a loose blueprint for global New Dealing and public works. Besides LBJ's "Great Society" for the United States, he invoked the promise of democracy in Saigon and in April 1965 proposed a $1 billion program for electrification in Indochina's Mekong Valley, a project even larger than FDR's Tennessee Valley Authority. It was an adventure in nation building, a naive preview of what his neoconservative heirs would promise the Tigris-Euphrates Valley nearly four decades later.

In *Promised Land, Crusader State,* historian Walter A. McDougall has described the delusionary do-gooding, Wilsonian uplift, and "welfare imperialism" that accompanied America's 1960s march into the Indochinese quagmire. The National Security Council declared it a goal of U.S. policy in Vietnam to "create in that country a viable and increasingly democratic society." Aides Jack Valenti and Richard Goodwin wanted to carry LBJ's War on Poverty to Asia. Secretary of Defense Robert S. McNamara, who had more faith in technocrats than in infantry colonels, "put more than a hundred sociologists, ethnologists and psychologists to work 'modeling' South Vietnamese society and seeking data 'sufficient to describe it quantitatively and simulate its behavior on a computer.'" The struggle for the third world, he said, "might well have to be considered the social scientists' war."[39]

Too many ambitions spoiled the policy soup. The economy had to soar, social welfare required huge funding, and South Vietnam had to be cleared of Vietcong and of North Vietnamese invaders. Yet Johnson did not want to spend too much money in Vietnam, because Congress would force him to cut the Great Society to pay for it. Deception replaced coherence.

Johnson's Texas mentality also imprinted itself through memorable, but counterproductive, phrases. When a soldier in Vietnam asked the visiting president which of the helicopters on the field was his, LBJ famously answered, "They're all my helicopters, son." Impatient with the war's progress, he admitted wanting "to nail that coonskin to the wall." Determined to be in control, he boasted that U.S. pilots "can't even bomb an outhouse without my approval."[40] He did not just escalate the war, he Texified it—applying a coat of good-ole-boy rhetoric that whetted the loathing on campuses from New England through the Great Lakes and west to the Pacific.

Notable public leaders who had earned their fame as generals—Charles de Gaulle, Douglas MacArthur, Dwight Eisenhower—had opposed or been leery of U.S. military commitment to an Asian land war in the 1960s. Johnson, something less than a second Clausewitz, undermined his bold words with a muddled strategy, a weakness his Texas successors would repeat in 1991 and 2003. Despite the large numbers of troops being committed, said one historian, "a basic ambiguity . . . had characterized America's policy since 1965. Militarily, Johnson had been seeking victory over the Vietcong. Diplomatically, he paid lip service to a negotiated settlement, which implied compromise."[41]

Public opinion respecting Vietnam was never mobilized around a clear, well-stated objective. The president might bemoan, as he did in 1966, that "there will be some 'nervous nellies' and some who will become frustrated and break ranks under strain, and some will turn on their leaders, and on their country and on our own fighting men."[42] Yet he so antagonized war supporters by the incomplete application of U.S. power that in 1968, when antiwar senator Eugene McCarthy's strong New Hampshire Democratic primary total signaled Johnson to retire, polls showed that more of the McCarthy voters had been hawks than doves![43] A 1974 survey of generals who had commanded in Vietnam found that "almost 70% of the Army generals who managed the war were uncertain of its objectives."[44]

This is not abstract history. Memories of early-1970s U.S. frustration in Vietnam became an important seedbed for aggressiveness with respect to Iraq in the 1990s. As a 1970 Republican U.S. Senate candidate in Texas, U.S. ambassador to the United Nations, and U.S. Liaison Office head in China, George H. W. Bush had been a strong supporter of commitment to the South Vietnamese. In April 1975, when Saigon finally fell to the North Vietnamese, creating a panicked exodus of Americans and the few Asians in a position to escape, Bush's close associate Theodore Shackley was the CIA station chief in Saigon. In Washington, Donald Rumsfeld was the White House chief of staff (for Gerald Ford) and Dick Cheney was the deputy chief of staff.

All were embarrassed or embittered—Bush in Beijing, Shackley in Saigon, and Rumsfeld, Cheney, and many others in the nation's capital. Between the end of April, when the last Americans fled Saigon, and May 15, when President Gerald Ford prematurely claimed victory in the miniwar over the Cambodian seizure of the U.S. merchant vessel *Mayaguez,* the White House kept being surprised or overtaken by events. Two detailed accounts—Olivier Todd's *Cruel April: The Fall of Saigon* (1987) and Ralph Wetterhahn's *The Last Battle: The* Mayaguez *Incident and the End of the Vietnam War* (2001)—barely mention George H. W. Bush, tucked away in China. However, White House chief of staff Rumsfeld drew brief but acid portraiture for first asserting that the fall of Saigon would give President Ford the credit for pulling the Americans out of Vietnam, and then celebrating a triumphant *Mayaguez* rescue before the ill-managed fighting had actually finished, leaving three U.S. Marines captive on Koh Tang to be executed by the Cambodians.[45]

The neoconservatives, most of them still in the Democratic Party's hawkish wing headed by Senator Henry "Scoop" Jackson, were equally stamped by failure in Vietnam and the vulnerability they believed the mid-1970s foreign policy implosion created for Israel and the United States.

Richard Perle, a principal aide to Jackson, would spend three decades trying to rebut the notion that neoconservatism, at its heart, had its psychological origins in Vietnam-era malaise.

The Iranian hostage crisis only intensified perceptions of U.S. impo-
tence, as did the ostensible "second Castro" success of Daniel Ortega,
elected president of Nicaragua in 1984. Although this outcome precipitated
open Reagan administration hostility, Congress refused to fund Nicaraguan
counterrevolutionaries. But because Lebanese Hezbollah radicals with ties
to Iran took a new set of American hostages in 1984, the Reagan administration edged into a triangular solution—a partial replay of the 1980 guns-
and-hostages arrangements. Its revelation in late 1986 by a Lebanese
newspaper began the Iran-Contra scandal.

To bribe Iran—still locked in a bloody war with Iraq—into pressuring
the Lebanese radicals to release their American hostages, a new round of
covert U.S. arms sales to Iran was arranged. Then, in order to fund the contras when Congress would not, some of the profits from the clandestine
Iranian deliveries were channeled to Nicaragua. In the process, multiple
federal laws were broken. After Republican former U.S. deputy attorney general Lawrence Walsh was chosen as the Iran-Contra special prosecutor in
December 1986, his staff counted at least three.[46]

Despite the illegal deliveries to Iran, if the ayatollahs were America's top
Middle Eastern foes, it made sense to bolster their wartime enemies—the
Iraqis. Through the 1980s, as we will see, George H. W. Bush would be in
the vanguard of this effort. Then, when Iraq itself jumped the rails in
August 1990, Bush, quickly braced by British prime minister Margaret
Thatcher, scripted a new confrontation: demonizing and defeating Iraq's
Saddam Hussein. All were aware of the precedent to be avoided. In 1991,
during the Gulf War, Bush promised, "This will not be another Vietnam."
After the seeming victory, he boasted, "We've kicked the Vietnam Syn-
drome for once and for all."[47]

Historian George C. Herring, in an article called "America and Vietnam: The Unending War" in the winter 1991–92 issue of *Foreign Affairs*,
thought otherwise. "Such was the lingering impact of the Vietnam War," he
explained, "that the Persian Gulf conflict appeared at times to be as much
a struggle with its ghosts as with Saddam Hussein's Iraq. President Bush's
eulogy for the Vietnam Syndrome may therefore be premature. Success in
the Gulf War no doubt raised the nation's confidence in its foreign policy
leadership and its military institutions and weakened long-standing inhi-

bitions against intervention abroad. Still, it seems doubtful that military victory over a nation with a population less than one-third of Vietnam in a conflict fought under the most favorable circumstances could expunge deeply encrusted and still painful memories of an earlier and very different kind of war."

Indeed, it did not expunge them. Herring's prediction would be confirmed as Saddam Hussein survived, renewing his control of Iraq even while Bush went down to defeat in 1992. Like fellow Texan LBJ's handling of Vietnam, Bush's 1991 war conduct would fail to backstop macho rhetoric with geopolitical success. With Saddam Hussein free to thumb his nose again, the Bushes, Rumsfeld, and Cheney, together with their neoconservative acolytes, would have to confront the aging ghosts of 1960s ineptness, fumbled bombing halts, a cruel April 1975 in Saigon, and the muddled *Mayaguez* rescue on another set of Middle East battlefields a decade later.

George I and the First Iraq War

The George H. W. Bush who took office in 1981 was the first vice president since World War II to have recently come from a senior federal responsibility—CIA director—rather than from Congress or a state governorship. This expertise helped to shape his day-to-day duties until the demands of his presidential campaign took over in late 1987. Aside from economic deregulation, his preferred subject matter as vice president involved global crises, intelligence, and terrorism. A fair part of his schedule dealt with international affairs: discussing Nicaragua with Lieutenant Colonel Oliver North; meeting Saudi ambassador Prince Bandar to arrange off-the-books Saudi funding for key U.S. projects; and making full-dress overseas trips, like one in 1984 to Pakistan to thank President Mohammad Zia ul-Haq, with more money and weapons, for his nation's vital supply pipeline to the mujahideen rebels fighting the Soviets in Afghanistan. It was not unlike what Bush had done as CIA director, although Bill Casey held that official position under Reagan.

By late 1987, as Bush prepared for his presidential bid, he found himself with political symptoms uncommon for a vice president: the early discomfort of several minor abrasions from international relations, ones that would later become scandal-infected and swell in importance. As we have seen, the October Surprise was already a small nick by 1987, thanks to former Iranian president Bani-Sadr and veiled references by ex-president

Carter. The Iran-Contra subject matter—illegal arms sales to Iran, illegal funding for the contras—became worrisome when first revealed in late 1986. However, congressional Democrats were soon bounding off after the faux fox of Oliver North as rogue operator. The special prosecutor named in December 1986, Lawrence Walsh, looked like a slowpoke. Oliver North and his midlevel co-conspirators were not indicted until March 1988. Bush, the imminent Republican presidential nominee, was in nobody's legal gunsights.

What eventually became Iraqgate—Bush's own culpability for building up Saddam Hussein, right through 1990, with weaponry and dual-use (civilian-military) technology—remained only a minor sensitivity. It couldn't deepen into a sore unless and until the Iraqi strongman turned into an open foe and the confrontation was unsatisfactorily resolved. Lastly, despite growing attention to the tie-ins between the demands of clandestine activity and the practices of corrupt banks like BCCI and Italy's Banca Nazionale del Lavoro (BNL)—Casey and Bush both had to know—as of 1987–88 those issues remained under control.

How this changed by 1992, however, was richly ironic. Instead of dwarfing and sidelining these scandals, the Gulf War wound up becoming, in part, a display case of the consequences of corruption and covert overindulgence. Especially among the well-read, the war's inconclusive end catalyzed awareness that before the Gulf War the Bush administration had winked permissively as, in the summer of 1990, Saddam Hussein maneuvered to gobble up a portion of Kuwait. In this larger context, the war became testimony to Bush's prior ineptitude, not just his coalition-building achievements. Iraqgate, as the sum of Bush's 1984–90 overindulgences of Iraq (and their cover-up) came to be known, was able to catch hold only in 1991 and 1992, *after* the fighting.

The election was manifestly influenced. Besides the weakness in the U.S. economy in 1991–92, a second reason why Bush lost, despite having enjoyed 90 percent job approval ratings right after the war, was the accumulating tarnish on his ethics and even his military success. By early 1992, all three Middle East–connected scandals—the October Surprise, Iran-Contra, and Iraqgate—were commanding national notice.

Here a brief recapitulation is in order because the political chronology was both complex and critical. We have seen how the October Surprise issue built in 1991 but then lost headway in June 1992, when the bipartisan task force in the House of Representatives exonerated Bush of allegations that he had flown to Paris in October 1980 to cut a deal with the Iranians. However, the Iran-Contra issue, which had minimally affected Reagan and Bush in 1988, mushroomed just before the November 1992 election, when Special Counsel Walsh filed a supplemental and superseding indictment against a major defendant, Defense Secretary Caspar Weinberger. For Bush, the blow was the claim in the new indictment that notes kept by Weinberger contradicted George H. W. Bush's claims of being "out of the loop" on the arms-for-hostages swap. Bush, it appeared, had been a participant. Clinton's lead quickly jumped from 3 points in the polls to 7.[48]

Parenthetically, after his defeat, Bush aggravated public discontent on Christmas Eve, a few weeks before leaving office, when he pardoned Weinberger and a half dozen others involved in Iran-Contra. Earlier Gallup polling had shown Americans opposed to a Weinberger pardon by 59 percent to 27 percent; postpardon Gallup sampling in December 1992 found half of those who had followed the news coverage believed that Bush's real motive in granting the pardons had been "to protect himself from legal difficulties or embarrassment resulting from his own role in Iran-Contra."[49] CNN political analyst William Schneider summed up: "Not only did he pardon his political allies, he pardoned them for illegal activities in which he himself may have been implicated."[50]

The third scandal, Iraqgate, was also the most prejudicial to the public's high-flying early-1991 perception of Bush as a successful Persian Gulf war leader. Discussion of Bush's prewar aid to Iraq had grown intense—witness the remarks with which a grave Ted Koppel had opened ABC News *Nightline* on June 9, 1992: "It is becoming increasingly clear that George Bush, operating largely behind the scenes through the 1980s, initiated and supported much of the financing, intelligence and military help that built Saddam's Iraq into the aggressive power that the United States ultimately had to destroy."[51] By September, Democratic vice presidential candidate Albert Gore would say that "George Bush wants the American people to see him as the hero who put out a raging fire. But new evidence now shows that he is the one who set the fire." In October, Gore charged the president with "presiding over a cover-up significantly larger than Watergate."[52] Bill Clinton, for his part, pledged to appoint a special prosecutor.

Between 1993 and 1996, three additional books on Iraqgate were published, following Kenneth R. Timmerman's pre-1992-election opener, *The Death Lobby: How the West Armed Iraq* (1991). Although Bush was out of office, these analyses put a devastating spotlight on the Gulf War's origins.

The most influential was *Spider's Web: The Secret History of How the White House Illegally Armed Iraq*, by *Financial Times* of London correspondent Alan Friedman, released in December 1993. Friedman detailed the pro-Iraqi activities of the U.S. State Department, as well as those of George H. W. Bush. His accusations elicited a pro-administration response entitled "The Myth of Iraqgate" in the spring 1994 issue of *Foreign Policy*. The author, Kenneth I. Juster, was the former deputy and senior adviser to Deputy Secretary of State Lawrence Eagleburger.

Juster's point, previously made in 1992 congressional testimony by Eagleburger and in ad hoc comments by President Bush himself, was that the administration had tried to use friendly relations to contain Saddam Hussein, but that had not worked out. True in part, this failed to rebut Friedman's many pages devoted to specific excesses and major misjudgments.

Another powerful exposé of Iraqgate, *Shell Game: A True Story of Banking, Spies, Lies, Politics—and the Arming of Saddam Hussein*, by former *Atlanta Journal-Constitution* reporter Peter Mantius, appeared in 1995. It shed more light on what had presumably agitated Juster and Eagleburger, previously the president of Kissinger Associates. Mantius, who had covered the arms-for-Iraq scandal through a local focus on related activities of the Atlanta branch of Italy's Banca Nazionale del Lavoro, added more information on Kissinger Associates.

According to Mantius, some of the BNL/Atlanta loans went to corporate clients of the Kissinger firm. Former secretary of state Kissinger himself had been a member of the BNL international advisory board between 1985 and 1991; and in 1989, two top Kissinger Associates officials, Eagleburger and Brent Scowcroft, became leading advocates for Iraq upon assuming their new Bush administration positions as deputy secretary of state and national security adviser.[53]

In short, this was big stuff—and the establishment closed ranks. Notwithstanding Bill Clinton's earlier promises of a special prosecutor, the Justice Department in early 1995 issued nothing more than a *Final Report on Iraqgate* drafted by Assistant Attorney General John Hogan. It "concluded that there had been no violations of laws," but admitted that the CIA's role was not entirely clear.[54] While this signaled that Democrats would lay off, the dodge riled some Republicans, who saw the Clinton administration extending the earlier cover-up.

Despite the partisan tones of 1992, several whistle-blowers were Republicans: *New York Times* columnist William Safire, the editors of the

American Spectator monthly, and Kenneth R. Timmerman, the Middle East expert who had published *The Death Lobby* back in 1991. In 2000, Timmerman would be a candidate for the Republican U.S. Senate nomination in Maryland. All howled over Clinton's "whitewash."

Safire, who called Iraqgate "the first global scandal," summarized that the "the leaders of three major nations [the United States, Britain, and Italy] are implicated in a criminal conspiracy: first, to misuse taxpayer funds and public agencies in the clandestine buildup of a terrorist dictator; then to abuse the intelligence and banking services of these nations to conceal the dirty deed; finally, to thwart the inexorable course of justice."[55] Three weeks after *Final Report* was released, the Justice Department decided to award $400 million compensation to the Banca Nazionale del Lavoro for the Iraq-connected losses of its Atlanta branch. This prompted Safire to charge that "Mr. Clinton's BNL bailout makes him a $400 million participant in Iraqgate."[56]

In November 1996, the conservative *American Spectator* published Kenneth Timmerman's "Whatever Happened to Iraqgate?" Charging the Clinton administration with "sweeping the 'Iraqgate' investigation under the rug," Timmerman described *Final Report* as "little more than a whitewash of the entire affair." One possible explanation, he contended, was that in 1990 Hillary Clinton, through her Little Rock–based Rose Law Firm, had become a director of LaFarge, a French multinational chemical company. LaFarge, it turned out, had a CIA-connected Ohio subsidiary whose Lake Erie waterfront property was used as a transshipment center for weapons components bound for Iraq. Any serious Clinton administration pursuit of Iraqgate could lash back at her, Timmerman theorized. The less controversial explanation, of course, was that by 1995 the Clinton administration itself needed Saddam Hussein as a devil figure. Unleashing an investigation that moved some of the 1990–91 culpability to George H. W. Bush would only complicate things.

Following the ups and downs of these three scandals over their quarter-century history led me to this double hypothesis: they offered, first, an alternative framework for weighing the origins of the 1991 Gulf War, and second, a partial explanation for why voters declined to credit Bush's war leadership in 1992. Collectively, the evidence of improper behavior by George H. W. Bush enlarged considerably during the decade after 1992, even as very few Americans were paying any attention. There is still room for doubt, but more for belief. Put differently, the scandals deserve to be a greater factor in interpreting the first Iraq war—and inquiring into the origins of the second—than they ever became in 1992 or 2000.

As part of this argument, the first Bush administration's early 1990 muddling toward an August confrontation with Saddam Hussein deserves a brief chronicle. Two inclinations stood out: the president's disbelieving reluctance to shut down the multiple U.S. favoritism to Iraq (weapons, advanced technology, chemical and biological supplies, massive loans, and shared military intelligence) and the State Department's down-to-the-wire commitment to signaling that an Iraq, economically drained by its 1980–88 war, would be permitted to adjust its boundaries with Kuwait and to seize a few disputed oil-production areas. Few more damning chronologies have been assembled.

During the first half of 1990, before Saddam Hussein invaded Kuwait in August, the Bush administration pushed aside reports that Iraq was manufacturing nuclear materials, purring over chemical weapons, and developing al-Abid guided missiles. Likewise rejected were proposals to curb or suspend U.S. assistance. On January 19, Bush voided a prohibition Congress had imposed on new Export-Import Bank financing for Iraq;[57] in April, National Security Adviser Brent Scowcroft objected to any limitation on sensitive technology sales that singled out Iraq;[58] late spring brought a decision against cutting off U.S.-Iraqi intelligence sharing;[59] and as July ended, the administration still opposed congressional efforts to vote economic sanctions against Baghdad, giving up only after Iraqi troops entered Kuwait.[60]

Morality had not been an administration qualm. On April 25, Secretary of State James Baker had declined to criticize Saddam Hussein's threat that he would use chemical weapons to deter nuclear attack. Indeed, U.S. policymakers were quite aware that Iraq had repeatedly relied on chemical weapons. The New York Times later reported that "a covert American program during the Reagan administration [1988] provided Iraq with critical battle planning assistance at a time when American intelligence agencies knew that Iraqi commanders would employ chemical weapons in waging the decisive battles of the Iran-Iraq war, according to senior military officers with direct knowledge of the program."[61]

Biological and nuclear weaponry also thrived on Washington's permissiveness. According to a 1994 Senate committee report, between 1985 and 1989 biological materials exported to Iraq included dozens of unweakened pathogenic agents (capable of reproduction) ranging from *Bacillus anthracis* to *Histoplasma capsulatum*. "It was later learned," said the committee report, "that these microorganisms exported by the United States were identical to those the United Nations inspectors found and removed from the Iraq biological warfare program."[62] In *Spider's Web,* correspondent Alan Friedman detailed how the Bush administration, in 1989 and early 1990, knew but seemed not to care that U.S. exports were assisting Iraq's nuclear weapons development. Two Iraqi nuclear scientists from Saddam's Al-Qaqaa nuclear research facility were even invited to Portland, Oregon, for a September 1989 U.S. Energy Department symposium on nuclear detonations.[63]

The so-called green lights given to Saddam Hussein's plans to nibble at Kuwait were open and public, even during the final two weeks. On July 20, Defense Secretary Cheney was obliged by the White House to back down from his previous day's statement that the United States would defend Kuwait if it was attacked.[64] During a press briefing on July 24, State Department spokesperson Margaret Tutwiler said: "We do not have any defense treaties with Kuwait, and there are no special defense or security commitments to Kuwait."[65] The next day, Saddam Hussein in Baghdad received the same message from the U.S. ambassador to Iraq, April Glaspie. She told him, "We have no opinion on the Arab-Arab conflicts, like your border disagreements with Kuwait."[66]

If Iraq attacked, the Iraqi leader insisted to Glaspie, it would be because Kuwait had already warred on Iraq through multiple oil provocations—digging slant wells into the Rumaila oil fields on Iraq's side of the border and overproducing (2.4 million barrels a day, versus its OPEC quota of 1.5 million) in order to depress oil prices and inhibit Iraq's economic recovery. These were complaints with which Washington was known to have some sympathy.

On July 28, CIA director William Webster visited President Bush to report that while an Iraqi invasion of Kuwait was imminent, the Iraqis were likely to annex only the disputed Rumaila oil fields, and Bubiyan and Warba, the two uninhabited islands that blocked Iraq's Persian Gulf approaches.[67] Far from exploding, Bush seems to have relaxed audibly enough to be overheard in the State Department. On July 31, Assistant Secretary of State for the Middle East John Kelly told a House Foreign Affairs subcommittee, "Historically, the U.S. has taken no position on the border disputes in the area, nor on matters pertaining to internal OPEC deliberations." Asked whether the United States had a treaty commitment that would require it to protect Kuwait from Iraqis crossing the border, Kelly said no.[68] Two days later, at two o'clock on the morning of August 2, Baghdad time, the Iraqis invaded.

A further context is important. Forty years earlier, when North Korea had invaded South Korea, congressional Republicans blamed a 1949 speech in which Secretary of State Dean Acheson had omitted Korea from the U.S. defense perimeter. Acheson's omission, they said, was an invitation. The invitations issued by James Baker's State Department in 1990, which lacked only vellum and fine engraving, were far more damning.

On the morning of the invasion, the first response from the Oval Office was ambiguous. The United States, said the president, had no intention of intervening militarily. Some in the State Department thought Saddam might be taking all of Kuwait only as a gambit to bargain to retain the limited objectives he had signaled earlier.

But later on August 2, before George H. W. Bush had committed himself to a firm response, he flew to Colorado to attend a conference where he would meet with another major leader involved in Persian Gulf affairs, British prime minister Margaret Thatcher. Most accounts of their conversation report only that the Iron Lady stiffened his resolve, saying, "George, now don't be wobbly." But one longtime Bush critic and home-state political rival, former governor John Connally, alleged in his autobiography that her most persuasive advice was bluntly political: "George," he has her saying, "I was about to be defeated in England [in 1982] when the Falkland conflict happened. I stayed in office for eight years after that."[69]

One way or another, Bush consolidated his position, saying late on August 2 that military intervention was indeed being considered. He telephoned King Fahd of Saudi Arabia to insist—contrary to intelligence estimates—that Iraq might attack that country next. When Bush went on U.S. television to explain these events, it was to say that King Fahd, afraid Saddam Hussein would attack Saudi Arabia, had asked for U.S. troops and help. And, said the president of the United States, "This will not stand, this aggression against Kuwait."

Some of Bush's advisers were shocked, reported journalist Bob Woodward. The president had made this decision personally and emotionally, rather than in consultation with Colin Powell and the other members of the Joint Chiefs of Staff. "Powell marveled at the distance Bush had traveled in three days," Woodward wrote. "To Powell, it was almost as if the President had six-shooters in both hands and was blazing away."[70]

Politically, though, there was a logic. If George H. W. Bush was going to reverse from weak conciliation into high-profile, two-fisted confrontation, he needed a stage full of new scenery and evil, large-scale plotting. Having the Saudis fearfully ask for U.S. troops to protect them against a rampaging Saddam Hussein was a start; so was likening the Iraqi leader to Hitler (a comparison requiring someone able to menace more than Kuwait). The Washington public relations firm of Hill and Knowlton, boasting former Bush chief of staff Craig Fuller as its chief operating officer, was hired—for some $10.7 million, it would later develop—to promote the rescue of Kuwait on behalf of a front group, the sheikhdom-funded "Citizens for a Free Kuwait."[71]

The result was one of the greatest travesties—and critical political successes—in the annals of media-age war making. In October 1990, a fifteen-year-old Kuwaiti girl, named only as "Nayirah," testified before the Human Rights Caucus of the U.S. House of Representatives that the Iraqi soldiers invading Kuwait tore hundreds of babies from hospital incubators and killed them. It turned out, after investigation by Amnesty International and others, that this was a lie. There were just a few incubators in Kuwait, and hardly any babies in them; Nayirah hadn't been to any hospital—she was the daughter of Saud Nasir al-Sabah, Kuwait's ambassador to the United States and a relative of the ruling family.[72]

In the meantime, according to one chronicle, President George H. W. Bush "quoted Nayirah at every opportunity. Six times in one month, he referred to '312 premature babies at Kuwait City's maternity hospital who died after Iraqi soldiers stole their incubators and left the infants on the floor' and to 'babies pulled from incubators and scattered like firewood across the floor.' Bush used Nayirah's testimony to lambaste Senate Democrats still supporting 'only' sanctions against Iraq . . . but who waffled on endorsing the policy Bush wanted to implement: outright bombardment."[73] The ploy worked—her testimony was cited in November by seven senators who switched to support the military resolution, which passed by six votes.

Geopolitics professor Edward Luttwak penned a cynical description: "Happily leaving behind all serious concern for the economy, and even more happily content to see photographs of Saddam Hussein replacing those of Neil Bush on the front pages, George Bush threw himself into crisis management on a full-time basis with boyish enthusiasm, barely turning aside to explain, most unconvincingly, the reason for it all."[74] In *The New Yorker,* Washington correspondent Elizabeth Drew reported the con-

cern that nagged many in the Senate: "When he [Bush] personalized the issue as one between himself and Saddam Hussein, when he swaggered and
did his Clint Eastwood routine, when he said that Hussein 'is going to get
his ass kicked,' he gave credence to the idea that he was proving something."[75] In retrospect, the president was hiding at least as much.

However, what most Americans instead remembered about the August
to December 1990 prewar period and then Desert Storm itself was Bush's
great diplomatic skill in lining up world leaders in a global coalition to
eject Saddam Hussein from Kuwait, and the unexpectedly lopsided military victory quickly achieved by the U.S.-led forces. From potentially painful
embarrassment in early August, Bush rocketed to 89 percent job approval
in February, the highest ever for a U.S. president. Nevertheless, clouds soon
appeared on the horizon: Others in the coalition didn't want to push on to
Baghdad; Saddam Hussein survived; Bush encouraged Kurds and Shiites to
revolt against Saddam, only to stand by as the Iraqi leader suppressed those
risings. The U.S. military triumph faded, and scandal began to eat into the
president's credibility.

Still, it must be said that George H. W. Bush was only beaten in 1992,
not shattered. He and his advisers believed that without special prosecutor
Walsh's preelection Iran-Contra announcement, they might have overtaken Clinton in the last days. When the public stopped following Bush's
scandals in late 1992 and turned its attention to Clinton's instead, the ex-
president's ratings started climbing again. His credibility resurged, with
most of the negative details fading from national memory. Saddam Hussein, for his part, was soon confirmed as a *bipartisan* bogeyman, whose
convenience as a target also came to serve Bill Clinton. In any event, the defeated president had a new supporter warming up in the bullpen.

George II and the Second Iraq War

To describe George W. Bush in 2003 as the first U.S. chief executive to re-
new hostilities with the same foreign leader who had embarrassed that executive's own presidential father could be called a truism—the sort of
axiom that need not be proved because of its self-evidence.

Or it might not. If few Americans had grasped the dynastization of
their politics, the creeping dynastization of U.S. war making was even less
analyzed—certainly in public debate. Equally to the point, the unusual
dynamics of inherited grudges helped to explain some of the new U.S. geo-

politics that emerged in 2001, especially its multitextured revenge component. Some of the revenge being sought by the Bush administration was familial; other portions were factional.

As we have seen, old colleagues and advisers of the elder Bush—Messrs. Cheney, Rumsfeld, Wolfowitz, Libby, Perle, and others—returned to their drawing boards in the mid- to late 1990s to reformulate the New World Order hypothesized during the first Bush administration. Their blueprint included a section on realigning the Middle East by overthrowing Saddam Hussein, as much legacy as realpolitik.

When terror struck on 9/11, Rumsfeld was one of those who wanted to make Iraq an immediate target. Cooler heads insisted that Afghanistan and Osama bin Laden came first. Once Afghanistan had been tamed, Iraq was next. By the spring of 2002, with Osama bin Laden hiding somewhere along the mountainous Afghan-Pakistani frontier, the more convenient bogeyman, Saddam Hussein, moved back out in front in the comparative finger-pointing of administration wrath and retribution. Bin Laden led back to potentially embarrassing past Bush dynasty contacts with the Saudis, the bin Laden family, and the Taliban. Journalists joked about Osama bin Who? and watched as Bush officials beat their new public relations war drum: *We must strike because Iraq and Al Qaeda are connected, and Saddam has arsenals of weapons of mass destruction that he could make available to terrorist groups.*

Experts were unsure on both points, especially the Iraq–Al Qaeda linkage. The public, however, was won over. By early 2003, as war approached, opinion polls showed that a large majority of Americans believed that Iraq's alleged weapons of mass destruction justified war. A poll taken by CBS News in early April even found a 53 percent majority calling Saddam Hussein "personally involved in the September 11 terror attacks," which almost no U.S. intelligence officials believed. In mid-March, the *Christian Science Monitor* had reported a tactic as successful as it was deceptive: "In his prime-time press conference last week, which focused almost solely on Iraq, President Bush mentioned Sept. 11 eight times. He referred to Saddam Hussein many more times than that, often in the same breath with Sept. 11. Bush never pinned blame for the attacks directly on the Iraqi president. Still, the overall effect was to reinforce an impression that persists among much of the American public: that the Iraqi dictator did play a direct role in the attacks."[76] So convinced, citizens were primed for another Iraq war, at least for one that succeeded and involved few U.S. casualties.

At first, after Baghdad fell in April, those conditions for approval appeared to be fulfilled. Americans initially shrugged off the failure to find weapons of mass destruction, just as they had earlier let slide their brief autumn 2002 insistence that Bush make war only with UN support. Taking Baghdad had required less than a month of fighting; in politics, what works out tends to be accepted.

Nevertheless, within a few months it became clear that the second Iraq war was following in one particularly dangerous set of footsteps: lack of presidential clarity and candor about the purpose for which the war was being fought. Military scholar Harry G. Summers, in his much-praised book *On Strategy: A Critical Analysis of the Vietnam War* (1982), noted that one examination of the official objectives of U.S. involvement between 1949 and 1967 found twenty-two different ones.[77] The nation building and democracy implanting were particularly anomalous.[78] As we have seen, even generals who held commands in Vietnam admitted to uncertainty of that war's objectives. Comparable confusion attended the justifications and objectives stated by the elder Bush in the 1990–91 confrontation with Iraq, not surprising given the weird circumstances in which Iraq seized Kuwait and the particular personal dislike between the U.S. and Iraqi presidents.

By March 2003, George W. Bush, in turn, rested his own imminent war with Iraq on three much-repeated premises: (1) Iraq's complicity with terrorists and possession of weapons of mass destruction; (2) the sheer evil of Saddam Hussein; and (3) the importance of ushering the people of Iraq and the Middle East into a more democratic era. A few U.S. publications, but not many, used the prewar weeks to reexamine the propaganda—not least the falsified Kuwait incubator episode—used twelve years earlier.

In a number of cases, George W. Bush followed approaches used earlier by his father. The elder Bush, once he had determined to fight Iraq, relabeled prior ally Saddam Hussein "a tyrant worse than Hitler." His son's emphasis on the Iraqi leader's great evil followed suit. That *both* Bushes personalized their animosity was a particularly revealing continuity. In March 2003, Dana Milbank of the *Washington Post*, after combing both men's speeches, reported the son's close repetition of his father's themes and even phraseology: to wit, pledging as short as possible a stay in Iraq, viewing the war as an opportunity to settle deep regional conflicts, describing Saddam's regime as "a nightmare," and invoking the universal desire of families to secure and improve their children's opportunities.[79]

Embracing yet another theme from 1990–91, allies of George W. Bush—neoconservatives in particular—accused war doubters of "appeasement." Even the weapons of mass destruction issue had its tactical debut back in the autumn of 1990, when the elder Bush found that a potential Iraqi nuclear threat produced the strongest public response for U.S. military intervention.[80]

Although the same theme worked again in 2003, its ultimate weakness lay in being put to the test once successful U.S. troops took over the country. When months went by and no weapons of mass destruction were found, their nonappearance began to crystallize questions about prewar misrepresentation by both coalition leaders, George W. Bush and British prime minister Tony Blair. Other motives, just as clearly, had been understated.

Back in 1990 and 1991, oil had been acknowledged as part of the U.S. concern about Iraq's goals in the Middle East. George H. W. Bush's oil-sector motivations were prominent over a long career. According to a detailed analysis by the *Los Angeles Times,* even his mid-November 1992 intervention in Somalia was motivated less by local starvation than by restoring the promising oil exploration rights granted to four U.S. firms (Conoco, Amoco, Phillips, and Chevron) by the previous Somali government.[81] Indeed, twentieth-century history and U.S. preoccupation with petroleum made the disavowals of 2003 seem disingenuous.

One could even call them deceitful. As one trenchant analysis noted, Richard Cheney had warned, in an August 1992 speech, that if Saddam Hussein got his hands on weapons of terror, he would "seek domination of the entire Middle East" and "take control of a great portion of the world's energy supplies." That speech, *The New Yorker* concluded, "was one of the last occasions on which the Bush Administration publicly acknowledged the link between energy policy and national security. Thereafter, it adopted the line that its decision to remove Saddam from power had, in the words of Defense Secretary Donald Rumsfeld, 'nothing to do with oil, literally nothing to do with oil.'"[82]

Oil had to be a factor in White House calculations, even if the motivation was less about short-term U.S. oil supplies and more about future geopolitical power—Washington's ambition to control the global oil flows without which potential rivals like the European Union and China could not challenge U.S. hegemony. In 2000, two-thirds of Persian Gulf oil went to Western industrial nations, especially in Europe. By 2015, according to

CIA estimates, three-quarters of the Gulf's oil will go to Asia, chiefly to China.[83] American hands would have to be on the pumps.

Beyond revenge and oil, however, important aspects of George W. Bush's involvement with Iraq differed from his father's. Comparing 2003 with 1990–91, the unilateralist evolution in U.S. diplomacy, the intensifying religious fundamentalism of the national Bush coalition, and the increasing weight of Bush family financial links to the Middle East all made for new circumstances. Few would have been attractive to the public as war explanations.

Dynastic and national revenge, however, was perceived to be near the top of the list in Europe, where local populations had a closer historical acquaintance with the motivations of hereditary rulers. Schoolchildren learned about long and bloody conflicts with names like the War of the Spanish Succession and the War of the Austrian Succession. In September 2002, Agence France-Presse provided especially full reportage of George W. Bush's statement to a Texas Republican dinner that war with Iraq was "a uniquely American issue" because Saddam Hussein was "the guy who tried to kill my dad."[84] Britain's conservative *Daily Telegraph* revisited that Texas speech in March 2003, reporting that "White House officials later said that reference was a mistake, allowing critics to argue that Mr. Bush was acting solely out of a desire for personal revenge. When Mr. Bush let slip recently that his wife Laura could also have been killed by the 175 pounds of plastic explosive placed in his father's car, it was clear that toppling Saddam was a matter of the heart as well as an affair of state."[85]

London and Paris sensitivities bespoke an old and valid recognition. The inherited foreign preoccupations and family quarrels of hereditary rulers had become fair political game as soon as there were councils of state or parliaments in which to raise them. The increasingly imperial and dynastic United States had not developed a parallel awareness. Yet one could plausibly argue that the pull on George W. Bush toward war with Saddam Hussein was as much a family legacy as were his admissions to Andover, Yale, and Skull and Bones.

A further spur to U.S. military action against Iraq was the mounting realization that the United States faced not only terrorism from the Middle East but a complicated, broader pattern of Islamic revenge, a facet of the fundamentalism discussed in chapter 7. To justify their hate, Osama bin Laden and others had spoken of making the United States, along with Britain and the collaborating Saudi and Persian Gulf royalty, pay for eight

decades of colonialism, imperialism, war, and subjection since the end of
the Ottoman Empire and the caliphate in 1918.

The Al Qaeda chief's personal anger hung on what he perceived as the
violation of Saudi Arabia—his homeland, and the birthplace of Islam—by
foreign (American) influences and military forces. Distaste for the Bush
family and desire to be revenged on it were logical components. As this
book has shown, albeit on a necessarily limited scale, no other political
family in the United States has had anything remotely resembling the
Bushes' four-decade relationship with the Saudi royal family and the oil
sheikhs of the Persian Gulf. The same late-spring 2003 polls that showed
regard for the United States plummeting in the Muslim world also revealed
that much of that disdain was for George W. Bush personally, not for the
American Republic or its people.

A few commentators have pursued the Bush-Saudi connection to far-
reaching, if not altogether documented, conclusions that several Bush-
Saudi ties provoked or could have motivated the Al Qaeda fundamentalists.
From 1992 to 1997, the Bush-connected Carlyle Group owned the Vinnell
Corporation, which trained and supported the Saudi National Guard, the
royal family's internal security force. In 2001, when the terrorists of 9/11
crashed two aircraft into the twin towers of the World Trade Center, WTC
security was being handled by Securacom (now Stratasec), a firm that from
1993 to 2000 had Marvin Bush as a director and major shareholder, along
with KuwAm, the previously mentioned Kuwait-American Corporation.
In 1997, security contracts with the World Trade Center and Washington's
Dulles Airport brought in 75 percent of Securacom's revenues.[86] A third
situation, more ambiguous in import, involved the role of the Carlyle
Group as an interface between its top managers and advisers—George H. W.
Bush, James A. Baker III, and Frank Carlucci—and the rich ($12 billion)
Saudi bin Laden family, with whom Bush, Baker, and Carlucci met fre-
quently as late as 1999–2001. What influence the bin Ladens applied for
what purpose remains conjecture.

Charles Freeman, president of the Middle East Policy Council and a
former U.S. ambassador to Saudi Arabia, has said of this relationship, "If
ever there were any company closely connected to the U.S. and its presence
in Saudi Arabia, it's the bin Laden Group. They're the establishment
Osama's trying to overthrow."[87] Other commentators, contrarily, felt that
some connections between the bin Ladens and their black-sheep relative
persisted.

Still others found the Bush–Carlyle–bin Laden connection innately reprehensible. At Judicial Watch, a conservative watchdog group, President Larry Klayman said, "The idea of the President's father, an ex-president himself, doing business with a company under investigation by the FBI in the terror attacks of September 11 is horrible. President Bush should not ask, but demand, that his father pull out of the Carlyle Group."[88] At the World Policy Institute, foreign policy specialist William Hartung deplored reluctance to investigate the Saudis by saying, "If there weren't all these other arrangements—arms deals and oil deals and consultancies—I don't think the U.S. would stand for this lack of cooperation."[89]

The boldest indictments cut to the quick. On the cusp of the U.S. invasion of Iraq in March 2003, Greg Palast, a muckraking commentator for BBC Television's *Newsnight,* raised the question "What made this new president [George W. Bush] take particular care to protect the Saudis, even to the point of stymieing his own intelligence agencies?" The answers, he said, kept coming back "Carlyle" and "Arbusto," the two prominent interfaces between the finances of the Bush family and those of the bin Laden family. "That connection influenced a policy that ordered our intelligence agencies to say, 'hands off the Saudis, hands off the Persian Gulf potentates.'"[90] Much the same point was made by journalist Joseph Trento, author of *The Secret History of the CIA,* who had contended in earlier remarks that "as CIA director, the President's father, George Herbert Walker Bush, joined with a Saudi prince to create a bank for covert operations to fight the Soviets through the Islamic cause in Afghanistan. The Bank of Credit and Commerce International collapsed in scandal, but its personalities and pieces became the vessels and conduits of the terrorist network."[91]

Radical-seeming when made, the Palast-Trento interpretation was bolstered in the summer of 2003 by the joint report of the House and Senate Intelligence Committees on the origins of the 9/11 attack and how it might have been prevented. Before the document was released, the Bush administration demanded major deletions, especially in the twenty-eight-page section dealing with the role played by the Saudis and other foreign governments. "I just don't understand the administration here," said New York Democratic senator Charles E. Schumer. "There seems to be a systematic strategy of coddling and cover-up when it comes to the Saudis."[92] Unfortunately, the October Surprise, Iran-Contra, and Iraqgate precedents justified concern that another potent scandal was gestating.

Meanwhile, the growing and related perception in Washington that popular discontent and upheaval were closing in on the House of Saud and the lesser Gulf emirates—in contrast to the optimism after the 1990–91 war—began to emerge as a little-discussed but vital underpinning of the decision to seize Iraq. Deputy Defense Secretary Paul Wolfowitz, in a comment sometimes distorted, allowed that "for bureaucratic reasons, we settled on one issue, weapons of mass destruction, because it was the one reason everyone could agree on," but another reason was that ousting Saddam would make it possible to base U.S. troops in Iraq and remove them from Saudi Arabia.[93] Removing the U.S. military presence from Saudi Arabia, of course, would meet an important Al Qaeda demand.

Historians eager to measure a further war ingredient—the extent to which George W. Bush's Middle East policy reflected either his own biblical beliefs or those of the huge fundamentalist and evangelical Christian mainstay of the Republican presidential coalition—had limited information with which to work. For sure, the U.S. Religious Right was a prop of the GOP's closeness to the Israeli Likud Party and its allies in that country's radical Right. In 1990, George H. W. Bush had been able to tailor his war coalition building to include many Islamic nations in addition to the oil sheikhdoms. His son's coalition, by contrast, was much narrower globally and much weaker among Islamic moderates. Within the United States, support for the war was far more disproportionately based on Christian fundamentalists and evangelicals.

Another aspect of the religious evolution was equally troubling. Although George H. W. Bush had been obliged to swing like a weather vane during the summer and autumn of 1990, he was a skilled diplomat—and no coded biblical scripture ever issued from his Episcopalian lips suggesting that he and God were copilots in warring on Iraq. By comparison, the degree to which George W. Bush, after 9/11, supposedly came to feel that the Almighty was speaking to him and had chosen him for a great role never stirred serious U.S. political debate, for all the attention that it received elsewhere in the world. The fact that almost half of U.S. Christians believed in Armageddon—a striking anomaly in the Western world—was enough to chill even a brave Washington legislator.

Central to the difference between the war policies of Bush *père* and those of Bush *fils* was how George I failed to go all the way to Baghdad in 1991, mistakenly letting Saddam Hussein survive. That lesson learned, George II did go all the way in 2003, proudly toppling Baghdad's great statue of Saddam. Unfortunately, he then wound up in a different but also unsatisfactory set of circumstances. Essential services broke down; guerrilla warfare broke out; American soldiers kept dying in ambushes and suicide bombings. All were reminders that the Bush dynasty's predilection has been for covert action, not nation building.

The United States' larger national record warranted caution. Outside of administering the Philippines for four decades, certainly at least a partial success, the United States has no record in Asia of building a nation that wasn't already successfully molded. Ethnically and religiously divided Iraq, assembled by a bunch of lines drawn in the post–World War I sands of what had been the Ottoman Empire, could be managed by a vicious strongman—Saddam Hussein proved that, at least. However, the prospect of its being turned into a democratic polity by a succession of American viceroys was an illusion nurtured by George W. Bush's defense intellectuals, despite the earlier U.S. disillusionment in Indochina. Historian Walter A. McDougall, author of *Promised Land, Crusader State,* noted before the postwar embarrassments of 2003, "Suffice it to say that no democracy, as Westerners understand the concept, has ever existed in the Arab world and only one (Turkey) in the whole Islamic world."[94]

Yet many Americans continued to march with the president—*Walker, Texas Ranger*—to the stirring cadence of "Themes from Hollywood's Great Westerns." Just days before U.S. troops moved into Iraq, Vice President Cheney opined that the notion of George Bush as a "cowboy" was "not necessarily a bad idea. . . . The fact of the matter is, he cuts to the chase, he is very direct, and I find that very refreshing." It was a foolish symbolism, soon abandoned. Instead, the postwar confusion and death along the Tigris and the Euphrates, while necessarily awaiting a fuller verdict of history, showed signs of becoming the third less-than-successful Texas-launched U.S. war—one more confrontation fought with rhetorical six-guns, political deceit, and frontier determination to "nail that coonskin to the wall," "kick ass," "smoke 'em out," or run down "the evil ones," but failing in terms of larger conceptualization and strategic planning. Three successive mistakes began to leave the realm of coincidence. Retired Marine General Anthony Zinni, who headed the U.S. Central Command from 1997 to 2000, lamented that Iraq "reminds me of Vietnam. Here we have some strategic thinkers who have long wanted to invade Iraq. They saw an opportunity, and they used the imminence of the threat and the association with terrorism and the 9/11 emotions as a catalyst and a justification. It's another Gulf of Tonkin."[95]

Whereas Vietnam turned embarrassing after two to three years of heavy fighting, and the first Iraq war appeared inadequately managed with the hindsight of a year and a half, the second Iraq war may have produced rapid global reversals that few Americans comprehended. Early but worrisome evidence came in the postwar worldwide polling by the Pew Research Center that showed huge numbers of Muslims had been won over to bin Laden and away from support for the U.S. war on terrorism. In virtually every Muslim nation, lopsided ratios wished that the Iraqis had fought harder.[96]

Not long after George W. Bush's election in 2000 made his family into the first real dynasty in American presidential politics, the crisis of 9/11—including terrorism, U.S.-Saudi ties, and the question of replacing Saudi oil and bases with new facilities in Iraq—took over his presidency. Although this was something none of those involved could have expected, it also spotlighted some hitherto little-debated dynastic disabilities. Clearly, the Bush family's place in U.S. history must rise or fall on its ability to deal with the Middle East. The concern must be over how those same controversial talents and conflicts of interest will be remembered in histories of the twenty-first-century fortunes of the United States.

Machiavelli and the American Dynastic Moment

A republic, if you can keep it.

> Benjamin Franklin, on being asked in 1787
> whether the Constitutional Convention
> had created a monarchy or a republic

I'll play the orator as well as Nestor,
Deceive more slyly than Ulysses could,
And, like a Sinon, take another Troy.
I can add colors to the chameleon,
Change shapes with Proteus for advantages,
And set the murderous Machiavel to school.

> Shakespeare, *Henry VI*

The political thinker Niccolò Machiavelli (1469–1527), long a believer in the famous Florentine Republic of the Renaissance, began to lose faith in his later years as the tides of imperial power and ambition—French, German, and Spanish—swept across the Italian peninsula, washing away the old republican politics of city-states like Florence and Siena too small to survive on their own. Unlike Machiavelli's less-well-known books, which embraced republican politics and institutions, his most famous volume, *The Prince,* was dedicated to Lorenzo de' Medici, the duke of Urbino.[1] It encapsulated the techniques, from amorality and fraud to religion, by which the ascendant princely rulers might govern most successfully.

As the 2004 presidential election took shape, another such Machiavellian moment was at hand. U.S. president George W. Bush, while hardly a

Medici, was a dynast whose family heritage included secrecy and calculated deception. Harkening to the increasingly imperial self-perception of the United States, the president's theorists and tacticians boasted of taking the advice of Machiavelli and the Chinese strategist Sun Tzu. The late Lee Atwater, chief political adviser to the elder Bush, and Karl Rove, strategist for the younger Bush, friends and collaborators, were both devotees of Machiavelli and *The Prince*, hardly a coincidence.[2] Not a few latter-day Republicans have sought to cast politics in military terms.

More than two centuries earlier, the founding fathers of the United States—avid readers of political theory and the chronicles of the old Roman, Florentine, and Dutch republics—worried about how the new republic they had created in 1787 would manage. Of the first three founders to become presidents, John Adams was the particular student of what has since become relevant again: the definitions, internal balances, and vulnerabilities of the republic as a form of government. George Washington, great leader rather than philosopher, made his practical contribution to republican government in the late 1780s by turning down the crown that some had urged him to take. Thomas Jefferson preferred to busy himself with importuning some kind of revolution every twenty years or so to clean out the Augean stables of banking, aristocracy, and incipient monarchy.

None of the three would have welcomed the events of the 2000 election. But Adams was the institutional worrywart. While he was serving as U.S. minister to Britain from 1783 to 1787, his preoccupation with republics and their perils led him to research and write a book, *A Defence of the Constitutions of Government of the United States of America,* which was principally a history of those republics that had so far existed in the Western world. Printed just in time to be available to the delegates arriving at Philadelphia's Constitutional Convention in the summer of 1787, his work described not only the architecture of republics but the forces that had sapped and destroyed previous examples. It was something of a Bushian anticipation. Prominent sapping and debilitating factors were the rise of hereditary offices, aristocracies, and rulers. Luxury, great wealth, and corruption were other dangers, along with imperial ambitions and wars.

Which obviously returns us to the outlook, republican or otherwise, for a United States of the early twenty-first century caught up in elements of dynastization. How much so, and for how long, is not yet clear. Yet a further insight can be gleaned from the second institutional face of the U.S. political upheaval of 2000: *restoration.*

The turn-of-the-century United States did not simply drift into a dynastic bent by electing a slew of sons and daughters to Senate seats previously filled by parents or siblings—or, for that matter, by picking as chief executive the son of a man who had been a president or senator long before. What the erstwhile republic of Adams, Jefferson, and Madison did in 2000, as we have seen, was restore to the Oval Office the eldest son and near namesake of a president from the same party who had been ejected just eight years earlier.

Historically, such restoration of a ruling family has followed some national trauma. The very few restorations of ruling houses in Western Europe, for example—the English Stuarts in 1660, the French Bourbons in 1815—involved enough of a cultural, political, and psychological watershed to endure for some fifteen to thirty years.[3] Neither was a mere flash in the pan. But they were unable to last longer, because restoration itself has been a national blind alley, its appeal a chimera. The restored dynasts displayed many of the same biases and tendencies that had undone the deposed kings. Indeed, unhappiness with both restorations eventually led to new upheavals—the Glorious Revolution of 1688 in England and the Parisian street barricades of 1830.

Where the United States stands amid its own upheaval is a question the next decade or so must resolve. The French and English precedents suggest that restored, smug conservatism—a common denominator—can expect more than a four-year presidential term to indulge its excesses and wear out any welcome. Besides, the current evidence that dynasticism is likewise affecting the Democratic Party, through the appeal of Senator Hillary Clinton, supports the notion that great-family politics is still unfolding, not retreating, in the United States.

The upshot, some speculate, may be a second term for the Bush dynast and then a match between the remaining heirs, Floridian Jeb Bush and Senator Clinton, in 2008. The founding fathers would cringe, to be sure, but portions of the national psyche have seemed accepting, as discussed in this book's early chapters.

The other possible denouement, that small-r republican voters might turn on the restored Bush chief executive after one term or during a second, would represent a speeding-up of the prior restorationist clock. Still, several political time frames or procedures make it at least possible. In terms of motive, national disillusionment likely would have to crest around constitutional, legal, and moral issues arising out of the alleged misrepresentations and deceptions used by George W. Bush to take the United States into the second Iraq war in 2003, with some conceivable effects from the scandals and Iraq war antecedents during his father's term in office.

In 1992, as we have seen, the elder Bush was defeated for reelection at least in part because of his culpability and evasiveness in three war- and national-security-related scandals: October Surprise, Iran-Contra, and Iraqgate. As of 2004, most Americans have forgotten them, but a second-generation failure would fan their memory.

In addition to the quadrennial presidential election, a second, more remote means exists for removing a chief executive over a rising perception of war-related abuses. Professor Raoul Berger was trenchant in his 1973 classic *Impeachment:* "In our own time, the impeachment of President Truman, apparently for his conduct of the Korean War, was suggested by its staff to the Republican high command. There have been reiterated demands for the impeachment of President Nixon, arising out of dissatisfaction with his program for disengagement from the war in Vietnam. President Kennedy concurred with Attorney General Robert Kennedy that if he had not moved to expel Soviet nuclear missiles from Cuba at the time of the confrontation with Khrushchev, 'he would have been impeached.'"[4]

In the summer of 2003, as public unhappiness with apparent prewar deceit rose in the United States and Britain, voices on both sides of the Atlantic—lonely ones, to be sure—invoked this drastic remedy. John Dean, of onetime Watergate notoriety, opined that "if Bush has taken Congress and the nation into war based on bogus information, he is cooked." In Britain, Labour MP Malcolm Savidge told a U.S. interviewer that should allegations prove true, "that would clearly be a more serious issue than even Watergate" and could "fit into the definition of high crimes and misdemeanors which we in Britain used to have as a basis for impeachment, and which, of course, you still have as a basis of impeachment." Scott Ritter, a former UN weapons inspector in Iraq, an ex-marine major and registered Republican, urged George W. Bush's impeachment for lying to Congress. Florida senator Robert Graham, a former chairman of the Senate Intelligence Committee, also touched vaguely on the possibility of impeachment.[5]

U.S. presidential politics being a roller coaster to match any found in amusement parks, no one could assume that mid-2003 frustration previewed the circumstances of 2004. But just as popular sentiment is fickle, the time limitation on scandals is fluid. Should Americans conclude that negligence with some deliberate aspects helped bring about 9/11, or that the president, for personal reasons or through willful misrepresentation, embroiled the United States in a Persian Gulf debacle, such an inference could haunt even a reelected George W. Bush through a second term. In this matter, we need only remember how his father, facing reelection in 1991–92, was haunted by lingering episodes of alleged misbehavior that had taken place in 1980–81, 1984–86, and 1984–90.

His father's scandals could have a double significance for George W. Bush, the sins-cum-precedents of a presidential father conceivably being visitable on a son—especially a son who has chosen to reenact some of the doubtful elements of his father's presidency. Manifestly, this is legal and constitutional terra incognita. These paragraphs are explanation only, not prediction. The context of global terrorism makes prediction ill advised.

Should the restorationist, getting-even type of conservatism that has characterized the George W. Bush administration be a major issue in 2004 or continue through an additional term in 2005–8, the incumbent could also face renewed questions of legitimacy. War conduct aside, there remains the haunting memory of the 2000 election and the suspended Florida recount, in which the U.S. Supreme Court by a 5–4 vote awarded dubious victory to the contender finishing *second* in the national popular vote.

Any souring public perception of Bush's motives in invading Iraq could revitalize an underlying legitimacy issue. Evidence that 9/11 itself might not have happened if the Bushes had not had so many close, embarrassing, and constraining ties to the Saudis could be a dangerous wedge. Indeed, in a legitimacy sense, 9/11 was a godsend to Bush. As chapter 3 discussed, many serious observers believe that the media consortium recounting the 2000 Florida election undervotes and overvotes abandoned the latter part of the recount in September 2001 for reasons of procedural patriotism—a clear Gore victory through countable overvotes would have severely damaged Bush's legitimacy at a time when an embattled, just-attacked United States could not have afforded that kind of division.

Even though the members of the media consortium have not admitted such motivation, public opinion polls have continued to report that 35 to 40 percent of Americans decline to call Bush a legitimately elected president. In August 2003, a CBS/*New York Times* poll put the figure at 38 percent.[6] A particularly difficult circumstance for Bush would be a Middle

Eastern policy failure that rubbed raw the legitimacy issue and persuaded the media consortium to reopen the overvote question.

Here, too, presidential dynastization limns a more extended frame of reference. Among the many father-son echoes in the annals of the Bush family is electoral taint—how both generations took national power in elections with a whiff of theft and whispers of conspiracy. This book's discussion in chapter 9 of the 1980 October Surprise and the alleged role of vice presidential nominee George H. W. Bush in making an election-determining deal with the Iranians, while too brief to provide more than cursory evidence, does suggest a possible continuity. The Bushes appear to be a family that approaches a presidential election as something to be won with a CIA manual, not earned with commitment to Lincolnian precepts or popular sovereignty.

The rest of the agenda visible in Bush II—and in the broader programmatic regime that has emerged since 2000—has a distinct cousinship to Bush I. While the attack of 9/11 is responsible for much of the national security pressure, it explains only a small part of the rightward trend in matters of secrecy, speech, detention, and private-sector warfare.

The advent of imperial America, as we have seen, goes beyond a simple response to 9/11. The lure and pursuit of empire, John Adams found, was corrosive of earlier republics. In Rome, an imperial spirit preceded the actual office of emperor. In the generations leading up to Julius Caesar, what began as a republic was remolded by expansion, loss of virtue, luxury, concentration of wealth, extended terms of office, and finally monarchy. Kindred changes overtook the weakening Dutch Republic of the eighteenth century.

The excitement with which many American conservatives and neoconservatives greeted the prerogatives and accoutrements of empire in the turn-of-the-century United States seemed to grow out of similar inclinations. However, despite a resurrected Anglophone lexicon of Eurasian pivotalism and advanced Great Game theory, the dross reality of Texas-style chicken-fried empire—George W. Bush *imperator,* sprawling Sun Belt megachurches instead of Gothic Westminster, Bible-thumping Virginia ayatollahs, Pentagon intellectuals-in-residence, doctrines of preemptive war, and Texas Ranger unilateralism—quickly sent serious historians reaching for less flattering analogies.

One view offered by Pulitzer Prize–winning Japan specialist John W.

Dower compared Bush-era America with the right-wing Japanese regime symbolized by Emperor Hirohito and World War II prime minister Hideki Tojo—a regime of triumphant nationalism that first took over Manchuria and part of China, then seized Southeast Asia and attacked Pearl Harbor. It, too, was terrorist suppressing, military in orientation, given to patriotic cultism, and caught up in the East Asian equivalent of Manifest Destiny. A second parallel, drawn by Anatol Lieven of the Carnegie Endowment for International Peace, perceived U.S. projects and attitudes as little resembling sophisticated British imperialism but rather "much more reminiscent of Wilhelmine Germany"—the saber-rattling era of Kaiser Wilhelm II (1888–1918), a militarist with more than a tinge of megalomania.[7] Unfair as these analogies may seem in brief capsules, they furnish a balance to the Anglo-Roman self-conceptions of the Bush, Cheney, and Rumsfeld advisers.

Parallel concerns about the United States' becoming a garrison state, for most of the late twentieth century a bugbear imagined by the Left, developed an aura of at least partial truth. The overwhelming shadow that the $400-billion-a-year U.S. military establishment casts over any conceivable international rival—be it the growing European Union or a hypothetical combination of Russia, China, and the Axis of Evil—is matched by the preponderance of the U.S. intelligence community. By one expert account, "The estimated 2000 intelligence budget of $30 billion was larger than all Russian military expenditures combined, and it dwarfed the puny amount Moscow spent on its relatively effective intelligence services. The United States spent five times as much on intelligence as the whole of Europe combined, and no other region of the world could begin to compete with that level of expenditure."[8]

With no Soviet-type great-power rival to stave off, the impulse has become protoimperial—Pax Americana in the mold of Pax Romana. The strain on the domestic institutions of the U.S. Republic is already a developing corollary. Here, too, appropriate and necessary national responses to terrorism have been major contributors. Even so, the expansion of military jurisdiction within the United States and the growing argument for mercenary and paramilitary forces seem to draw as much on viceregal and proconsular mind-sets as on manifest national security needs.

It may be salutary, then, that the Department of Defense has decided to set up Northcom, a military command for the domestic United States. But it may also be an unfortunate augury. Yet, just as with the Department of

Homeland Security, what *could* develop is the question mark. Civil libertarians worry about the military patrolling streets, making arrests, and conducting house-to-house searches, hitherto a great nightmare of Anglo-Saxon law and politics. Fears also sharpened following the government's mid-2003 decision to use military commissions to try terrorism suspects. One conservative-leaning publication flatly deplored how the president was "setting up a shadow court system outside the reach of either Congress or America's judiciary, and answerable only to himself."[9]

Disapproval also met the widening domestic reach envisioned in Bush administration proposals for additional "antiterrorist" legislation to be called the Domestic Security Enhancement Act. The *New York Times* had earlier pointed out that "the CIA is now permitted to read secret grand jury testimony without a judge's prior approval. It can obtain private records of institutions and corporations seized under federal court-approved searches."[10] Further extension seemed unnecessary.

The Center for Public Integrity, which leaked a draft of the Domestic Security Enhancement Act, explained that the act would authorize secret government arrests, wiretaps, and searches. It would also provide that any citizen, native born as well as foreign born, who supports even the lawful activities of an organization labeled "terrorist" by the executive branch would be presumptively stripped of citizenship and subject to deportation.[11]

Mounting demands for mercenary forces—which even Niccolò Machiavelli thought ill advised—have also stirred unease. There is a reasoned thesis, to be sure. Lieutenant Colonel Eugene Smith, a CENTCOM (Middle East Command) officer writing in a recent military quarterly, discussed this issue in "The New Condottieri and U.S. Policy: The Privatization of Conflict and Its Implications." His broad premise is that "niche wars, for instance, are on the rise around the globe, pitting governments and non-government forces against each other." As such forms of armed conflict multiply and spread, the lines between public and private, government and people, military and civilian become as blurred as they were in the sixteenth and seventeenth centuries. "Already, the new era is marked by a decrease in conventional warfare with large armies and an increase in conflicts characterized as Military Operations Other Than War (MOOTW)."[12]

MOOTW, alas, appears to be bureaucracy-speak for the dissolution of lines between the military, business, and civilian sectors that President Eisenhower warned against in 1961. The rise of such conflicts would also

recall the warfare that destroyed most of the remaining municipally centered republics such as Florence and Siena as it spread across fifteenth- and
sixteenth-century Italy. The republican institutions of the United States
could also be expected to suffer.

Latter-day imperialists show little concern. In 2003, neoconservative
writer Robert Kaplan enthused over the prospect for achieving supremacy
by stealth warfare. Global imperial efficacy, he said, would require the CIA
and Special Forces to "operate in the shadows and behind closed doors."
Congress and the rule of domestic and international law should be quietly
ignored, democratic consultations minimized. Propaganda, in turn, should
be perfected. The model should be successful late-twentieth-century U.S.
activity in Latin America—in Nicaragua, El Salvador, Honduras, and
Chile. Even Cuba was a learning process.[13]

Of course, it is hard to know whether Kaplan is a Bush apologist, or
George W. Bush is a Kaplan exemplar. One can fairly call the Bushes a CIA
dynasty; three generations of their line have thrilled to the romance of
Langley-funded soldiers of fortune parachuting into Central American
valleys, upending "unacceptable" governments, airlifting weaponry to de-
serving warlords, or charging through the Cuban surf.

Within the United States, government secrecy has been rising like an
antirepublican phoenix. Listing actions that ranged from George W. Bush's
2001 executive order restricting public access to the papers of former presidents to Vice President Cheney's refusal to name the corporate executives
his energy policy task force met with, the *New York Times* concluded in
2002 that "the Bush team's inclination to keep information under wraps
goes far beyond the reaction to terrorist attacks or even what can be regarded as traditional efforts to conduct government affairs out of the lime-
light."[14] Indeed, this penchant for secrecy and apparent elimination of
records and documents has a multigenerational history in the Walker-
Bush family, which is set out in appendix B. Secrecy, obviously, has been a
guardian angel of calculated deception.

One larger, all-important question is whether this sort of clandestine
mentality and its accompanying high-budget secret operations have brought
about the triumph of what supporters trumpet as American democracy, or
rather the global arousal of what Professor Chalmers Johnson has called
blowback—the fierce and terrorist-mobilizing resentment incited by U.S.
policies, bombings, wars, and covert operations, especially over the last

three decades. Neither side has won this debate; indeed, it has hardly been opened.

But we know its outlines. Covert operations protagonists contend, most importantly, that the multiple insurgencies they launched against the Soviet Union and its clients in the 1980s—from Central America to the hills of Afghanistan—helped weaken the Soviets militarily and economically, to the point where the Soviet Union effectively imploded in 1989–91. The United States thereupon won the cold war.

The counterargument, equally simplified, is that the U.S. defense buildup of the 1980s, in which military outlays increased from $157.5 billion in fiscal year 1981 to $303.6 billion in fiscal year 1989, could be said to have spent the Soviets under the table, essentially breaking the back of their economy and defense effort.[15] Not only did the U.S. covert actions play merely a minor role—this minimizes the effect of the Russian disaster in Afghanistan—but they generated a much larger number of problems that carried over into the post–cold war era and sapped the American triumph.

While there will always be two serious sides to this disagreement, the changing vein of analysis since the horrors of 9/11, together with the unexpected U.S. embarrassments and difficulties that followed the second Iraq war in 2003, appears to have renewed attention to blowback—the local backlash against half a century of U.S. policy in the Middle East and its environs. By one thesis, the seemingly successful insurgency that chased the Soviets from Afghanistan ultimately produced the Taliban and Al Qaeda. By another, the controversial U.S. military presence in Islam's Saudi Arabian holy lands helped breed Osama bin Laden and the men who attacked the World Trade Center. In Iran, the CIA coup that stymied the Iranian political upheaval of 1953 and restored the shah may have strangled an early opportunity for some regional democratic evolution and eventually led to the ayatollahs. The supposed liberation of Iraq in 2003 unleashed guerrilla warfare and produced a massive anti-American surge in Islamic nations from North Africa to Indonesia. One side effect may have been to print recruiting posters for a generation of suicide bombers.

With respect to the future of the American Republic—the suggestion of not a few of the historical perils that John Adams cataloged back in the 1780s—it is all too easy to imagine our own era as a watershed. In 1975, the historian J. G. A. Pocock wrote a book, *The Machiavellian Moment*, pointing out that the Florentine had penned his great works, *The Prince* and *The*

Discourses, in the early sixteenth century at a time when his beloved republic was confronting its own philosophical and governmental finitude. French, German, and Spanish imperial power was overrunning Europe, including Italy, through a scale of wealth and military capacity that doomed many of the old city-states.[16] Florence, one such, surrendered its republican status in the 1530s and took the Medici as hereditary rulers.

The possibility that the United States could edge toward its own Machiavellian moment in an early-twenty-first-century milieu of terrorism, neoimperialism, and dynastization is not far-fetched. As we have seen, Rove, the Bush dynasty's own political plotter, has been an avid reader of Machiavelli. While the analysis in *The Discourses* upholds republicanism, the advice Machiavelli gives in *The Prince* was dedicated to the Medicis and designed to work in the new princely, aristocratic, and neo-imperial milieu of sixteenth-century Italy.

Chapter 4, in its discussion of Bush domestic policy and "compassionate conservative" rhetoric, has already referred to Machiavelli's advice that the Prince should lie but must "be able to disguise this character well, and to be a great feigner and dissembler." Moreover, "to see and hear him, he [the Prince] should seem to be all mercy, faith, integrity, humanity and religion. And nothing is more necessary than to seem to have this last quality. . . . Everybody sees what you appear to be, few feel what you are."

Other advice dwells on the merits of fraud, hypocrisy, faithlessness, and related practices, and twentieth-century academicians have noted Machiavelli's appeal to leaders like Hitler, Stalin, and Mussolini.[17] Doubtless there are also hundreds of copies of *The Prince* at the CIA. Which makes it revealing, and arguably ill advised, that the two political advisers to the two Bush presidents should claim it as a bible of sorts.

Even in religion, Machiavelli's advice to emphasize it is relevant to the early-twenty-first-century United States. His career in Florence overlapped that of Friar Girolamo Savonarola, the Religious despot who ruled the gasping republic from 1494 to 1498 with a politics of fighting sin and immorality. Doubtless the youthful Machiavelli absorbed how close Savonarola came to achieving a theocracy even in republican Florence. Not a few Americans see a little bit of Savonarola in George W. Bush.

The advent of a Machiavelli-inclined dynasty in what may be a Machiavellian Moment for the American Republic is not a happy coincidence, but one that demands attention. Luckily, the arrival of a U.S. presidential election every fourth year typically brings with it an uncommon intensity of national debate, so perhaps attention will be paid.

Since the events and upheavals of 2000–2001, the United States has had an abundance of unfolding transformations to discuss—in economics, national security, and even religion. Of these, many can be considered and managed separately. But one is pervasive enough to make its impact felt almost everywhere: the extent to which national governance has, at least temporarily, moved away from the proven tradition of a leader chosen democratically, by a majority or plurality of the electorate, to the succession of a dynastic heir whose unfortunate inheritance is privileged, covert, and globally embroiling.

ACKNOWLEDGMENTS

Several of the most successful U.S. presidencies have in themselves become centers of scholarship. References to Lincoln scholars are frequent, but similar citations can be found for experts on Washington, Jefferson, and FDR.

Perhaps some day people will talk of Clinton and Bush scholars—but not for a while. In any event, this book is rooted in the concept that the Bushes have become a dynasty of disinformation and that serious portraiture involves going behind a facade thrown up over many decades. There are a few Bush cousins who might, in the right mood, be candid—mostly disgruntled grandchildren of George H. Walker, the old buccaneer—but in the end I did not travel that route.

Besides my own background of many years in Republican politics, I found particular utility in the following books on the Bushes. For the forty-first president, the best two are Herbert Parmet's *George Bush: The Life of a Lone Star Yankee* and the portrait by Michael Duffy and Dan Goodgame entitled *Running in Place: The Status Quo Presidency of George Bush*. For the forty-third, I relied on *First Son* by Bill Minutaglio of the *Dallas Morning News; Revenge of the Bush Dynasty* by Elizabeth Mitchell; *Ambling into History* by Frank Bruni of the *New York Times; Boy Genius,* by Lou Dubose, Jan Reid, and Carl Cannon; and *Bush's Brain: How Karl Rove Made George W. Bush Presidential* by James Moore and Wayne Slater. At the same time, of course, much of the most detailed and devastating coverage of George W. Bush has come not in books but from the Internet and the British national press (which is obliged to restrain its coverage of Britain's royal family and therefore concentrates its dissection on America's).

However, to get behind the Bush facade historically, much of my research has been into subjects like oil, finance, World War I, U.S. financial and business interlocks during the 1920s and 1930s, Yale and Skull and Bones, Wall Street ties to Germany, World War II, the OSS and the CIA, the armaments business, the rise of the military-industrial complex, Bush family ties to the Middle East (and the Persian Gulf in particular), the political role of rogue banks (UBC, BCCI, BNL), the Vietnam failure as a genesis of neoconservative and Bushian involvement in the Persian Gulf, the rise of fundamentalism in the world and of the Religious Right in the United States, Bush connections to religious radicalism (the Moonies, Dominionism, and Christian Zionism), and the threads connecting the October Surprise, Iran-Contra, and Iraqgate scandals to the two undeclared wars with Iraq and latter-day terrorism. It has been an education, one with some psychological rewards: I didn't like the Bushes when I was involved in GOP politics before their two presidencies, and now I better understand why.

This book would not have reached rapid fruition without the help of a number of others. My agents, Bill Leigh and Wes Neff, were indispensable in making speedy arrangements. My perspicacious editor at Viking Penguin, Wendy Wolf, saw the book in the outline and guided its evolution, and senior production editor Bruce Giffords made all the trains run on time. My able research assistant, Eric Ditzian, spent many hours in Manhattan and Washington libraries and archives.

APPENDIX A
Armaments and the Walker-Bush Family, 1914–40

Eight decades ago, a half century before anyone had ever heard of the Bank of Credit and Commerce International (BCCI) or Iran-Contra, George Herbert Walker, the founding father and spiritual progenitor of the Bush clan, had been the first to place the elements on the family escutcheon: arms deals, clandestine shipments, foreign covert operations, rogue banks, and money laundering.

The years preceding World War I convinced many of America's richest families that there were profits to be made in arms and war production. As the U.S. role in the world ballooned, monied Americans were also lured by investment vehicles claiming to draw on foreign political intelligence and identify overseas opportunities. If the Rockefellers, Harrimans, Morgans, and Stillmans of National City Bank were at the center, the Walker and Bush families were part of their supporting cast.

This appendix is designed to backstop references in several chapters to the interlocking directorates of ten or so companies involved in armaments, banking, overseas investment, shipping, and commercial relations with Germany and the Soviet Union. The table on page 336 shows how, at various times in the 1920s and 1930s, George Herbert Walker and Prescott Bush were officers or directors of more than a half dozen of these firms.

The guns of August 1914 brought proceeds of thunderous proportions. One beneficiary, Marcellus Hartley Dodge, who had recently inherited control of the Remington Arms–Union Metallic Cartridge Company, by 1915 found the size of wartime demand mandating further expansion and investment. Luckily, Dodge's father-in-law, financier William Rockefeller (John D. Sr.'s brother), and Dodge's brother-in-law Percy Rockefeller, together with their Stillman relations, controlled the nation's largest bank, New York–based National City.[1] They helped Remington expand and reorganize, and Percy Rockefeller and James A. Stillman become Remington directors.

Now let us widen the new horizon. The Rockefellers and Stillmans—in cooperation with the Morgan-linked Guaranty Trust Company, also New

The National City Bank–Harriman–Walker Axis: Interlocking Corporate Directors

To illustrate the interlock, those persons serving each of the nine companies as a director for at least one year between 1916 and 1941 are listed because of these principal institutional associations: From **National City Bank,** William Rockefeller, Percy Rockefeller, James Stillman, James A. Stillman, Frank Vanderlip; from **W. A. Harriman and Company,** W. Averell Harriman, E. R. Harriman, George H. Walker, Prescott Bush; from **Remington Arms,** Samuel Pryor; from **American International Corporation,** Matthew Brush. All director/officer data is from various volumes of *The Directory of Directors in the City of New York.*

NATIONAL CITY BANK	W. A. HARRIMAN AND COMPANY (ALSO W. A. HARRIMAN SECURITIES CORPORATION)	AMERICAN INTERNATIONAL CORPORATION	REMINGTON ARMS
W. Rockefeller	P. Rockefeller	P. Rockefeller	P. Rockefeller
P. Rockefeller	W. A. Harriman	J. A. Stillman	J. A. Stillman
J. Stillman	E. R. Harriman	F. Vanderlip	S. Pryor
J. A. Stillman	G. H. Walker	G. H. Walker	M. Brush
F. Vanderlip	M. Brush	M. Brush	
	S. Pryor	J. Stillman	

AMERICAN SHIP AND COMMERCE CORPORATION (SHIPPING, HAMBURG-AMERIKA)	UNION BANKING CORPORATION (GERMAN-OWNED NEW YORK BANK)	GEORGIAN MANGANESE CORPORATION (SOVIET MINING CONCESSION)	BARNSDALL CORPORATION (SOVIET OIL CONCESSION)
W. A. Harriman	G. H. Walker	P. Rockefeller	G. H. Walker
G. H. Walker	S. Pryor	S. Pryor	M. Brush
S. Pryor	P. Bush	E. R. Harriman	
		M. Brush	
		G. H. Walker	

HARRIMAN FIFTEEN CORPORATION (HOLDING COMPANY)
W. A. Harriman
G. H. Walker
P. Bush

Note: Other small companies that have been left out include Harriman Thirty and Silesian-American Corporation. In 1933, after a merger, W. A. Harriman and Company became Brown Brothers Harriman. Prescott Bush was a vice president of W. A. Harriman and Company but not a director; he became a partner in Brown Brothers Harriman.

York based—took a leading role in the organization of an ambitious new venture in 1915. This was the American International Corporation, which was liberally funded by prominent industrialists and financiers to invest in U.S. war industries and pursue overseas opportunities. William and Percy Rockefeller, along with National City chairman James Stillman and his son James A. Stillman, all became directors of AIC. The new company launched or bought several major war-production enterprises: Allied Machinery Corporation, American International Shipbuilding, New York Shipbuilding, and the Symington Forge Corporation, a major government contractor for shell forgings.[2] AIC also bought into United Fruit, with its web of political connections in Latin America.

In a kindred move, AIC bought control in 1917 of Amsinck and Company, a New York investment bank run by German Americans. What made it attractive was the firm's strong pre-1917 ties to German intelligence operations in the United States.[3] Other AIC directors and officers, notably William Boyce Thompson and William Franklin Sands, undertook thinly disguised political and intelligence-type missions to Europe and Russia.[4] Investment banker David Francis, the U.S. ambassador to Russia (and an old St. Louis associate of George Herbert Walker), was so close to National City Bank and AIC that his activities elicited criticism from the State Department.[5]

W. Averell Harriman, age twenty-seven and just four years out of Yale, had his own ambitions: in 1917, he took advantage of wartime demand and government contracts to jump into shipbuilding, a vocation that escaped the shadow of his late father's huge reputation in railroading. Harriman built ships during the war, and after its conclusion began gathering a large fleet of merchant ships and liners, consolidated in 1920 under the name United American Lines. Central to these sweeping ambitions was a deal with Germany's once-proud Hamburg-Amerika line, now in postwar disarray. Harriman and his new colleague George H. Walker would supply Hamburg-Amerika with ships if it would act as the European agent for Harriman's own shipping lines.

Here we must clarify the emerging corporate frameworks. As a holding company for buying into Hamburg-Amerika, Harriman used a recent acquisition, the American Ship and Commerce Corporation, in which Harriman and Walker both became directors. The grander framework for Harriman's overall domestic and international business ambitions, organized in 1919, was W. A. Harriman and Company, which immediately garnered additional influential sponsorship.

For one thing, the new firm merged in 1920 with Morton and Company, which interlocked with Guaranty Trust. More important, positions in W. A. Harriman and Company were taken by both Guaranty Trust and National City Bank. The former had passed under Morgan control only in 1912, when Harriman's mother sold the Morgans her 40 percent share (enough of a connection continued, however, that Averell Harriman himself was made a Guaranty Trust director in 1916).

The ties to National City Bank were at least as strong. Both the Rockefellers and the Stillmans had been allies of E. H. Harriman, Averell's father, in the railroad financial wars of the 1890s. In Texas, where the Stillmans had made their first fortune in cotton brokering, William Rockefeller, Jacob Schiff (Kuhn Loeb), James Stillman, and E. H. Harriman were regarded as the "Big Four" of southwestern railroading.[6] National City had handled Harriman's grand reorganization of the Union Pacific Railroad in 1897.

The outline extends to New Haven and Yale. After W. A. Harriman and Company was organized in 1919, National City's Percy Rockefeller—Skull and Bones, 1900 (the only Rockefeller to be tapped)—soon joined fellow Bonesman Harriman (1913) on the board. Harold Stanley, president of Guaranty Trust from 1921 to 1928, was also Skull and Bones (1908). As the 1920s unfolded, Harriman, Rockefeller, and Stanley represented a study in youth, riches, connections, and the hubris of an emerging elite. Coincidence is an unlikely explanation of either the Harriman firm's global ambition or its 1920s dominance by Skull and Bonesmen.

Before noting the rest of the interlocking institutions, however, we must weave in the vital supporting players below the Rockefeller and Harriman level. All four hailed from the Midwest: George Herbert Walker, of course, had been chosen as president of W. A. Harriman and Company in 1919; Samuel F. Pryor, a friend of Walker's from St. Louis, became president of Remington Arms during the war; and Matthew Brush of Minnesota emerged as president first of American International Shipbuilding and then, in 1923, of the parent company, American International Corporation. In addition, Ohio-born Prescott Bush, Walker's son-in-law, was named vice president of W. A. Harriman and Company in 1926, after two years at AIC-connected U.S. Rubber.

Now we can complete the list of networked firms. American Ship and

Commerce, which held shares in the Hamburg-Amerika line, has already been noted. Another was a principal Harriman-Walker holding company: the Harriman Fifteen Corporation. Two more were Russian mineral development companies: Georgian Manganese Corporation and the Soviet oil concession holder Barnsdall Corporation (jointly owned by W. A. Harriman and Company, Lee Higginson and Company, and Guaranty Trust). The last was a U.S. bank set up by W. A. Harriman and Company for Germany's Thyssen steel interests: the Union Banking Corporation (together with its affiliate, the Holland-American Trading Company). Prescott Bush's closest involvement was with Harriman Fifteen and Union Banking Corporation.

Fritz Thyssen's connections with this network were multiple but vague. Besides the Union Banking Corporation, Thyssen was probably one of the German investors in Georgian Manganese Corporation. He received copies of some Georgian Manganese documents, and German steelmakers were eager to share access to Russian manganese production. The enigma is the Thyssen relationship to the Hamburg-Amerika line and Remington Arms during the 1920s and early 1930s, when Fritz Thyssen was one of the major funders of Adolf Hiter and the Nazi Party. Remington Arms chairman Samuel Pryor was simultaneously a board member of American Ship and Commerce, Union Banking, and Georgian Manganese.

Taken together, extraordinary capacities were conjoined: armaments, shipping, shipbuilding, banking, political intelligence gathering, money laundering, and strategic minerals development. Of the nine companies listed in the table, four were pillars: National City Bank, W. A. Harriman and Company, AIC, and Remington Arms. The interlock of directors is striking. According to the *New York City Directory of Directors,* Percy Rockefeller spent many years as a board member at each of these pillars; George Herbert Walker, many years at two (AIC and W. A. Harriman); James A. Stillman, a few years at three (National City, Remington, and AIC); and Samuel Pryor of Remington, many years at two (W. A. Harriman and Remington). But the pattern of interlock becomes even more interesting when it is extended to the boards of the five smaller companies with the specific German, Russian, and holding company relationships.

Matthew Brush, president of the American International Corporation from 1923 to 1933, had his closest connections with Averell Harriman and George Herbert Walker during the years when Harriman and Walker were getting involved in Soviet oil and manganese operations, and then trying to secure the maximum return and successful withdrawal of capital from the Soviet Union. In addition to heading AIC, Brush, in the mid- to late 1920s, was also a director of Georgian Manganese, chairman of Barnsdall, and director and chairman of the finance committee of W. A. Harriman Securities Corporation.

Like Harriman and Walker, Brush had a taste for foreign intrigue. In 1923 and 1924, when Wall Street was focused on assessing and arranging German investments, Brush was briefly chairman of Amsinck, the small German-American investment bank owned by AIC that before 1917 had been an asset of German intelligence.[7] In the late 1920s, AIC named as a new director Gordon Auchincloss, who during World War I had been second in command of U-1, the U.S. State Department's intelligence division.[8]

Of the two big financial institutions, Guaranty Trust acted most avidly in the Soviet Union. One of its vice presidents, Max May, left in 1922 to become director of the foreign division of Ruskom, the Russian Commercial Bank.[9] Guaranty Trust was also one of the three major investors in Barnsdall, which briefly held the post–World War I Soviet oil concession.

National City Bank, by contrast, was German oriented. In 1932, a Brookings Institution survey of U.S. investment bank profits from German loans found National City topping the list, with profits almost twice those of second-place Dillon Read.[10] To be sure, Percy Rockefeller served for a number of years on the board of Georgian Manganese. However, Harriman and Walker had raised some of Georgian's capital through the firm's Berlin office, and German interest was high.

Arms and ammunition maker Samuel Pryor was the sole outsider to serve on the both smaller Harriman-Walker boards—American Ship and Commerce, and Union Banking Corporation—that dealt with the firm's German connections. Although American Ship and Commerce disposed of its ships and its original relationship with Hamburg-Amerika in the mid-1920s, it held a large block of stock in the German shipping company and continued to nominate its single director through the mid-1930s. One can imagine, as U.S. Senate investigators speculated in 1934, that the guns and ammunition finding their way to German buyers around 1932 might have been facilitated by these interrelationships. Corporate regulation was so minimal in those days that few records have survived.

As for the Union Banking Corporation, where George Herbert Walker and Samuel Pryor were directors during its early years (1925–33), no one knows how much money traveled from Germany through Holland to New York, what it did when it got there, or how much of it returned to the *Vaterland* and for what purposes. The ownership chain reached from Berlin's August Thyssen Bank to Rotterdam's Bank voor Handel en Scheepvart, to UBC, and doubtless there was some money laundering. Parenthetically, Prescott Bush took up director's roles in Union Banking and Harriman Fifteen shortly after George Walker retired from W. A. Harriman in the early thirties, so there may have been a considerable continuity of knowledge.

National City Bank, a major investor in Germany during the 1920s, continued to pursue such opportunities in the 1930s, sometimes in collaboration with Brown Brothers Harriman, the successor firm to W. A. Harriman and Company. Several publications have identified Henry Mann, a German with access to Hitler, as being a German deal finder for National City Bank and Brown Brothers Harriman through 1940.[11] After Percy Rockefeller died, his son Avery in 1936 established Schroeder, Rockefeller and Company, investment bankers, in partnership with the German-connected New York banking firm of J. Henry Schroeder.[12] Although incorporated in the United States, it had family ties to the Schroeder banks in England and Germany.

Despite these small successions, the old corporate entente of the 1920s lost its importance in the 1930s because of the Depression, the deaths of Percy Rockefeller and Samuel Pryor, and the retirements of George Herbert Walker and Matthew Brush. The American International Corporation became a passive investment trust. Harriman Fifteen, where George Walker was still president, settled into a substantially similar mode. Remington was bought by Du Pont in 1933, and American Ship and Commerce faded away. But in their day, they represented a considerable preview of techniques and devices that would emerge again in the last quarter of the twentieth century.

APPENDIX B
Deception, Dissimulation, and Disinformation

In the third year of George W. Bush's term, the approaching 2004 national elections unleashed an unprecedented array of U.S. political writing: a flow of books alleging (and by some yardsticks establishing) that the president of the United States was a serial prevaricator. Commentators hurled the ultimate L-word—"liar"—with abandon.

The purpose of this appendix is to tie that debate to the book's related but broader thesis: that George W. Bush's behavior, far from being entirely his own product, is rooted in the dynasty's four-generation evolution and concomitant pattern of deception, dissimulation, and disinformation. This is the new dimension. Of the last eight U.S. presidents, three besides the two Bushes—Lyndon Johnson, Richard Nixon, and Bill Clinton—had personal reputations as at least intermittent liars or deceivers. U.S. voters, having become somewhat inured to such manipulation, may see only more of the same. What makes the Bush pattern different, deeper, and more worrisome is that it has been almost a century in the making.

Consider first the motivational incubators of these attitudes. Five stand out.

Family and Business Connections: Far from being middle class or self-made, as the two Bush presidents have sometimes implied, three generations of Bushes and Walkers were wealthy enough to have significant Rockefeller ties—Samuel Bush in Ohio was closely involved with Frank Rockefeller (John D. Sr.'s brother) and Standard Oil; George H. Walker was associated with Percy Rockefeller (son of John D. Sr.'s brother William); and George H. Walker Jr. got some of the financing for George H. W. Bush's oil ventures from Godfrey S. Rockefeller, a John D. grandson. Sam Bush's Ohio firm, Buckeye Steel Castings, made money out of World War I armaments, even while Sam was in Washington regulating ordnance and forgings (on pp. 94–95 of *A History of Small Business in America,* Professor Mansel Blackford notes that Buckeye "earned rich profits turning out gun casings and other products"). George H. Walker was a business buccaneer who had a considerable need to hide the details of what he was up to. The Harriman-Walker business relationships with the Soviets during the 1920s were frowned on by Washington authorities, and the 1920 Harriman-Walker deal with the Hamburg-Amerika line was deemed so pro-German that Kermit Roosevelt, Teddy Roosevelt's son, resigned as secretary of the Harriman-Walker American Ship and Commerce Corporation rather than participate.[1] Prescott Bush also had to keep a lid on his 1930s involvement with German-connected corporations. The last two Bush generations have also blurred and glossed over controversial business connections and practices.

Military Intelligence and National Security: The Walker and Bush ties to a community notorious for dissimulation and disinformation also go back to World War I. As chapter 6 noted, former Justice Department official John Loftus has contended that Prescott Bush, ostensibly a newly commissioned artillery officer, was brought into military intelligence through British auspices, those of Stewart Menzies, who by World War II was the head of MI-6. By the period 1917–18, some of Bush's friends from Yale and Skull and Bones were already working closely with the British. As for George H. W. Bush, the alternatives entertained in chapter 6 were that he might have been taken into the OSS before naval flight school, that a CIA connection might have been made at Yale, or that his company Zapata Offshore could have become at least partially a CIA front sometime in the 1950s or early 1960s. The CIA's attempt in the 1980s to say that it was a different George Bush who had worked for it in the early 1960s was distinctly unconvincing. Such covert relationships on the part of both Bushes would have nurtured the practices that are textbook stuff at the CIA.

Skull and Bones as a Fount of Elitism, Hubris, and Secrecy: In its half-century heyday, Yale's number one secret society stood for all three attitudes, well documented in several books and studies. In George H. W. Bush's case, prior to Yale he belonged to another secret society, AUV, at Andover. These societies had a considerable overlap with the OSS and the CIA, for which they were good preparation. Bonesmen, in particular, were conditioned to level with each other and to keep secrets from (or deceive) outsiders. Walter Isaacson and Evan Thomas, in their book *The Wise Men*, described how seriously W. Averell Harriman took the society: "So complete was his trust in Bones's code of secrecy that in conversations at annual dinners he spoke openly about national security affairs. He refused, however, to tell his family anything about Bones. Soon after she became Harriman's third wife in 1971, Pamela Churchill Harriman received an odd letter addressing her by a name spelled in hieroglyphics. 'Oh, that's Bones,' Harriman said. 'I must tell you about that sometime. Uh, I mean I can't tell you about that.' When Harriman carried secret dispatches between London and Moscow during World War Two, he chose as the combination on his diplomatic case the numerals 322, the society's secret number."[2]

Posturing as Candidates: Hiding controversial business practices was one thing, but when Prescott Bush ran for the Senate from Connecticut in 1950 and 1952, he faced a different challenge: reassuring a public caught up in mid-twentieth-century democratic values. Because of Averell Harriman's high positions in the Truman administration, the Democrats were not free to attack Bush on earlier controversies that involved W. A. Harriman and Company or the subsequent Brown Brothers Harriman, but George W. Bush's grandfather did cover up and distort his family background, which voters would not have found appealing. In 2001, the *Boston Globe* quoted Prescott Bush as having told the compiler of an oral history during his elective years that "my father wasn't able to support me. He had a modest income, but he couldn't support his adult children, and I didn't want him to anyway. So that's why I abandoned the law."[3] This is transparent flim flam, hinting at the hypocrisies of subsequent generations and the evolution of "kinder and gentler"policies and "compassionate conservatism" discussed in chapter 4.

Tactical Machiavellianism: There is no evidence that Prescott Bush was a reader of the famous Florentine. George H. W. Bush might have been, because of his apparent CIA connections, even before he became Director of Central Intelligence under Gerald Ford. At any rate, Lee Atwater, political adviser to the forty-first president, was a man who reread Machiavelli yearly. Karl Rove, the even more influential adviser to number forty-three, is widely known as a Machiavelli aficionado. For that matter, Machiavelli himself has become more relevant in the upheaval years of the early twenty-first century than he was in the transitional America of the George H. W. Bush presidency. Here it is useful to repeat advice quoted earlier in this book: "A prince must take great care that nothing goes out of his mouth that is not full of the above-named five qualities, and, to see and hear him, he should seem to be all mercy, faith, integrity, humanity and religion."[4] Machiavelli's underlying advice, however, is to practice deceit, because the most successful princes—he names Cesare Borgia and Pope Alexander VI—have been relentless deceivers. "However, it is necessary to be able to disguise this character well, and to be a great feigner and dissembler; and men are so simple and so ready to obey present necessities that one who deceives will always find those who allow themselves to be deceived."[5] In short, "the experience of our times shows those princes to have done good things who have had little regard for good faith, and have been able by astuteness to confuse men's brains."[6] Still another chronicler has pointed out Machiavelli's tribute to fraud in *The Discourses*, book 2, chapter 13: "Machiavelli's writings contain numerous discussions of the indispensable role of fraud in political affairs, ranging from analyses of deceptions and stratagems in war to the breaking of treaties to the varied types of fraud met with daily in civil life. . . . He generalizes that 'from mean to great fortune, people rise rather by fraud than by force.'"[7]

As we move closer to the present day, some of these themes and connections have been scrutinized. However, this has not been done in any comprehensive manner.

Two second-echelon dissimulations—hiding substantial early Rockefeller and Standard Oil connections and minimizing attention to Samuel Bush, George H. Walker, and their armaments tie-ins—have been duly noted. Some further focus on George H. Walker's and Prescott Bush's ties to pre–World War II Germany remains in order. Chroniclers of Averell Harriman have tended to skip over his firm's involvement with the Hamburg-Amerika line, Thyssen steel, and the Union Banking Corporation. George H. Walker left even fewer tracks, and during his life he was of little or no interest to the national press.

Prescott Bush's role at Brown Brothers Harriman in the 1930s and early 1940s has been virtually ignored, except by writers like John Loftus and Mark Aarons. However, as noted earlier, Burton Hersh in *The Old Boys: The American Elite and the Origins of the CIA* makes reference to Henry Mann and his European lieutenant, E. V. D. Wright. Mann is described as "until 1940 the deal-maker around the Third Reich for Brown Brothers Harriman and National City Bank."[8] In Antony Sutton's *Wall Street and the*

Rise of Hitler, the Union Banking Corporation, of which Bush was a director through 1942, is described on pp. 103–7 as sharing German Nazi directors with Thyssen's Vereingte Stalwerke. E. R. Harriman, also a Brown
Brothers Harriman partner, recalled UBC as just an "unpaid courtesy for a
client" believed to be a friend of Charles Lindbergh, according to a short
p. 73 discussion in *Duty, Honor, Country,* the 2003 biography of Prescott
Bush. However, Sutton, in his book, notes a relevant U.S. Senate report:
*Hearings Before a Subcommittee of the Committee on Military Affairs: Elim-
ination of German Resources for War.*[9] One Sutton footnote suggests, "For
yet other connections between the Union Banking Corporation and German enterprises, see Ibid. (U.S. Senate Report), pp. 728–730."[10] Unfortunately, very few records remain to describe what went on in the 1930s.

Jumping ahead to the 1970s and 1980s, the Bushes have also been at
pain to minimize their relations to two much more substantial latter-day
rogue banks, the Bank of Credit and Commerce International and the
Banco Nazionale di Lavoro, which have been connected to global weapons
transactions and to U.S. scandals like Iran-Contra and the Iraqgate arms
buildup of Saddam Hussein. In *False Profits* by Peter Truell and Larry Gurwin and *The Outlaw Bank* by Jonathan Beaty and S. C. Gwynne, the authors approach the possibility that George Bush, as CIA director, may have
been involved in the 1970s emergence and success of BCCI. As noted in
chapter 9, Truell and Gurwin suggest that after Bush left the CIA and became chairman of the executive committee of the First International Bank
of Houston in 1977, "he sometimes marketed to international banks in
London, including several Middle Eastern institutions. Some speculate
that he met with BCCI officers at this time."[11] Beaty and Gwynne dwell on
how Bush, while running the CIA in 1976, enlisted as a CIA asset James
Bath, the U.S. representative of major BCCI investor Khalid bin Mahfouz,
as well as the BCCI-linked bin Laden family.[12] Both sets of authors underscore that one of Bush's major 1976 priorities at the CIA was expanding its
cooperation with Saudi intelligence, at the time run by Sheikh Kamal Adham, who also had close financial ties to BCCI.

The possibility that George H. W. Bush was an architect, not a victim or
dupe, of BCCI's emerging and corrupting international role would help to
explain why Bush could have been so centrally involved in the three major
political scandals of the 1980s—October Surprise (1980–81), Iran-Contra
(1984–86), and Iraqgate (1981–90)—that partly involved covert financing
of clandestine arms deals and relationships with Iraq and Iran. When

George H. W. Bush left office after the 1992 election, Washington policy-makers and observers for the most part put aside the three controversies despite the fact that, as chapter 9 shows, evidence was continuing to mount. But although his 1992 defeat in a sense rescued Bush from the scandals, his son's restoration in 2000 renewed their political and legal relevance. Under the new dynastic circumstances, potential vulnerability mandated a major new federal emphasis on secrecy in government.

These changes have been widely cataloged. The Bush family has had a longstanding interest in ensuring loyalist control of the SEC and the Justice Department to squelch special prosecutors and investigations—back in the late 1980s, journalist Jonathan Kwitny wryly remarked on how the 1960–66 SEC filings for Bush's Zapata Offshore corporation had been inadvertently destroyed in 1981.[13] Then, in 2001, George W. Bush's inauguration ushered in a new preoccupation with suppressing public access to the papers of former presidents and information on White House and departmental decision making. In November 2001, George W. Bush signed an executive order restricting public access to the papers of former presidents, following up his earlier decision to ship his own Texas gubernatorial papers off to his father's presidential library at Texas A&M University, where they became inaccessible. Texas A&M is a second-string Texas University with close Bush ties. Its president is former CIA director Robert Gates, a Bush loyalist whom critics have sought to tie to the October Surprise, Iran-Contra, and Iraqgate alike.

Attorney General John Ashcroft, for his part, promulgated new restrictions on what agencies must release under the Freedom of Information Act. Civil liberties lawyers complained that 9/11 was becoming an unwarranted cloak for secrecy. If national security was obviously involved, dynastic security had become a hidden new context.

NOTES

INTRODUCTION

1. Doug Hannah, a Bush friend since childhood, has found that an attention problem runs in the family: "They have an attention span of about an hour." When he and George were boys, he remembers, "Mr. Bush would pick us up to take us to the movies and he would leave after an hour and twenty minutes. George would sometimes want to leave [ball games] in the fifth inning." Gail Sheehy, "The Accidental Candidate," *Vanity Fair,* October 2000.

CHAPTER 1: The Not-Quite-Royal Family

1. "Family Values Award," *Mother Jones,* September–October 2002, p. 63.
2. Richard Brookhiser, *America's First Dynasty: The Adamses, 1735–1918* (New York: Free Press, 2002).
3. Chuck Concini, "Personalities," *Washington Post,* November 10, 1988.
4. "Bush Has Royal Relatives," Associated Press, September 18, 2002.
5. Herbert Parmet, *George Bush: The Life of a Lone Star Yankee* (New York: Scribner's, 1997), p. 21.
6. Mansel G. Blackford, *A Portrait Cast in Steel* (Westport, Conn.: Greenwood Press, 1982), p. 48.
7. Parmet, *Lone Star Yankee,* p. 20.
8. Vincent P. Carosso, *Investment Banking in America: A History* (Cambridge, Mass.: Harvard University Press, 1970), pp. 84–85.
9. Nini Harris, "D. D. Walker and Family," *St. Louis Senior Circuit News,* 2002, p. 2.
10. Ron Chernow, *The House of Morgan* (New York: Simon & Schuster, 1990), p. 188.
11. Grosvenor Clarkson, *Industrial America in the World War* (Boston: Houghton Mifflin, 1923), p. 501.
12. Harper Barnes, *Standing on a Volcano: The Life and Times of David Rowland Francis* (St. Louis: Missouri Historical Society Press, 2001), p. 245.
13. Walter Isaacson and Evan Thomas, *The Wise Men* (New York: Simon & Schuster, 1986), p. 84.
14. *St. Louis Globe-Democrat,* October 12, 1920.
15. Parmet, *Lone Star Yankee,* p. 34.
16. Nicholas King, *George Bush: A Biography* (New York: Dodd, Mead, 1980), p. 19.
17. Michael Kranish, "Powerful Alliance Aids Bushes' Rise," *Boston Globe,* April 22, 2001.

18. Ibid.
19. Joseph Alsop, *I've Seen the Best of It* (New York: W. W. Norton, 1992), p. 18.
20. King, *George Bush: A Biography,* p. 20.
21. Isaacson and Thomas, *The Wise Men,* p. 81.
22. Alsop, *I've Seen,* p. 18.
23. Isaacson and Thomas, *The Wise Men,* p. 29.
24. Mickey Herskowitz, *Duty, Honor, Country: The Life and Legacy of Prescott Bush* (Nashville: Rutledge Hill Press, 2003), p. 67.
25. *The Directory of Directors in the City of New York,* various vols. (New York: The Directory of Directors Company), published semiannually at first, then after World War II annually.
26. Fitzhugh Green, *George Bush: An Intimate Portrait* (New York: Hippocrene, 1989), p. 6.
27. Ibid., p. 9.
28. Ibid., p. 22.
29. "3 High Military Honors," *(Columbus) Ohio State Journal,* August 8, 1918.
30. Green, *Intimate Portrait,* p. 109.
31. Ibid., p. 124.
32. Michael Duffy and Dan Goodgame, *Marching in Place* (New York: Simon & Schuster, 1992), pp. 41–43.
33. Frank Bruni, *Ambling into History* (New York: HarperCollins, 2002), p. 4.
34. Green, *Intimate Portrait,* p. 66.
35. King, *George Bush: A Biography,* p. 20.
36. Parmet, *Lone Star Yankee,* p. 31.
37. Green, *Intimate Portrait,* p. 123.
38. Ibid., p. 134.
39. Parmet, *Lone Star Yankee,* p. 168.
40. Quoted in "Name Roster," www.metareligion.com.
41. Green, *Intimate Portrait,* pp. 161–162.
42. Parmet, *Lone Star Yankee,* p. 221.
43. Paul A. C. Koistinen, *Mobilizing for Modern War, 1865–1919* (Lawrence: University Press of Kansas, 1997), pp. 297–298.
44. Isaacson and Thomas, *The Wise Men,* p. 21.
45. Ibid., p. 108.
46. Robert Sobel, *The Life and Times of Dillon Read* (New York: Dutton, 1991), p. 51.
47. Clarkson, *Industrial America,* p. 63.
48. Sobel, *Dillon Read,* p. 53.
49. Isaacson and Thomas, *The Wise Men,* p. 89.
50. Nancy Lisagor and Frank Lipsius, *A Law unto Itself* (New York: Paragon House, 1989), pp. 64–86.
51. Isaacson and Thomas, *The Wise Men,* p. 112.
52. Sobel, *Dillon Read,* pp. 103–111.
53. John Loftus and Mark Aarons, *The Secret War Against the Jews* (New York: St. Martin's Press, 1994), pp. 63–64.

54. Christopher Simpson, *The Splendid Blond Beast* (New York: Grove Press, 1993), p. 64.

55. Loftus and Aarons, *Secret War,* p. 60.

56. Antony Sutton, *Wall Street and the Rise of Hitler* (Seal Beach, Calif.: '76 Press, 1976), p. 74.

57. "Thyssen Has $3,000,000 Cash in New York Vault," *New York Herald Tribune,* July 31, 1941.

58. Loftus and Aarons, *Secret War,* pp. 360–361.

59. Darwin Payne, *Initiative in Energy: The Story of Dresser Industries* (New York: Simon & Schuster, 1979), pp. 232–233.

60. Gridiron Club Parody of George Bush, March 1988, quoted in Kevin Phillips, *The Politics of Rich and Poor* (New York: Random House, 1990), p. 210.

61. Elizabeth Mitchell, *Revenge of the Bush Dynasty* (New York: Hyperion, 2000), p. 15.

62. Sheehy, "The Accidental Candidate."

63. Mitchell, *Revenge,* p. 97.

64. "Bush Received Quick Air National Guard Coalition," *Los Angeles Times,* July 4, 1999.

65. Ibid.

66. J. H. Hatfield, *Fortunate Son* (New York: Soft Skull Press, 2000), pp. 303–310.

67. Mitchell, *Revenge,* p. 145.

68. Ibid., p. 195.

69. Gregory Palast, "Bush Family Finances," *London Observer,* November 26, 2000.

70. "At the Height of Vietnam, Graduate Picks the Guard," *Washington Post,* July 28, 1999.

71. *Time,* June 21, 1999, quoted in Mitchell, *Revenge,* p. 198.

72. Richard Hofstadter, *American Political Tradition* (New York: Knopf, 1948). The table of contents lists the dual characterizations in his chapter headings.

CHAPTER 2: **The Dynastization of America**

1. Debora Silverman, *Selling Culture* (New York: Pantheon, 1986), pp. 12–13.

2. Ibid., p. 152.

3. Robert R. Davenport, *The Hereditary Society Bluebook,* 1994 ed. (Baltimore: Genealogical Publishing Co., 1993).

4. Ibid.

5. Quoted in Robert H. Frank, *Luxury Fever* (New York: Free Press, 1999), p. 37.

6. Daniel Gross, "America's Growing Love Affair with Its Own Aristocracy," *Los Angeles Times,* February 18, 2001.

7. Silverman, *Selling Culture,* p. xii.

8. Michael Novak, *Choosing Our King* (New York: Macmillan, 1974), p. 2.

9. Ibid., p. 19.

10. Ibid., p. 23.

11. Ibid., p. 52.

12. Lewis Lapham, *The Wish for Kings* (New York: Grove Press, 1993), pp. 154–155.

13. "Victory Is in the Blood for 'Aristocratic' Republican," *Guardian,* November 6, 2000.

14. Walter A. McDougall, *Promised Land, Crusader State* (New York: Houghton Mifflin, 1997), pp. 1–12.

15. Charles Maier, "An American Empire," *Harvard Magazine,* November–December 2002, pp. 28–30.

16. John W. Dower, "The Other Japanese Occupation," *The Nation,* July 7, 2003, p. 11; Anatol Lieven, "The Empire Strikes Back," *The Nation,* July 7, 2002, p. 25.

17. Lev Grossman, "Feeding on Fantasy," *Time,* December 2, 2002.

18. "Religion and Cultural Studies" section book listings, *Duke University Press Catalogue* for 2003, pp. 7, 26–29.

19. For listings of claimant houses, see John E. Morby, *Dynasties of the World* (Oxford, England: Oxford University Press, 2002).

20. George Packer, *Blood of the Liberals* (New York: Farrar, Straus, and Giroux, 2000), p. 26.

21. Brooks Adams, *The Law of Civilization and Decay* (New York: Knopf, 1943), p. 45.

22. "Wealth Gap," *Wall Street Journal,* September 13, 1999.

23. Paul Krugman, "The End of Middle Class America," *New York Times Magazine,* October 20, 2002, pp. 64–65.

24. "Trust Yourself," *Forbes,* October 12, 1998, pp. 62–64; see also p. 47.

25. "The Apple Falls Close to the Tree," *New York Times,* November 14, 2002.

26. Lisa Keister, "Estate Tax as Robin Hood," *American Prospect,* May 21, 2001.

27. William H. Gates Sr. and Chuck Collins, *Wealth and Our Commonwealth* (Boston: Beacon Press, 2002), p. 86.

28. Ibid., p. 103.

29. "The Sons Also Rise," *New York Times,* November 22, 2002.

30. Gross, "America's Growing Love Affair."

31. Ibid.

32. Michael Kinsley, "Dad, Can I Borrow the Scepter?" *Time,* November 11, 2002.

33. *Mother Jones,* September–October 2002, p. 64.

34. Bill Minutaglio, *First Son* (New York: Three Rivers Press, 2001), p. 245.

35. Ibid., pp. 261–262.

CHAPTER 3: **The First American Restoration**

1. Gerald Pomper, *The Election of 1992* (Chatham, N.J.: Chatham House, 1993), pp. 1–2.

2. Minutaglio, *First Son,* p. 237.

3. Herskowitz, *Duty, Honor, and Country,* p. 24.

4. Ibid., p. 42.

5. Ibid.

6. Ibid., p. 150.

7. Parmet, *Lone Star Yankee,* p. 36.

8. Minutaglio, *First Son,* p. 69.

9. Ibid., p. 140.

10. Ibid., p. 123.

11. Mitchell, *Revenge,* p. 210.

12. Minutaglio, *First Son,* p. 147.

13. Ibid., p. 231.

14. Mitchell, *Revenge,* p. 234.

15. Ibid., p. 9.

16. "Oops, They've Done It Again," *Washington Post,* January 21, 2001.

17. Louis Harris survey, January 1993, www.harrisinteractive.com.

18. Irwin L. Morris, *Votes, Money, and the Clinton Impeachment* (Boulder, Colo.: Westview, 2002), p. 53.

19. Oran B. Smith, *The Rise of Baptist Republicanism* (New York: New York University Press, 1997), p. 199.

20. Ibid., p. 192.

21. Lou Dubose, Jan Reid, and Carl Cannon, *Boy Genius* (New York: Public Affairs, 2003), pp. 89–90.

22. Ibid., p. 119.

23. "Bush Junior's Skeleton Closet," www.realchang.org/bushjr.htm.

24. Minutaglio, *First Son,* p. 331.

25. Hatfield, *Fortunate Son,* p. 285.

26. Ibid., p. 287.

27. Bruni, *Ambling into History,* p. 101.

28. Minutaglio, *First Son,* p. 300.

29. Mitchell, *Revenge,* p. 6.

30. Ibid., p. 66.

31. Ibid., p. 330.

32. Dubose, Reid, and Cannon, *Boy Genius,* p. 156.

33. Hatfield, *Fortunate Son,* pp. ix–xxi.

34. "Bush Family Fortune," British Broadcasting Corp., July 19, 2003.

35. Walter Robinson, "One-Year Gap in Bush's National Guard Duty," *Boston Globe,* May 23, 2000.

36. Julia Malone, "The Juanita Broaddrick Charges: Too Hot for the Press to Handle?" www.newsmax.com/articles, June 24, 1999.

37. Morris, *Votes, Money,* p. 51.

38. Associated Press/ICR Poll, www.icrsurvey.com, July 2000.

39. "Speakers Consider Role of Religion in Elections," *Rice News,* February 15, 2001.

40. "After All These Years," *New York Times,* December 31, 2002.

41. Calvin Trillin, "New Federal Hires," *The Nation,* December 30, 2002, p. 6.

42. Jonathan Atter and Howard Fineman, "A Dynasty's Dilemma," *Newsweek,* July 29, 2002, p. 29.

43. In Europe as NATO Commander, Eisenhower could not campaign but was so popular that he could win in New Hampshire in 1952 without appearing.

44. Jake Tapper, *Down and Dirty* (New York: Little, Brown, 2001), p. 65.
45. Ibid., pp. 123–124, 149–150.
46. David Corn, "The Florida Fog," *The Nation,* March 19, 2001.
47. The intriguing but not legally weighty evidence that Harris's office deleted computer files related to the Florida recount through supposedly innocous "reformatting" was discussed in a number of August 2001 analyses by the *New York Times,* CBS News, the AP, and the Florida media, but this direction of inquiry, like the recount itself, was set aside after 9/11.
48. Tapper, *Down and Dirty,* pp. 428–429.
49. Ibid., p. 184.
50. Corn, "The Florida Fog."
51. Lloyd Robinson, *The Stolen Election* (New York: Forge Books, 2001), pp. 164–168.
52. Tapper, *Down and Dirty,* p. 451.
53. Ibid., pp. 453–454.
54. Ibid., p. 453.
55. Ibid., p. ix.
56. "Bush Spent Four Times as Much," Associated Press, July 27, 2002.
57. "How Bush Took Florida," *New York Times,* July 15, 2001.
58. *The Nation,* September 30, 2002.
59. "Did Al Gore Win After All?" *London Telegraph,* October 21, 2001.
60. "Disdain for Bush Simmers," *New York Times,* August 4, 2003.
61. *Bush et al. v. Gore et al., an application for a stay,* December 9, 2000, concurring opinion of Justice Scalia.
62. Jack N. Rakove, ed., *The Unfinished Election of 2000* (New York: Basic, 2001), p. 77.
63. Ibid., p. 76.
64. "Infallible Justice," *The Nation,* October 7, 2002, p. 9.

CHAPTER 4: Texanomics and Compassionate Conservatism

1. "Income Gap Continues to Grow," Center for Public Policy Priorities, Austin, Texas, www.cppp.org, January 18, 2000.
2. "More Misery in Store for Texas Poor," *Houston Chronicle,* February 15, 2003.
3. "Capital Chronicle," *Austin Chronicle,* February 14, 2003.
4. Parmet, *Lone Star Yankee,* p. 102.
5. "Houston Searches for Remedies," *New York Times,* September 24, 2000.
6. Dubose, Reid, and Cannon, *Boy Genius,* p. 93.
7. Public Campaign, Washington, D.C., *Corruption Perception Index* no. 20, www.publiccampaign.org, August 3, 2001.
8. Michael Lind, *Made in Texas* (New York: New American Books, 2003), p. 82.
9. Eric Pooley, "Bush in Texas," *Time,* February 21, 2000.
10. Dubose, Reid, and Cannon, *Boy Genius,* p. 84; Minutaglio, *First Son,* p. 305.
11. "From W. with Love," *Time,* March 26, 2001.
12. Lind, *Made in Texas,* pp. 91, 189.

13. Minutaglio, *First Son*, p. 31.
14. Payne, *Initiative in Energy*, pp. 232–233.
15. Ibid. Training under Reimer would have been meant to give Bush the larger overview of the company in which he would be expected to reach top management.
16. Harry Hurt III, "George Bush, Plucky Lad," *Texas Monthly*, June 1983, p. 193.
17. Minutaglio, *First Son*, p. 29.
18. Margaret Warner, "Bush Battles the Wimp Factor," *Newsweek*, October 19, 1987.
19. Mitchell, *Revenge*, p. 147.
20. Thomas Petzinger, *Oil and Honor* (New York: G. P. Putnam's Sons, 1987), p. 41.
21. Sarah Bartlett, *The Money Machine* (New York: Warner Books, 1991), p. 268.
22. Ibid., p. 9.
23. Ibid., p. 14.
24. Hurt, "George Bush, Plucky Lad," p. 194.
25. Parmet, *Lone Star Yankee*, p. 111.
26. Bush got $1.1 million for his share of Zapata Offshore in 1966 (before taxes). He would have done much better financially by staying in business, but as other comments have made clear, he was hungry to pursue a U.S. Senate seat and the presidency.
27. Minutaglio, *First Son*, p. 108.
28. Ibid., p. 199.
29. Parmet, *Lone Star Yankee*, p. 300.
30. Duffy and Goodgame, *Marching in Place*, p. 66.
31. Too litle attention has been paid to these Bush associations. Discussions of his relations with Kravis appear in Bartlett's *The Money Machine* and his relations with Liedtke and Pickens in Petzinger's *Oil and Honor*.
32. "George Bush's Ruling Class," *Common Cause Magazine*, April–May 1992, p. 8.
33. The two relevant studies of Bush's Buckeye Steel Castings by Ohio business professor Mansel G. Blackford are *A Portrait Cast in Steel: Buckeye International and Columbus, Ohio, 1881–1980* (Westport, Conn.: Greenwood Press, 1982) and *A History of Small Business in America* (Chapel Hill: University of North Carolina Press, 2003), pp. 81–94.
34. Barnes, *Standing on a Volcano*, pp. 119, 205.
35. Isaacson and Thomas, *The Wise Men*, p. 214.
36. Mitchell, *Revenge*, p. 185.
37. Robert Sherrill, "What Fertilized the Bushes?" *Texas Observer*, July 12, 1991.
38. "Bush Family Value$," *Mother Jones*, September–October 1992, p. 8.
39. Ibid., p. 11.
40. Ibid., p. 16; see also Jack Colhoun, "The Family That Preys Together," *Covert Action Quarterly* (summer 1992), p. 8.
41. Mitchell, *Revenge*, p. 247.
42. "Broken Promises Plague Parks," *New York Daily News*, October 12, 2002, sports section.
43. Mitchell, *Revenge*, p. 248.

44. By some analyses, the government's 1988 foot-dragging in taking action against Silverado reflected a strategy of avoiding embarrassment to George H. W. Bush in that year's election. But some say that Silverado, like so many activities the Bush sons involved themselves in, had a CIA connection. Rodney Stich, a former government investigator, contended that Silverado was a CIA proprietary on p. 114 of his 2001 book, *Defrauding America* (Alamo, Calif.: Diablo Western Press, 1993).

45. "Influence and Bailouts a Business Tradition in Bush Family," *St. Petersburg Times,* October 29, 2000.

46. Louis Dubose, "O Brother Where Art Thou?" *Austin Chronicle,* March 16, 2001.

47. Adam C. Smith, "Ex-Partner of Jeb Bush Hid Assets Abroad," *St. Petersburg Times,* April 6, 2002.

48. "Influence and Bailouts."

49. Colhoun, "The Family That Preys Together," p. 3; "President's Uncle Shares Bush Family Ties to China," *USA Today,* February 18, 2002.

50. *Wall Street Journal,* March 11, 1991, p. 46B.

51. "State Fines Bush's Brother," *Boston Globe,* July 26, 1991.

52. Knut Royce, "Bush Violated Securities Laws Four Times," *The Public I,* November 2001, p. 1.

53. Michael Kranish, "Harken Board Was Told of Risks," *Boston Globe,* October 30, 2002.

54. Duncan Campbell, "The Bush Dynasty and the Cuban Criminals," *Guardian,* December 2, 2002.

55. *Congress and the Nation, 1945–64* (Washington, D.C.: Congressional Quarterly, 1965), pp. 203, 366, 488, 1141.

56. Parmet, *Lone Star Yankee,* pp. 31–32.

57. Minutaglio, *First Son,* p. 70.

58. Parmet, *Lone Star Yankee,* p. 114.

59. Ibid., p. 116.

60. Ibid., p. 309.

61. Ibid., p. 107.

62. Ibid., p. 208.

63. Minutaglio, *First Son,* p. 193.

64. Samuel Lubell, *The Future While It Happened* (New York: W. W. Norton, 1973), p. 62.

65. Oran Smith, *The Rise of Baptist Republicanism,* p. 78.

66. Bruni, *Ambling into History,* p. 89.

67. "God and the Tax Cut," *Boston Globe,* May 22, 2001.

68. Tamar and Martha Hennessy, "Distorting the Message of Dorothy Day," *Rutland (Vermont) Herald,* May 23, 2001.

69. National Election Studies data from Michael Emerson and Christian Smith, *Divided by Faith* (New York: Oxford University Press, 2000), pp. 95–105.

70. Oran Smith, *The Rise of Baptist Republicanism,* pp. 165–175.

71. Minutaglio, *First Son,* p. 289.

72. Ibid., p. 343.
73. "In His Address, Bush Lingers on a Promise to Care," *New York Times,* January 21, 2001.
74. "A President Puts His Fath in Prayer," *New York Times,* February 9, 2003; "Bush Links Faith and Agenda," *Washington Post,* February 11, 2003.
75. Jack Beatty, "Governing from His Biography," *Atlantic,* May 2002, p. 27.
76. Bob Herbert, "Suffer the Children," *New York Times,* July 11, 2002.
77. Frank Rich, "Bonfire of the Vanities," *New York Times,* December 21, 2002.
78. "President's Compassionate Conservatism Agenda Lags," *Washington Post,* December 26, 2002.
79. Ibid.
80. "The Education Election," *New York Times,* November 10, 2002.
81. David Broder, "Bush's Tax Brush-off," *Washington Post,* March 9, 2003.
82. Drake Bennett and Heidi Pauker, "All the President's Lies," *American Prospect,* May 2003, p. 29.
83. James Moore and Wayne Slater, *Bush's Brain: How Karl Rove Made George Bush Presidential* (New York: John Wiley & Sons, 2003), pp. 31, 43.
84. Niccolò Machiavelli, *The Prince* (New York: Mentor Books, 1952), p. 102.
85. Ibid., p. 103.
86. Ibid.
87. Duffy and Goodgame, *Marching in Place,* p. 11.
88. Ibid., p. 62.
89. Moore and Slater, *Bush's Brain,* p. 138.
90. Eric Alterman, "State of Disunion," *The Nation,* February 10, 2003, p. 10.

CHAPTER 5: **The Enron-Halliburton Administration**

1. Blackford, *History of Small Business,* p. 86 (see chap. 4, n. 33).
2. Antony Sutton, *America's Secret Establishment* (Billings, Mont.: Liberty House, 1986), p. 150.
3. *The Directory of Directors in the City of New York,* 1925–35.
4. Ibid.
5. Minutaglio, *First Son,* pp. 24–25.
6. Anthony Sampson, *The Seven Sisters* (New York: Bantam Books, 1976), p. 74.
7. Ibid., p. 113.
8. Payne, *Initiative in Energy,* pp. 229–272.
9. Parmet, *Lone Star Yankee,* p. 299.
10. Robert Bryce, *Pipe Dreams* (New York: Public Affairs, 2002), p. 78.
11. Ibid., pp. 86–87.
12. "Enron's Many Strands," *New York Times,* February 3, 2002.
13. "Bush Had Dealings with Lay, Enron Ventures in the 1980s," *Chicago Tribune,* March 6, 2002.
14. Ibid.
15. Bryce, *Pipe Dreams,* p. 86.

16. Ibid., pp. 72–73.
17. Robert Scheer, "Bush to Lay: What Was Your Name Again?" *Los Angeles Times,* January 15, 2002.
18. "Blind Faith: How Deregulation and Enron's Influence on Government Looted Billions from Americans," *Public Citizen,* December 2001, p. 10.
19. Seymour Hersh, "The Spoils of War," *New Yorker,* September 6, 1993, p. 70.
20. Bryce, *Pipe Dreams,* pp. 105–107.
21. Ibid., p. 88.
22. "Letters Show Ideas and Gifts Exchanged by Bush and Lay," *New York Times,* February 16, 2002.
23. Bryce, *Pipe Dreams,* p. 90.
24. John Hoefle, "Bush Crew and Enron," www.differentvoices.com, 2001, p. 3.
25. "Enron Ran Global Game of Finance, Report Says," *Chicago Tribune,* March 22, 2002.
26. David Morris, *Seeing the Light* (Minneapolis: Institute for Local Self-Reliance, 2001), pp. 34–45.
27. Bryce, *Pipe Dreams,* p. 92.
28. "Blind Faith," p. 8.
29. Ibid., p. 11.
30. "Lobby Watch," *Texans for Public Justice,* December 4, 2001, p. 1.
31. Ibid., p. 2.
32. Ibid.
33. Vikki Kratz, "Energy Companies Fuel Local and State Campaigns," *Capital Eye,* June 2001, p. 1.
34. "Blind Faith," p. 15.
35. Hank Gutman, "Bush's Biggest Donors Had Links to Enron," *Statesman of Calcutta,* February 15, 2002.
36. Bryce, *Pipe Dreams,* p. 273.
37. "Blind Faith," p. 11.
38. Dubose, Reid, and Cannon, *Boy Genius,* p. 105.
39. "Utilities Lick Wounds After Encounter with Sharp-Toothed Power Traders," *Washington Post,* July 28, 1998.
40. Morris, *Seeing the Light,* p. 45.
41. Ibid.
42. *Newsletter of Congressman Peter DeFazio,* May 24, 2001.
43. "Chronology of Administration Dealings with Enron," *Washington Post,* January 22, 2002.
44. Bryce, *Pipe Dreams,* p. 302.
45. Daniel Armstrong, "The Real Deal About Enron, an Interview with Catherine Austin Fitts," www.sandersresearch.com/html/mappingtherealdeal, February 2003.
46. "In Tough Times, a Company Finds Profits in Terror War," *New York Times,* July 13, 2002.
47. Ibid.

48. Knut Royce and Nathaniel Heller, "Cheney Led Halliburton to Feast at Federal Trough," Center for Public Integrity, www.publicintegrity.com, August 2000, p. 1.

49. Ibid., p. 2.

50. "In Tough Times."

51. Mafruza Khan, "Business on the Battlefield: The Role of Private Military Companies," *Corporate Research E-Letter* no. 30, www.corpresearch.org, December 2002.

52. Ibid.

53. "Cheney's Former Company Wins Afghanistan Contracts," *CorpWatch*, May 2, 2002.

54. "Halliburton Profile," *Cooperative Corporate Research*, www.cooperativeresearch. org, p. 6.

55. Ibid., p. 6.

56. Ibid., p. 12.

57. Ibid., p. 6.

58. Ibid., p. 11.

59. Ibid., p. 11.

60. Royce and Heller, "Cheney Led Halliburton to Feast," p. 1.

61. "The Cheney Loyalty Test," *Mother Jones*, March–April 2003, pp. 19–20.

CHAPTER 6: **Armaments and Men: The Bush Dynasty
and the National Security State**

1. Antony Sutton, *Wall Street and the Bolshevik Revolution* (Western Australia: Veritas Publishing, 1981), pp. 83, 91.

2. Matthew Ware Coulter, *The Senate Munitions Inquiry of the 1930s* (Westport, Conn.: Greenwood Press, 1997), p. 67.

3. K. D. Kirkland, *Remington* (New York: Exeter Books, 1988), p. 46.

4. *The Directory of Directors in the City of New York*, 1916–33.

5. *The Directory of Directors in the City of New York*, 1936–39.

6. Coulter, *Senate Munitions Inquiry*, p. 45.

7. Kirkland, *Remington*, p. 46.

8. Ibid., p. 50.

9. Sutton, *Wall Street and the Bolshevik Revolution*, pp. 15, 65–66, 71–88.

10. *The Directory of Directors in the City of New York*, 1925–33.

11. Koistinen, *Mobilizing for Modern War*, pp. 281–287.

12. Ibid., p. 298.

13. Hodgson's words are quoted in Alexandra Robbins's book about Skull and Bones, *Secrets of the Tomb* (New York: Little, Brown, 2002), p. 184.

14. Simpson, *The Splendid Blond Beast*, pp. 47–48.

15. Ibid., p. 64.

16. Mark L. Chadwin, *The War Hawks* (New York: W. W. Norton, 1968), p. 27; Richard J. Whalen, *Founding Father* (New York: New American Library, 1966), p. 293.

17. Chadwin, *The War Hawks,* p. 28.
18. Whalen, *Founding Father,* pp. 344, 357.
19. Simpson, *The Splendid Blond Beast,* pp. 122–123.
20. Ibid., p. 129.
21. Daniel Yergin, *The Prize* (New York: Simon & Schuster, 1991), p. 395.
22. Loftus and Aarons, *Secret War,* pp. 75–77.
23. Burton Hersh, *The Old Boys: The American Elite and the Origins of the CIA* (St. Petersburg, Fla.: Tree Farm Books, 2002), p. 70. While Allen Dulles was on the board of the J. Henry Schroeder Bank, John Foster Dulles appears to have done only legal work for the bank.
24. Loftus and Aarons, *Secret War,* p. 361.
25. Antony Sutton, *Wall Street and the Rise of Hitler,* pp. 79–80.
26. Simpson, *The Splendid Blond Beast,* pp. 81–83.
27. Sutton, *Wall Street and the Rise of Hitler,* pp. 126–132.
28. Simpson, *The Splendid Blond Beast,* p. 124.
29. Gregory Hooks, *Forging the Military-Industrial Complex* (Urbana: University of Illinois Press, 1991), pp. 100–106.
30. Isaacson and Thomas, *The Wise Men,* p. 214.
31. Hooks, *Forging the Military-Industrial Complex,* p. 312.
32. Ibid., p. 257.
33. C. Wright Mills, *The Power Elite* (New York: Oxford University Press, 1956), pp. 213–214.
34. Isaacson and Thomas, *The Wise Men,* p. 29.
35. Letter from Prescott Bush to Mrs. Allen Dulles reproduced in Bruce Adamson, *The Adamson Report,* vol. 10 (Santa Cruz, Calif.: privately published, 1995), exhibit 1-P.
36. Payne, *Initiative in Energy,* pp. 176–177.
37. Adamson, *The Adamson Report,* vol. 10, exhibits 4-I, 4-P, 4-Q, 4-T, and 4-U.
38. Robin Winks, *Cloak and Gown* (New York: Morrow, 1987), p. 23.
39. Loftus and Aarons, *Secret War,* p. 361.
40. Rhodri Jeffreys-Jones, *Cloak and Dollar* (New Haven, Conn.: Yale University Press, 2002), pp. 60–70.
41. "Thyssen Has $3,000,000 Cash in New York Vault," *New York Herald Tribune,* July 31, 1941.
42. Letter to Lewis E. Rubin, chief, Management and Liquidation Branch of the office of the Alien Property Custodian, U.S. Justice Department, Washington, from C. Gordon Lamude, manager of the New York office, File no. D-49-283, July 25, 1952, describes the process of the dissolution of the corporation and the cancellation of the one share of stock held in the name of Prescott Bush.
43. Winks, *Cloak and Gown,* pp. 23–24.
44. Lewis Laphan, "The Boys Next Door," *Harper's,* July 2001.
45. Winks, *Cloak and Gown,* p. 35.
46. Loftus and Aarons, *Secret War,* p. 592.
47. Anthony Kimery, *Covert Action Information Bulletin* (summer 1992).

48. *The Directory of Directors in the City of New York,* 1924–35.

49. *The Directory of Directors in the City of New York,* 1934–52.

50. "Cuban Revolution," *New York Review of Books,* April 28, 1966.

51. "West Indies Sugar Directors Approve Plan to Liquidate," *Wall Street Journal,* January 5, 1960.

52. Adamson, *The Adamson Report,* vol. 10, p. 16.

53. Jonathan Kwitny, "The Mexican Connection," *Barron's,* September 19, 1988.

54. Ibid.

55. Loftus and Aarons, *Secret War,* p. 367.

56. Ibid., p. 368.

57. Parmet, *Lone Star Yankee,* p. 111.

58. Adamson, *The Adamson Report,* vol. 10, p. 19.

59. Carl Jensen and Project Censored, *Twenty Years of Censored News* (New York: Seven Stories Press, 1997). A short reference can also be found in Carl Jensen and Project Censored, *Censored: The News That Didn't Make It—and Why* (New York: Four Walls, Eight Windows, 1994), p. 185, citing Bush's role as a "CIA Asset" as one of the top censored stories of that election year.

60. Joseph McBride, "The Man Who Wasn't There," *The Nation,* July 16–23, 1988.

61. Joseph McBride, "The Man Who Wasn't There," *The Nation,* August 13–20, 1988.

62. Ibid.

63. *Wall Street Journal,* December 15, 1959; also "West Indies Sugar Directors."

64. Ron Rosenbaum, "I Stole the Head of Prescott Bush! More Scary Skull and Bones Tales," *New York Observer,* July 17, 2000.

65. Loftus and Aarons, *Secret War,* p. 371.

66. H. R. Haldeman, *The Ends of Power* (New York: Times Books, 1978), p. 64.

CHAPTER 7: **The American Presidency and the Rise of the Religious Right**

1. Gabriel Almond, R. Scott Appleby, and Emmanuel Sivan, *Strong Religion: The Rise of Fundamentalisms Around the World* (Chicago: University of Chicago Press, 2003), pp. 1–2.

2. Ibid., p. 17.

3. Ibid., pp. 116–134.

4. The multiple volumes of studies published by the Fundamentalism Project range far beyond the Christian, Jewish, and Islamic examples, although chapter 7 singles out those three because of their potentially explosive convergence in the Middle East.

5. Minutaglio, *First Son,* pp. 210–224.

6. Ibid., p. 211.

7. Ibid., pp. 219–220.

8. James Guth and John Green, *The Bible and the Ballot Box* (Boulder, Colo.: Westview Press, 1991), p. 32.

9. Ibid., p. 23.

10. Ibid., p. 207.

11. Ibid., pp. 16–19, for a discussion of the parachurch network.

12. John C. Green and John Dilulio, "Evangelicals in Civil Life: How the Faithful Voted," Ethics and Public Policy Center, www.eppc.org, January 2001, p. 3.

13. Almond, Appleby, and Sivan, *Strong Religion,* p. 1.

14. Ibid., p. 27.

15. Guth and Green, *Bible and Ballot Box,* p. 76.

16. Ibid., p. 85.

17. Almond, Appleby, and Sivan, *Strong Religion,* p. 20.

18. Quoted in Kevin Phillips, *Post-Conservative America* (New York: Random House, 1982), p. 187.

19. Kevin Phillips, *Mediacracy* (New York: Doubleday, 1974), pp. 56–58.

20. For 1956 through 1980, the estimates of the national split in Baptist vote by Albert J. Menendez show the Democrats collapsing to 24.2 percent in 1968 and 25.5 percent in 1972. These elections, and not those of 1980, represent the beginning of the Democratic hemorrhage among Baptists. See Kevin P. Phillips, *Post-Conservative America* (New York: Random House, 1982); pp. 187–88.

21. Garry Wills, *Under God: Religion and American Politics* (New York: Touchstone, 1991), p. 60.

22. John Green, Mark Rozell, and Clyde Wilcox, *Prayers in the Precincts* (Washington, D.C.: Georgetown University Press, 2000), p. 42.

23. Ibid., p. 1.

24. Green and Dilulio, "Evangelicals in Civil Life," p. 7.

25. Ibid., pp. 7–8.

26. B. J. Almond, "Speakers Consider the Role of Religion," *Rice News,* February 15, 2001, p. 2.

27. None of the Muslim samplings in Florida are large enough to be reliable, but they suggest a lopsided support for Bush. Some GOP activists, only half tongue-in-cheek, insist that the Muslim vote gave Bush Florida and the presidency, a wry historical twist.

28. Thomas Edsall, "Blue Movie," *Atlantic,* January–February 2003.

29. Green and Dilulio, "Evangelicals in Civil Life," p. 3.

30. "Religious Right Finds Its Center in Oval Office," *Washington Post,* December 24, 2001.

31. Ibid.

32. Ibid.

33. Ibid.

34. Paul Kengor, "God & W. at Pennsylvania Avenue," *National Review Online,* March 5, 2003.

35. Ibid.

36. Bruce Lincoln, *Holy Terrors* (Chicago: University of Chicago Press, 2003), pp. 30–32.

37. Howard Fineman, "Bush and God," *Newsweek,* March 10, 2002, p. 28.

38. This evaluation came from Steve Hassan, a journalist who authored *The Truth About Sun Myung Moon* (2000) and maintains a Moon-watching Web site, www.factnet.org.

39. Chris Mooney, "W's Christian Nation," *American Prospect,* June 1, 2003.

40. "AIDS Panel Choice Wrote of Gay Plague," *Washington Post,* January 24, 2003.

41. "Jesus and the FDA," *Time On-Line,* October 5, 2002.

42. "Ashcroft Appointments Assailed," *Washington Post,* September 5, 2002.

43. Almond, Appleby, and Sivan, *Strong Religion,* p. 2.

44. Ehud Sprinzak, *The Ascendance of Israel's Radical Right* (New York: Oxford University Press, 1991), p. 13.

45. Ian S. Lustick, *For the Land and the Lord* (New York: Council on Foreign Relations Press, 1988), p. vii.

46. Almond, Appleby, and Sivan, *Strong Religion,* p. 5.

47. "The President Rides Out," *London Observer,* January 26, 2003.

48. "God and Diplomacy," *Economist,* February 8, 2003, p. 33.

49. Ken Silverstein and Michael Scherer, "Born-Again Zionists," *Mother Jones,* September–October 2002, p. 61.

50. "New Scrutiny of Religion in Bush's Policies," *Christian Science Monitor,* March 17, 2003.

51. Silverstein and Scherer, "Born-Again Zionists," p. 60.

52. Gershom Gorenberg, *The End of Days* (New York: Free Press, 2000), pp. 7–29.

53. "Examining Fundamentalism," www.miftah.org, August 2002.

54. "Christian Zionism," course outline, Earlham University, www.earlham.edu, fall 1997, p. 5.

55. Lincoln, *Holy Terrors,* p. 115.

56. "Reactions to Verbal Attacks on Muslims," www.religioustolerance.org, May 9, 2003, pp. 2–3.

57. Ibid., p. 1.

58. Paul Marshall, *Their Blood Cries Out: The Growing Worldwide Persecution of Christians* (Dallas: Word Publishing 1997); Nina Shea, *In the Lion's Den: Persecuted Christians and What the World Can Do About It* (Nashville: Broadman and Holman, 1997).

59. "The President Rides Out," p. 6.

60. Bob Woodward, *Bush at War* (New York: Simon & Schuster, 2002), p. 67.

61. Fineman, "Bush and God," p. 28.

62. "A President Puts His Faith in Providence," *New York Times,* February 9, 2003, "Week in Review."

63. "Religious Leaders Uneasy with Bush Rhetoric," *Pittsburgh Post-Gazette,* February 12, 2003.

64. *La Nacion,* November 26, 1996, cited in "Bush Praises Sun Myung Moon," Reuters (Buenos Aires), November 25, 1996.

65. Robert Parry, "The Dark Side of Rev. Moon," *Consortium News,* www.consortiumnews.com, October 11, 2000, p. 2.

66. "Evangelicals Unaware Inaugural Event Was Sponsored by Unification Leader," *Baptist Press News,* January 23, 2001.

67. Parry, "Dark Side of Rev. Moon," p. 5.

68. Harold Meyerson, "Reaping the World's Disfavor," *Washington Post,* June 11, 2003; "They Don't Like Us. Worse, They Don't Trust Us," *Washington Post,* June 15, 2003.

69. Lincoln, *Holy Terrors,* p. 20.

70. Ibid.

71. Richard J. Neuhaus, "Religious Freedom in a Time of War," *First Things,* www.firstthings.com, January 2002.

72. Sprinzak, *Ascendance,* p. 4.

73. Ibid., p. 11.

74. Ibid., p. 13.

75. Ibid., p. 16.

76. Lustick, *Land and Lord,* pp. 11, 15.

77. Ibid., p. 10.

78. Andrew Lang, "The Politics of Armageddon," *Convergence,* 1985, p. 4.

79. "New Scrutiny of Religion."

80. Debora Caldwell, "George W. Bush, Presidential Preacher," *Beliefnet,* February 17, 2003, p. 1.

81. Ibid., p. 2.

82. "Is Bush Too Christian?" www.pastornet.net, March 15, 2003, p. 2.

83. Welton Gaddy, "Statement on President or Preacher," Interfaith Alliance, www.interfaithalliance.org, February 11, 2003, p. 1.

84. Martin Marty, "The Sin of Pride," *Newsweek,* March 10, 2003, p. 32.

85. "Israeli Experts Fear Apocalyptic Holy War," press agencies, www.arabia.com/news, January 8, 2000.

86. Sprinzak, *Ascendance,* p. 3.

87. Lincoln, *Holy Terrors,* pp. 102–103.

88. The poll appears in "Prophecy: What the Bible Says About the End of the World," *Newsweek,* November 1, 1999.

89. Gorenberg, *The End of Days,* p. 3.

90. Ibid., pp. 43–45.

91. Ibid., pp. 185–191.

92. R. Scott Appleby, "Religious Fundamentalisms and Global Conflict," Foreign Policy Association, www.fpa.org/topics, October 5, 2001, p. 4.

93. Ibid., p. 7.

CHAPTER 8: **Indiana Bush and the Axis of Evil**

1. Coulter, *Senate Munitions Inquiry,* p. 9.

2. Peter Hobkirk, *Like Hidden Fire* (New York: Kodansha, 1994), p. 22.

3. Sampson, *The Seven Sisters,* p. 82.

4. Hobkirk, *Like Hidden Fire,* p. 60.

5. Ibid., pp. 105–120; Yergin, *The Prize,* p. 173.

6. Yergin, *The Prize,* p. 173.

7. Ibid., p. 176.

8. Ibid., pp. 179–182.

9. Ibid., p. 188.

10. Ibid., p. 182.

11. Ibid., p. 183.

12. Sampson, *The Seven Sisters,* p. 72.

13. Yergin, *The Prize,* p. 183.

14. Sampson, *The Seven Sisters,* p. 73.

15. "Bars Concessions in Baku Oil Field," *New York Times,* March 11, 1925.

16. Yergin, *The Prize,* p. 334.

17. Ibid., pp. 340, 394, 337.

18. Ibid., pp. 373, 376, 377.

19. Ibid., pp. 326, 356.

20. Ibid., pp. 346–347, 357–364.

21. Ibid., pp. 382–393.

22. Michael Klare, *Resource Wars* (New York: Henry Holt, 2001), p. 39.

23. Christopher Cerf and Micah Sifry, *Iraq War Reader* (New York: Touchstone, 2003), pp. 580–583.

24. "Bush Planned Iraq Regime Change Before Becoming President," *Glasgow Sunday Herald,* September 15, 2002.

25. Klare, *Resource Wars,* p. 28.

26. Boris L. Rumer, "The Gathering Storm in Central Asia," *Orbis* 37, no. 1 (winter 1993): 89.

27. Dianne Smith, "Central Asia: A New Great Game," U.S. Army War College Strategic Studies Institute, June 17, 1996.

28. Klare, *Resource Wars,* pp. 90–92.

29. "Why Are We Really in Somalia," *Los Angeles Times,* January 18, 1993.

30. Richard Dreyfuss, "The Thirty-Year Itch," *Mother Jones,* March–April 2003, p. 41.

31. Karl E. Meyer, *Dust of Empire* (New York: Public Affairs, 2003), pp. 118–119.

32. "Harriman Defends German Ship Deal," *New York Times,* October 6, 1920.

33. Karl E. Meyer and Charlene Blair Brysac, *Tournament of Shadows* (Washington, D.C.: Counterpoint, 1999), p. xxiv.

34. Ibid., pp. 569–570.

35. Meyer, *Dust of Empire,* p. 7.

36. Zbigniew Brzezinski, *The Grand Chessboard* (New York: Basic Books, 1997); Ilan Berman, "Slouching Toward Eurasia," *Perspective* 12, no. 1 (September–October 2001): 15.

37. Coulter, *Senate Munitions Inquiry,* p. 32.

38. Ibid., pp. 42, 45, 49.

39. Ibid., pp. 59–63.

40. David Eisenhower, foreword to Gregg Walker, David Bella, and Steven Sprecher, *The Military-Industrial Complex* (New York: Peter Lang, 1992), pp. ix–xi.

41. Paul A. C. Koistinen, "The Industrial Military Complex in Historical Perspective: The Interwar Years," *Journal of American History* 56 (March 1970): 831–839.

42. Coulter, *Senate Munitions Inquiry*, p. 128.

43. Charles Higham, *Trading with the Enemy* (New York: Dell, 1984), p. 114; Burton Hersh, *Old Boys*, p. 143.

44. Michael Klare, *Arms Supermarket* (Austin: University of Texas Press, 1984), p. 128.

45. Ibid., p. 150.

46. Ibid., p. 129.

47. Ibid., p. 48.

48. Meyer, *Dust of Empire*, p. 136.

49. James Adams, *Engines of War* (New York: Atlantic Monthly Press, 1990), p. 128.

50. Ibid., pp. 149–150.

51. Ibid.

52. Klare, *Resource Wars*, p. 65.

53. Chalmers Johnson, *Blowback* (New York: Metropolitan Books, 2000), p. 8.

54. Anthony Sampson, *The Arms Bazaar: From Lebanon to Lockheed* (New York: Viking, 1977), p. xx.

55. Nafeez Ahmed, *The War on Freedom* (Joshua Tree, Calif.: Media Messenger, 2002), p. 29.

56. Johnson, *Blowback*, p. 9.

57. "Rusk Offers Hope to Cuban People," *New York Times*, October 10, 1962.

58. Pete Brewton, *The Mafia, the CIA, and George Bush* (New York: SPI Press, 1992), p. 223.

59. Jonathan Beaty and S. C. Gwynne, *The Outlaw Bank* (New York: Random House, 1993), p. 227.

60. "Family Ties: How Oil Firm Linked to a Son of Bush Won Bahrain Drilling Pact," *Wall Street Journal*, December 6, 1991.

61. Beaty and Gwynne, *The Outlaw Bank*, p. xxiii.

62. Peter Truell and Larry Gurwin, *False Profits* (New York: Houghton Mifflin, 1992), p. 117.

63. Hooks, *Forging the Military-Industrial Complex*, p. 127.

64. Walker, Bella, and Sprecher, *The Military-Industrial Complex*, p. 158.

65. Thom Shanker, "U.S. Again Leads World in International Weapons Sales," *New York Times*, September 26, 2002.

66. Eugene B. Smith, "The New Condottieri and U.S. Policy: The Privatization of Conflict and Its Implications," *Parameters*, winter 2002–2003, pp. 104, 107.

67. Dan Briody, *Iron Triangle* (New York: John Wiley, 2003), pp. 60–68.

68. Michael C. Ruppert, "Halliburton Corporation's Brown and Root," www.FromtheWilderness.com, October 24, 2000.

69. Oliver Burkeman and Julian Burger, *Guardian*, October 31, 2001.

70. Ibid.
71. Seymour Hersh, "Lunch with the Chairman," *New Yorker,* March 17, 2003, p. 76.
72. "A Fusillade of Defense IPOs," *Boston Globe,* May 17, 2002.
73. "From Ridge Aide to Security Lobbyist," *New York Times,* April 26, 2003.
74. Margie Burns, "Bush Family Dipping into Security Pie," *Prince George's Journal,* December 1, 2002.
75. Tim Shorrock, "Selling (Off) Iraq," *The Nation,* June 23, 2003, p. 12.
76. Naomi Klein, "Downsizing in Disguise," *The Nation,* June 23, 2003, p. 10.
77. Robert Dreyfuss, "Orbit of Influence," *American Prospect,* March–April 1996, p. 30.
78. Ibid., p. 31.
79. Ann Louise Bardach, *Cuba Confidential* (New York: Random House, 2002), p. 313.
80. Ibid., pp. 314–315.
81. Ellis D. Slater, *The Ike I Knew* (privately published, 1980), pp. 240–241.
82. David Eisenhower, foreword to *The Military Industrial Complex,* pp. ix–xi.
83. Margie Burns, "Bush-Linked Company," *Prince George's Journal,* February 4, 2003.
84. Alan Friedman, *Spider's Web* (New York: Bantam, 1993), pp. 168, 210.

CHAPTER 9: The Wars of the Texas Succession

1. *Dallas Morning News,* October 24, 1964.
2. Truell and Gurwin, *False Profits,* p. 365.
3. Bill Peterson, *Washington Post,* March 1, 1980.
4. Parmet, *Lone Star Yankee,* p. 221.
5. Russel S. Bowen, *The Immaculate Deception* (Carson City, Nev.: America West, 1991), pp. 54–56.
6. Ken Silverstein, "Licensed to Kill," *Harper's,* May 2000, p. 52.
7. Joseph Persico, *Casey* (New York: Viking, 1990), p. 192.
8. Hamilton Jordan, *Crisis* (New York: Putnam, 1982), p. 361.
9. Interview with Richard V. Allen, quoted in Gary Sick, *October Surprise* (New York: Times Books, 1991), p. 24.
10. Robert Parry, "History on the Ballot," www.consortiumnews.com, November 15, 2000.
11. "The October Surprise," *The Other Americas Radio,* transcript, p. 5, www.sumeria.net.
12. Ibid., p. 2.
13. Robert Parry, "The Ladies' Room Secrets," www.consortiumnews.com, December 5, 1995, p. 2.
14. Robert Parry, "Disappearing History," *In These Times,* August 19, 1996, pp. 10–11.
15. Truell and Gurwin, *False Profits,* pp. 303–304.
16. Parry, "Disappearing History,"

17. Robert Parry, "History on the Ballot," www.consortiumnews.com, November 5, 2000.
18. Robert Parry, "October Surprise X-Files: Russia's Report," www.consortiumnews.com, December 5, 1995.
19. Jack Colhoun, "Israeli Spy Cover-up Crumbles," www.consortiumnews.com, October 14, 1999.
20. Robert Parry, "October Surprise X-Files, Part II," www.consortiumnews.com, 1997, p. 1.
21. Parry, "History on the Ballot," p. 3.
22. Abolhassan Bani-Sadr, *My Turn to Speak: Iran, the Revolution and Secret Deals* (Dulles, Va.: Brassey's, 1991), quoted in Harvey Wasserman, "Bush's Impendding Watergate," www.oldvalleyadvocate.com, May 23, 1991.
23. "The October Surprise," p. 5.
24. Parry, "History on the Ballot," pp. 3–4.
25. "The October Surprise," p. 6.
26. The Alibi Club dinner is noted in Sick, *October Surprise,* p. 81.
27. Elsa Walsh, "The Prince," *New Yorker,* March 24, 2003, p. 48.
28. Beaty and Gwynne, *The Outlaw Bank,* p. 275.
29. Robert Kaiser, "Royal Family's Wealth Invested in West," *Washington Post,* February 18, 2002.
30. Jonathan Ashley, "Eyes on America," www.truthout.org, October 9, 2001.
31. Seymour Hersh, "The Spoils of War."
32. Burns, "Bush-Linked Company," pp. 1–2.
33. Margie Burns, "Secrecy Surrounds a Bush Brother's Role," *American Reporter,* January 20, 2003.
34. "Periscope," *Newsweek,* February 4, 2002.
35. "Bush Planned Iraq 'Regime Change' Before Becoming President," *Glasgow Sunday Herald,* September 15, 2002.
36. "Bush Personalizes Conflict," Agence France-Presse, September 27, 2002.
37. Lind, *Made in Texas,* p. 155.
38. Ibid., p. 142.
39. McDougall, *Promised Land,* pp. 173, 187, 188, 189.
40. Ralph Wetterhahn, *The Last Battle* (New York: Carroll & Graf, 2001), p. 45.
41. Allan J. Matusow, *The Unraveling of America* (New York: Harper & Row, 1984), p. 393.
42. Ibid., p. 382.
43. Ibid., p. 392.
44. Harry G. Summers Jr., *On Strategy* (Novato, Calif.: Presidio Press, 1982), p. 105.
45. Olivier Todd, *Cruel April* (New York: W. W. Norton, 1987), p. 281.
46. Lawrence Walsh, *Firewall* (New York: W. W. Norton, 1997), p. 65.
47. Spencer C. Tucker, ed., *The Encyclopedia of the Vietnam War* (New York: Oxford University Press, 2000), p. 52.
48. Lawrence Walsh, *Firewall,* p. 460.

49. Ibid., pp. 476, 504–505.

50. Ibid., p. 505.

51. Russ W. Baker, "Iraqgate," *Columbia Journalism Review,* March–April 1993.

52. Friedman, *Spider's Web,* p. 245.

53. Peter Mantius, *Shell Game* (New York: St. Martin's Press, 1995), pp. 45–53.

54. Ibid., p. 234.

55. William Safire, *New York Times,* December 7, 1992.

56. William Safire, "Clinton and Iraq," *New York Times,* February 7, 1995.

57. Friedman, *Spider's Web,* p. 157.

58. Ibid., p. 162.

59. Ibid., p. 168.

60. Ibid., pp. 162–64.

61. "Officers Say U.S. Aided Iraq in War Despite Use of Gas," *New York Times,* August 18, 2002.

62. William Blum, "What the *New York Times* Left Out," www.counterpunch.com, August 20, 2002.

63. Friedman, *Spider's Web,* p. 155.

64. Murray Waas, "Who Lost Kuwait?" *The Village Voice,* www.sfbg.com, January 22, 1991, p. 5.

65. Ibid.

66. Ibid.

67. Ibid., p. 1.

68. Ibid., p. 6.

69. John B. Connally and Mickey Herskowitz, *In History's Shadow* (New York: Hyperion, 1993), p. 331.

70. Bob Woodward, *The Commanders* (New York: Simon & Schuster, 1991), p. 261.

71. Tom Regan, "When Contemplating War, Beware of Babies in Incubators," www.csmonitor.com, September 6, 2002.

72. Mitchell Cohen, "How Bush Sold the Bombing of Iraq," www.counterpunch.com, December 28, 2002, pp. 1–2.

73. Ibid.

74. Roger Hilsman, *George Bush Versus Saddam Hussein* (Novato, Calif.: Presidio Press, 1992), p. 250.

75. Ibid., p. 254.

76. "The Impact of Bush Linking 9/11 and Iraq," *Christian Science Monitor,* March 14, 2003.

77. Summers, *On Strategy,* p. 98.

78. Ibid., p. 78.

79. "President Makes Use of Familiar Phrases," *Washington Post,* March 9, 2003.

80. Hilsman, *George Bush Versus Saddam Hussein,* p. 75; Friedman, *Spider's Web,* pp. 173–74.

81. "Why Are We Really in Somalia?"

82. John Cassidy, "Letter from Iraq," *New Yorker,* July 14, 2003, p. 71.

83. Dreyfuss, "The Thirty-Year Itch," p. 44.

84. "Bush Personalizes Conflict," Agence France-Press.

85. "Unfinished Business for the Bush family," *London Daily Telegraph*, March 18, 2003.

86. "Secrecy Surrounds a Bush Brother's Role in 9/11 Security," *American Reporter*, January 20, 2003.

87. Victor Thorn, "The Bush–Bin Laden Family Connection," *BabelMagazine.com*, October 13, 2002.

88. Ibid.

89. "U.S. Ties to Saudi Elite May Be Hurting the War on Terrorism," *Boston Herald*, December 10, 2001.

90. Greg Palast, "See No Evil," *TomPaine.com*, March 1, 2003; Greg Palast, "What About Saudi Arabia," *Buzzflash* interview, May 21, 2003.

91. Jean-Charles Brisard and Guillaume Dasquié, *Forbidden Truth* (New York: Thunder's Mouth Press/Nation Books, 2002), pp. x–xi.

92. "Panel Says 9/11 Attack Might Have Been Prevented," *New York Times*, July 25, 2003.

93. Sam Tanenhaus, interview with Paul Wolfowitz, *Vanity Fair*, July 2002.

94. Walter McDougall, "What the U.S. Needs to Promote in Iraq," *Foreign Policy Research Institute*, May 2003, p. 6.

95. Michael Elliott, "So, What Went Wrong?" *Time Europe*, October 6, 2003, p. 26.

96. Meyerson, "Poll: Support for U.S. at New Low," Associated Press, June 4, 2003.

AFTERWORD: **Machiavelli and the American Dynastic Moment**

1. Machiavelli, *The Prince*, p. 35. The dedication was to "Lorenzo the Magnificent, son of Piero di Medici." This, unfortunately for Machiavelli, was not the same Lorenzo referred to as "the Magnificent" in the history books. He was the Medici duke of Urbino, a ruler Machiavelli wanted to flatter.

2. Rove's recollection of Atwater saying that he reread Machiavelli every year appears in Moore and Slater, *Bush's Brain*, p. 138.

3. After English king Charles I was executed in 1649, his son Charles II was restored in 1660. His second son, King James II, was forced to flee in 1688 by the "Glorious Revolution" of that year. In France, after Louis XVIII, the brother of the executed Louis XVI was restored in 1815; his family's restoration lasted fifteen years until the reactionary brother, Charles X, was forced to flee by the revolutionaries of 1830.

4. Raoul Berger, *Impeachment* (Cambridge, Mass.: Harvard University Press, 1973), p. 299.

5. "Where's the Accountability?" www.inreview.com, June 9, 2003, cites both John Dean's comments published on a CNN Web site and Malcolm Savidge's interview with Brian Williams of MSNBC. The account of Ritter's charges is from Jan Barry, "Scott Ritter May Be the Bush Re-election Team's Worst Nightmare," www.informationclearinghouse.info, May 5, 2003.

6. "Disdain for Bush Simmers."

7. Dower, "The Other Japanese Occupation"; Lieven, "The Empire Strikes Back."

8. Jeffreys-Jones, *The CIA and American Democracy,* p. 17.

9. "Unjust, Unwise, Un-American," *Economist,* July 12, 2003, p. 9.

10. "The CIA Widens Its Domestic Reach," *New York Times,* January 20, 2002.

11. David Cole, "Patriot Act's Big Brother," *The Nation,* March 17, 2003.

12. Eugene Smith, "The New Condottieri and U.S. Policy," p. 1.

13. Robert Kaplan, "Supremacy by Stealth: Ten Rules for Managing the World," *Atlantic,* July–August 2003.

14. "When Government Doesn't Tell You," *New York Times,* February 3, 2002, "Week in Review."

15. Historical tables, *Budget of the U.S. Government, Fiscal Year 2000* (Washington D.C.: Government Printing Office, 1999), Table 6.1, pp. 107–8.

16. J. G. A. Pocock, *The Machiavellian Moment* (Princeton, N.J.: Princeton University Press, 1975), pp. vii, viii, 93.

17. Machiavelli, *The Prince,* pp. 8, 20–21.

APPENDIX A: Armaments and the Walker-Bush Family, 1914–40

1. Time line of life of Marcellus Hartley Dodge, www.columbia.edu.

2. Sutton, *Wall Street and the Bolshevik Revolution,* pp. 129–30.

3. Ibid., pp. 65–66.

4. Ibid., pp. 71–78, 132, 135.

5. Ibid., pp. 54–56.

6. Handbook of Texas Online, James Stillman, www.tsha.utexus.edu.

7. *The Directory of Directors in the City of New York,* 1921–22, 1923–24.

8. *The Directory of Directors in the City of New York,* 1930–31, 1931–32.

9. Sutton, *Wall Street and the Bolshevik Revolution,* pp. 61-62.

10. Robert R. Kucinski, *Bankers' Profits from German Loans* (Washington, D.C.: Brookings Institution, 1932); p. 127.

11. Burton Hersh, *The Old Boys,* p. 133.

12. Higham, *Trading with the Enemy,* pp. 42–43; Sutton, *Wall Street and the Rise of Hitler,* p. 81.

APPENDIX B: Deception, Dissimulation, and Disinformation

1. "Harriman Defends German Ship Deal," *New York Times,* October 6, 1920.

2. Isaacson and Thomas, *The Wise Men,* p. 82.

3. Kranish, "Powerful Alliance Aids Bushes' Rise."

4. Machiavelli, *The Prince,* p. 103.

5. Ibid., p. 102.

6. Ibid., p. 101.

7. James Burnham, *The Machiavellians* (Chicago: Regnery Gateway, 1943), pp. 66–67.

8. Burton Hersh, *The Old Boys,* pp. 65–66, 133.

9. U.S. Senate, *Hearings Before a Subcommittee of the Committee on Military Affairs: Elimination of German Resources for War, Report Pursuant to S. Res. 107 and 146,* July 2, 1945, Part 7, 78th Congress and 79th Congress (Washington, D.C.: Government Printing Office).
10. Sutton, *Wall Street and the Rise of Hitler* (Seal Beach, CA: '76 Press, 1976) p. 201, nn. 20–21.
11. Truell and Gurwin, *False Profits,* p. 365.
12. Beaty and Gwynne, *The Outlaw Bank,* pp. 228–29.
13. Kwitny, "The Mexican Connection."

INDEX